Black Resettlement and the American Civil War

Based on sweeping research in six languages, *Black Resettlement and the American Civil War* offers the first comprehensive, comparative account of nineteenth-century America's greatest road not taken: the mass resettlement of African Americans outside the United States. Building on resurgent scholarly interest in the so-called colonization movement, the book goes beyond tired debates about colonization's place in the contest over slavery, and beyond the familiar black destinations of Liberia, Canada, and Haiti. Striding effortlessly from Pittsburgh to Panama, Toronto to Trinidad, and Lagos to Louisiana, it synthesizes a wealth of individual, state-level, and national considerations to reorient the field and set a new standard for Atlantic history. Along the way, it shows that what haunted politicians from Thomas Jefferson to Abraham Lincoln was not whether it was right to abolish slavery, but whether it was safe to do so unless the races were separated.

Sebastian N. Page is a historian of the United States and Atlantic world during the nineteenth century. He is the co-author of *Colonization after Emancipation: Lincoln and the Movement for Black Resettlement*.

CAMBRIDGE STUDIES ON THE AMERICAN SOUTH

Series Editors:

Mark M. Smith, *University of South Carolina, Columbia*
Peter Coclanis, *University of North Carolina at Chapel Hill*

Editor Emeritus:

David Moltke-Hansen

Interdisciplinary in its scope and intent, this series builds upon and extends Cambridge University Press's longstanding commitment to studies on the American South. The series offers the best new work on the South's distinctive institutional, social, economic, and cultural history and also features works in a national, comparative, and transnational perspective.

Titles in the Series

Black Resettlement and the American Civil War

SEBASTIAN N. PAGE

University of Oxford

CAMBRIDGE
UNIVERSITY PRESS

CAMBRIDGE
UNIVERSITY PRESS

University Printing House, Cambridge CB2 8BS, United Kingdom

One Liberty Plaza, 20th Floor, New York, NY 10006, USA

477 Williamstown Road, Port Melbourne, VIC 3207, Australia

314–321, 3rd Floor, Plot 3, Splendor Forum, Jasola District Centre,
New Delhi – 110025, India

79 Anson Road, #06–04/06, Singapore 079906

Cambridge University Press is part of the University of Cambridge.

It furthers the University's mission by disseminating knowledge in the pursuit of
education, learning, and research at the highest international levels of excellence.

www.cambridge.org
Information on this title: www.cambridge.org/9781107141773
DOI: 10.1017/9781316493915

First published 2021

A catalogue record for this publication is available from the British Library.

ISBN 978-1-107-14177-3 Hardback

For the Pelican!

Contents

Figures and Maps

Figures

Maps

Acknowledgments

"The library has just bought microfilm copies of the records of the American Colonization Society. Why don't you find out what it was up to during the Civil War?" Those words from Jay Sexton started a project that ranged much further than I would ever have imagined, and took much longer than I would ever have dreaded. Perhaps an eternity of labor is a fitting punishment for those undergraduates who ask their supervisor for ideas for a thesis. As I committed to the topic (and then some!) for my graduate studies, Richard Carwardine became an ever more important advisor. He was joined in that respect by Richard Blackett, whose Grand Tour–like research into black emigration made possible the whistle-stop excursion that is Chapter 2. Still, I researched much of this book in Washington, DC, home to none of those people and to no institution where I have ever held an affiliation. (Though I probably have squatter's rights to parts of the Library of Congress by now.) How lucky I am, then, for the friendship of Anna Sproul-Latimer and Irene Upshur, who made almost a year's research so much more sociable than it might have been. It is thanks to their warm welcome whenever I go back that I call Arlington, Virginia, my home from home.

I knew from the second year of my doctoral course, when Phillip Magness and I discovered the sources that we would present in *Colonization after Emancipation*, that I had been sucked into a topic that no dissertation could ever encompass. It is a testament to the mercy of my examiners, Nicholas Guyatt and David Turley, that they approved an effort that somehow covered less than one-tenth of the material included in this book in eleven-tenths the number of words. Anyone who wishes to gawp at such a prolix document should head to the Vere Harmsworth

Library, where Jane Rawson or one of her wonderful team of Judy Warden, Johanna O'Connor, Martin Sutcliffe, and Richard Purkiss will call it up.

Otherwise, I have accumulated debts to so many librarians, colleagues, and even strangers who offered me their couch that I could not fairly specify any more people, beyond a quintet at Cambridge University Press: Deborah Gershenowitz, Cecelia Cancellaro, Rachel Blaifeder, and two anonymous readers. Nevertheless, I recognize three broad areas of help: emotional, financial, and institutional. The first, as ever, is the support of friends and family. The second is the generosity, in chronological order, of the Arts and Humanities Research Council, the Peter Parish Memorial Fund, the Rothermere American Institute (especially the anonymous benefactor who funded my fellowship there), and The Queen's College, Oxford. The third is the education that I received a few hundred yards away at Corpus Christi College, where I studied for my undergraduate, master's, and most of my doctoral degree. Those familiar with Christian iconography, or foxed by why a Briton would acknowledge, before all else, the great state of Louisiana (which I have never had the pleasure of visiting), might have already divined the origins of this book's dedication. It has been some years since I left Corpus, but that just makes me all the keener to acknowledge its place in my intellectual development.

When I started at the college, alongside another future Americanist, David Sim, Corpus had no reputation for scholarship on the United States. Given the multivalent medievalist that is John Watts, that was no defect in itself. But over just a few years, I had the pleasure of watching Oxford's smallest college attract an outsized cluster of experts in US history: Jay Sexton, Richard Carwardine (an old member, back as the college's president), Nigel Bowles, Stephen Tuffnell, Skye Montgomery, Alice Kelly, and Katherine Paugh.

May the hive buzz forever.

Terminology

For the most part, this book uses "African American" and "black" interchangeably, though it is more precise whenever it (also) refers to the black populations of places other than the United States. Furthermore, it features both "freepeople" and "freedpeople": the former were those African Americans who had been free for a long time, perhaps their entire lives, while the latter were those freed recently, even prospectively (such as by the Emancipation Proclamation or by colonizationist slaveholders who stipulated slaves' emigration as the price of their freedom).

As befits a book that focuses on foreign countries as much as on the United States, it uses both "immigration" and "emigration," depending on whether the sense is more one of people arriving or leaving. If both directions are pertinent, then it uses the neutral "migration." The names and spellings of polities are the common English forms of the day, but "Hayti" is "Haiti" because of its sheer recurrence, while "Santo Domingo" is "the Dominican Republic" wherever it does not refer to the restored Spanish colony of 1861–5.

Abbreviations

For personal papers, footnotes normally cite the item, the name of the collection, and the archive. The reader should assume that such collections, whether available on microfilm, online, or as only the original manuscripts, are easily navigated with a finding aid or the obvious search terms, and that the item comes under the main series of correspondence unless stated otherwise. For personal papers arranged in a more complex manner, and for institutional records, footnotes offer more detail.

ACS	American Colonization Society Records, LC
AL	Abraham Lincoln Papers, LC
AR	*African Repository*
BF	Blair Family Papers, LC
BL	Blair and Lee Family Papers, Princeton University
CG	*Congressional Globe*
CO123/456	Colonial Office Records, series 123, book 456 (example)
CWAL	Roy P. Basler, ed., *The Collected Works of Abraham Lincoln* (New Brunswick, NJ, 1953–5)
FDP	*Frederick Douglass' Paper*
FO123/456	Foreign Office Records, series 123, book 456 (example)
HCPP 1812 (34)	House of Commons Parliamentary Paper, session of 1812, paper 34 (example)
LC	Library of Congress
NARA	National Archives and Records Administration, Washington, DC
NARA II	National Archives and Records Administration, College Park, MD

NYPL	New York Public Library
PRFA	*Papers Relating to Foreign Affairs*
RG12/34/56	Record Group 12, entry 34, box or book 56 (example)
RG12/M34/56	Record Group 12, microfilm series 34, reel 56 (example, "M" publication)
RG12/T34/56	Record Group 12, microfilm series 34, reel 56 (example, "T" publication)
TNA	The National Archives, Kew, United Kingdom
WAA	*Weekly Anglo-African*
WHS	William Henry Seward Papers, University of Rochester

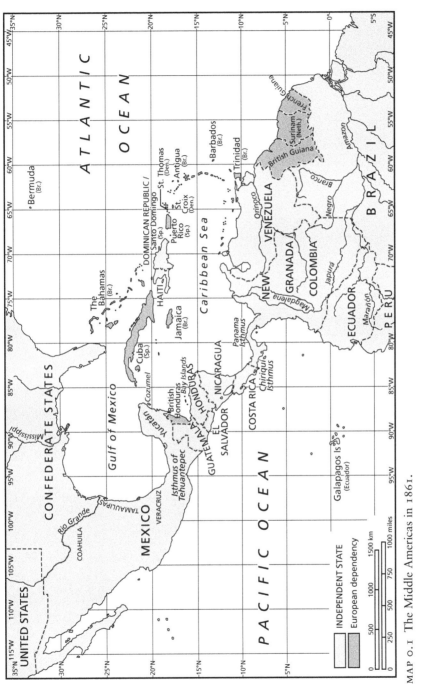

MAP 0.1 The Middle Americas in 1861.

Introduction

From the Revolution to the Civil War, white Americans entertained the strangest of notions: their black compatriots, who comprised one-fifth of the population in 1770 and still one-seventh by 1860, could, would, and should leave the United States for some other land. Stranger yet, the same blacks whom whites thought too degraded to ever form part of the American nation would civilize other peoples, thanks, ironically, to the American influences that they had imbued.[1] That belief was called "colonization," at once an ideology, a movement, and, most famously, the eponymous project of the American Colonization Society (ACS), established in 1816–17.[2] In the 1820s, the northern reformers and southern slaveholders who had founded the ACS secured a settlement in west Africa for black Americans, which they named Liberia. Although these "colonizationists" – that is to say, the supporters of colonization, as distinct from the colonists themselves – would be the best-known face of the movement, the ACS (and Liberia) was far from the only scheme (and location) that Americans had in mind. Indeed, the major contribution of this book is to chronicle the full geographic and institutional range of the drive for black resettlement.

In the labor-hungry Americas of the nineteenth century, it was remarkable that a movement to expel part of the workforce even existed,

---

[1] Hugh Davis, "Northern Colonizationists and Free Blacks, 1823–1837: A Case Study of Leonard Bacon," *Journal of the Early Republic* 17 (1997), 662; Samuel E. Cornish and Theodore S. Wright, *The Colonization Scheme Considered* (Newark, 1840), 15–16.
[2] Eric Foner, "Abraham Lincoln, Colonization, and the Rights of Black Americans," in Richard J. Follett et al., eds., *Slavery's Ghost: The Problem of Freedom in the Age of Emancipation* (Baltimore, 2011), 34.

let alone inspired humanitarians, politicians, and the public.[3] That lesser-known manifestation of "American exceptionalism" reflected a combination of demographic, economic, and intellectual factors peculiar to the United States and its cultural hinterland (in certain respects), Canada.[4] Uniquely among the western Atlantic polities that permitted slavery by 1861 (which otherwise meant Brazil, Cuba, Puerto Rico, and Surinam), the United States saw its enslaved population keep growing by natural reproduction – the only way that it *could*, once Britain and the United States had each banned the transatlantic trade in 1807–8. Although ending the slave trade was the obvious complement to removing those foreign "Africans" (in reality, African Americans) already present in the United States, that virtual precondition might not have sufficed, on its own, to encourage so many white Americans to try exiling their black neighbors.[5] But the United States of the long nineteenth century was also blessed with the bulk of Europe's emigrants to the Americas, a demographic luxury that allowed politicians from the northern states (where slave agriculture was less significant than in the southern states) to agitate for the western territories of the ever-receding frontier to be reserved for white settlers, who would shun living alongside black competitors.

Congress endorsed that "free soil" impulse with the Northwest Ordinance (1787), banning slavery from those territories east of the Mississippi that would become Illinois, Indiana, Ohio, Michigan, and Wisconsin, as well as with the Missouri Compromise (1820), banning slavery from those territories west of the Mississippi (gained from France in the Louisiana Purchase of 1803) that lay above 36°30′N. Granted, at the same time, Congress allowed slavery to expand into the southerly lands where the institution would prove more valuable. Moreover, the federal government could not prevent any *state*, as a territory became once admitted to the Union, from exercising its sovereignty by adopting slavery. Despite congressmen's concessions to southerners' property

---

[3] Seymour Drescher, *Abolition: A History of Slavery and Antislavery* (New York, 2009), 140; Alexis de Tocqueville and Henry Reeve, trans., *Democracy in America* (New York, 1839), 373–4.

[4] Nicholas Guyatt, "Tocqueville's Prophecy: The United States and the Caribbean, 1850–1871," in Jörg Nagler et al., eds., *The Transnational Significance of the American Civil War* (New York, 2016), 205–6, 221.

[5] Christa Dierksheide, *Amelioration and Empire: Progress and Slavery in the Plantation Americas* (Charlottesville, 2014), 27.

rights, however, advocates of slavery's expansion found themselves on the ideological defensive until the late antebellum period.

Political debates over slavery had assumed such an antislavery default because they were steeped in an Anglo-American tradition of abolitionism (in its limited, pre-1830s sense), which had emerged as a formal movement on both sides of the Atlantic during the American Revolution. By the 1770s, many white Americans, north and south, agreed that slavery was inefficient compared with free labor. (They would doubt that piety after 1793, when the invention of the cotton gin birthed a new slave economy, and dismiss it after 1834, when the abolition of slavery in the British West Indies nearly destroyed the old sugar industry.) They also thought bondage unrepublican, by depriving slaveholders of the economic independence required of virtuous citizens, and unchristian, by denying that God had "made of one blood all nations of men," as the Bible had it. Yet while metropolitan Britons could emancipate their colonial slaves without having to live alongside them, and while ancient slaveowners could manumit those whose servile status had never been based on racial difference, white Americans felt unable to do either.[6] In the words of the slaveholder, intellectual, and third president, Thomas Jefferson, "among the Romans, emancipation required but one effort. The slave, when made free, might mix with, without staining, the blood of his master. But with us a second is necessary, unknown to history. When freed, he is to be removed beyond the reach of mixture."[7] For the rest of his life, Jefferson worried about the "blot" of America's own black population, and supported colonization – at least, notionally.

Jefferson's concerns were echoed by other white Americans, who embraced black resettlement whenever they probed the social, cultural, and racial foundations of their nation. During the nineteenth century, thinkers throughout the Atlantic world moved from an inclusionary, civic understanding of nationalism, in which the nation comprised all men (though usually not women) who attested shared political values, to an exclusionary, ethnic one, in which the nation comprised those united by lineage, language, and religion. Despite African Americans' claims to a *cultural* Anglo-Saxonism, ethnic definitions of the American nation self-evidently left less room than the civic one for a racial minority whose ancestors had, in fact, usually arrived in the United States earlier than had

[6] David Brion Davis, *Inhuman Bondage: The Rise and Fall of Slavery in the New World* (New York, 2006), 176.
[7] Thomas Jefferson, *Notes on the State of Virginia* (Boston, 1802), 199.

whites'.[8] (Moreover, even the civic definition could exclude former slaves, whom, Jefferson alleged, bondage had left unfit to participate in politics.)[9] While an increasingly diverse range of European immigrants precluded the narrowly Protestant, British-descended homogeneity that nativists desired, virtually all white men could agree, unsurprisingly, that their government should be one of, by, and for white men. And in reality, compared with those countries south of the Rio Grande, it *was*. The precursor colonies of the United States had been settler colonies, dominated by white immigrants who had dispossessed Native Americans and imported Africans only as slaves, so white Americans could just about contrive to treat "race" in (literally) black and white terms. By contrast, the Spanish and Portuguese colonies had been conquest colonies, in which limited numbers of Iberian immigrants had, by necessity, formed interracial relationships. Accordingly, Latin American norms acknowledged a smoother spectrum of color, though with the darkest-skinned still at the "inferior" end, than did Anglo-American mores. That was why, even as white "United Statians" (a term that this book ultimately avoids) attempted to expel their black compatriots, Latin Americans contemplated, albeit with misgivings, extending a home to the putative exiles.

It takes no expert to surmise that white Americans' expulsive impetus, though ever present in US race relations, was almost always a frustrated one. Indeed, that fact imbues the movement for black resettlement with its true significance, for that very record of failed colonization efforts attests to whites' inability to imagine a biracial society outside, and sometimes even within, the framework of black slavery. Yet Euro-Americans also discerned mechanisms other than colonization for "whitening" the United States, even as African Americans grew in number from 750,000 in 1790 to 4,500,000 in 1860 (of whom 4,000,000 were slaves). Where slavery had once seemed an obsolete institution, which the states from Pennsylvania northward had, by 1804, moved to extirpate, a viable US cotton industry from the 1790s sealed the fate of the Southwest as a land defined by bondage. Moreover, Congress's territorial restrictions of 1787 and 1820 were matched by its acquiescence in slavery's expansion

---

[8] Dale T. Knobel, "'Native Soil': Nativists, Colonizationists, and the Rhetoric of Nationality," *Civil War History* 27 (1981), 325; Paul Quigley, *Shifting Grounds: Nationalism and the American South, 1848–1865* (New York, 2011), 6, 31; Jay Rubin, "Black Nativism: The European Immigrant in Negro Thought, 1830–1860," *Phylon* 39 (1978), 199–200.

[9] Brian Steele, *Thomas Jefferson and American Nationhood* (New York, 2012), 180–1.

into more lucrative lands, while the Compromise of 1850 and Kansas–Nebraska Act of 1854 removed the Missouri Compromise's 36°30′N prohibition altogether.[10] But the workings of the internal slave trade, which drained slaves from the cornfields of Maryland, Virginia, and Missouri to the cotton plantations of Alabama, Mississippi, and Louisiana, achieved much of what the booster-colonizationists of the upper South had desired.[11] The one-way traffic that characterized the internal slave trade had been ensconced by the US ban on new slaves from Africa, and so underpinned the main alternative to colonization, known as "diffusion." This was an idea that Virginians had articulated as early as 1798 and that became popular during the sectionally charged debates of 1820 over the admission of Missouri as a slave state. Diffusion, southern congressmen claimed, would not only save them from a growing population of restive blacks in the older states, but hasten emancipation by spreading slavery too thinly for it to survive.[12]

Yet if the logistics of mass colonization perplexed racial separatists, so did the sophistry of diffusion, which would expand slavery in order, supposedly, to weaken it. Diffusion also came with a deadline: it could work for only as long as the United States had space.[13] By the 1840s and 1850s, expansionists proposed the obvious answer, not caring much whether US troops or unauthorized "filibusterers" annexed the independent states of Central America and European colonies of the Caribbean. Part of the expansionists' logic was their pseudo-scientific belief that black people gravitated toward the tropics, which was to endorse a form of diffusionism with which colonizationists could agree – only, where the former envisioned blacks in the tropics in a state of slavery, the latter did so in one of freedom.[14]

Given the speculative basis of all ideologies of US expansion, there could be no clear sectional alignment on the merits of annexationism, its southern tinge notwithstanding. Even South Carolina's most famous exponent of proslavery and states' rights, Senator John Calhoun, opposed seizing the whole of Mexico following the Mexican-American War

---

[10] Edward E. Baptist, *The Half Has Never Been Told: Slavery and the Making of American Capitalism* (New York, 2014), 8, 29–30, 155.
[11] Lacy K. Ford, *Deliver Us from Evil: The Slavery Question in the Old South* (New York, 2009), 73–6; Walter Johnson, "The Future Store," in his *The Chattel Principle: Internal Slave Trades in the Americas* (New Haven, 2004), 20.
[12] Dierksheide, *Amelioration and Empire*, 44–7.   [13] Davis, *Inhuman Bondage*, 277.
[14] Robert E. Bonner, *Mastering America: Southern Slaveholders and the Crisis of American Nationhood* (New York, 2009), 32–7.

(1846–8), because of the difficulties that he perceived of incorporating a large ethnic minority into the Union.[15] In the 1850s, his fellow inhabitants of the Palmetto State, James Henry Hammond and James De Bow, worried that the expansion of American slavery into the tropics would accelerate the drain of slaves from the upper South, and so disturb the delicate political balance between free and slave states.[16] Indeed, whites' debates about distributing black people over space engulfed late antebellum politics. Historians should not treat the relative importance of its distinct (but overlapping) schools of thought as a zero-sum consideration: it was no coincidence that the campaigns for territorial slavery, black colonization, tropical expansion, and even the reopening of the Atlantic slave trade all peaked in the 1850s.[17]

In light of America's unknowable future at mid-century, it was also no coincidence that the practically hardest, but intellectually simplest answer to the "race question," black expatriation, garnered the support that it did from political centrists. Self-styled moderates prayed that the venture would unite the sections of North and South, not only by removing the ostensible source of antagonism between them, but also by requiring material sacrifice from each. Statesmen lauded a scheme that, moreover, combined a lofty providential fantasy – that, with initial help, African Americans could replicate the self-sustaining migration that had driven oppressed Europeans to America – with the political malleability of its avowed focus on free blacks.[18] For a proslavery planter in the lower South, that might mean the few local freepeople, whose anomalous example risked prompting his own slaves to rebel; for a booster in the upper South, that might mean the slaves on his own plantation, or even those throughout the state, freed in waves and on condition of their emigration; and for an evangelical in the North, that might mean every slave in America, freed and sent to Africa to bring Christianity, civilization, and commerce to the presumably benighted natives. And despite their critics' refrains, colonizationists could contend that mass removal had become more viable, not less, by 1850. If the spread of slavery had, in

---

[15] Steven Hahn, *A Nation without Borders: The United States and Its World in an Age of Civil Wars, 1830–1910* (New York, 2016), 139–40.

[16] Lacy Ford, "Reconsidering the Internal Slave Trade: Paternalism, Markets, and the Character of the Old South," in Johnson, *Chattel Principle*, 154–60.

[17] Walter Johnson, *River of Dark Dreams: Slavery and Empire in the Cotton Kingdom* (Cambridge, MA, 2013), 399–406.

[18] Nicholas Guyatt, *Providence and the Invention of the United States, 1607–1876* (New York, 2007), 183–94.

one respect, made the work of resettlement harder, then the decrease in African Americans as a proportion of the population, the growth of charitable organizations, a string of favorable political precedents (such as Indian removal), and the emergence of superior forms of transport (such as the steamship) had at once made it easier. Who was to say that colonization could not succeed?[19]

Lots of people, it turned out – not least the inhabitants of those countries that were supposed to accept African American immigrants. Across the Atlantic world, foreign governments and those acting in their name (whether authorized or not) beheld with everything from horror to elation what one Colombian described as an impetus "entirely peculiar" to the United States.[20] The two countries populated and governed wholly by black people, the west African republic of Liberia and the West Indian autocracy (usually) of Haiti, welcomed African American immigrants – the former having no existence without them. Meanwhile, the two contiguous neighbors of the United States, the republic of Mexico and the British colonies that comprised Canada, had little choice but to accept African American immigrants, often fugitives from US slavery. But more distant lands could exercise greater control in the matter. Although the rulers of the heterogenous states of Ibero-America scrutinized any influx liable to darken the population, the administrators of the struggling post-emancipation European West Indies grasped at any prospect of additional labor, while, however, comparing the merits of African Americans with those of "free" (in reality, bonded) workers from Africa, China, and India.

Furthermore, both national and imperial governments moved to restrain the commercial, often US-based interests that lobbied for the migration of black Americans, since such investors were too often willing to risk diplomatic crisis for personal gain. Stakeholders unilaterally surrendered geostrategic locations and sovereign prerogatives to American actors, or blithely risked the host polity's relations with the southern section of the United States – during the Civil War, a power in its own right, the Confederacy. Before 1861, foreign recruiters of African Americans might incur a lawsuit by inadvertently accepting fugitive

[19] Joanne Pope Melish, *Disowning Slavery: Gradual Emancipation and "Race" in New England, 1780–1860* (Ithaca, 1998), 193–4.
[20] "Inmigración de libertos norte-americanos a Chiriquí," *La Estrella de Panamá*, November 29, 1862.

slaves; after 1861, they might provoke war by deliberately trafficking Confederate slaves freed under Union auspices, the so-called contrabands.

Although politicians tried to keep the sensitive diplomacy of colonization within the corridors of power, their plans could hardly escape the notice of their would-be beneficiaries, African Americans. For the most part, blacks objected to whites' presumption in trying to exile them, especially when "back" to an Africa that, following the closure of the slave trade, fewer and fewer had ever seen. While resettlement plans were usually doomed for want of concurrent consent from slaveholders, politicians, and funders, the (largely withheld) consent of African Americans was always the greatest limiting factor on such schemes. But where enslaved southerners had to resist expatriation without fanfare, and often faced the stark choice between an unknowable freedom in Liberia and continued bondage in the United States, free northerners proclaimed their objections to the ACS from its founding. Yet, like their white counterparts, black Americans were engaged in an inchoate, even chaotic process of nation-building. Theirs was self-evidently a nation *within* a nation, a duality that, if anything, divided black separatists and black integrationists by a common language. Although African Americans preferred to invoke civic forms of nationalism, asserting their birthright citizenship long before the Civil Rights Act (1866) and Fourteenth Amendment to the US Constitution (1868) did the same, they also flirted with nationalism's ethnic bases, exploring their commonality with the other peoples of Africa and the African diaspora. During the intensified white oppression of the 1820s and 1850s, several thousand African Americans emigrated to Canada, Liberia, and Haiti, each of which appealed to a different facet of their identities as African *and* American. But the settlers' fraught interactions with the natives of Liberia and Haiti, in particular, confirmed what opponents of emigration had long maintained: African Americans were, first and foremost, Americans, as prone as their white compatriots to the sense of cultural superiority that that entailed.

For a century from 1770, almost every American institution, black and white, public and private, state and federal, engaged with the drive to resettle African Americans, even if fitfully or fleetingly. Along with a host of hitherto obscure figures, colonization implicated a number of well-known individuals: US presidents from Thomas Jefferson to Abraham Lincoln, black abolitionists from James Forten to Frederick Douglass, and global leaders from Earl Russell, Britain's foreign minister during the Civil War, to Dom Pedro II, the emperor of Brazil for half a century. If sometimes just for a moment, black resettlement affected lands from

Canada to Argentina, the Danish West Indies to the Niger Valley, and Haiti to Liberia. Some Americans even proposed that blacks remove to Australia, Cyprus, and Poland.[21] Colonization was notorious in its own day, and has not wanted for academic interest since the very dawn of the American historical profession.[22] Why, then, has it taken a century and a half for a scholar to write the first comprehensive, comparative survey of the long-acknowledged revival of colonization during the Civil War era?

This book has surely benefited from the growth of Atlantic history, though it also straddles a number of specializations within US history proper, such as black history, Civil War history, and the history of reform movements.[23] More than a mastery of a disparate scholarship, however, what this book needed was a researcher willing to overcome their incredulity about the entire venture of black resettlement. For, despite a secondary literature that has exploded even since the turn of the millennium, colonization remains the butt of derision from many historians, who misdirect their criticism of "unrealistic" historical actors toward those colleagues who would study the same. Get beyond scholars' pained expressions (an image born of personal experience), and their objections seem to be threefold.

First, colonization was impractical. Between the Revolution and the Civil War, the black population of the United States increased by more than 3,500,000. In the same period, slightly more than 20,000 African Americans emigrated to Liberia, Haiti, and the British West Indies (combined) via formal emigration agencies, and a similar number to Canada on their own initiative.[24] How can those individual, even anecdotal stories of migration hold any importance compared with the headline event, the ultimate freedom, on American soil, of 4,000,000 slaves?

[21] "Meeting of the State Council, in Behalf of Colored Americans," *Liberator*, February 24, 1854 (Australia); W. Winthrop to W. H. Seward, No. 49, September 8, 1862, Despatches from U.S. Consuls in Malta, RG59/T218/5, NARA II (Cyprus); Cassius Clay, *The Life of Cassius Marcellus Clay* (Cincinnati, 1886), 1:440 (Poland).

[22] Beverly C. Tomek, "The Past, Present, and Future of Colonization Studies," in Tomek and Matthew J. Hetrick, eds., *New Directions in the Study of African American Recolonization* (Gainesville, 2017), 11–17.

[23] Don H. Doyle, "The Atlantic World and the Crisis of the 1860s," in his *American Civil Wars: The United States, Latin America, Europe, and the Crisis of the 1860s* (Chapel Hill, 2017), 1.

[24] Nicholas Guyatt, "Rethinking Colonization in the Early United States," in Tomek, *New Directions*, 329; Michael Wayne, "The Black Population of Canada West on the Eve of the American Civil War: A Reassessment Based on the Manuscript Census of 1861," *Social History* 28 (1995), 470.

Second, colonization was evasive. Adherents of the ACS were mealy-mouthed about whether they meant to end slavery – no surprise, given the diametric views they had to navigate. Not as eloquent in their speech or elegant in their stance as the institution's overt opponents, it is tempting to dismiss them as on the wrong side of history.

Third, colonization was, arguably, immoral – but certainly amoral, and confusing for that reason. Colonizationists usually admitted blacks' natural rights, but were so resigned to the persistence of other whites' prejudice – always that of meaner whites than themselves, in their imagination – that they could only suggest that blacks emigrate.[25] Whenever mobs destroyed black homes, lawmakers disfranchised black voters, or masters insisted on deporting black slaves as the price of their freedom, colonizationists shrugged and handed out pamphlets extolling their preferred destination.

Why, then, study a movement of such seeming irrelevance to the story of American freedom? The answer is simple: it is our duty as historians to rescue proponents of black resettlement from what E. P. Thompson so memorably called "the enormous condescension of posterity." At the same time, it is not our duty to rehabilitate them or to invoke the discipline's stock platitude that we should not apply the standards of the present to the past. Colonizationists knew full well that the preamble of the Declaration of Independence promised more to black Americans than whites were willing to concede (at least, in the United States). What the black abolitionist David Walker called the "colonizing trick" was the proffer not of unreflective racists but of thoughtful, would-be enlightened Americans.[26] It was not an eccentricity of marginal relevance, but an idea that, like all ideas, did not exist in isolation, and that dampened what might have been a more ardent integrationism on the part of antislavery "moderates." It was not the inevitable product of some backward age but a conscious artifice, which we know because its opponents mustered every last criticism – moral, political, and logistical – that we, too, would make.

The separatist impulse makes for history at its most frustrating, and nowhere more so than in its zenith during the Civil War, when two and a

---

[25] Annette Gordon-Reed, "The Resonance of Minds: Thomas Jefferson and James Madison in the Republic of Letters," in Frank Shuffelton, ed., *The Cambridge Companion to Thomas Jefferson* (New York, 2009), 189–90.

[26] David Kazanjian, *The Colonizing Trick: National Culture and Imperial Citizenship in Early America* (Minneapolis, 2003), 1–2.

half centuries of American bondage were, hindsight tells us, about to draw to a close. That awkward juxtaposition defies two of our tendencies as historians: to perceive change rather than continuity, and difference rather than similarity. When we emphasize change and difference, we elevate the importance of our own period of study, and preempt the accusation that we have been insensitive to contrast. Yet it is those two habits that have prevented historians from acknowledging the sheer persistence and kindred nature of the many schemes for black resettlement.

Our need to perceive change impels us to treat the end of slavery as the epochal moment when the light of self-evident truths finally shone through the darkness of antebellum America. Yet those truths had long had their vocal champions, notably African Americans, whom nothing had vexed like the offer of civic equality through racial outsourcing. Black abolitionists protested the ACS's plans from 1817 and, belatedly joined by white allies, seemed to have claimed antislavery for the principle of "no expatriation" by the mid-1830s. So when, just a decade later, whites troubled by the sectionalism arising from the Mexican-American War once more considered ousting their black neighbors, they revived an idea long discredited by its adversaries. And when politicians proved willing, during the Civil War itself, to emancipate, enlist, and even enfranchise African Americans, few of them stopped believing that blacks would eventually part from their white compatriots. How much further might the architects of what James McPherson has called the "second American Revolution" have gone if they *had*?

At the same time, our need to perceive difference makes us overlook the underlying cohesion of the separatist impetus because of the (sometimes literally) skin-deep differences between the various projects for black removal. Partly, that is the result of the loaded lexicon that contemporaries used for such schemes, be it "colonization," "deportation," "emigration," "expatriation," or "transportation." Two distinctions, in particular, continue to exercise scholars. One is a more modern preoccupation, but the other is a convention that dates to the period concerned, and so deserves more careful consideration.

The first distinction, which would have some merit in diplomatic history proper, is that "colonization" must involve one polity asserting sovereignty over territories gained from another. In truth, the word merely comes from the Latin *colonus*, a farmer. The "colonies" of ancient Rome were agricultural outposts, and the sense of "political dependencies" an addition, though not a substitution, of the eighteenth century.[27] Moreover, in a world of flexible maps and fluid migrations, only clairvoyants could have known which movements would result in annexation and which not. For example, the American "Colonization" Society disavowed sovereignty over Liberia by the mid-1840s, while the Central American republics protested Abraham Lincoln's colonization schemes because they feared that even immigrants who swore loyalty to their new government might invoke US protection.

The second distinction is that "colonization" must refer to the white-led movement for black resettlement, and "emigration" to its black-led counterpart. Certainly, we should acknowledge important differences. Where white colonizationists usually hoped to remove the entire black population in the fullness of time (even as they accepted that they would have to start small), black emigrationists treated relocation as one option among many, and better kept to an enterprising minority. Where those whites still loyal to colonization from the 1830s usually remained supporters for life, blacks changed their mind about emigration as their prospects in the United States waxed and waned. Such vacillations met with accusations of betrayal from stalwart integrationists, so it should not surprise us that black emigrationists never declared themselves for "colonization," the word of the hated ACS. But even colonizationists rarely supported outright coercion, abolitionists' most serious charge against them; conversely, emigrationists had to request the financial, political, and practical help of colonizationists more than they would have liked. We do not dismiss black agency or black identity by upholding the semantic distinction between "colonization" and "emigration," as this book does, while, at the same time, not using it to denote fundamental differences. Others might disagree, but to overcome colonization's woeful legacy of divisiveness, we might at least choose to coexist on the same ground.[28]

And what is that ground? That, from the antebellum period through the Civil War, there was an embarrassment of projects aimed at removing African Americans from the United States. This book treats that

---

[27] Barbara Arneil, *Domestic Colonies: The Turn inward to Colony* (Oxford, 2017), 5.
[28] For the debate over terminology, see Martha S. Jones, *Birthright Citizens: A History of Race and Rights in Antebellum America* (New York, 2018), 37–8; Floyd J. Miller, *The Search for a Black Nationality: Black Emigration and Colonization, 1787–1863* (Urbana, 1975), vii; Wilson Jeremiah Moses, *The Golden Age of Black Nationalism, 1850–1925* (New York, 1978), 32–3; and Ousmane K. Power-Greene, *Against Wind and Tide: The African American Struggle against the Colonization Movement* (New York, 2014), xix.

phenomenon as "resettlement," not just because of the debate surrounding "colonization" and "emigration," but because other aspects of racial separatism, such as the state laws that forbade the immigration of African Americans or the pseudo-science that forecasted their gravitation southward, put little effort into determining their destination, the *true* prerequisite of colonization. Moreover, the work of black resettlement involved many more countries than the United States and Liberia, whose usage of "colonization" was at least idiomatic, even if not incorrect as such.

Despite the unavoidable chronological overlap between chapters, there is, in fact, a long arc to this book. But it is not, as Martin Luther King, Jr., once remarked (in paraphrasing an 1853 sermon by a white abolitionist, Theodore Parker), one that bends toward moral justice. Rather, it bends toward the ever more viable locations that Americans – white politicians, certainly, but black emigrationists too – considered for black resettlement. Chapter 1 addresses the most familiar face of the colonization movement, the white-run ACS and its west African settlement of Liberia, as well as the all too obvious limitations of the Liberian project by 1861. Chapter 2 likewise covers the antebellum period, but from the perspective of (mostly northern) African Americans, who emigrated in their thousands to Canada and Haiti after 1850, and some of whom even reconsidered Africa, despite its tainted association with the ACS. But the colonizationists of the new, antislavery Republican Party, whose support for resettlement is treated in Chapter 3, spurned Liberia for the independent states of Latin America, with the catastrophic results charted in Chapter 4. In response, Republican policy makers changed their focus again, to the European colonies of the West Indies, which Chapter 5 shows to have received, some years earlier, more African American immigrants than scholars had realized. For all that, though, the politicians revisited in Chapter 6 need only have left it to natural forces, or so they came to believe, to prevent black immigration northward, even promote black emigration southward. While we see emancipation, total and unqualified, as the proudest legacy of the Civil War, white northerners saw their real triumph as having contained the geography of black freedom.

We might prefer to view the colonizationist revival as a tortuous diversion from the moral high road to an integrated America, especially given the iconic Lincoln's enthusiasm for the idea. But what if *Reconstruction* were the anomaly, diminishing the normality of antebellum separatism only by false contrast? What if African Americans once again responded to a white onslaught on their rights with emigrationism, from the late nineteenth century and into the twentieth? What if plans for distant resettlement were just an earlier form of what we know as segregation, scaled up for a globe that had seemed to offer more space? What if the expulsive pressures that the authorities applied to African Americans prefigured those that they exert today on unauthorized immigrants, and even on American-born members of minority groups? What if racial integration were the exception in US history, and separation the rule?

This book can only ever be part of a longer story.

I

The Revival of "Colonization," to 1861

By 1850, for most white Americans, black resettlement meant one organization and one destination: the American Colonization Society (ACS), founded over the winter of 1816–17, and Liberia, the west African exclave that it negotiated with native peoples in 1821–2.

Beyond such matters of fact, historians have agreed on almost nothing about the ACS. They even dispute the identity of its founder, because its inaugural gathering, the culmination of a separatist impulse present since the American Revolution, drew together such a diverse range of reformers and slaveholders, who tasked themselves with "removing the free people of color, with their own consent."[1] There ended any clarity of purpose, through the Civil War and beyond.

FAULT LINES

Was such a migration supposed to benefit whites, or blacks? To civilize the United States, or Africa? To spread Christianity, or republicanism? The society's journal, the *African Repository*, never tired of raising and miraculously resolving such false dilemmas.[2] But from the outset, the

---

[1] Douglas R. Egerton, "'Its Origin Is Not a Little Curious': A New Look at the American Colonization Society," *Journal of the Early Republic* 5 (1985), 463–80; Nicholas Guyatt, *Bind Us Apart: How Enlightened Americans Invented Racial Segregation* (New York, 2016), 378–9n32; Matthew Spooner, "'I Know This Scheme Is from God': Toward a Reconsideration of the Origins of the American Colonization Society," *Slavery and Abolition* 35 (2014), 559–75.
[2] Carl Patrick Burrowes, "Black Christian Republicanism: A Southern Ideology in Early Liberia, 1822 to 1847," *Journal of Negro History* 86 (2001), 30–44.

ACS's chosen terrain contained two fault lines that demanded more skillful evasion.

First, did the "free people of color" embrace those slaves who might be freed on condition of emigrating, as well as the already free? The former definition might seem antislavery in its purpose, since it allowed masters to act on their guilt over the "peculiar institution" by freeing their slaves while stipulating that they also be sent away, to the presumable benefit of both races. Conversely, it might seem proslavery – and the removal of the already free, unambiguously so – since it banished those whose newfound freedom might inspire slaves to claim their own liberty. Little wonder that Henry Clay, slaveholder, statesman, and future president of the society, suggested to his fellow drafters that they make no reference to emancipation in the ACS's constitution.

Two centuries later, the jury is still out. In recent years, most historians have thought that a "moderate" antislavery underpinned the colonization movement and that most masters who freed their slaves and sent them to Liberia probably would not have done so except on that condition (or *could* not have done otherwise, by state law).[3] Moreover, slavery's defenders made little time for an idea that smacked of danger for the institution. Yet viewing the question laterally, it is harder to dismiss abolitionist charges that promulgating separation increased white prejudice against African Americans and forestalled greater unity behind a more assertive, nonexpulsive antislavery.[4] For slaves, manumission conditional on emigration also made a mockery of "consent," but even for free blacks, that word had "a power of mischief above all others," as the black abolitionist and former slave, Frederick Douglass, put it.[5]

Second, was colonization a work of government, or of charity – public, or private? That fault line also ran back to the ACS's earliest days, after US Representative Charles Mercer, a Virginia politician and one of two "candidates" for founder of the ACS, inveigled the society's way into

---

[3] Eric Burin, *Slavery and the Peculiar Solution: A History of the American Colonization Society* (Gainesville, 2005), x; Samantha Seeley, "Beyond the American Colonization Society," *History Compass* 14 (2016), 95–6.

[4] Andrew Diemer, "'A Desire to Better Their Condition': European Immigration, African Colonization, and the Lure of Consensual Emancipation," in Beverly C. Tomek and Matthew J. Hetrick, eds., *New Directions in the Study of African American Recolonization* (Gainesville, 2017), 250.

[5] Claude A. Clegg, *The Price of Liberty: African Americans and the Making of Liberia* (Chapel Hill, 2004), 189–90; "Persecution on Account of Faith, Persecution on Account of Color," January 26, 1851, in John W. Blassingame and John R. McKivigan, eds., *The Frederick Douglass Papers* (New Haven, 1979–92), 2:309.

resettling "recaptives," those survivors of the illegal transatlantic slave trade intercepted at sea. Under Mercer's own Slave Trade Act (1819), they would now be returned to a US agent on the coast of Africa, regardless of their provenance *within* that continent.[6] Since 1808, the United States had outlawed the importation of slaves, and the recent debates over the admission of Missouri left congressmen grateful for the only solution that did not draw the federal government into implicit commentary on domestic slavery, which either selling the recaptives or freeing them on American soil would have done.[7] Indeed, it was under the auspices of the Slave Trade Act that the US Navy secured its foothold in Liberia in the first place.

The prevailing mood of anti-imperialism and strict constructionism meant that the US government always rebuffed any suggestion that *it* had founded a colony. President James Monroe (1817–25), for whom Liberia's capital, Monrovia, is named, argued that he had merely enabled a venture by a private organization. Further shipments of recaptives and additional ACS dealings with the US Navy strained that distinction, however. The "colonial question" perplexed not only American diplomats, who, during the 1840s, had to handle British inquiries over Liberia's status, but also colonizationists themselves, who had to depict the settlement as neither a dependency unworthy of republican support, like Sierra Leone, its neighbor and Britain's own receptacle for recaptives, nor a normal US territory on track for statehood.[8]

In practice, the extent of federal support for the ACS followed wider political trends. During the 1820s, colonizationists had presented their work as part of Clay's "American System" of internal improvements, but their ever-bolder proposals provoked a backlash from the lower South. In 1830, President Andrew Jackson (1829–37) subjected the ACS to a hostile audit, which found that it had misappropriated the recaptives fund by improving the colony and funding the emigration of free black Americans.[9]

---

[6] Eric Burin, "The Slave Trade Act of 1819: A New Look at Colonization and the Politics of Slavery," *American Nineteenth Century History* 13 (2012), 1–14.

[7] Hazel Akehurst, "Sectional Crises and the Fate of Africans Illegally Imported into the United States, 1806–1860," *American Nineteenth Century History* 9 (2008), 97–122.

[8] For the role of the US government, see David F. Ericson, "The American Colonization Society's Not-So-Private Colonization Project," Bronwen Everill, "Experiments in Colonial Citizenship in Sierra Leone and Liberia," and Brandon Mills, "Situating African Colonization Within the History of U.S. Expansion," in Tomek, *New Directions*, 111–28, 184–205, 166–83, respectively.

[9] Burin, *Peculiar Solution*, 17–18.

Other developments also steered the work of colonization away from the center and toward the states, whose jurisdiction over local race relations was beyond mainstream dispute. The white backlash from the deadliest slave rising in US history, Virginia's Nat Turner's Rebellion (1831), prompted 1,300 black southerners to flee to Liberia over less than two years. The insurrection also prompted legislators, in Virginia and farther afield, to review the competing merits of colonization and diffusion, the rival scheme that would remove those dangerous, bottled-up African Americans by dispersing them westward, across the growing Union. The upper South, whose black population contained a higher proportion of freepeople than the lower South's, would hereafter take an active interest in colonization, which offered to exchange black natives and the torpor of slavery for white immigrants and the vitality of free labor. Virginia, Tennessee, and Maryland appropriated money for colonization, the last earmarking $200,000 for the already free *and* recent manumittees.[10]

While legislators in the upper South warmed to colonization, reformers in the North cooled on it. With his *Thoughts on African Colonization* (1832), Boston's William Lloyd Garrison began an exodus of antislavery whites from colonizationism to immediatist abolitionism, which demanded emancipation without delay or deportation. Indeed, the ACS itself proved susceptible to sectional fissure between its northern staff and southern managers, though the former prevailed by the early 1830s thanks to administrative subterfuge by the *Repository*'s editor, Connecticut clergyman Ralph Gurley. But given the sustained assault on a precariously national organization from both proslavery and antislavery quarters, nothing seemed able to stop the ACS's mounting debts or its fragmentation into separate state societies. In 1838, the ACS achieved a semblance of unity by adopting a new constitution, making the society a federation of state auxiliaries represented in proportion to their financial contributions. From now on, the ACS's bottom line would be private philanthropy and leadership at the local level, as befitted the age of Jackson, though colonization never mustered the same degree of female support as the era's other reform movements. Yet should the winds change once more, there was nothing to stop the society's leaders from appealing for public support, be it state or federal, or for tighter central control of the organization.[11]

---

[10] Ibid., 19–20; Christopher Michael Curtis, *Jefferson's Freeholders and the Politics of Ownership in the Old Dominion* (New York, 2012), 134–46.

[11] Burin, *Peculiar Solution*, 21–5; Bruce Dorsey, "A Gendered History of African Colonization in the Antebellum United States," *Journal of Social History* 34 (2000),

Antebellum Revival

Until the mid-1840s, the forecast remained much the same for the ACS. Its cutbacks shrank the number of emigrants, who increasingly comprised manumittees, not freepeople, as conscientious masters raised in the wake of the Revolution liberated their slaves by will. By contrast, free African Americans' interest in emigrating to Liberia was moribund. There things might have stood, but for the Mexican-American War (1846–8), which fomented the two-decade revival of separatism covered in this book.[12]

As northerners and southerners disputed whether slavery should be allowed into the lands lately acquired by the United States, moderates turned once more to colonization, the solution that would have removed the problem by removing African Americans. So severe was the crisis culminating in the Compromise of 1850 that national politicians once more dared to speak of colonization and emancipation in the same breath.[13] "If any gentleman from the South shall propose a scheme of colonization ... I should ... incur almost any degree of expense," promised Daniel Webster of Massachusetts, a member of the US Senate's "Great Triumvirate."[14] He achieved nothing but to tarnish his antislavery credentials, as did other abolitionist (re)converts to colonization, notably the editor of the *New-York Tribune*, Horace Greeley; the author of *Uncle Tom's Cabin* (1852), Harriet Beecher Stowe; and the Alabama slaveholder-turned-immediatist, James Birney.[15]

More cautiously than Webster, President Millard Fillmore (1850–3) planned to endorse emancipation and colonization in his valedictory annual message, now known as the State of the Union, but excised that passage after consulting his cabinet. Even Fillmore's draft had recognized a tenet of mainstream antebellum politics, and one with which colonizationists heartily agreed: while the federal government might offer financial help, each state must decide for itself whether to abolish slavery within its

---

77–103; Karen Fisher Younger, "Philadelphia Ladies' Liberia School Association and the Rise and Decline of Northern Female Colonization Support," *Pennsylvania Magazine of History and Biography* 134 (2010), 235–61.

[12] Burin, *Peculiar Solution*, 25–7.

[13] Douglas R. Egerton, "Averting a Crisis: The Proslavery Critique of the American Colonization Society," *Civil War History* 43 (1997), 142–56.

[14] *CG* 31 Cong., 1 Sess., Appendix, 276 (March 7, 1850).

[15] Leon F. Litwack, *North of Slavery: The Negro in the Free States, 1790–1860* (Chicago, 1961), 254–6; "*Frederick Douglass' Paper* is requested ...," *FDP*, February 26, 1852.

bounds.[16] Shortly after Fillmore's aborted announcement, a North
Carolina Whig, Representative Edward Stanly, played to the prevalent
states' rights mindset with a bill releasing federal funds on condition that
the states spend part on colonization.[17] But as tempers in Washington
cooled, at least until the Kansas–Nebraska Act (1854) rekindled the
debate over territorial slavery, the initiative swung back away from the
federal government.

Local Colonizationism

In statehouses, the greater homogeneity of local interests meant that the so-
called negro question was a less contentious one than in Congress, but also
a more chronic one. It was obvious, to all but true believers, that the ACS
would never remove enough African Americans, especially as long as it
adhered to black voluntarism (however nominal). So politicians revived the
"black laws," which barred African Americans from entering the individual states and territories. Such legislation had emerged in the early nineteenth century and represented, as abolitionists alleged, the counterpart
push to colonization's pull.[18] Yet during the antebellum period, white
Americans failed, by both accident and design, to coordinate measures of
colonization and exclusion, logically the "positive" and "negative" com-
plements to each other. Politicians' continued failure to whiten America
should not, however, hide the depths of white animus against blacks during
the 1850s. Ultimately, lawmakers might not have put African Americans to
the sword, but they dangled the sword of Damocles over them, from one
place to another, time and time again. Whenever legislators thundered that
they had lost patience with voluntarism and that they would instead
consider coercion, was not that threat *itself* coercion?[19]

The heartland of black exclusion was the upper South and lower
North, the two regions that would be the most affected by presumptive
changes in racial demography. In the upper South, a new generation of
modernizers looked to the free states and redoubled in their predecessors'
conviction that slavery, and with it, black people, had to disappear before

---

[16] "Mr. Fillmore's Views Relating to Slavery," December 6, 1852, in Frank H. Severance,
     ed., *Millard Fillmore Papers* (Buffalo, 1907), 1:322–3.
[17] *CG* 32 Cong., 2 Sess., 424–6 (January 27, 1853).
[18] Martha S. Jones, *Birthright Citizens: A History of Race and Rights in Antebellum
     America* (New York, 2018), 45–8; "Oppressive Legislation – Colonization," *National
     Era*, May 27, 1852.
[19] Jones, *Birthright Citizens*, 57–8.

the local economy might flourish. In the lower North, whites looked uneasily to those same slave states, fearing that the upper South would send northward a wave of manumittees. Such concerns pervaded politics along the Mason-Dixon Line and into the territories, as far as the Pacific states of California (admitted 1850) and Oregon (1859), which also worried about transoceanic immigration from China.[20] Yet prejudice reached a fever pitch in the uneasy border zone between slavery and freedom that was the Ohio Valley.[21] Although not unique even for the free states, the black laws of Ohio, Indiana, and Illinois were notorious and, unlike their equivalents in the slave states, lacked the plausibility of protecting slavery.

Yet even if the states *could* forbid African Americans from entering their bounds, *should* they? That was a question that state politicians tackled at length, thanks to a wave of constitutional conventions instigated by electorates eager to reframe government for changing conditions, especially on the "negro question." To be sure, northern congressmen had always challenged US territorial legislatures that sought to exclude free blacks, with Ohio (1803), Missouri (1821), and Iowa (1846) having had to excise exclusionary clauses from their draft constitutions to smooth their path to statehood. (Following their admission to the Union, they had swiftly reinstituted black laws.) Indeed, it was a sign of antebellum whites' belief in imminent upheaval, not to say a spur to like-minded legislators elsewhere, that Congress *did* admit Florida (1845) and Oregon with constitutions that already excluded free blacks. Once part of the Union, the states were sovereign in internal matters of racial discrimination, though the immigration of free blacks from states that considered them citizens, both of their own state and therefore of the United States, sparked occasional disputes. But for the most part, state-level politicians debated only whether exclusion acts were self-defeating in their cruelty, or whether a convention could oblige a future legislature to pass them.[22]

The second-generation Illinois and Indiana Conventions, held in 1847 and 1850–1, respectively, left the decision to voters, each putting its exclusionary article to a separate ratification from the rest of the constitution. Such sidestepping betrayed delegates' curious mixture of

[20] Najia Aarim-Heriot, *Chinese Immigrants, African Americans, and Racial Anxiety in the United States, 1848–82* (Urbana, 2003), 1–14.

[21] Matthew Salafia, *Slavery's Borderland: Freedom and Bondage along the Ohio River* (Philadelphia, 2013), 1–8.

[22] Eugene H. Berwanger, *The Frontier against Slavery: Western Anti-Negro Prejudice and the Slavery Extension Controversy* (Urbana, 1967), 25, 43, 95.

confidence in popular white supremacism and concern at how just one clause might jeopardize the rest of their handiwork. They need not have worried. In both states, voters approved the article along with the main document. In Illinois, the ban on black immigration passed by 61,000 to 16,000; in Indiana, by a searing 114,000 to 22,000. Legislators then had to write those provisions into law, which took until 1852 in Indiana and 1853 in Illinois. Within the Ohio Valley, only the Buckeye State itself moved in the other direction, repealing its black laws in 1849 when the antislavery Free Soilers, who held the balance in the assembly, struck a bargain with the Democrats, who betrayed their principles in return for power. Exclusionists fought back, however, from Ohio's own convention the next year through the Civil War.[23]

While abolitionists blamed colonizationists for stoking the sentiments that had fired the black laws, the ACS's officers looked askance at such legislation. To some extent, the political alignments of the Second Party System limited the usefulness to the ACS of the overarching exclusionary drive. The Democrats, who believed in white supremacism and fiscal rectitude, dominated the Midwest, especially the southern counties that would suffer any black influx, but the party refrained from matching its racial proscriptions with the taxes necessary to find African Americans a new home.[24] Conversely, the Whigs were happy to raise levies for the Liberian project, but their firmer opposition to ordering the exclusion of African Americans obviated the demand.[25] But quite apart from doubting the efficacy of the loophole-laden black laws, many colonizationists were troubled by their inhumanity. "I felt the [exclusion] provision ... oppressive and voted against the adoption of the Constitution on that ground," recalled one Hoosier colonizationist, Calvin Fletcher.[26] "We by no means give our sanction to the stringent measures that have been adopted by

[23] Ibid., 43–51; Leonard Erickson, "Politics and Repeal of Ohio's Black Laws, 1837–1849," *Ohio History* 82 (1973), 171–5; Paul Finkelman, "Ohio's Struggle for Equality before the Civil War," *Timeline* 23 (2006), 37–43; Stephen Middleton, *The Black Laws: Race and the Legal Process in Early Ohio* (Athens, OH, 2005), 151–6.

[24] A. H. Brown, pub., *Debates of the Convention of Indiana* (Indianapolis, 1850), 2:1792, 1816.

[25] For the Whigs and colonization, see Daniel Walker Howe, *The Political Culture of the American Whigs* (Chicago, 1979), 134–7; Thomas D. Matijasic, "Whig Support for African Colonization: Ohio as a Test Case," *Mid-America* 66 (1984), 79–91; and James Brewer Stewart, "The Emergence of Racial Modernity and the Rise of the White North, 1790–1840," *Journal of the Early Republic* 18 (1998), 206–8.

[26] Entry, September 12, 1862, in Gayle Thornbrough, ed., *The Diary of Calvin Fletcher* (Indianapolis, 1972–81), 7:530.

some of the States," observed the *Repository*, in rare commentary on domestic politics.[27] In their own, blinkered way, the clergymen who staffed the ACS were troubled by laws banning the immigration of African Americans, and outraged by those mandating their expulsion.[28]

Yet there was one state initiative that colonizationists could applaud: raising money for the cause. "It was never imagined that the Colonization Society would be able to accomplish all the good contemplated, by *private resources* alone," announced the ACS's financial secretary, William McLain, hailing a resurgence in public funding.[29] In 1850, partly through McLain's own lobbying, Virginia became the first in a series of states to assign money to colonizing its free blacks, earlier appropriations having expired everywhere except Maryland. While the *Repository* hailed "an example worthy of imitation by every State in the Union," it also rued the law's limitations, a portent of the stinginess shown by later states when setting the terms of their appropriations. Virginia's law did not cover half the cost of sending an emigrant to Liberia, and would even swell the state treasury on account of another of its provisos, a poll tax on free black men. Neither did it extend to those blacks who might become free, as distinct from the already free.[30] Several upper South states followed suit, with Maryland appropriating $10,000 (1852); Missouri, $3,000 (1855); and Kentucky, $5,000 (1855). Among the free states, New Jersey voted $1,000 and later $4,000; Pennsylvania, $2,000; and Indiana, a total of $15,000 in three installments from 1853. Colonizationist lobbying in Ohio, Illinois, Iowa, and New York yielded nothing, however. No state ever exhausted its appropriations, which were invariably limited to its own inhabitants rather than awarded outright to the ACS. Only Indiana and Maryland kept up a colonization drive worthy of the name, thanks, respectively, to enthusiastic individuals and to a state society that worked closely with government.[31]

Local colonizationism was usually ephemeral, especially in newer states with more pressing concerns and, necessarily, no history of involvement in the movement's earlier phase.[32] "We in the West have a great many objects of charity ... we have churches and schoolhouses to build,"

---

[27] *AR* 29 (1853), 163.
[28] *AR* 23 (1847), 45–6; *Maryland Colonization Journal* 10 (1860), 137–45.
[29] *AR* 25 (1849), 66.　　[30] *AR* 26 (1850), 98–103.
[31] Ira Berlin, *Slaves without Masters: The Free Negro in the Antebellum South* (New York, 1974), 355–6; Berwanger, *Frontier against Slavery*, 57; Philip J. Staudenraus, *The African Colonization Movement, 1816–1865* (New York, 1961), 243–4.
[32] Berwanger, *Frontier against Slavery*, 53–4.

one Iowan wrote McLain.[33] Dignitaries formed state societies to great acclaim in the *Repository*, only for such organizations never to reconvene.[34] With greater persistence, white sympathizers offered their services to the ACS as roving agents to solicit donors and recruit emigrants. Yet they usually lost interest once they discovered that they could not support themselves on the stipulated one-third share of donations, or that they had not discovered the elusive gift of persuading their black compatriots to leave for another continent.[35] "I take the ground with them that I approve all that has been done ... to remove them – and I do it *as their friend*, to avoid harsher measures that *must come*," explained a recruiter in the Shenandoah Valley, who did not appreciate just how complicit in coercion he really was – or how to tailor his remarks to an audience.[36] Other agents gave up when faced by no-shows for the overland journeys to Baltimore and New Orleans, the ports from which ships for Liberia usually sailed, or by rivals claiming the same patch, a common outcome of the distinct efforts of the national and state societies.[37]

Local Agent, Central Problem: Mitchell

From its difficult relationship with subordinate agencies and insubordinate agents, the central ACS knew all too well that colonization was not an idea on which it held a monopoly, but one that others could adopt, adapt, and adulterate. During the 1850s, it lamented less those many converts whose zeal burned out, and more one whose ardor failed to cool: the Rev. James Mitchell, Methodist minister, sometime colonization agent for the state of Indiana, and all-round scourge of the society (Figure 1.1). Mitchell was a paradoxical man. A Protestant sectarian who had emigrated from Ulster, he overcame his own nativism to join the Catholic-friendly Democratic Party; a staunch partisan, he called on voters to support colonizationists of all stripes, which usually meant Whigs; a shrewd operator, he entertained dogmatic notions of racial destiny and conspiracy theories about abolitionists, Catholics, and the "aristocrats"

[33] A. W. McGregor to W. McLain, April 12, 1855, reel 75, ACS.
[34] S. S. Howe to McLain, April 23, 1856, reel 79, ACS.
[35] Entry, August 31, 1850, Journal of the Executive Committee, reel 292, ACS.
[36] R. W. Bailey to McLain, December 5, 1850, reel 63, ACS; Ellen Eslinger, "The Brief Career of Rufus W. Bailey, American Colonization Society Agent in Virginia," *Journal of Southern History* 71 (2005), 39–74.
[37] *AR* 31 (1855), 353–5; McLain to J. Mitchell, June 15, 1854, reel 196, ACS.

FIGURE 1.1 James Mitchell (1818–1903). Methodist minister, colonizationist, and administrator.
Mathew Brady Photographs, RG111/T252/2, NARA II

of the Old World and the South.[38] Moreover, Mitchell vacillated on how far he would go to make African Americans leave. He voted against Article XIII, Indiana's exclusionary clause, despite happily citing it to intimidate black Hoosiers – but he later argued that coercion might become necessary.[39]

Over a twenty-year career in colonization, Mitchell made friends and enemies in equal measure. "I dislike him," admitted Calvin Fletcher. "He always approaches me … as if I was in the field to buy [the] good opinions of others."[40] "The sooner you cut connection the better," Mitchell's first boss, Benjamin Kavanaugh, told McLain, pointing to the minister's taste for meddling in national policy rather than attending to

[38] R. J. M. Blackett, *The Captive's Quest for Freedom: Fugitive Slaves, the 1850 Fugitive Slave Law, and the Politics of Slavery* (New York, 2018), 107–11; Mark E. Neely, Jr., "Colonization and the Myth That Lincoln Prepared the People for Emancipation," in William A. Blair and Karen Fisher Younger, eds., *Lincoln's Proclamation: Emancipation Reconsidered* (Chapel Hill, 2009), 57–63; James Mitchell, *To the Friends of Colonization* (Springfield, IL, 1853), 1; Mary E. Mitchell, *Memoirs of James Mitchell: Statesman, Educator, Minister* (n.p., n.d.), 4–8.

[39] James Mitchell, *The Educational Claims of the Children of the Non-Slave-Holding Whites of the South* (Atlanta, 1891), 11, and *Letter on the Relation of the White and African Races* (Washington, DC, 1862), 25.

[40] Entry, June 15, 1854, in Thornbrough, *Diary of Fletcher*, 5:236.

the duties of a local agent.[41] Awkwardly for the course of history, however, theirs were not the only opinions on the adoptive American. "James Mitchell ... I know, and like," wrote the new occupant of the White House, Abraham Lincoln, in 1861.[42]

Even if Mitchell had never met Lincoln, the former's activities would fill a book on their own, thanks in no small part to his penchant for self-promotion. Introducing himself to McLain in 1848, the Rev. Mitchell had claimed that he would not have joined the colonizationist cause had it not enjoyed the "sanction of God."[43] Ironically, in view of later developments, he also scorned local initiatives that acted independently of the central ACS.[44] It is not worth charting Mitchell's turbulent relationship with the parent organization, or counting his many colonization agencies – and abrupt resignations from them.[45] Suffice it to say that his mainstays were his fellow Democrat, Governor Joseph Wright of Indiana (1849–57), and the state colonization board that they fostered from 1852 with the help of generous legislators. Otherwise, Mitchell proved cantankerous, even toward colleagues. His closest collaborators were two black assistants and emigrationists, William Findlay and, once Findlay had settled in Liberia, John McKay, who ultimately remained in Indiana.[46] Even McKay was not exempt from sabotage by his superior, while Mitchell's temporary replacement as secretary of the board, another white minister, Thornton Mills, despaired of working without interference from the man who had preceded – and would succeed – him.[47]

By his own choosing, Mitchell had no perpetual allies, but he did have eternal interests. Among them was a distinctive sense of political geography, a fixation on setting national colonization policy by triangulating sectional sentiments. He sought (and received) an ACS agency for the Old Northwest, and hoped to cooperate with the handful of colonizationists that the 1850s had produced in the Southwest, in order to reduce the "eastern" influences of abolitionism and nullification, the theory of states'

---

[41] B. T. Kavanaugh to McLain, April 23, 1851, reel 64, ACS.
[42] A. Lincoln to W. H. Seward, October 3, 1861, *CWAL*, 4:547.
[43] Mitchell to McLain, May 30, 1848, reel 56, ACS.
[44] Mitchell to McLain, March 25, 1850, reel 61, ACS.
[45] Mitchell to McLain, August 1, 1850, reel 62, October 21, 1851, reel 66A, and July 27, 1854, reel 73, ACS; *AR* 29 (1853), 49, and *AR* 31 (1855), 77.
[46] Emma Lou Thornbrough, *The Negro in Indiana: A Study of a Minority* (Indianapolis, 1957), 82–9.
[47] Thornton A. Mills, *Report of the Secretary of the State Board of Colonization*, in Joseph J. Bingham, pub., *Documents of the Assembly of Indiana* (Indianapolis, 1857), 2:333–5; T. A. Mills to McLain, October 26, 1855, reel 77, ACS.

rights proposed by South Carolina's John Calhoun.[48] Although Mitchell founded satellite societies in Wisconsin and Michigan, and strayed as far as the District of Columbia and Canada, he devoted the most attention to Indiana's western neighbor, which never pushed its black laws to their logical conclusion by funding colonization.[49] "The state of Illinois has always been regarded as sound and liberal on this subject," he told the people of Springfield in the summer of 1853, "but ... the enterprise has been at a stand for a year or two past."[50] While in town, Mitchell asked a local pastor, the Rev. Dodge, if Illinois had any politician who could help him like Wright had in Indiana. "Yes, I think we have – an attorney named Abraham Lincoln," replied Dodge.[51]

The resultant meeting between Mitchell and Lincoln was not the latter's first taste of colonization. Probably present at the founding of a short-lived state society in 1845, Lincoln had helped transfer a donation to the ACS in 1848, when his single term on Capitol Hill had placed him just a few blocks from the society's headquarters, staffed by Ralph Gurley and William McLain.[52] In 1852, Lincoln uttered his first recorded words on colonization in a eulogy for Henry Clay. Quoting the "Great Compromiser" himself, Lincoln praised Clay's vision of the "ultimate redemption of the African race and African continent."[53] Privately, Lincoln was more ambivalent about Clay, having once traveled to Clay's home of Lexington, Kentucky, only to hear him deliver a passionless address on colonization.[54] Yet it made sense for an ambitious Whig to pose as Clay's heir, and Lincoln genuinely agreed with his strain of moderate antislavery, which combined colonization, compensation (for the slaveowners), and gradualism (which would guard against social disruption by freeing slaves a few at a time). In 1853, then, when

[48] James Mitchell, *Report on Colonization for 1860*, in John C. Walker, pub., *Documents of the Assembly of Indiana* (Indianapolis, 1861), 2:152; Mitchell to McLain, May 8, 1850, reel 62, and McLain to Mitchell, January 25, 1853, reel 194–5, ACS.

[49] Entry, September 27, 1853, Proceedings of the State Board of Colonization, General Assembly Miscellaneous Records, Indiana State Archives; Mitchell to McLain, September 21, 1853, reel 71, ACS.

[50] Mitchell, *To the Friends*, 1.

[51] "Lincoln and the Negro," *St. Louis Daily Globe-Democrat*, August 26, 1894.

[52] Michael Lind, *What Lincoln Believed: The Values and Convictions of America's Greatest President* (New York, 2005), 105; McLain to J. B. Crist, June 24, 1848, reel 188, ACS.

[53] "Eulogy on Henry Clay," July 6, 1852, *CWAL*, 2:132.

[54] Noah Brooks, *Abraham Lincoln* (New York, 1901), 68–9; Marvin R. Cain, "Lincoln's Views on Slavery and the Negro: A Suggestion," *Historian* 26 (1964), 503–4; Phillip W. Magness, "The American System and the Political Economy of Black Colonization," *Journal of the History of Economic Thought* 37 (2015), 194.

Mitchell took to the pulpit of Dodge's church to espouse colonization to a congregation that included Lincoln, he was preaching to the converted.

LIBERIA: DEPENDENCE AND INDEPENDENCE

National Identity

And what of Liberia, Henry Clay's wellspring of redemption for Africans and African Americans alike – that eponymous "land of the free," in contrived Latin?[55]

For a small colony, it was a busy one, home to multiple sources of authority, which clashed as much as they collaborated: the agents of the central ACS, their state-society counterparts, religious missionaries (of different sects), native Africans (of distinct nations), and, of course, the settlers themselves. By the mid-nineteenth century, the colonists had successfully asserted their primacy over all local rivals, but had no sooner done so than they divided over long-brewing issues of colorism and elitism. Moreover, political independence did nothing to lessen Liberia's economic, cultural, and diplomatic dependence on a mother country that took an unusual degree of interest in a technically independent state.

The earliest victory for the settlers was over their spatially, if not always spiritually, closest allies: missionaries infused with the spirit of the Second Great Awakening, the evangelical revival that drove American Protestants to try to convert the world.[56] In 1810, graduates of Williams College, Massachusetts, had founded the American Board of Commissioners for Foreign Missions, an ecumenical venture of the reformed churches, which would dispatch missionaries to what are now India, Sri Lanka, and Hawaii. But the board prized, above all other missions, that at Liberia, which promised to repay the ethical debt to Africa that America had incurred in the slave trade. In theory, mission work in Liberia provided a rare point of unity between America's races, sections, and denominations, which even the secular emollience of

---

[55] *AR* 33 (1857), 34.
[56] For missions in Liberia, see Erskine Clarke, *By the Rivers of Water: A Nineteenth-Century Atlantic Odyssey* (New York, 2013); Edmund M. Hogan, *Catholic Missionaries and Liberia: A Study of Christian Enterprise in West Africa, 1842–1950* (Cork, 1981); and Eunjin Park, *"White" Americans in "Black Africa": Black and White American Methodist Missionaries in Liberia, 1820–1875* (New York, 2001).

colonization in US politics could not match.[57] In practice, missionaries and settlers, and the US-based agencies to which they reported, often found themselves at loggerheads.

In 1839, Liberia achieved the unenviable distinction of furnishing the American Board with its first-ever closure of a post. The mission failed (quite literally) for instructive reasons. A Presbyterian evangelist, John Leighton Wilson, had settled at Liberia in 1834, buoyed by high hopes of saving souls with a gospel that would penetrate deep into the African interior. Instead, he despaired as the colonists – whom the South Carolinian (and slaveholder) Wilson treated, admittedly, with some dis-dain – exploited the natives, seized their lands, and rebuffed his protests as the bleating of a white hypocrite who should not impede black politicians. For their part, the native Grebo viewed the missionaries and settlers as Americans alike, and equally complicit in colonialism.[58] Other mission-aries in Liberia, even those who doubled up as colonial officials or were themselves black, concurred with Wilson's eventual conclusion: missions would fare better at a distance from the settlers, who preferred to develop their new homes than to spread the word of God, and should appeal to Africans with a basic Christian message rather than trying to acculture them as Americans.[59] Duly yielding, the missionaries allowed the colon-ists to switch their focus to more secular sources of white cooperation, competition, and condescension: the ACS and its auxiliaries.

In 1847, Liberia declared an independence that dispelled none of the haziness of its previous, quasi-colonial status. Originally pushed toward self-governance by the near-bankrupt ACS of the late 1830s, colonists welcomed the chance to break free from white dictatorship and fulfill their destiny as black republicans. In 1839, the society itself had revamped the settlement as the Commonwealth of Liberia, and, in 1842, acquiesced in the appointment of Liberia's first black governor, Joseph Jenkins Roberts (a former resident of Norfolk, Virginia), following his white predecessor's death.[60]

---

[57] Ben Wright, "'The Heathen Are Demanding the Gospel': Conversion, Redemption, and African Colonization," in Tomek, *New Directions*, 51–2, 55.
[58] Clarke, *Rivers of Water*, 57, 86, 118, 142–3; 173; Emily Conroy-Krutz, *Christian Imperialism: Converting the World in the Early American Republic* (Ithaca, 2015), 151–78.
[59] Andrew N. Wegmann, "'He Be God Who Made Dis Man': Christianity and Conversion in Nineteenth-Century Liberia," in Tomek, *New Directions*, 73–83.
[60] James Wesley Smith, *Sojourners in Search of Freedom: The Settlement of Liberia by Black Americans* (Lanham, 1987), 189.

Always inclined toward independence, Roberts had sought to extinguish foreign and indigenous claims along the nearly 400 miles of coast over which his government asserted its attenuated authority. That brought him into conflict with French and British traders, who argued that Liberia, not being a sovereign state, could not ban their activities. The dispute reached the highest offices, with London asking Washington to clarify the colony's status, only for the latter to disavow any formal connection to Monrovia. The ACS had then agreed with Roberts that the colonists had little choice but to join the family of nations. Having secured a slim majority in a referendum to declare Liberia's independence from the ACS, Roberts asked the Legislative Council to call a convention, which drafted a constitution modeled on that of the United States. Ratified in 1847, with some resistance from the southern settlements, the new government went into effect. Roberts was elected Liberia's first president, remaining so until 1856.[61]

Yet every step in Liberia's long path to meaningful self-rule revealed its ambiguous place in the world. A colony founded by outcasts from the United States reveled in its Americanness, not only in its cloned government but also in a flag comprising red and white stripes, with a white star on a blue background in the top-left corner.[62] A settlement challenged by British politicians, and defended by American philanthropists, soon found itself welcomed by British philanthropists as a bulwark against the slave trade, but unrecognized by American politicians, who feared inflaming white southerners.[63] An African republic issued a declaration of independence indicting America for relegating blacks to an inferior caste, but defined its own citizens as "originally the inhabitants of the United States," elevating a mere 3,000 Americo-Liberians over the sixteen ethnicities that comprised Liberia's 250,000 natives. For all the pan-Africanism of the country's most notable black apologists, the journalist Edward Wilmot Blyden and the missionary Alexander Crummell, more typical

---

[61] Ibid., 190–203.
[62] For Americo-Liberian identity, see M. B. Akpan, "Black Imperialism: Americo-Liberian Rule over the African Peoples of Liberia, 1841–1964," *Canadian Journal of African Studies* 7 (1973), 219; Amos J. Beyan, *The American Colonization Society and the Creation of the Liberian State: A Historical Perspective, 1822–1900* (Lanham, 1991), xi; Ben Schiller, "U.S. Slavery's Diaspora: Black Atlantic History at the Crossroads of 'Race,' Enslavement, and Colonisation," *Slavery and Abolition* 32 (2011), 199–212; and Howard Temperley, "African-American Aspirations and the Settlement of Liberia," *Slavery and Abolition* 21 (2000), 78.
[63] Katherine Harris, *African and American Values: Liberia and West Africa* (Lanham, 1985), 68–70; Tom W. Shick, *Behold the Promised Land: A History of Afro-American Settler Society in Nineteenth-Century Liberia* (Baltimore, 1980), 104–7.

was the colonist who thought it "something strange … that these people of Africa are calld our ancestors."[64] Indeed, scholars have long treated Liberia as an imperialist state in all but name on account of the immigrants' exploitation of the indigenes.[65]

Recognition

The irony of Monrovia's quasi-imperialism was lost on Liberians and their American friends, who spent fifteen years trying to get Washington to recognize a government that even a foe of emancipation, Secretary of State Abel Upshur, thought entitled to Americans' "sympathy and solicitude."[66] Southerners panicked over a precedent that pointed to the US recognition of Haiti – like Liberia, a black state, but unlike Liberia, one founded by slaves who had revolted, not repatriated.[67] "To acknowledge the independence of the Republic of Liberia … will be very unfortunate," warned Virginia's Senator James Mason.[68] Specifically, recognition would permit black diplomats to stroll Washington's lily-white colonnades. "It is felt that the presence of a colored foreign minister would be inconvenient … [and] that he could neither be excluded from society nor made comfortable in it," explained John Pinney, secretary of the ACS's most influential auxiliary, the New-York State Colonization Society.[69]

Colonizationists discerned several ways to force the United States to acknowledge its misbegotten child. They orchestrated pseudo-spontaneous flurries of petitions from citizens, counties, and states.[70] They pestered the presidents, gaining muted support from Zachary Taylor (Whig, 1849–50), Millard Fillmore (Whig, 1850–3), and James Buchanan (Democrat, 1857–61). Unsurprisingly, they met with refusal from the one Democrat-cum-slaveholder, James Polk (1845–9), but

---

[64] P. Skipwith to J. H. Cocke, April 22, 1840, in Bell I. Wiley, ed., *Slaves No More: Letters from Liberia, 1833–1869* (Lexington, 1980), 53.

[65] Akpan, "Black Imperialism," 217–18; Gus J. Liebenow, *Liberia: The Evolution of Privilege* (Ithaca, 1969), 18–21.

[66] A. P. Upshur to H. S. Fox, September 25, 1843, H. Exec. Doc. 162, 28 Cong., 1 Sess. (1844), 9.

[67] Charles H. Wesley, "The Struggle for the Recognition of Haiti and Liberia as Independent Republics," *Journal of Negro History* 2 (1917), 369–83.

[68] CG 32 Cong., 2 Sess., 1064 (March 3, 1853).

[69] "Diplomacy of Liberia," *New-York Colonization Journal*, June 1854.

[70] Petitions for the Recognition of Liberia, RG59/161/1, NARA II; McLain to J. T. Hargrave, August 4, 1849, reel 189, ACS.

attributed the reticence of New Hampshire's Franklin Pierce (Democrat, 1853–7) more to his cabinet than to Pierce himself.[71] They also lobbied friendly congressmen, who agreed with them that certain bills touching on Liberia might draw Washington into a relationship with Monrovia that, at some point, it could no longer deny.

Yet such schemes forever fizzled, as political centrists came to celebrate the Compromise of 1850 as a cure for sectionalism rather than a prescription for more medicine. In 1849, Secretary of State John Clayton had commissioned Ralph Gurley to travel to Liberia and report on its progress. It seems that Clayton's superior, President Taylor, was about to submit a treaty with Liberia to the Senate when he suddenly died, killing the prospects of Gurley's ensuing appeal for US recognition.[72] In 1850, a Tennessee Democrat, Representative Frederick Stanton, presented a memorial by one Joseph Bryan of Alabama, asking the United States to establish a line of steamers to Liberia. Although the enterprise might boost American commerce and carry the mails, Stanton backed it for "removing the free persons of color … and suppressing the slave trade," which the navy might achieve by arming those vessels.[73] The ACS remained aloof from a proposal that it had not originated and that attracted southerners interested in removing only the already free.[74] In any case, the mooted ships of the "Ebony Line" foundered on congressional hostility against sponsored steamer services.[75]

Thereafter, the ACS resorted to stealth. During 1852–3, it colluded with naval officers keen to explore the great unknown, to western eyes, of the African interior.[76] Such expeditions might as well anchor in Liberia, which could then demand recognition as the price of cooperation. Unfortunately, politicians did not share old hands' tact in avoiding the

---

[71] McLain to A. D. Pollock, August 2, 1849, reel 189, E. Whittlesey to McLain, March 16, 1852, reel 67, McLain to J. Tracy, July 28, 1853, reel 194–5, and entry, October 18, 1860, Journal of the Executive Committee, reel 292, ACS; entry, January 19, 1848, in Milo M. Quaife, ed., *The Diary of James K. Polk during His Presidency, 1845 to 1849* (Chicago, 1910), 3:306–7.

[72] Harris, *African and American Values*, 69; R. R. Gurley to J. M. Clayton, February 15, 1850, S. Exec. Doc. 75, 31 Cong., 1 Sess. (1850), 33; *AR* 38 (1862), 236.

[73] H. Rep. 438, 31 Cong., 1 Sess. (1850), 3, 10.

[74] Entry, April 20, 1850, Journal of the Executive Committee, reel 292, ACS; S. Misc. Doc. 18, 31 Cong., 2 Sess. (1850), 3, 10.

[75] McLain to S. Wright, September 8, 1852, reel 193, ACS.

[76] Richard K. MacMaster, "United States Navy and African Exploration," *Mid-America* 46 (1964), 191–7; McLain to J. J. Roberts, November 19, 1852, reel 239, ACS.

word "colonization" when necessary.[77] In 1853, on his penultimate day in Congress, a New Jersey Whig, Senator Jacob Miller, asked to amend a naval appropriations bill by adding $125,000 to explore the country east of Liberia and colonize free African Americans. Denying all ulterior motives, Miller nevertheless seized his chance to explain why the United States should recognize Liberia. "There is a 'Monroe doctrine' as to colonization in Africa, as well as to colonization in America," he argued.[78] Far from persuading his colleagues, though, Miller had to strike the reference to colonization, only to watch even his amended motion fail on a tied vote.[79]

With his fellow Senate colonizationists, Henry Clay and Daniel Webster, having died the previous year, Miller's effort marked high water for the deluge of attempts to persuade the United States to recognize Liberia.[80] Colonizationists kept trying anyway. William McLain asked Clay's successor as president of the ACS, John Latrobe, a Baltimore lawyer and former president of the Maryland State Colonization Society, to lobby his southern contacts. "Liberia could not . . . ask less than a full, unqualified recognition," explained McLain, but to avoid offense to either government, it might "transact all its business . . . with the U. States Govt. by and through white men; and the U. States should transact all its business with . . . Liberia by and through colored men."[81] In a similar vein, in 1854 the ACS appointed a committee, drawn from its lengthy roster of (honorific) vice presidents, with politicians from the slave states in three of the five slots. Despite the society's hopes that an inbuilt southern majority would forestall future controversy, all three of its appointees refused to serve in view of the crisis over the Kansas–Nebraska Act.[82] Thereafter, only the secretary of the Massachusetts Colonization Society (and Congregationalist minister), Joseph Tracy, kept fighting the good fight. He investigated whether Congress had dragged the United States into acknowledging Liberia by upgrading the commercial agency at Monrovia to a consulate, but found that it had not, in that Pierce had kept its holder at agent rank. From then on, Tracy could only condemn the US presidents' cowardice in claiming that it was not for them, but for congressmen, to acknowledge a foreign state.[83]

[77] W. P. Foulke to McLain, February 3, 1854, reel 72, ACS.
[78] *CG* 32 Cong., 2 Sess., Appendix, 231–4 (March 3, 1853).
[79] *CG* 32 Cong., 2 Sess., 1065 (March 3, 1853).
[80] McLain to Roberts, November 19, 1852, reel 239, ACS.
[81] McLain to J. H. B. Latrobe, April 9, 1853, reel 194–5, ACS.   [82] *AR* 31 (1855), 45–6.
[83] T. R. Marvin, pub., *Seventeenth Annual Report of the Massachusetts Colonization Society* (Boston, 1858), 12–13; *AR* 38 (1862), 236; Tracy to McLain, September 29, 1855, reel 77, and Tracy to Roberts, February 17, 1857, reel 235, ACS.

Colonizationists' efforts to persuade Washington to recognize Monrovia's independence should not obscure Liberians' own struggle to get their American associates to do the same. Even in 1847, both sides had harbored misgivings about the settlement's semi-separation from the ACS.[84] "He does not intend to give any more money," reported Tracy of one erstwhile donor. "The work is done – the enterprise has succeeded.... Such was the drift of his talk."[85] Meanwhile, a Georgia correspondent of the society feared that independence would allow Monrovia to reject those "troublesome" blacks whose putative deportation drove his own support for colonization.[86] For their part, Liberians took umbrage at the ACS sending them a (blatantly self-interested) draft constitution, as though it could not trust them to produce one themselves.[87] Even Liberia's own version met with some abstentionism at the polls, because it did not clarify that the ACS would cede its public land holdings to the new government.[88] Such apparent niceties would fester precisely because all parties could see that Liberia would continue to depend on American infusions of immigrants and funds. Lauding "a total severance of the ACS from all political connexion with the colony," the author of the 1847 declaration of independence and editor of the *Liberia Herald*, Hilary Teage, simultaneously reminded readers not "to suppose for a moment that the society contemplates a cessation of its operations here."[89]

If only the struggle for control had been allowed to unfold between just one government and one organization. Granted, the relationship between Monrovia and the central ACS needed adjusting sooner than any other. In 1848, Roberts came to Washington to hammer out an arrangement with the society's directors. They agreed that the ACS would surrender all public lands, but retain the right to settle emigrants on the previous terms, and to approve the site of any new towns. Awkwardly, the ACS had to speak for the federal government (which could not treat with a negotiator it did not recognize), and so asserted the right of the United States to keep landing recaptives.[90] Unsurprisingly, all parties concurred by the 1850s that the agreement between Liberia and the ACS had resolved nothing.

[84] Brandon Mills, "'The United States of Africa': Liberian Independence and the Contested Meaning of a Black Republic," *Journal of the Early Republic* 34 (2014), 91–7.
[85] Tracy to McLain, December 3, 1847, reel 53, ACS.
[86] J. J. Flournoy to McLain, May 27, 1847, *AR* 23 (1847), 225.
[87] Smith, *Sojourners*, 198.   [88] Roberts to McLain, October 9, 1847, reel 154, ACS.
[89] *AR* 23 (1847), 16–17.   [90] *AR* 24 (1848), 257–9.

Roberts's ongoing battle against the claims of other powers, international and indigenous, could not fail to remind him that his country lay atop contested terrain. Yet Monrovia's most disheartening dispute was one imported entirely from America: states' rights. During the ACS's internal tumult of the 1830s, independent colonization societies had emerged in several states and founded their own settlements in Liberia (Map 1.1).[91] The bellwether was Maryland, whose state chapter broke from the parent board in 1833, alleging financial mismanagement. The Maryland society then colonized Cape Palmas, more than 250 miles to the southeast of Monrovia. Splinter societies in New York and Pennsylvania, explicitly opposed to slavery and fired by a shared spirit against spirits, joined forces to make a toehold for temperance at Bassa Cove, between Monrovia and Cape Palmas. In 1838, the pair rejoined the fold as auxiliaries, per that year's changes to the ACS constitution, while Bassa Cove itself was incorporated into the Commonwealth of Liberia.[92] The same fate befell the fledgling colony of "Mississippi in Africa," a joint venture of the Mississippi and Louisiana societies, but "Maryland in Liberia" would attach itself to the Monrovia government only as late as 1857. Indeed, it was the Maryland colony where the frustrated missionary John Leighton Wilson had fought so hard against local administrators.[93]

The antebellum revival of state societies threatened to add yet more tiles to the Liberian mosaic.[94] American advocates of settling emigrants from the same state in the same place pointed to donors' desire to see discernible results for their money, and to emigrants' own wishes to replant their former communities intact, where possible.[95] The most prominent drive was for an "Ohio in Africa," the pet idea of David

[91] Staudenraus, *Colonization Movement*, 231–7.

[92] Eli Seifman, "The United Colonization Societies of New York and Pennsylvania and the Establishment of the African Colony of Bassa Cove," *Pennsylvania History* 35 (1968), 23–44; Beverly C. Tomek, *Colonization and Its Discontents: Emancipation, Emigration, and Antislavery in Antebellum Pennsylvania* (New York, 2011), 93–5, 128–9, 167–71.

[93] For the Maryland colony, see Penelope Campbell, *Maryland in Africa: The Maryland State Colonization Society, 1831–1857* (Urbana, 1971), and Richard L. Hall, *On Afric's Shore: A History of Maryland in Liberia, 1834–1857* (Baltimore, 2003). For the Mississippi colony, see Alan Huffman, *Mississippi in Africa: The Saga of the Slaves of Prospect Hill Plantation and Their Legacy in Liberia Today* (New York, 2004).

[94] Robert S. Hamilton, *Discourse on the Scheme of African Colonization* (Cincinnati, 1849), 14, 16–17; W. D. Shumate to Kavanaugh, December 3, 1851, *AR* 28 (1852), 50.

[95] D. Christy to McLain, August 27, 1848, reel 56, ACS.

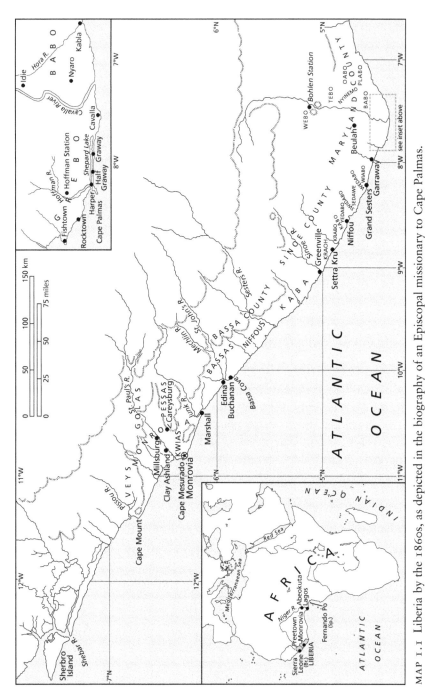

MAP 1.1 Liberia by the 1860s, as depicted in the biography of an Episcopal missionary to Cape Palmas. Based on George Townshend Fox, *A Memoir of the Rev. C. Colden Hoffman* (London, 1868), 169

Christy, one of the more overtly racist colonizationists and author of *Cotton Is King* (1855), a book beloved of proslavery ideologues.[96] Predictably, James Mitchell, William Findlay, and John McKay commandeered Christy's plan and substituted Indiana's imprimatur even as they tried to draw the entire Midwest into their scheme.[97] Moreover, where Christy failed to gain funding from the Ohio legislature, Mitchell succeeded with that of Indiana.[98]

Tempering his parochialism with a dose of internationalism, Mitchell encouraged his superior, Governor Wright, to negotiate directly with President Roberts to surrender Grand Cape Mount, to the northwest of Monrovia. "Public sentiment here is opposed to transferring it for the exclusive use and benefit of emigrants from any individual State," replied Roberts. He feared that the natives, who resented Liberia's clampdown on the lucrative slave trade, would attack any Americans who settled nearby. Again voicing Mitchell's own concerns, Wright wrote Roberts of his disappointment, claiming that Indiana would have readily paid for the requisite defenses had the terms of its appropriation covered anything more than the emigrants' passage and a plot of land.[99] The mothballed Mitchell sent McKay to Liberia in order to haggle, and asked the assembly of Indiana to relax the terms of its appropriation, but all to no avail.[100]

At the offices of the ACS, McLain encouraged Roberts to resist Mitchell's promise of large allotments for Hoosier farmers, which would cast aspersions on the society's standard offer to emigrants.[101] Yet the ACS was, like Mitchell, quite guilty of arranging from afar the lives, livelihoods, and living spaces of those blacks who had bid farewell to the United States – and to its white rulers. The society forever rued how settlers eschewed the kind of agriculture that would have made them virtuous tillers of the soil, and how they instead grew, or just traded,

---

[96] Edward Wesley Shunk, "Ohio in Africa," *Ohio State Archaeological and Historical Quarterly* 51 (1942), 79–88; Christy to McLain, November 8, 1848, reel 57, ACS.

[97] M. H. Smith to Christy, October 16, 1851, reel 66A, ACS.

[98] Berwanger, *Frontier against Slavery*, 54–5.

[99] Roberts to J. A. Wright, July 5, and Wright to Roberts, September 27, 1853, *AR* 30 (1854), 14–17.

[100] A. H. Brown, pub., *Report of Rev. John McKay* (Indianapolis, 1854), 13–15, 40; James Mitchell, *Circular to the Friends of African Colonization*, containing his *Communication to the Indiana State Board of Colonization* (Jeffersonville, 1855), 5–8.

[101] McLain to Roberts, January 27, 1853, reel 239, ACS.

export crops such as sugar, palm oil, and coffee.[102] "We cannot too strongly urge the *superlative importance* of a regular, systematic, and persevering course of agricultural industry," intoned an ACS brochure.[103] In truth, many farmers would have happily resumed growing American crops with American techniques, but the climate, soil, and pests of the west African tropics thwarted such efforts. Beasts of burden died, corn would not grow, and imported tools wore out quickly.[104]

Mortality

During the 1850s, a more pressing challenge than agriculture sowed discord between Liberia and the ACS. "The excitement here from the mortality of the emigrants is considerable," Monrovia's secretary of state, John Lewis, warned William McLain. "What alterations are necessary by the ACS to prevent ... such a direful calamity?"[105] The net increase in the Americo-Liberian population had always masked a large number who had not survived tropical fevers, especially malaria, and especially in their first year of acclimation.[106] After an 1843 survey revealed only 2,400 colonists to show for the 4,600 immigrants since Liberia's founding, the ACS never again ran a census.[107] Even those who saw the hand of providence in the frequent deaths of white missionaries had to concede a certain biracialism to such sacrifice: "perhaps many more white as well as colored laborers will fall at their posts before Ethiopia shall have fully stretched out her hands unto God," an image taken from the sixty-eighth psalm so beloved of colonizationists.[108] Until Ethiopia did so, Liberia and America would have to produce some ideas.

Scientists had not yet grasped that it was mosquitoes that spread malaria, but the settlers could see that the disease was somehow connected to the low-lying swamps of Liberia's coast and to the rainy season

---

[102] William E. Allen, "Rethinking the History of Settler Agriculture in Nineteenth-Century Liberia," *The International Journal of African Historical Studies* 37 (2004), 436; Santosh C. Saha, "Agriculture in Liberia during the Nineteenth Century: Americo-Liberians' Contribution," *Canadian Journal of African Studies* 22 (1988), 224–5.

[103] ACS, pub., *Information about Going to Liberia* (Washington, DC, 1852), 6.

[104] Burin, *Peculiar Solution*, 151.

[105] J. N. Lewis to McLain, July 20, 1854, reel 156, ACS.

[106] For thorough statistics, see Antonio McDaniel, *Swing Low, Sweet Chariot: The Mortality Cost of Colonizing Liberia in the Nineteenth Century* (Chicago, 1995).

[107] Shick, *Behold the Promised Land*, 27.

[108] Conroy-Krutz, *Christian Imperialism*, 47; AR 30 (1854), 282.

of May through October.[109] In 1825, an early colonist, Lott Cary, had noted that newcomers seemed to suffer from the "very unfavorable season ... in which they leave America."[110] Thereafter, the society tried to dispatch vessels between November and April, but by the mid-1850s, mounting reports of a virtual deathtrap impelled the Pennsylvania and New York societies to investigate for themselves.[111] Their agents returned with a sobering assessment. "The Receptacles for the emigrants on their landing in Liberia ... are in the most wretched condition ... [and a] fearfully large proportion of cases are terminated in death," John Pinney told the ACS. "To be silent ... would be treason to humanity," he continued, mincing no words for an organization more accustomed to self-congratulation than self-criticism.[112]

The ACS proposed three solutions. The first was already in hand: a plan to acquire its own ship, which could offer a more salubrious berth than did chartered vessels, and deliver passengers in better health to start with. Although the "Ebony Line" had not been the society's idea, it had made some colonizationists wistful for a steamer, which would slash the duration of the transatlantic crossing and the chance for contagion to take hold.[113] Their colleagues were skeptical. It was not "the *best* plan, but ... the best practicable," Gurley tried to reassure McLain.[114] "Is there an extensive association of unchained Bedlamites on this subject?" demanded Tracy, his characteristic caution piqued by some of the more ambitious tenders from shipbuilders.[115] Despite founding a joint stock company to raise funds for a steamer, the ACS eventually opted for a sail ship, launched in 1856 in the wake of a generous bequest.[116] As far as possible, the *Mary Caroline Stevens* would weigh anchor in Baltimore biannually, and avoid summer sailings.

The second solution was to improve the "receptacles," the buildings in which immigrants were acclimated before being sent to their permanent homes. Given that Liberians had found the seniority of ACS agents obnoxious even prior to independence, Ralph Gurley trod gently when he asked Roberts's successor, Stephen Benson (1856–64), whether Monrovia would

---

[109] Burin, *Peculiar Solution*, 146–7.
[110] L. Cary to anon., June 15, 1825, *Christian Advocate* 4 (1826), 42.
[111] Burin, *Peculiar Solution*, 97.
[112] Entry, June 19, 1855, Journal of the Executive Committee, reel 292, ACS.
[113] J. S. Smith to McLain, August 8, 1854, reel 156, ACS.
[114] Gurley to McLain, November 23, 1854, reel 74, ACS.
[115] Tracy to McLain, March 27, 1857, reel 235, ACS.
[116] Staudenraus, *Colonization Movement*, 243; *AR* 31 (1855), 90.

accept an ACS appointee to manage the new facilities.[117] Moreover, a lack of necessary skills and materials meant that, while Liberians might have wanted to make the receptacles, the units would have to be prefabricated in the United States.[118] Still, replacing shambolic buildings could only prove so contentious, and a white Methodist missionary of known tolerance to African fevers, John Seys, sailed out with his proto–flat packs and erected them in short order.[119] More problematic was the ACS's policy of detaining recent arrivals in the receptacles against their will, as a family of expatriate New Yorkers attested.[120]

The third and most controversial solution was to found new communities in the higher land of the Liberian interior, which colonizationists (incorrectly) imagined free of epidemics. It was a bold departure for the ACS, which had always been littoral-minded, planting new footholds along the seaboard in order to check the slave trade.[121] Although the parent society had contemplated elevated townships as early as 1855, the New York, Pennsylvania, and New Jersey auxiliaries seized the idea and made it their own.[122] "I have never been confident of the wisdom of that movement," admitted Tracy in 1857. "It would have been absolutely ruinous, had not some of us succeeded in reducing it to a fourth part of its original magnitude."[123] The officers of the ACS compromised by having Seys, once he had installed his receptacles, proceed upriver to lay out an experimental town, Careysburg (named for Lott Cary), over the dry months of 1856–7.[124] But the site proved no more immune to disease than the coast, and conferred other disadvantages. "If the People makes more then they want for themselves thir is no way to convate it to market which is Monrovia.... People comes to this Country Poor and thay remaine Poor," wrote one Liberian, James Skipwith, of the higher lands.[125]

---

[117] Gurley to S. A. Benson, March 13, 1856, reel 231, ACS.

[118] Smith to McLain, May 11, 1856, reel 156, ACS.

[119] Willis D. Boyd, "The American Colonization Society and the Slave Recaptives of 1860–1861: An Early Example of United States-African Relations," *Journal of Negro History* 47 (1962), 117.

[120] Pinney to Gurley, October 21, 1857, reel 83, ACS.

[121] Burin, *Peculiar Solution*, 147-8.

[122] McLain to Benson, January 25, 1855, reel 239, and Gurley to J. Hall, March 24, 1856, reel 231, ACS.

[123] Tracy to J. H. Snowden, February 13, 1857, reel 235, ACS.

[124] *AR* 33 (1857), 83–7, 114–18, 194–7.

[125] J. P. Skipwith to Cocke, July 10, 1860, in Wiley, *Slaves No More*, 96–7.

Within the Liberian government, Roberts had broadly favored the society's experiment, but delegated the proposal to then–Vice President Benson, who rejected it. "The natives might be tempted . . . to stir up some difficulty so as to gratify their avarice," warned Benson, fearful that they would attack immigrants who were still acclimating.[126] From 1856, Benson held an office that allowed him to give full voice to his objections. "You must have formed a very poor opinion of my integrity," he scolded Seys, protesting the unilateralism of the Careysburg project.[127] Benson's fears about premature expansion were quite sound. In 1853, the colonists of Maryland in Liberia, troubled by the death of their talismanic governor, John Brown Russwurm (1836–51), and by the lethargy of the state society once Latrobe had assumed the presidency of the ACS, had followed Monrovia's example and declared their independence. No sooner had they done so than the local Kru and Grebo attacked. Calling on Monrovian troops for assistance, the administrators at Cape Palmas hurriedly annexed the Maryland settlement to the rest of Liberia.[128] Meanwhile, the Liberian legislature passed a law imposing the costs of defending interior settlements on the ACS, which suspended the scheme.[129]

Recaptives

A final test of the triangular relationship between the United States, the ACS, and Liberia arose from their shared opposition to the international slave trade. Until 1859, the limiting factor on its suppression had always been the United States, which had taken lightly its obligations to Britain (and to humanity), under the Webster–Ashburton Treaty (1842), to maintain an adequate naval squadron off the African coast.[130] Bullishly, the ACS had always pronounced colonization the miraculous means of stopping the trade at source, until, in 1854, it transpired that senators planned to abrogate the relevant article of the treaty in return for their backing colonization, a suggestion that they assumed had come from the ACS itself.[131] Naturally, the society's unsolicited lobbyist turned out to be

---

[126] *AR* 32 (1856), 12–13, 39.
[127] Benson to J. Seys, December 9, 1856, Records of Foreign Service Posts, RG84/Liberia/ 16, NARA II.
[128] Campbell, *Maryland in Africa*, 211–37.   [129] *AR* 33 (1857), 183–6.
[130] Don E. Fehrenbacher, *The Slaveholding Republic: An Account of the United States Government's Relations to Slavery* (New York, 2001), 173–80.
[131] *AR* 30 (1854), 225–8.

none other than James Mitchell, whose machinations now-Senator Clayton disavowed on its behalf.[132] Having survived that scare, the ACS became more cautious about exaggerating Liberia's hold over the coast of west Africa.[133] As long as politicians had paid only lip service to fighting the trade, colonizationists had also indulged in glib pieties about their own ability to arrest it. After all, lax enforcement by the US Navy meant that Liberia had not taken a shipload of recaptives since 1845.

That changed at the end of the 1850s. Under antislavery pressure to retort proslavery demands to reopen the trade, and keen to preempt the Royal Navy's grounds for boarding US-registered merchant ships, the Buchanan administration moved part of the fleet closer to the slave-hungry island of Cuba, a Spanish colony. The president was shocked to discover that once he looked for slavers, he found them. American warships had averaged only one prize per year during 1851–8, but took five in 1859 and fifteen in 1860. For the first time, the federal government had encountered large numbers of Africans rescued under its own Slave Trade Act. For those slavers intercepted near Cuba, US officials had to condemn the ships and detain their human cargoes in the sultry atmosphere of the lower South.[134]

The navy had only to land one vessel, the *Echo*, in the choleric atmosphere of Charleston, South Carolina, for James Buchanan to follow James Monroe's precedent and arrange for the ACS to send the freed slaves to Liberia. He advanced the society $45,000, pleading with Congress to retroactively appropriate the sum for a group that "could [not] be removed, with any regard to humanity, except to Liberia."[135] As Africans accrued – they would reach 5,500 by April 1861 – Congress made an open-ended agreement with the ACS in 1860 to send the recaptives straight back, without ever landing them in the United States if possible. The bill passed both houses handily, but with bad grace from many southerners.[136] "Charity begins at home," lectured Senator

---

[132] CG 33 Cong., 1 Sess., 1591–3 (July 1), and 1604 (July 5, 1854).

[133] John H. Haley, "The Later Years of the American Colonization Society (1850–1865)," dissertation, Old Dominion University (1971), 129.

[134] Fehrenbacher, *Slaveholding Republic*, 180–8; Sharla M. Fett, *Recaptured Africans: Surviving Slave Ships, Detention, and Dislocation in the Final Years of the Slave Trade* (Chapel Hill, 2017), 22–3; Ted Maris-Wolf, "'Of Blood and Treasure': Recaptive Africans and the Politics of Slave Trade Suppression," *Journal of the Civil War Era* 4 (2014), 61.

[135] CG 35 Cong., 2 Sess., Appendix, 8 (December 6, 1858).

[136] Fehrenbacher, *Slaveholding Republic*, 188–9.

Jefferson Davis. "I have no right to tax our people in order that we may support and educate the barbarians of Africa."[137] In the House, a Virginia Democrat, William Smith, asked "whether the compulsory return of these negroes to Africa is an act recognizing their freedom or slavery?" Yet the enormous implications of his pedantry were precisely what many southerners wished to avoid, even by 1860.[138]

Congress had harked back to precedent when faced once again with the recaptives problem. For the ACS and a newly independent Liberia, history could provide no such guidance. "We are alarmed!" Benson told the society. In language redolent of Davis's, he worried that "thousands of raw savages, exceeding the numbers of Americo-Liberians, may thus be landed within a few months ... [and then] thrown upon the government to support."[139] In reality, all that prevented Liberia being overwhelmed was the recaptives' mortality on the return passage, and Washington's annulment of the African Squadron at the outbreak of the Civil War, which left sailors chasing secessionists rather than slavers.[140] But the society was sympathetic to Liberia's plight. As ever, ACS administrators requested recognition as the price of handing American officials an expedient, but Buchanan refused to acknowledge Monrovia through such underhand means.[141] When Benson demanded that the ACS transfer its contracts with the United States to Liberia, the society's board capitulated and sent a Maryland colleague, James Hall, to Monrovia. In December 1860, Hall arranged with Benson that the ACS would henceforth count as an intermediary in the recaptives business and that Liberia could use any leftover appropriations for its own purposes. In short, the ACS had finally acknowledged its former colony's independence.[142]

Although missionaries and farmers hailed the arrival of the recaptives, who brought hands to clasp in prayer and hold a shovel, the influx helped transform Liberian politics in ways that would topple its ruling classes twice over.[143] Along with the manumittee-heavy immigration of the late 1840s and 1850s, the infusion of recaptives darkened Liberia's overall complexion, storing up a challenge for the light-skinned establishment of former freepeople such as Roberts, which had embedded itself in the

---

[137] *CG* 36 Cong., 1 Sess., 2304 (May 24, 1860).   [138] Ibid., 2643 (June 5, 1860).
[139] Karen Fisher Younger, "Liberia and the Last Slave Ships," *Civil War History* 54 (2008), 435.
[140] Fehrenbacher, *Slaveholding Republic*, 189–91.
[141] Entry, October 18, 1860, Journal of the Executive Committee, reel 292, ACS.
[142] Boyd, "American Colonization Society," 118–26.
[143] Beyan, *Colonization Society*, 136–7; Younger, "Last Slave Ships," 438–9.

1820s.[144] As color began to inflect politics, and economic woes to trouble Liberia, those former recaptives who had integrated with Americo-Liberians enabled a new alliance, the True Whigs, to achieve hegemony in the 1870s. That party's dominance would in turn come to a violent end as late as 1980, when soldiers of indigenous background murdered the president, a descendant of the colonists. Unimaginable in 1847, the coup showed that different Liberians held different ideas about what constituted independence – and how they might go about declaring it.

PROSLAVERY: EXPULSION AND ENSLAVEMENT

In what ways, if any, was Liberian colonization unique? After all, the nineteenth century was altogether one of mass migration, racial "destinies," and religious mission to distant lands. Like migrants the world over, Americans who moved to Liberia were propelled by push and pull factors: repulsion from their old home and the attraction of a new one.[145] Arguably, Liberia's true claim to distinction was as a settler colony that never received enough settlers, condemning it to geopolitical vulnerability and economic underdevelopment by the late nineteenth century. For no other colonial venture was so subject to sustained attack in its metropole, and from such diametric quarters.[146]

During the 1850s, most abolitionists just reiterated their contempt whenever colonizationists spoke up. Neither side had much new to say in the latest round of the pamphleteering war, which had started with William Lloyd Garrison's *Thoughts* and not abated since. Indeed, the decade's only novelty lay in some of the *authors* of those arguments. Frederick Douglass thought James Birney's advice to emigrate to Liberia, which Birney had tried to differentiate from "colonization," identical to what John Pinney and Ralph Gurley would have said.[147] For the first time, however, the ACS had to engage with irrefutable accounts of an infrastructure overwhelmed by the immigration of just a few hundred Americans each year, and to publish frank advice to voyagers as well as paeans to the nobility of its own project. "They should

[144] Clegg, *Price of Liberty*, 246.
[145] Bronwen Everill, "'Destiny Seems to Point Me to That Country': Early Nineteenth-Century African American Migration, Emigration, and Expansion," *Journal of Global History* 7 (2012), 58–9.
[146] Shick, *Behold the Promised Land*, 135–6.
[147] "Mr. Birney on Colonization," *FDP*, February 12, 1852.

understand that they are going to a comparatively new country," the ACS announced of would-be recruits, and "must carry with them the courage and energy to bear the burdens."[148] For the propaganda war was not just about trading blows with abolitionists, but also about canvassing African Americans, who would sooner listen to the gnawing disaffection of black returnees than to the glowing descriptions of white recruiters.[149]

Southern Ideology

What defined the 1850s for the ACS was not the ongoing attacks of abolitionists, but a fresh assault from the forces of proslavery, which, by mid-century, had jettisoned their one-time defensiveness to proclaim slave labor more economically productive and socially harmonious than its free counterpart.[150] Slavery was at the heart of an emerging southern nationalism, which white southerners found easier to define not by what they supported (a source of friction between them) but by what they opposed: "foreign" threats to the South's peculiar institution. Those external dangers might emanate from individuals, such as the freeperson Denmark Vesey, the alleged ringleader of the 1822 Charleston "conspiracy"; from organizations, such as the ACS, which evidently encouraged emancipation, whatever it claimed; and even from the US government, whose Constitution northerners invoked to assert the rights of free blacks visiting the South.[151] Differences of economic interest across the South meant that proslavery sentiments could never coalesce into a political program, instead flourishing in the religious, commercial, and literary press.[152] As a result, the only proslavery measures to sweep the South prior to the Civil War were reactive, even reactionary, and concerned the place of the foreigners within: the freepeople.

Still, if free blacks could rouse slaves with notions of liberty, then so could white colonizationists. As early as the 1820s, the ACS's common-law marriage to the federal government had worried planters in South Carolina, a state whose black-majority demographics through the Civil

---

[148] ACS, *Information about Going to Liberia*, 9.   [149] Burin, *Peculiar Solution*, 69–70.

[150] Robert E. Bonner, *Mastering America: Southern Slaveholders and the Crisis of American Nationhood* (New York, 2009), 106–8.

[151] Paul Quigley, *Shifting Grounds: Nationalism and the American South, 1848–1865* (New York, 2011), 9, 31–2, 56.

[152] Bonner, *Mastering America*, 102.

War imbued its politicians with a siege mentality.[153] An Edisto Island planter, Whitemarsh Seabrook, worried that the ACS's backroom dealings with Capitol Hill would make "the extinguishment of the relation of master and servant ... the work of a day."[154] One of his peers, William Harper, discerned a more insidious threat: although the society's self-appointed mission was impractical, its "eternal tirades upon the injustice and horrors of slavery" would incite ignorant slaves to rebel.[155] By the 1830s, though, defenders of slavery happily dismissed colonization as impossible.[156] Following Nat Turner's Rebellion, the Virginia assembly had considered emancipation with deportation, the last time in the antebellum South that state-led abolition would command widespread support. Reviewing the legislature's debates, a professor at the College of William and Mary, Thomas Dew, scoffed at colonization's insurmountable logistics and fallacious premise of taking bondspeople from "slavery and ignorance ... to the condition of freemen."[157] The consensus among proslavery thinkers that his work cemented for the next two decades – even Harper thought that "after President Dew, it is unnecessary to say a single word on the practicality of colonizing our slaves" – disparaged the scheme's irrationality in theory, but overlooked the danger in practice as long as the states allowed masters to free their slaves on condition of removal.[158] Yet to acknowledge that freedpeople might indeed choose to go to Africa would have been to admit that a benign, even benevolent institution failed to inspire gratitude in its wards.

By the eve of the Civil War, planter-intellectuals, who had watched the ACS's revival with mounting concern, struggled to maintain their silence on colonization. In 1858, a French slaver, the *Regina Coeli*, was anchored at Cape Mount when its cargo rebelled. Hastily accusing Liberia of complicity in the traffic, South Carolina's Senator James Henry Hammond alleged that the crew of the *Regina Coeli* had purchased not native Africans, but rather "the colonists ... who, sick of freedom, prefer

---

[153] Christa Dierksheide, *Amelioration and Empire: Progress and Slavery in the Plantation Americas* (Charlottesville, 2014), 123–38; Egerton, "Averting a Crisis," 143.
[154] Whitemarsh B. Seabrook, *A Concise View of the Critical Situation* (Charleston, 1825), 6–7.
[155] William Harper, "Colonization Society," *Southern Review* 1 (1828), 228–30.
[156] Burin, *Peculiar Solution*, 114–15.
[157] Dierksheide, *Amelioration and Empire*, 57–65, 76–87; Thomas R. Dew, *Review of the Debate in the Virginia Legislature of 1831 and 1832* (Richmond, 1832), 77.
[158] Burin, *Peculiar Solution*, 115–16; William Harper, "Memoir on Slavery," in Lippincott and Grambo, pub., *The Pro-Slavery Argument* (Philadelphia, 1853), 88.

any form of slavery."[159] John Latrobe refuted him on Stephen Benson's behalf, but the ACS's newfound candor about Liberia's shortcomings also allowed Edmund Ruffin, a prominent Virginia "fire-eater," to land some easy blows. Quoting an agent of the Kentucky Colonization Society, Alexander Cowan, Ruffin highlighted Liberia's pitiful provision for recent arrivals and its exploitation of native labor.[160] He confided to his diary his pride in handing ammunition to critics of the recaptives appropriations, which Congress then had under consideration.[161] Yet Ruffin's *African Colonization Unveiled* (1859) concluded on a different note: the longer that Americans supported Liberia, "the more complete will be the experiment of ... the negro intellect." In other words, the black settlement's continued travails furnished cheering signs of inexorable racial degeneration.[162]

Yet such polemicists overcompensated for their very real worries for the institution of slavery. For all his avowed disdain, Ruffin was troubled by how colonization inspired masters to free their slaves. Singling out the society for its unique ability, in the South, to circulate publications lauding manumission, Ruffin denounced the ACS's appeal to Christian slaveowners' "vanity, ostentation, self-righteousness, and self-worship."[163] In condemning emancipation as a selfish act, he echoed the burgeoning biases of southern jurists, who, by 1860, would all but choke ACS operations in the slave states. Previously, southern state law had tended to ban "domestic" manumissions (those acts of emancipation that would have let freedpeople stay in the state), while permitting "foreign" ones (those that forced them to leave). Such a compromise honored slaveholders' property rights (here, their right to alienate their chattels), while limiting the growth of the free black population.[164]

From around 1840, however, a movement emerged in the lower South to outlaw postmortem manumission, a common practice that allowed masters to make full use of their slaves in life, while escaping, in death, the anger of a righteous God (should He see fit), of disseized (and often litigious) heirs, and of nearby planters whose own slaves would surely

---

[159] *AR* 35 (1859), 33.
[160] Alexander M. Cowan, *Liberia, as I Found It* (Frankfort, 1858); Edmund Ruffin, *African Colonization Unveiled* (Washington, DC, 1859), 26–9.
[161] Entry, January 28, 1859, in William K. Scarborough, ed., *The Diary of Edmund Ruffin* (Baton Rouge, 1972–89), 1:276.
[162] Ruffin, *African Colonization Unveiled*, 32.   [163] Ibid., 5.
[164] Memory F. Mitchell, "Off to Africa – With Judicial Blessing," *North Carolina Historical Review* 53 (1976), 269.

hear that freedom was coming to the neighborhood. In legal cases over contested wills, the antebellum tide ran against individual masters' freedom of action, and toward the safety of the wider community of slaveholders. By the outbreak of war, state bans on manumission had reached their apogee. "It is becoming impossible to emancipate any body by will," William McLain told John Pinney, "and those disposed to emancipate while living, are surrounded with such obstacles ... as render it almost impossible."[165] If the courts had once feared circumscribing the rights of slaveowners, they now feared acknowledging the agency of black Americans, a dangerous implication of emancipatory wills' frequent offer of continued enslavement in America or a potentially pyrrhic freedom in Africa.[166]

Southern Politics

Of course, the judges meant only to interpret the laws passed by legislators. And during the 1850s, southern lawmakers had supported the Liberian project, *if* they had, with one object in mind: removing free blacks, whose very existence was an affront, even an oxymoron, to proslavery thinkers. Nearly 500,000 strong in 1860, those African Americans who had eluded slavery, whether by birth, manumission, or flight, were split equally between the free and the slave states, and, within the latter, concentrated in the upper South.[167] While planters vaunted the South's living example of racial coexistence, theirs was a model premised strictly on the white enslavement of blacks. Both free blacks and the nonslaveholders who comprised three-fourths of the South's white population were, therefore, troubling anomalies in proslavery schemas. Unless enabled to enter the ranks of the slaveholding classes (by enslaving freepeople or "fresh" Africans, per a reopened Atlantic trade), or unburdened of the economic competition posed by free blacks, white southerners such as North Carolina's Hinton Rowan Helper, author of the deportationist *Impending Crisis of the South* (1857), would always prove susceptible to the idea of emancipation with colonization.[168]

[165] McLain to Pinney, May 30, 1859, reel 201–2, ACS.
[166] Burin, *Peculiar Solution*, 121–40; Emily West, *Family or Freedom: People of Color in the Antebellum South* (Lexington, 2012), 154.
[167] William W. Freehling, *The Road to Disunion* (New York, 1990–2007), 2:185.
[168] David Brown, *Southern Outcast: Hinton Rowan Helper and "The Impending Crisis of the South"* (Baton Rouge, 2006), 105–15; Walter Johnson, *River of Dark Dreams: Slavery and Empire in the Cotton Kingdom* (Cambridge, MA, 2013), 375–81.

Legislators found it easier, ethically and politically, to propose the expulsion rather than the enslavement of free blacks. Virginia was the first to broach mandatory exile, no surprise from a state whose colonization society, refounded in 1849 after years of inactivity, had explicitly devoted its efforts to the already free.[169] Indeed, as early as 1846, Governor William Smith (1846–9), of later recaptives-begrudging fame, had proposed that the Commonwealth's individual counties vote on banishing their black residents.[170] When the *Repository* lambasted that "utterly repugnant" idea, most Virginians nodded, but Smith had at least put the idea of expulsion into circulation.[171] Heeding an appeal by one of his successors to improve on the desultory numbers sent to Liberia, the legislature debated removal during 1851–3, and contemplated hiring out free blacks to fund their own exile. "If this population is ever to be removed ... there should be no longer delay," warned the statehouse's preeminent deportationist, John Rutherfoord, who undermined his own case by conceding the moral gravity of compulsion.[172] Other lawmakers agreed with his apprehensions more than his argument, citing the folly of expelling part of the workforce, and voted against his bill – but tempered their decision by renewing the colonization law.[173]

The inexorable logic of proslavery and the pitiful results of colonization pointed to another answer, though: "removing" free blacks, as a category, by enslaving them, a deed that the Virginia assembly could base on at least a burlesque of volition if it allowed them to choose between selecting a new master and leaving for Liberia.[174] As national politics succumbed to sectionalism, lawmakers throughout the South soured on the old compromises such as colonization. In 1858, the Old Dominion's assemblymen again defeated a proposal to expel free blacks, but this time, they also refused to renew the colonization provisions. "Not only politicians, but Christian men and ministers of the gospel ... have changed very much lately," reported one Virginia colonizationist. "There is nothing more desired ... than that Liberia shall turn out to be a Humbug."[175]

---

[169] William A. Link, *Roots of Secession: Slavery and Politics in Antebellum Virginia* (Chapel Hill, 2003), 154–7.
[170] Ted Maris-Wolf, *Family Bonds: Free Blacks and Re-Enslavement Law in Antebellum Virginia* (Chapel Hill, 2015), 33.
[171] *AR* 23 (1847), 45.
[172] John C. Rutherfoord, *Removal from the Commonwealth of the Free Colored Population* (Richmond, 1853), 19.
[173] Berlin, *Slaves without Masters*, 360–4.   [174] Maris-Wolf, *Family Bonds*, 76–7.
[175] W. H. Starr to Gurley, June 25, 1858, reel 84, ACS.

The same year, the legislatures of North Carolina and Missouri debated expulsion for the first time.[176]

If levels of reactionary agitation had been anything to go by, Maryland should have been the first to cross the Rubicon by issuing its free blacks an ultimatum of placing themselves under a master or leaving for one of the many other states that would not take them. For the Old Line State was on the cusp of joining its tiny neighbor, Delaware, in containing more free blacks than it did slaves. From late 1858, a slaveholder from the proslavery Eastern Shore (and chairman of the assembly's committee on the black population), Curtis Jacobs, led a continual drive to enslave free black Marylanders.[177] As it happened, though, Arkansas was first to cast the die, setting its free black residents a deadline of January 1, 1860, to find themselves on the road or in chains. Demands for expulsion had already gained momentum throughout the South, when, in October 1859, the militant abolitionist John Brown raided the arsenal at Harper's Ferry, Virginia, in an attempt to spark a slave insurrection. Fearing that more northern plotters would stir rebellion, the southern states stampeded to expel or enslave their free black residents. Such legislation ultimately failed everywhere, an outcome that would have been unimaginable at the mania's peak, once a modicum of basic decency and rudimentary economics found a foothold in one or more of the lower house, upper house, and governor's mansion. With war looming, even Arkansas repealed its expulsion law in early 1861. It turned out that the Rubicon *could* be recrossed, though doing so was easier for leery legislators than for the 800 freepeople who had already fled the state.[178]

Colonizationists could do little but survey a landscape at once alien to them and yet entirely of their making. In Maryland, James Hall confused even himself with his denunciations of the state's free-black enslavement bill: "we admit the existence of this class an evil, but wheretofore and to what extent? *Comparatively*, only, is it an evil."[179] In early 1860, the ACS

---

[176] Berlin, *Slaves without Masters*, 370–1.

[177] Barbara Jeanne Fields, *Slavery and Freedom on the Middle Ground: Maryland during the Nineteenth Century* (New Haven, 1985), 63–89; Freehling, *Road to Disunion*, 2:190–8; Jones, *Birthright Citizens*, 143–5; Curtis W. Jacobs, *The Free Negro Question in Maryland* (Baltimore, 1859), 14–28, and *Speech on the Free Colored Population of Maryland* (Annapolis, 1860), 26, 29.

[178] Jonathan M. Atkins, "Party Politics and the Debate over the Tennessee Free Negro Bill, 1859–1860," *Journal of Southern History* 71 (2005), 245–78; Berlin, *Slaves without Masters*, 371–80; Cameron and Co., pub., *Speech of Jordan Stokes in the Senate of Tennessee* (Nashville, 1860), 13–14.

[179] *Maryland Colonization Journal* 10 (1860), 138.

recorded that "such obstacles now exist ... in the southern states, that our supply of emigrants from that source is almost entirely cut off," but sent its traveling secretary, John Orcutt, to see whether he could enroll the Arkansas refugees.[180] He found them in Cincinnati. "They all listened with interest to what I had to say about Liberia," reported Orcutt. The refugees were too prescient, however, to grant him success: "some of them entertain the idea that the offensive law ... will be repealed and they shall return to their homes."[181] And with that damp squib sputtered the ACS's last initiative before the war that its officers feared from the outset would obviate its operations.

Ambition and Introspection

The ACS's impotence forced its leaders to reflect on its place in a wider movement for black resettlement that it no longer controlled, and perhaps never had. If slave-state legislators had disrupted the ACS's external operations, it was a free-state businessman and Quaker, Benjamin Coates, who now disquieted its internal unity. Hailing from Pennsylvania, the one state where it had remained possible for individuals to support both abolition and colonization, Coates complicated matters by proposing an expedition to the Niger Valley that would complement the work of the ACS, but remain distinct from it.[182] Inspired by the similar, earlier scheme of a British abolitionist, Thomas Fowell Buxton, as well as by the recent explorations of a Georgia missionary, Thomas Bowen, Coates suggested sending black American pioneers to grow cotton in what he supposed the unusually fertile soil of west Africa, in order to undersell slave produce.[183] By keeping the ACS at arm's length and stressing that voyagers must be volunteers, Coates turned emigration-minded black New Yorkers to the African Civilization Society (a name borrowed from Buxton's venture), founded in 1858.[184]

Colonizationists tried to fathom the new movement's connection to their own. Coates admitted that many black Americans considered "the

---

[180] Statement of the Executive Committee, January 17, 1860, reel 286, ACS.
[181] J. Orcutt to McLain, February 25, 1860, reel 88, ACS.
[182] Benjamin Coates, *Cotton Cultivation in Africa* (Philadelphia, 1858).
[183] Emma J. Lapsansky-Werner and Margaret Hope Bacon, eds., *Back to Africa: Benjamin Coates and the Colonization Movement in America, 1848–1880* (University Park, 2005), 19–47; Howard Temperley, *British Antislavery, 1833–1870* (Columbia, SC, 1972), 42–61.
[184] Tomek, *Colonization and Its Discontents*, 181–6.

African Civilization Society only African Colonization under another name, which it really is, except that it professes to be anti-slavery."[185] In 1857, Ralph Gurley, for one, had been intrigued by what was then more like Bowen's idea, probably because it offered the "high open country north of Lagos" that Monrovia's recent law against interior settlements had prohibited within Liberia.[186] By 1858, John Pinney's appetite had also been whetted: based in New York, he could not fail to notice local black interest in the Niger expedition.[187] Typically, his Boston counterpart was unmoved. "It operates badly, distracting the attention and dividing the action of our friends," tutted Joseph Tracy.[188] As with the earlier movement to found interior settlements, Tracy (rightly) identified the New York and Pennsylvania societies as Coates's main allies. Only, Tracy thought that, this time, they meant to sideline the ACS altogether. At the head office, William McLain modestly hoped that his own organization would never turn its back on Liberia.[189] In any case, the Civil War intervened and the Niger plan went awry.

Amid clampdowns on the manumission and locomotion of blacks, it was the existing states of the American Union, not the putative colonies of an African empire, that caused the society more trouble. For all its lobbying of politicians from its Pennsylvania Avenue headquarters, the ACS had never been at the center of colonization's revival, which had unfolded in the states. For the leadership, it was a familiar enough picture. During the 1830s, a young Gurley had warned, "if the state societies take colonization into their hands, we are a nullity."[190] Twenty years later, hindsight could show him that, from the ashes of the old regime, a new one had risen. Concurrent, state-level agencies enjoyed the flexibility that the cause needed to survive, be it the Pennsylvania chapter that included avowed abolitionists or the Alabama chapter that refused to affiliate to the parent society for its presumably pernicious views on slavery.[191]

At the same time, nothing thwarted white Americans' desire to remove their black compatriots more than did local governance. States passed laws prodding the black population to leave, only for their neighbors to pass laws forbidding it to enter. So emigrants to Liberia needed a white

[185] B. Coates to Gurley, January 13, 1859, reel 85, ACS.
[186] Gurley to Pinney, April 21, 1857, reel 232, ACS.
[187] Pinney to Gurley, November 8, 1858, reel 85, and March 15, 1860, reel 88, ACS.
[188] Tracy to Latrobe, November 19, 1858, reel 235, ACS.
[189] McLain to F. Butler, September 19, 1859, reel 201–2, ACS.
[190] Seifman, "United Colonization Societies," 33n29.
[191] Tomek, *Colonization and Its Discontents*, 163; *AR* 28 (1852), 142.

agent to escort them to port, past suspicious sheriffs and belligerent bystanders, only to encounter further hostility at the quayside, often from black opponents of colonization. Although the ACS had always acted tactfully when organizing embarkations from southern ports, that all-pervasive localism reared its head again in the form of increased municipal restrictions, which left open only Baltimore by the end of the 1850s. That was too far for most manumittees to travel, if their state even allowed their owners to free them anymore.[192]

While eager in principle to see their black brethren depart, whites were awfully good at denying them the means – financial, legal, and logistical – of doing so. Perhaps only the federal government could cut the Gordian knot of the states' self-sabotage. By 1860, the leaders of the ACS had come full circle to 1817, and considered a petition to the US government for help in rehoming the Arkansas exiles (and what looked likely to be their counterparts across the South). Inevitably, Tracy was skeptical. The ACS constitution should be amended "to write out all reference to Congress, to the General Government, and to the State Governments," he told Gurley. "Any attempt to induce Congress to aid us ... would cause us to be regarded as an organization for abolition."[193] Gurley ignored Tracy, and introduced himself to a member of the US Senate. "I have noticed the interest you have been pleased to express in the condition and prospects of our free people of color," he told James Doolittle, a Wisconsin Republican. "We are not bound by our Constitution to confine our colonization movements to Africa, yet great moral considerations ... have induced the society to give them solely that direction," added Gurley.[194]

Why the secretary of the ACS found himself writing to a politician from a state that had neither slavery nor an active colonization society nor more than a dozen years of statehood behind it, as well as having to make the case for Africa as opposed to some other destination, is the subject of Chapter 3.

[192] Blackett, *Captive's Quest*, 127–32; Burin, *Peculiar Solution*, 112–14.
[193] Tracy to Gurley, February 10, 1860, reel 236, ACS.
[194] Gurley to J. R. Doolittle, February 16, 1860, reel 234, ACS.

2

The Revival of "Emigration," to 1862

By 1850, for most African Americans, black resettlement meant the ACS and Liberia. It also meant Canada, Haiti, Jamaica, Mexico, Trinidad, and the American West. It meant a topic for open debate, and one for enforced unity; a belief in black solidarity, and a faith in western superiority. It meant mission to the benighted, and self-rule for the enlightened; hope, for those who left, and disappointment, for those who returned. It meant betrayal of the enslaved, and an enlarged struggle for their freedom.

Above all, black resettlement meant an investigation of what it even meant to be black. But white oppression, by its very nature, did not allow African Americans to explore their growing consciousness in isolation. If the premise of colonization imposed a general African identity on the diverse ethnicities brought to the Americas, then the premise of the black laws, which admitted no grades of color, imposed a blackness that was, at once, inflexible and unpredictable, with individuals passing for white in one state, decade, or courthouse, but not another.[1] Conversely, while the emergence of black churches, black conventions, and black newspapers provided independent forums for African Americans, the last of these was liable to the intrusion of white voices passing for black, and so raised chronic doubts about the authenticity of purportedly black commentary. As long as whites hoped to cajole rather than compel blacks to emigrate, however, the discursive traffic had to flow both ways, with white separatists adjusting to black goals as well as vice-versa. If the poor lifespan of

[1] John Ernest, *A Nation within a Nation: Organizing African-American Communities before the Civil War* (Chicago, 2011), 12, and *Chaotic Justice: Rethinking African American Literary History* (Chapel Hill, 2009), 38–40.

the era's African American newspapers left black intellectuals unduly reliant on white sources of information, then the low numbers of emigrants to Liberia left colonizationists reliant on stressing African Americans' capacity for greatness, rather than their unfitness for the United States, the tenor of earlier colonizationist material.[2]

That mutual dependence, an ironic form of racial co-existence for a movement that denied the very possibility of the same, was the hallmark of the last antebellum decade. During the 1850s, many black northerners, inhabiting a precarious world less amenable to abstract ideals than that of their white allies, changed their mind more than once whether, where, and when to emigrate. They debated the matter all the more furiously for invoking the same concepts. Those black Americans who supported foreign emigration did not oppose domestic integration, just as those who supported geographic fixedness did not oppose black independence from white institutions.[3]

Such flux was far from unique to African Americans. The nineteenth century was a nationalist one, during which peoples across Europe and the Americas started to think that they *were* peoples, linked by political, civic, and ideological values, on the one hand, and religious, ethnic, and cultural affinities, on the other.[4] Those two strands intertwined awkwardly for black Americans, devoted to the birthright that they asserted as would-be citizens of the United States, but also intrigued by their distant kin of the African diaspora.[5] In 1853, the most famous opponent of emigration, Frederick Douglass, described African Americans as "a nation, in the midst of a nation." A year earlier, the most famous supporter of emigration, Pittsburgh physician and journalist Martin Delany, had used near-identical words: "a nation within a nation," comparable to minorities such as the Poles in the Russian Empire, the Hungarians in the Austrian Empire, and the Irish in the United Kingdom. But where Douglass would have empowered the nation through protest, Delany would have done so by relocating it outside the United States.[6] And since nobody knew how much of the world's surface would end up under the

---

[2] Dickson D. Bruce, Jr., *The Origins of African American Literature, 1680–1865* (Charlottesville, 2001), 135–55, 269.
[3] Raymond L. Hall, *Black Separatism in the United States* (Hanover, 1978), 1–2.
[4] Philip S. Foner, *History of Black Americans* (Westport, 1975–83), 3:133.
[5] Martha S. Jones, *Birthright Citizens: A History of Race and Rights in Antebellum America* (New York, 2018), 10–11.
[6] Robert S. Levine, *Martin Delany, Frederick Douglass, and the Politics of Representative Identity* (Chapel Hill, 1997), 60.

Stars and Stripes, black Americans struggled all the more to disentangle their notions of sovereignty and separatism.

At the dawn of the 1850s, most African Americans opposed black-led "emigration" as well as white-led "colonization." Yet even that unity was, in part, a fiction wreaked after 1830 by community leaders keen to distance themselves from Africa, which had been coopted by the obnoxious ACS, and, to a lesser extent, from Haiti, the site of a failed emigration movement of the 1820s.[7] Emigration*ism* had already been stirring in the late 1840s, when, in 1850, emigration itself became necessary for many black Americans because of the newly tightened Fugitive Slave Act.[8] In 1857, Washington again assailed African Americans with the Supreme Court's *Dred Scott* ruling, which answered a decades-old question about blacks' US citizenship with a firm, if constitutionally fallacious, "no." Meanwhile, the states' support for exclusion and colonization seemed to point to a white conspiracy against black freedom. Although emigrationism embodied so much more than mere reaction to oppression, white Americans' own drive to resettle blacks loomed large over African Americans' plans for their own departure.

Indeed, the rancor of the 1850s lay in blacks' awareness that whites were forever looking for colonization's missing catalyst: African American consent, however tokenistic it might be.[9] If the black nation was, to quote Benedict Anderson's aphorism, an imagined community, then the danger was that *whites* might do the imagining, as well, and take the consent of a black minority as that of the majority. Although it feels intuitive to agree with Mary Ann Shadd, a champion of removal to Canada, when she argued that emigrationists' positions "should be examined and not be cried down," it is also easy to understand why a critic of one of her fellow emigrationists, Martin Delany, asked why Delany could not arrange his own venture quietly, "and not attempt to give [his] little movement a national character?"[10] Yet during the 1850s, those African Americans who would have stifled migratory sentiments lost the battle.[11]

[7] Matthew J. Hetrick, "Rewriting Their Own History; or, the Many Paul Cuffes," in Beverly C. Tomek and Hetrick, eds., *New Directions in the Study of African American Recolonization* (Gainesville, 2017), 290.

[8] Joanne Pope Melish, *Disowning Slavery: Gradual Emancipation and "Race" in New England, 1780–1860* (Ithaca, 1998), 267–8.

[9] Bruce, *Origins*, 143.

[10] "The Emigration Convention," *Provincial Freeman*, July 5, 1856; "Emigration Convention," *FDP*, November 18, 1853.

[11] Howard H. Bell, "Negro Nationalism: A Factor in Emigration Projects, 1858–1861," *Journal of Negro History* 47 (1962), 49.

Why were *words* so important? As one commentator put it, "there is gigantic talk of emigration, but I really would like to see some of its noted leaders emigrate themselves."[12] "How happens it that you are here ... still talking loudly about leaving?" demanded an antagonist of one journalist who claimed to have supported emigration for fifteen years.[13] Yet words mold ideas, and ideas mold imagined possibilities, for better and for worse. Words also connected a racial minority spread thinly outside the slave states, whether those words were articulated in the black press, from black pulpits, or at black conventions, state and national platforms where delegates discussed the problems that African Americans faced.[14] All three forums had once been strongholds of opposition to resettlement, but became contested terrain during the 1850s. Black newspapers, in particular, were so influential (and have provided such an important source) that scholars have wondered whether the presumed slump in emigrationist activity from 1830 to 1850 was more apparent than real (as the content of Chapter 5 would indeed suggest), the figment of editorial excision by the anti-emigrationists who ran the publications in question.[15] By contrast, the new titles of the 1850s, such as the *Voice of the Fugitive* and the *Provincial Freeman*, supported emigration, while the *Weekly Anglo-African* and the *Christian Recorder*, the official organ of the AME Church, presented both sides of the argument, a novelty in itself.[16] Likewise, the national convention movement, which had started at Philadelphia in 1830, had once provided a stage for affirming assimilationism and promoting domestic outlets for black frustration, such as benevolent institutions.[17] White lampoonery of black politics demanded

---

[12] "Our Albany Letter," *WAA*, March 24, 1860.
[13] M. T. Newsom, pub., *Arguments, Pro and Con, on the Call for a National Emigration Convention* (Detroit, 1854), 23.
[14] Philip S. Foner and George E. Walker, eds., *Proceedings of the Black State Conventions, 1840–1865* (Philadelphia, 1979–80), 1:xi–xviii; Eric Gardner, *Black Print Unbound: "The Christian Recorder," African American Literature, and Periodical Culture* (New York, 2015), 14–15.
[15] Howard H. Bell, "A Survey of the Negro Convention Movement, 1830–1861," dissertation, Northwestern University (1953), 126–9; Kwando M. Kinshasa, *Emigration vs. Assimilation: The Debate in the African American Press, 1827–1861* (Jefferson, NC, 1988), 1–2.
[16] Gilbert Anthony Williams, *"The Christian Recorder," Newspaper of the African Methodist Episcopal Church: History of a Forum for Ideas, 1854–1902* (Jefferson, NC, 1996), 82.
[17] Jane H. Pease and William H. Pease, *They Who Would Be Free: Blacks' Search for Freedom, 1830–1861* (New York, 1974), 119–21.

nothing less than shows of unity at such occasions.[18] Yet that anti-emigrationist monopoly also dissolved when Martin Delany, disappointed at the orthodox stance of Frederick Douglass's Rochester Convention (1853), called his own the next year at Cleveland, forbidding opponents of emigration from even attending.[19] So another stronghold of solidarity became a vacuum, filled by an upsurge in the state-level conventions that had flourished during an earlier hiatus in the national organization, and by a factionalism that soon divided emigrationists from each other, too.[20]

The best way to gauge the intensity of the 1850s is to place the decade in a longer-term perspective. By 1862, only two living black leaders, George Downing and James McCune Smith, had constantly held their ground against the allure of expatriation.[21] Within the lifetime of nearly everyone named in this chapter, however, blacks' interest in emigration fluctuated with their prospects in the United States. Tellingly, emigrationism peaked again with the "end" of Reconstruction in the late 1870s and the emergence of Jim Crow segregation laws in the 1890s.[22] That pattern suggests that, despite those 1970s scholars who saw the antebellum period as the formative era of "black nationalism," most African Americans were indeed American at heart: in favorable or fair times, they hoped for elevation at home.[23] Not all emigrationists became emigrants, and only a few of the well-known emigrants never returned to the United States.[24]

[18] Bruce, *Origins*, 152; Patrick Rael, *Black Identity and Black Protest in the Antebellum North* (Chapel Hill, 2002), 33–4.

[19] "Call for National Emigration Convention of Colored Men," *Provincial Freeman*, March 25, 1854.

[20] Ernest, *Nation within a Nation*, 107–20.

[21] Bell, "Negro Convention Movement," 223.

[22] For postwar emigrationism, see Kenneth C. Barnes, *Journey of Hope: The Back-to-Africa Movement in Arkansas in the Late 1800s* (Chapel Hill, 2004); Steven Hahn, *A Nation under Our Feet: Black Political Struggles in the Rural South from Slavery to the Great Migration* (Cambridge, MA, 2003); Nell Irvin Painter, *Exodusters: Black Migration to Kansas after Reconstruction* (New York, 1977); and Edwin S. Redkey, *Black Exodus: Black Nationalist and Back-to-Africa Movements, 1890–1910* (1969).

[23] For proponents of "black nationalism," see Rodney Carlisle, *The Roots of Black Nationalism* (New York, 1974); Floyd J. Miller, "'The Father of Black Nationalism': Another Contender," *Civil War History* 17 (1971), 310–19; and Wilson Jeremiah Moses, *The Golden Age of Black Nationalism, 1850–1925* (New York, 1978). For the concept's critics, see Tunde Adeleke, *UnAfrican Americans: Nineteenth-Century Black Nationalists and the Civilizing Mission* (Lexington, 1998), and Theodore Draper, *The Rediscovery of Black Nationalism* (London, 1971).

[24] R. J. M. Blackett, *Beating against the Barriers: Biographical Essays in Nineteenth-Century Afro-American History* (Baton Rouge, 1986), 394.

Moreover, no advocate of resettlement broke free from a certain elitist mindset, best described as that of the black, (culturally) Anglo-Saxon Protestant. Emigrationists condescended not only to those foreign peoples who supposedly needed the "three Cs" – Christianity, civilization, and commerce – but also to their own followers, who supposedly needed forceful leadership. As such, most pioneers planned the selective emigration of an elite cadre of black Americans, and not mass removal.[25] (In fairness, anti-emigrationists could also strike superior notes: "some whose presence in this country is necessary to the elevation of the colored people will leave us ... [and the] worthless will remain to help bind us to our present debasement," worried Douglass to Gerrit Smith, a white abolitionist from New York.[26]) Black Americans also struggled to run emigration schemes independently of white support, which complicates any distinction that historians might make between "emigration" and "colonization" in projects' actual execution, however important that difference to blacks' self-image. Remarkably, the antebellum era's largest biracial cause, other than the Christian mission that underpinned all social reforms, was not abolition, suffrage, or self-reliance, but black resettlement – not least because it incorporated all those struggles.

During the 1850s, that unexpected expression of Atlantic antislavery showed up in three theaters: Canada, west Africa (Liberia and the Niger Valley), and Haiti, with black Americans' interest peaking in that order. The first represented a convenient refuge, but also a haven for those keen to exercise Anglo-American political rights; the second, the ideal location for a mission to blacks' ancestral homeland; and the third, an opportunity to reinforce an infamous base of black militancy. By the 1850s, none of those options was new, but they offered African Americans new opportunities and challenges. Two further targets for black emigrationists, Central America and the British West Indies, are considered in Chapters 4 and 5.

SEEKING A REFUGE: CANADA

If anyone wanted evidence that emigration was better left to individuals than to institutions, they had only to follow the North Star. "Since

---

[25] Floyd J. Miller, *The Search for a Black Nationality: Black Emigration and Colonization, 1787–1863* (Urbana, 1975), 268–9.
[26] F. Douglass to G. Smith, January 21, 1851, in Philip S. Foner, ed., *The Life and Writings of Frederick Douglass* (New York, 1950–5), 2:151.

1816 there have not been more than 6,000 transported to Africa, while Anti-Slavery has forwarded to Canada ... near 20,000," observed one reporter in 1848.[27] Although contemporaries usually overestimated the number who had crossed the border, underestimated the proportion who had been free rather than enslaved, and inflated the number of "conductors" working on the so-called Underground Railroad, the flow of fugitives, which had increased after abolition in the western British Empire (1834), increased again with the Fugitive Slave Act (1850).[28] Of the destinations surveyed in this chapter, only Canada offered the convenience of contiguity, and took as many African Americans through the Civil War as Liberia and Haiti combined. Similar to the United States in so many respects, Canada would stand and fall, in black eyes, by its willingness to offer the equality that the United States should have done. Yet white Canadians' response disabused African Americans of such hopes, even if local prejudice did not eject as many black immigrants as historians once thought.[29]

Unlike the other destinations treated in this book, the provinces of Canada, which Britain would federate in 1867, were always the object of more emigration than of emigrationism. At the end of the Revolutionary War and its successor conflict, the War of 1812, Nova Scotia had taken in enslaved African Americans who had fought on Britain's side in return for their personal freedom.[30] For those African Americans who considered whether to stay in the United States to fight for further freedoms, such as the vote, the Great White North came as an afterthought to the smaller, black souths of Liberia and Haiti, which, however, commanded little confidence after 1830. The Canadian option came to prominence, then, in an era of newfound opposition to "emigration," from which tainted designation many African Americans excluded removal northward, however idiosyncratically. The first national convention met in response to Cincinnati's expulsion of its black residents (1829) and endorsed their plans to move to Canada, all the while condemning "foreign emigration." Even Samuel Cornish, the New York–based editor of the first black-run newspaper, *Freedom's Journal*, and a staunch opponent of emigration, conceded that refugees had to go *somewhere*. A rare, overt emigrationist

[27] "Isaac T. Hopper and David Ruggles," *North Star*, April 14, 1848.
[28] Eric Foner, *Gateway to Freedom: The Hidden History of America's Fugitive Slaves* (New York, 2015), 11–15.
[29] Michael Wayne, "The Black Population of Canada West on the Eve of the American Civil War: A Reassessment Based on the Manuscript Census of 1861," *Social History* 28 (1995), 461–85.
[30] Robin W. Winks, *The Blacks in Canada: A History* (New Haven, 1971), 24–60, 114–41.

of the 1830s, Pittsburgh's Lewis Woodson, advocated Canada for unemployed urban blacks, arguing that it would hardly betray the slaves to found a colony that then saved the entire race from extinction.[31] Unsurprisingly, the Toronto Convention (1851) advocated relocation to the land that had hosted it, while even Frederick Douglass conceded that African Americans could plant themselves "at the very portals of slavery" if they stayed close to the United States.[32]

In the wake of the Fugitive Slave Act, Canada's newest residents found it easier to justify migration. "Let us … mould the destiny of the whole Africo American race … with a centre of unity in Canada," proposed a boot-maker and imminent immigrant, James Theodore Holly.[33] "We … solicit your friendly aid in behalf of an improved plan of colonizing," wrote Henry Bibb, a fugitive slave in Canada, to Henry Clay, after encountering an escapee from Clay's own estate.[34] For his part, Samuel Ringgold Ward, who had fled slavery as a child but only recently moved from New York to Canada, thought that with blacks' improvement in a similar country "must go down for ever the old, oft refuted lie, of our incapacity for social equality with the Anglo-Saxons."[35] Was he right? Would black Americans take to white Canadians, and white Canadians to black Americans?

Planned Settlements

Like those who had arrived before 1850, the immigrants soon discovered limits to whites' welcome, not least since most blacks gathered in Canada West (prior to 1841, "Upper Canada," and today, part of Ontario), which was separated from the slave states by only the state of Ohio and Lake Erie. Having reached British lines, the earliest fugitives tended to go no farther. They had little money, preferred to remain where the soil was the most like what they knew, and positioned themselves to return with ease to the United States should conditions change. Black Americans formed settlements across the Detroit River, at Amherstburg, Windsor, and Colchester; across the Niagara River, at Welland and St. Catharines; and in the center of the peninsula running between them, along the shores of Lake Erie, at Chatham, Dresden, and London (Map 2.1). Immigrants

---

[31] Bruce, *Origins*, 163–74; Miller, *Black Nationality*, 88–9, 101.
[32] "The Future Prospects of the Negro People," May 11, 1853, in Foner, *Writings of Douglass*, 2:252.
[33] "Interesting Letter from Vermont," *Voice of the Fugitive*, July 2, 1851.
[34] "To the 'Hon.' Henry Clay," ibid.
[35] "For the Voice of the Fugitive," ibid., November 6, 1851.

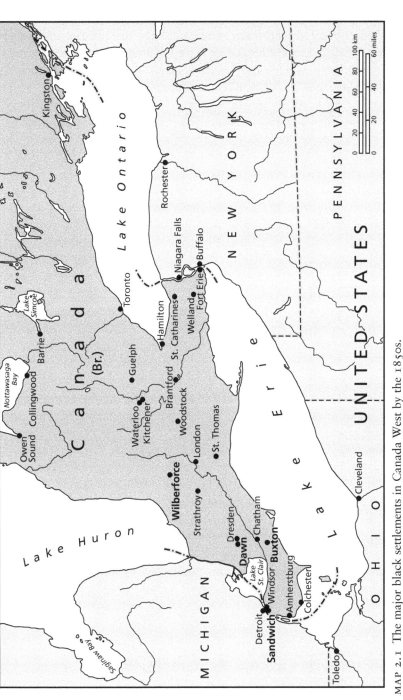

MAP 2.1 The major black settlements in Canada West by the 1850s.
Based on Colonial Church and School Society (West London Branch), pub., *Mission to the Free Colored Population in Canada* (London, 1855), frontispiece.

arrived in small bands, mostly from the upper South, and had often stayed a while in one of the northern states; until the harsher Act of 1850, fugitive slaves had rarely needed to leave the United States with haste. For slaves, then, unlike for free African Americans, emigration had represented a more conscious choice *before* 1850.[36]

Despite the initiative that immigrants had showed in even reaching Canada, they were unlikely to escape the paternalism of Victorian philanthropists for long. Prior to the Civil War, reformers founded four Canadian communities that each offered a plot of land, a basic education, and a taste of self-reliance. Unlike the leaders of the notorious utopian ventures of the 1820s at Nashoba, Tennessee, and New Harmony, Indiana, the directors of the Canadian communities did not mean to inculcate a primitive socialism in their residents, but, rather, a business acumen that would allow them to flourish in a capitalist world.[37]

The first community, Wilberforce, was founded in haste by the victims of Cincinnati's 1829 expulsion law, a seeming portent of the forcible removal that critics of colonization had prophesied.[38] With the clock ticking on their eviction, black Cincinnatians sent two delegates, Israel Lewis and Thomas Cresap, to investigate Upper Canada. "Tell your Republicans on your side of the line that we do not know men by their color," its governor reputedly told them. They offered to buy 4,000 acres from a land company, only to find, as banished blacks so often did, their native legislature unwilling to foot the bill – and the city mayor unhappy to see valuable workers depart. In fact, black Cincinnatians were so confident that he would overturn the law that only 200 ultimately went to Wilberforce, and perhaps another 800 to its environs. "In one year, this self-created, independent settlement will have received a greater accession of strength, than has been given to the colony at Liberia during the last twelve years," enthused a Baltimore colonizationist and mentor to the young William Lloyd Garrison, Benjamin Lundy, who had turned against Africa in favor of destinations more acceptable to black opinion. In reality, Wilberforce would fail by 1836, Israel Lewis having exhausted philanthropists' patience with his fraudulent fundraising. The poor example that he set would see almost a decade elapse before anyone

[36] Winks, *Blacks in Canada*, 144, 153.
[37] William H. Pease and Jane H. Pease, *Black Utopia: Negro Communal Experiments in America* (Madison, 1963), 18.
[38] Bruce, *Origins*, 176–8.

attempted another such colony. Still, Wilberforce had at least planted the idea of cooperative communities in reformers' minds.[39]

If the name "Wilberforce" had celebrated abolitionism's glorious past, then that of the second venture, Dawn, hailed its bright future. Located near Dresden, Dawn would eclipse its predecessor's fame, partly because one of its residents, Josiah Henson, claimed to have inspired Harriet Beecher Stowe's eponymous cabin-dweller, Uncle Tom. Like Wilberforce, Dawn originated in Ohio, where Hiram Wilson and his fellow abolitionists at the biracial Oberlin College decided to raise money to educate the fugitives. Accordingly, a manual labor school, the British-American Institute, opened its doors in 1842. Inverting municipal norms, the community was to serve the school, in turn governed by Dawn's trustees. The institute acquired 300 acres on the Sydenham River, named for the first governor general (1839–41) of the unified Province of Canada; the black settlers, who went on to number 500, acquired 1,500 acres in their own right, where they grew tobacco, wheat, and oats. The community had its own sawmill and made a modest success of lumbering. While handling a sale of timber to sponsors in Boston, Henson started to show signs of untrustworthiness, though not on the same scale as Wilberforce's Israel Lewis. Wilson, too, acted craftily, claiming to oppose the "begging ministers" who solicited from door to door, a practice that many fundraisers abhorred, while using the same method himself.

In 1840, abolitionists on both sides of the Atlantic had splintered at London's World Anti-Slavery Convention over growing resentment at Garrison's feminism, apoliticism, and anticlericalism. The ensuing fault lines ran as far as the communities of Canada West. Accused of hostility to Garrison, Hiram Wilson fell from the settlers' favor, and reports of their differences closed donors' purses. Scouting for new supporters, Josiah Henson went to London, and found the British and Foreign Anti-Slavery Society (BFASS) willing to assume management of Dawn, as long as it could appoint its own superintendent, John Scoble. Since the BFASS had been founded as a vehicle for Garrison's opponents, Scoble was in no better position than Wilson had been to end the strife at Dawn. Accused of paternalism by the settlers, and challenged for the position of manager, Scoble could not breathe new life into the experiment. From 1854, all-engulfing animosity left few of Dawn's residents unwilling to point the finger at one another. Meanwhile, neutral observers opined that they

---

[39] Pease, *Black Utopia*, 46–62; Winks, *Blacks in Canada*, 144–62.

might have learned more resourcefulness had they been left to support themselves from the outset.[40]

That lesson about misguided benevolence started to sink in for reformers, though not quickly enough, for the third of the failed projects, the Refugee Home Society. The RHS originated in a black convention held at Windsor in 1846 under Isaac Rice, a missionary who would also become involved in the dispute at Dawn. The convention chose a tract north of Amherstburg, some of it already owned by blacks, and established the Sandwich Mission. Sponsored by white Michiganders keen to help what would have been a local cause but for a national border, the mission bought lands and wrote a constitution allowing elected overseers to advise the trustees, who would be appointed by the scheme's backers. Settlers were to spurn the bar and the Bar: alcohol was banned, as were legal actions between one resident and another, at least until the trustees had tried to arbitrate.

For reasons unclear, the Sandwich Mission collapsed as an independent project, and, after 1852, was swallowed up in the larger organization that was the RHS. The society bought 2,000 acres within three years, reselling half to some 150 colonists, though with inadequate contiguity to foster a real community. Like Dawn, the settlement succumbed to factionalism. In 1854, the residents protested an increase in the RHS's surveying charges and a decrease in the term that it had allowed them to improve their land. Moreover, as its name implied, the cash-strapped Refugee Home Society accepted only fugitives and not free blacks, who might have helped it with their own funds. When the impoverished settlers failed to meet their debts, the society sued them, flatly ignoring its own ideal of arbitration, only to incur a surprise defeat in court – which ruined its finances.[41]

It was fourth time lucky for Canada's organized communities. The honorable exception showed that such settlements needed a devoted leader: in this case, William King, a Scotch-Irish immigrant whose unsolicited inheritance of slaves, through his Louisianan wife, had troubled his Presbyterian conscience enough for him to free and settle them near Chatham. He named his village Elgin, after the province's governor general (1847–54), and its concurrent mission Buxton, after Thomas Fowell Buxton (like Wilberforce, a luminary of British antislavery).

---

[40] Ernest, *Chaotic Justice*, 92–4; Pease, *Black Utopia*, 63–83; Winks, *Blacks in Canada*, 178–81, 195–204.
[41] Pease, *Black Utopia*, 109–22; Winks, *Blacks in Canada*, 204–8.

Crucially, King parted from precedent by placing fundraising in the hands of a joint stock company, which would dissolve itself once it had bought enough land. He did not rush to found an industrial institute, which he thought would discourage African Americans from breaking out of menial trades. Rather, he reserved school hours for fostering literate, active citizens, insisting that his charges become British subjects, and established a community court to air grievances in private. The Ulsterman also knew the dangers of sectarianism, encouraging denominations other than his own to found churches. Visitors during the 1850s praised Elgin's orderliness, such that the colony almost redeemed the all too visible shortcomings of Wilberforce, Dawn, and Sandwich.[42]

Like its predecessors, however, Elgin never outgrew its founding framework of white leadership.[43] For the three older communities, the ironies abounded. Established abroad, they had to send a constant stream of fundraisers back to the United States. Intended to steer African Americans toward independence and integration, they fostered only dependence and segregation. Designed to permit respectful differences of opinion in private, they aired their bitter divisions in public. However much local whites might mock the communities, other blacks were always the more scathing, especially since the four communities accounted for only a fraction of black immigrants to Canada, most of whom did perfectly well without such heavy-handed help. At the heart of African Americans' debate over the planned settlements was whether blacks in Canada should define themselves as American expatriates or British subjects; as victims of past oppressions or authors of their own future.

On the one side were James Theodore Holly and Henry Bibb, editors of the *Voice of the Fugitive*, and on the other were Samuel Ringgold Ward and Mary Ann Shadd, editors of the *Provincial Freeman*. Their differences showed up in the names of their newspapers, the former betraying an identity as exiles from America, and the latter embracing one as residents of Canada.[44] Opposed to the communal experiments for assuming that blacks lacked self-reliance, Shadd directed her fire at the RHS, in which Bibb was heavily involved. "It is not needed at all as Government offers land cheaper," she told the American Missionary Association. "It

---

[42] Pease, *Black Utopia*, 84–108; Winks, *Blacks in Canada*, 208–12.
[43] Howard Law, "'Self-Reliance Is the True Road to Independence': Ideology and the Ex-Slaves in Buxton and Chatham," *Ontario History* 77 (1985), 113.
[44] Jane Rhodes, *Mary Ann Shadd Cary: The Black Press and Protest in the Nineteenth Century* (Bloomington, 1998), 70–99.

arrays the whites against the blacks, because of the superior political privileges sought.... It keeps active the begging system, and thus diverts the gifts of benevolent persons from their proper course."[45] It *was* hard to ask for money with dignity, and Shadd's praise for Elgin proved that solicitation vexed her more than separatism in itself.[46] Defending the RHS, Bibb ventured that "strangers in a foreign land ... [prefer] being associated with those who may have come from the same region."[47] Meanwhile, Frederick Douglass could only rue the factionalism north of the border.[48]

Prejudice

Whatever the merits and demerits of separate communities, blacks could only assimilate as far as white Canadians allowed them. Until the late 1830s, locals had tolerated black immigrants, but, by the 1840s, disliked them, and, by the 1850s, disparaged them, with the inconsistency that only prejudice could muster: while some whites arraigned the arrivals for returning to the United States as soon as possible, others upbraided them for planning never to leave. Moreover, from the 1840s, Irish immigrants fulfilled the menial labor needs of a society that was, in any case, outgrowing the frontier phase. As land became more expensive, African Americans drifted to the towns, where whites started to demand the informal segregation that British law did not formally allow.[49] By 1848, the Rev. Henry Highland Garnet, a radical abolitionist from New York (Figure 2.1), described "colorphobia" as a fact of life in Canada.[50] Yet, unlike in the United States, blacks were allowed to serve in the militia, without even segregation, and helped rout Upper Canada's Mackenzie Rebellion (1837), the pro-American sympathies of which left them in no doubt of their own. Back in New York, Samuel Cornish cited those adoptive Canadians' actions against a republican rising as evidence of

---

[45] M. A. Shadd to G. Whipple, December 28, 1852, American Missionary Association Collection, Tulane.
[46] "Rev. Wm. King – The Buxton Settlement," *Provincial Freeman*, April 15, 1854.
[47] "Colored Schools, etc., in Canada," *Voice of the Fugitive*, February 26, 1852.
[48] "Voice of the Colored People of Sandwich," *FDP*, April 8, 1853.
[49] Winks, *Blacks in Canada*, 143–4.
[50] Henry Highland Garnet, *The Past and the Present Condition, and the Destiny, of the Colored Race* (Troy, 1848), 27.

FIGURE 2.1 Henry Highland Garnet (1815–1882). Presbyterian minister,
abolitionist, and emigrationist.
National Portrait Gallery, Smithsonian Institution

black *Americans*' loyalty to a political system that should duly reward
them with equal rights.[51]

White Canadians' prejudice crystallized at the founding of the fourth
planned settlement, Elgin. In 1849, before King had even bought any
land, the local council petitioned the provincial assembly to reject his
proposal, which was "highly deleterious to the morals and social condition" of Canada West. Mindful of Britain's pretensions to moral superiority on race relations, a meeting at Chatham resolved that blacks should
enjoy all the privileges of citizenship, but somewhere else, and that
American slaves should be set free, but in their own country. The instiga-
tor was Edwin Larwill, a local politician and real estate speculator,
who had drawn up a long list of preemptive charges: more black immigrants would repel their white counterparts, provoke war with the United
States, claim political privileges, marry white women, and commit
petty crime. Yet Larwill had chosen his enemies unwisely, for settlers at

[51] Ikuko Asaka, *Tropical Freedom: Climate, Settler Colonialism, and Black Exclusion in the
Age of Emancipation* (Durham, 2017), 66; Bradley Miller, "British Rights and Liberal
Law in Canada's Fugitive Slave Debate, 1833–1843," in Tony Freyer and Lyndsay
Campbell, eds., *Freedom's Conditions in the U.S.-Canadian Borderlands in the Age of
Emancipation* (Durham, 2011), 152.

Elgin owned enough land to vote, and would account for the margin of his defeat at the next election.[52] And given their newfound ability to cast a ballot, black refugees in Canada also experienced something else familiar to white Americans during the 1850s: political realignment. Previously, the immigrants had voted for Conservative candidates, to demonstrate their devotion to the regime that had given them a home: "they mostly vote against the friends of freedom," as Ward rued to Douglass.[53] Mary Ann Shadd regretted that Larwill, a Conservative, had tested her loyalties, but warned that the alternative, the Reform Party, admired American republicanism, with its own hypocrisy on race.[54] But when another Conservative proposed resettling the black residents of Toronto on a local island, the scheme's putative victims protested such a blatant variant of the "black hearted scheme of the American Colonization Society."[55] By 1861, blacks in Toronto had declared for the Reform Party.[56]

Yet prejudice permeated more than politics, and black immigrants began to wonder whether they would ever escape it. "Some of this horrid state of feeling pervades Canada, from its proximity to ... the States," noted Henry Bibb, in part exculpating white Canadians.[57] Ward agreed that such sentiments were essentially derivative, but also thought them, by dint of the same, more gratuitous than in the United States.[58] During the 1850s, black immigrants to Canada became less willing to attribute blame to American influences, with one settler appalled to find prejudice, "that mildew-like feeling," already present in distant Vancouver, where black Californians had recently moved to escape their state's exclusion law.[59] In different parts of Canada, white militiamen rioted against serving with black comrades, steamer captains ejected blacks from the cabin, and teachers started segregating schools, though often at the behest of the refugees, whose children inevitably lagged behind their free peers.[60]

---

[52] Winks, *Blacks in Canada*, 213–14.
[53] "Letters from Canada," *FDP*, December 18, 1851.
[54] "A Descendant of the African Race," *Provincial Freeman*, May 12, 1855.
[55] "Meeting of Colored People in Toronto," *Mirror of the Times*, August 22, 1857.
[56] "Meeting of Colored Electors," *Toronto Globe*, June 27, 1861.
[57] "Color-Phobia in Canada," *Voice of the Fugitive*, May 21, 1851.
[58] "Canadian Negro Hate," ibid., November 4, 1852.
[59] Robert W. O'Brien, "Victoria's Negro Colonists – 1858–1866," *Phylon* 3 (1942), 15–18; F. Smithea to A. de Cosmos, *British Colonist*, June 10, 1859.
[60] Jason H. Silverman, *Unwelcome Guests: Canada West's Response to American Fugitive Slaves, 1800–1865* (Millwood, 1985), 127–45.

Quite apart from the prejudice in Canada itself, black immigrants never felt safe from the United States, either. As long as the federal and state governments could issue extradition warrants, fugitive slaves had cause to doubt the protective fabric of the Union Jack. Abolitionists were disappointed by the Webster–Ashburton Treaty (1842), which enumerated the offenses liable to extradition from the British Empire to the United States (and vice-versa), even though it excluded fugitive slaves' usual "crimes" of desertion, mutiny, and revolt on board ship. (As to American warrants for robbery, Canadian courts continued to exempt theft that the named person had committed in order to escape slavery, such as stealing a horse.)[61] No shade of law, though, could prevent the US annexation of Canada, which contemporaries saw as a matter of time. Although Ward acknowledged that annexation would subject Canada to the Fugitive Slave Act, he also thought that that law had alienated white Canadians enough that they would protect their black neighbors by force.[62] Martin Delany disagreed, maintaining that "the Canadians are descended from the same common parentage as the Americans"; should the United States annex Canada, "the colored man ... is forever doomed." Declaring for emigration in his *Condition, Elevation, Emigration, and Destiny of the Colored People* (1852), Delany conceded that fugitive slaves should keep choosing Canada, but saw it as a stopgap pending a safer destination in Central or South America.[63]

Emigrationists Divide

The Cleveland Convention (1854), which Delany assembled to endorse his own brand of emigrationism, deepened the divisions between the expatriate factions. Holly and Bibb supported Delany, but had lost influence within Canada to Shadd and Ward, who questioned why African Americans needed a nationality of their own when Britain offered one open to all colors. Meeting in August 1854, the National Emigration Convention, to accord the Cleveland meeting its official name, seated delegates from eleven states and Canada – though almost half were from Delany's hometown, Pittsburgh. Indeed, a majority of the attendees were westerners, by the geographic standards of the day, and were keener on

[61] Winks, *Blacks in Canada*, 168–76.
[62] S. R. Ward to B. Coates, *FDP*, November 19, 1852.
[63] Martin Robison Delany, *The Condition, Elevation, Emigration, and Destiny of the Colored People of the United States* (Philadelphia, 1852), 48–9, 189–92.

challenging their eastern counterparts as the public voice of black America than on actually emigrating.[64] The convention's report – in reality, Delany's handiwork – advocated removal to those parts of the Americas where African Americans could "constitute by necessity of numbers, the ruling element of the body politic," the mark of which would be their ability to hold office, not just cast a vote. If moving south proved unfeasible, Delany added, then going north to Canada would be the next best option.[65]

If the debates at Cleveland confirmed Delany's break with Frederick Douglass over emigration, they also brought Shadd closer to Delany. In light of Bibb's premature death and Holly's departure from Canada, she had already won the argument north of the border, but now surrendered south of it, as Douglass refused to accept her distinction between Delany's emigrationism, premised on a new, black-controlled state, and her (exported) integrationism, premised on an existing but (officially) race-blind polity. For his part, Delany also moved in Shadd's direction – quite literally, as he cast aside his concerns about the potential US annexation of Canada and emigrated to Chatham in 1856. Yet even as his movement broadened, it dissolved, with Holly turning to a missionary form of emigration in reaction to Delany's strident secularism. A second Cleveland Convention, in 1856, attracted fewer delegates than two years earlier, with even Delany absent through illness, but it enlarged the bureaucracy of the emigration movement and transferred the convention's operations to Chatham. Yet the mental migrations of Delany, Shadd, and Holly ensured that Canada's triumph as the go-to destination for African Americans would prove short-lived, for it lacked the ethnic, cultural, and, in some respects, political appeal of west Africa and Haiti. By the end of the 1850s, those movements exerted the stronger appeal on black intellectuals in Canada and the United States.[66]

What is there to say of black experiences in Her Majesty's dominions? If white Canadians had missed an opportunity to show themselves above prejudice, they had largely accepted another, to acknowledge that their new neighbors were at least equal in the eyes of the law. If black Americans in Canada had missed an opportunity to show themselves

---

[64] Miller, *Black Nationality*, 140–5.
[65] Robert M. Kahn, "The Political Ideology of Martin Delany," *Journal of Black Studies* 14 (1984), 429–33; Martin Robison Delany, *Political Destiny of the Colored Race on the American Continent* (1854), in Frank A. Rollin, ed., *Life and Public Services of Martin R. Delany* (Boston, 1883), 329, 367.
[66] Miller, *Black Nationality*, 157–69.

above factionalism, they were far from alone in the annals of antislavery. Removed, for the time being, from the reach of the "Slave Power," what centripetal force could possibly have acted on them?[67]

While African Americans warmed to Canada after 1850, they remained cold toward Africa. The decade's increased emigration to Liberia was mostly one of emancipated but expedited slaves, whose contributions to a debate dominated by northerners would have always been limited, had black activists (or their own masters) even allowed them a hearing. From 1858 to 1862, however, a number of northern intellectuals accepted, even embraced, emigration to west Africa, especially to the Yoruba region of the Niger Valley. In effect, they acknowledged their identity as partly African, a label they had rejected for three decades to retort the ACS.[68]

In so doing, they harked back almost a century, for some of the earliest schemes for Africa had originated with black New Englanders in the 1770s. At the height of the slave trade, such advocates often thought less in terms of rekindling an ancestral connection, and more in terms of returning to their literal birthplace. Moreover, black emigrationists of the early republic looked without compunction to white support, be it the seventy-five Bostonians who, in 1787, petitioned the state of Massachusetts for assistance in reaching Africa, "where we shall live among our equals," or the Quaker businessman Paul Cuffe, who, in 1813, lobbied Congress with President James Madison's (1809–17) blessing. Although the War of 1812 prevented Cuffe persuading Capitol Hill to support a plan that involved bolstering the British colony of Sierra Leone, he dispatched thirty-eight emigrants anyway. Cuffe died in 1817, having added the idea of civilizing mission to one that his eighteenth-century forebears had understood more as flight from oppression. Latterly, he also resolved to found a separate, American settlement. Having influenced Robert Finley, a white New Jersey theologian and Charles Mercer's "rival" for founder of the ACS, Cuffe had as good a claim as theirs to that accolade, albeit a posthumous one. Only, the

---

[67] Winks, *Blacks in Canada*, 231, 261.

[68] Bruce, *Origins*, 154–5, 249; Ernest, *Chaotic Justice*, 155; Melish, *Disowning Slavery*, 251–2; Benjamin Quarles, "Black History's Antebellum Origins," *Proceedings of the American Antiquarian Society* 89 (1979), 101.

society never adopted the explicit antislavery that had featured in Cuffe's later thinking.[69]

From the earliest days of the ACS, however, African Americans opposed their white compatriots telling them where to go. In Georgetown, Richmond, and Philadelphia, local blacks assembled to protest the organization's formation, with 3,000 gathering at Philadelphia's Bethel Church. Since two of the city's loudest detractors of the society, James Forten and Richard Allen, the founder of the AME Church, had in fact collaborated with Cuffe, they set another precedent for opponents of emigration, namely, that community leaders should feel free to rewrite the record whenever wider opinion indicated that they should. Nevertheless, the project that would become Liberia drew in another of Cuffe's associates, Baltimore minister Daniel Coker, as well as Richmond missionary Lott Cary, both instrumental to the early colony's survival. The society scored a coup in 1829 when John Brown Russwurm, the editor of *Freedom's Journal* since Cornish's resignation, announced his decision to move to Liberia, and promptly shut down the newspaper. No immigrant of Russwurm's stature followed until two decades later, though.[70]

Liberia Revisited

From the late 1840s, state legislators oppressed blacks all the harder, which explains much of the increased emigration to Liberia during the antebellum period.[71] But would Liberia ever exercise a positive pull on African Americans? Would "the love of liberty ever bring them there," to paraphrase that country's motto? In 1847, an Illinois meeting of black Baptists sent a resident of Springfield, Samuel Ball, to investigate Liberia. He reported that, while no land was better for those with means, none was worse for those without.[72] The same year, Liberia's newfound independence from the ACS raised the possibility that erstwhile opponents

---

[69] Miller, *Black Nationality*, 3–53; W. Bryan Rommel-Ruiz, "Colonizing the Black Atlantic: The African Colonization Movements in Postwar Rhode Island and Nova Scotia," *Slavery and Abolition* 27 (2006), 349–65.

[70] Miller, *Black Nationality*, 48–74, 82–9; Julie Winch, *A Gentleman of Color: The Life of James Forten* (New York, 2002), 187–206.

[71] Ousmane K. Power-Greene, *Against Wind and Tide: The African American Struggle against the Colonization Movement* (New York, 2014), 95–9.

[72] S. S. Ball, *Report on the Condition and Prospects of the Republic of Liberia* (Alton, IL, 1848), 12–14.

might come to love the sin while still hating the sinner. "My imaginary objection is blown to the winds," confessed one George Baltimore, who had worried that the society would transfer Liberia to the United States sooner than allow it independence.[73] Martin Delany, at that point an opponent of emigration, was unimpressed: "[Liberia] is lauded to the skies as an evidence of the capacity of the colored man for self-government [while] Hayti has for the last fifty years fully demonstrated this truth," he wrote his then-ally Frederick Douglass.[74] Where Douglass confessed his pride in Liberia's progress (whatever his feelings about the ACS), Delany described President Joseph Jenkins Roberts as a "fawning servilian to the negro-hating Colonizationists."[75] Meanwhile, James Pennington, a fugitive slave and adoptive Brooklynite, worried that any emigrants to Africa would one day be skewered on the bayonets of British expansionists.[76]

However formidable whites' machinery for promoting Liberian colonization, the cause lacked a platform in autonomous black politics. State conventions declaimed against Liberia, with delegates in New York resolving to send a ship to Africa to rescue those brethren "deluded" enough to have moved to such an unhealthy clime.[77] A Maryland meeting of 1852, which declared for Liberia above all other locations, was the exception that proved the rule.[78] Even once Delany and Douglass had parted ways, neither's convention would be amenable to unorthodox thinking on Africa. "No person will be admitted ... who would introduce the subject of emigration to ... Asia, Africa, or Europe," warned Delany's invitation to the Americas-focused Cleveland meeting.[79] In 1855, at the last national convention of Douglass's stay-and-fight school, a delegate read out a letter on the merits of African colonization, only for George Downing, a New York restauranteur whose premises marked an important stop on the Underground Railroad, to demand that it be burned.[80] In the more cosmopolitan states, it was not just black forums where black opponents of Liberia could gain a hearing. During the 1850s, one Lewis Putnam presented his Liberia Emigration and Agricultural Association to the governments of New York and New Jersey, claiming popular support for his minor outfit. It was the sort of tokenistic black-led venture that so

[73] *AR* 24 (1848), 150.
[74] M. R. Delany to Douglass, January 21, *North Star*, February 4, 1848.
[75] "Liberia," ibid., March 2, 1849.
[76] "Will You Burn Our Candle at Both Ends?," *FDP*, April 22, 1852.
[77] Foner, *Proceedings*, 1:90.   [78] Ibid., 2:43.   [79] Newsom, *Arguments*, 5–6.
[80] Power-Greene, *Against Wind and Tide*, 129–30.

haunted northerners, especially after it prompted New York's Governor Washington Hunt (1851–2) to appeal to the state assembly to fund colonization. In the decade's most vicious attack on a traitor to the cause (no mean feat), the New York–born and Glasgow-trained physician James McCune Smith panned the portly Putnam: "with the shrieks of his expatriated brethren of Virginia and Indiana ringing in the air, [he] pats his stomach, and softly hisses *ragout, ragout.*"[81] Using less lurid language, a deputation met Hunt, reminded him that his narrow electoral victory had likely depended on black votes, and persuaded him to disavow Putnam.[82]

Given reactions such as Smith's, it was a wonder that anyone thought aloud about emigrating to Africa. But they did. "I hesitate not to say, that my mind, of late, has greatly changed in regard to the American Colonization scheme," admitted Henry Highland Garnet in 1849. "I would rather see a man free in Liberia, than a slave in the United States."[83] In 1850, James Theodore Holly, then still a resident of Vermont, wrote the ACS secretary, William McLain, that he would happily move to Liberia, "provided I could make myself useful to the community." McLain told Holly to complete his studies first, and the youthful indiscretion of that future proponent of Canada and Haiti went no farther than Burlington.[84] In a similar vein, it was distance from the major African American communities that allowed New York's Alexander Crummell, then a student at the University of Cambridge, to make his own quiet decision to emigrate to Liberia. As recently as 1851, Crummell had told a London audience that Christ would redeem the world "by the influence of the Cross ... and not by colonies."[85] Yet he came to believe, as did most missionaries, that those agencies were complementary, not contradictory. Somewhere between his calling to Anglican mission, his doubts for his chances in the United States, and his frustration with Britain's own, more insidious forms of prejudice, Crummell slipped away to Liberia.[86]

---

[81] "From Our New York Correspondent," *FDP*, December 16, 1853.
[82] R. J. M. Blackett, *The Captive's Quest for Freedom: Fugitive Slaves, the 1850 Fugitive Slave Law, and the Politics of Slavery* (New York, 2018), 121–3.
[83] "The West – The West!," *North Star*, January 26, 1849.
[84] David M. Dean, *Defender of the Race: James Theodore Holly, Black Nationalist and Bishop* (Boston, 1979), 4–6.
[85] "Rev. Alexander Crummell ...", *Anti-Slavery Reporter*, June 2, 1851.
[86] Wilson Jeremiah Moses, *Alexander Crummell: A Study of Civilization and Discontent* (Amherst, 1992), 80–8.

Clashes in the Niger Valley

Whatever future Alexander Crummell foresaw in Africa, it probably did not include meeting Martin Delany there and hearing him all but apologize for everything he had ever said about Liberia. As late as 1855, Delany, who had written the preface for a searing account of the country by a returnee, had assailed colonization as "that most pernicious and impudent of all schemes."[87] It is unclear why, by 1858, he had changed his mind. But to increase his own influence in the emigration movement, Delany probably needed to distance himself from Holly's pro-Haiti wing, especially once he had left his Pittsburgh power base for Chatham. He might also have worried that white filibusters would get to colonize the Caribbean, always his main target, before black settlers did.[88] Yet Delany had always been interested in Africa, his *Condition* having planned an exploration of the eastern side of the continent, a none-too-subtle swipe at Liberia.[89] In the spring of 1858, Delany returned to that scheme, which had envisioned sending researchers to Africa while dispatching fundraisers to Britain and France, whose governments would, hopefully, welcome another foothold on the continent. Having read the work of Thomas Bowen, which had also inspired the Philadelphia colonizationist, Benjamin Coates, Delany changed his focus from east to west Africa, specifically to Yorubaland, in the Niger Valley.

Seeking companions, Martin Delany found several professionals enthusiastic in principle, but unwilling to leave their families for such a risky venture. He also struggled to raise money, turning to a wealthy grocer, Jonathan Myers, who represented a Wisconsin party that wished to move to Africa. Myers contacted Thomas Clegg, a merchant from northwestern England and promoter of cotton cultivation in west Africa, and outlined an "industrial colony" supported by a black-run company based at Kingston, Canada West. For his part, Delany asked the help of the American Missionary Association, offering to negotiate with natives for territory on which to establish "an Enlightened and Christian Nationality," a concession to religiosity that pained him all the more for the association's subsequent refusal of an award.[90]

---

[87] William Nesbit, *Four Months in Liberia, or African Colonization Exposed* (Pittsburgh, 1855), 3.
[88] Richard Blackett, "Martin R. Delany and Robert Campbell: Black Americans in Search of an African Colony," *Journal of Negro History* 62 (1977), 3.
[89] Delany, *Condition*, 221.   [90] Miller, *Black Nationality*, 174–9.

Delany was also disappointed by the response of the National Emigration Convention, which he roused from its slumbers for a third outing, at Chatham in 1858, in an attempt to convey the community's consent for his change of destination. With several of the earlier emigrationists absent, the presidency of the board of commissioners went to Ohio's William Howard Day, a journalist and teacher in attendance for other reasons, and not personally inclined toward emigration. The convention agreed with Day's reservations, endorsing efforts to research regions to which individuals might move, but resolving against mass removal, a compromise that opponents of emigration often proposed in order to preempt accusations that they had impinged on others' freedom of choice.[91] The convention also redefined itself as an association for the general welfare of the black inhabitants of the United States and Canada. Yet its very eclecticism allowed Delany to at least recover his place on the board as a special foreign secretary, while his rival Holly, optimistic that the Episcopal Church would support his own, Haitian project, withdrew from a convention that now offered him nothing.[92]

Commissioned to explore Africa, though expressly not to negotiate for territory, Delany could radiate a faint aura of collective approval for his idiosyncratic venture.[93] At this point, a white minister and soon-to-be agent of the New-York State Colonization Society, Theodore Bourne, announced that the "African Civilization Committee," a body once more inspired by Bowen, would cooperate with Delany's Niger Valley Exploring Party.[94] It is doubtful that Delany welcomed the committee's support, but Bourne's offer introduced him to Garnet's own, New York–based movement – and to its lesser scruples about accepting white dollars. Garnet had long maintained that blacks should stay and fight, but his calls for violent resistance were also the mark of a man who despaired of success through moral suasion, and so turned increasingly to expatriation. Although Garnet had viewed a mid-decade stint abroad, in Jamaica, as more missionary than migratory (Chapter 5), he had also come to think that the Presbyterian Church's foreign missions needed more than the efforts of individuals in order to succeed. In October 1858, Garnet's outfit merged with Bourne's committee, co-founding the African

---

[91] Blackett, *Beating against the Barriers*, 313–15.   [92] Miller, *Black Nationality*, 179–81.
[93] W. H. Day et al., "African Commission," August 30, 1858, in Rollin, *Life of Delany*, 306–7.
[94] "Niger Valley Exploring Party," *New-York Daily Tribune*, October 26, 1858.

Civilization Society, with Garnet as president and Bourne as secretary. The society was the Christian counterpart to the secular Niger Valley Exploring Party.[95] For all the pioneers he had tried to enlist, Delany ended up with just one: Robert Campbell, a Jamaican who had moved to Philadelphia and become a teacher.[96] Feeling no fealty to the United States, Campbell was in earnest about Africa, but thought Delany's plans premature. "It would affect me very immaterially whether ... the whole affair should end in smoke," announced Campbell, soon cutting ties with Delany.[97] Shortly afterward, Day did the same, eschewing emigration at the Ohio state convention of November 1858. Day's about-face forced Delany to form a shadow organization, the African Civilization Society of Canada, to rubber-stamp his own activities.[98] Happily, Campbell now returned to Delany's side, though he had since solicited white colonizationists and mooted a merger between the (black) Exploring Party and (biracial) Civilization Society.[99] By this point, even Delany was desperate enough to approach the hated ACS, acceding to Ralph Gurley's request that he visit Liberia before proceeding to Yorubaland. But the Colonization Society would not underwrite the expedition, disappointing Delany with its counteroffer of a free passage. He fared better with the ACS's New York auxiliary, however, and sailed for Liberia in May 1859.[100]

The peripatetic physician examined west Africa for nine months: first Liberia, as Gurley had asked, and then Yorubaland. Disembarking at Monrovia, Delany had to gloss over his notorious slurs against its government. Invited by Edward Wilmot Blyden to deliver a lecture, Delany claimed that he had never "spoken directly 'against Liberia,' as ... I have always acknowledged a unity of interest in our race wherever located."[101] Blyden responded magnanimously, asking whether other (former) opponents of emigration would also discover that the road to Damascus actually terminated at Monrovia: "shall Liberians at home ever enjoy the pleasure of sitting under the thrilling language of Frederick Douglass, of Samuel

---

[95] Miller, *Black Nationality*, 183–93.

[96] R. J. M. Blackett, "Return to the Motherland: Robert Campbell, a Jamaican in Early Colonial Lagos," *Phylon* 40 (1979), 375–6.

[97] Miller, *Black Nationality*, 193.

[98] Foner, *Proceedings*, 1:335; "African Civilization Society of Canada," *Provincial Freeman*, January 4, 1859.

[99] Blackett, "Delany and Campbell," 10–12.   [100] Miller, *Black Nationality*, 197–8.

[101] Delany to B. P. Yates et al., July 13, 1859, in M. R. Delany, *Official Report of the Niger Valley Exploring Party* (New York, 1861), 18.

R. Ward, or of H. H. Garnet?"[102] While Delany proved fluent in
Liberians' language of black nationhood, his mind was set on the
Yoruba region. Having completed a trip up the Cavalla River with
Alexander Crummell, Delany boarded a steamer for Lagos (in what is
now Nigeria), a bustling port under British protection and with the
potential to become "the great metropolis of this quarter of the
world."[103] He then sailed up the Ogun River to Abeokuta, home of the
Egba people and the heart of Yorubaland.

There he rejoined Campbell, who had left the United States before
Delany to seek support in Britain.[104] Like Delany, Campbell had had to
call on the services of the Liberian government, namely, its consul in
London, Gerard Ralston, a British abolitionist. Like Blyden, Ralston
hoped to turn the attentions of a Niger emigrationist westward to
Liberia, and introduced Campbell to Henry Christy, a philanthropist
who would become Campbell's most generous supporter. The Jamaican
flaunted his British subjecthood to secure support from Manchester
manufacturers, whose Cotton Supply Association sought new sources of
the fiber to reduce Britain's reliance on the southern United States. The
abolitionist appeal of free-labor cotton gained Campbell the ear of
Thomas Clegg and Louis Chamerovzow, secretary of the BFASS. The
cotton lobby also commandeered him a free berth on a government
steamer, the *Ethiope*, which allowed him to beat Delany to Lagos by
some time.[105]

Waiting for his companion, Campbell used the downtime well, intro-
ducing himself to the local authorities. Having intimated that the immi-
grants would be Canadian (and, therefore, British), he presented Her
Majesty's consul with a letter of recommendation from the Foreign
Office.[106] He also met an African-born Anglican missionary, Samuel
Crowther, who told him that the Egba would accept a settlement between
Abeokuta and Lagos – welcome news for an explorer desperate to move
inland. "Of Lagos or any other place on the coast I think very poorly,"

[102] "Martin R. Delany in Liberia," *WAA*, October 1, 1859.
[103] A. Crummell to C. B. Dunbar, September 1, 1860, in Alexander Crummell, *The Future of Africa* (New York, 1862), 269–70; Delany, *Official Report*, 56.
[104] Richard Blackett, "In Search of International Support for African Colonization: Martin R. Delany's Visit to England, 1860," *Canadian Journal of History* 10 (1975), 309–10.
[105] Sven Beckert, *Empire of Cotton: A Global History* (New York, 2014), 124; Miller, *Black Nationality*, 206–7.
[106] E. Ashworth to E. F. Lodder, June 11, 1859, Africa Correspondence, FO2/30, 115–17, TNA.

Campbell wrote a friend, echoing the ACS's own concerns with the conviction of a man in the throes of malaria.[107] He headed for the hinterland, accompanied by two of Crowther's sons, but had to wait two months in Abeokuta for Delany, who arrived in November 1859. With the Crowthers as witnesses, the explorers signed a treaty with the city's ruler, the alake.[108]

Not for the first (or last) time in the history of colonization, it was unclear whether African Americans would intersperse themselves among the existing inhabitants or form their own settlement. While the treaty's first article ceded "the right and privilege of settling in common with the Egba people," the second article undermined the first by stipulating that "all matters requiring legal investigation among the settlers be ... disposed of according to their customs."[109] Yet such legerdemain promised little, for the Egba had no concept whatsoever of transferring land. Although a kinship group might allow strangers into its domains, and to work as much land as they could, no Egba could dispossess his descendants. "There are two ideas incomprehensible to Europeans, but part and parcel of the African mind," observed the British explorer, Richard Burton, once he had heard of Delany's agreement. "The first ... is that a slave-born man is a slave for ever. The second is the non-alienation of land."[110] Neither precept boded well for a colony of African Americans, but Campbell and Delany ignored further omens, as well: their own illness and the violence of the Ibadan-Ijaye War, which together curtailed their travels into the interior. Still, they left Africa satisfied at their progress, and arrived at Liverpool in May 1860 to explore another foreign land and investigate whether those Britons who had funded a small exploration would bankroll large-scale emigration.[111]

Delany, Garnet, and Their Critics

Ethnic tension, internecine warfare, and cultural misapprehension dogged Martin Delany in Europe as well as Africa. He arrived in Britain to

---

[107] "Our Philadelphia Letter," *WAA*, January 14, 1860.
[108] Lamin Sanneh, *Abolitionists Abroad: American Blacks and the Making of Modern West Africa* (Cambridge, MA, 1999), 172–3.
[109] Robert Campbell, *A Pilgrimage to My Motherland: An Account of a Journey among the Egbas and Yorubas of Central Africa, in 1859–60* (New York, 1861), 144.
[110] Richard F. Burton, *Abeokuta and the Camaroons Mountains: An Exploration* (London, 1863), 1:96.
[111] Miller, *Black Nationality*, 216.

discover the common but infuriating assumption that he had traveled under the auspices of the African Civilization Society, a simplification spread by Theodore Bourne, working the lucrative British circuit, and seemingly validated by the inclusion of Robert Campbell in Delany's party.[112] Bourne knew that, more than Christianity, civilization, or commerce in general, Britons were preoccupied with a fourth C: cotton, which he spun as Abeokuta's true appeal. Met with an enthusiastic public response, Bourne wrote Garnet, "let colored men arouse; England is ready to back them ... 'with a million pounds sterling, all in good time.'" Since Delany could not afford to antagonize the Civilization Society or its British friends, he feared that he would be unable to dispel a misconception that hurt his ethnic pride. Ironically, he found an answer in two inhabitants of Canada, from whose vicinity he hoped to depart: William King and William Howard Day, who had crossed the Atlantic to raise money for the Elgin settlement. King was impressed by the missionary aspect of the Niger plan, and probably hoped that Elgin would get to train the planter-pioneers, while Day discerned that Delany's more exciting cause would widen his own access to British benefactors. In that Day, the decade's outstanding waverer on emigration (again, no mean feat), remained president of the now-notional Chatham Convention, Delany could point audiences to him to demonstrate that African Americans were acting on their own initiative. Meanwhile, the white Bourne could compete for only so long with two blacks who had, moreover, visited the country in question. The Civilization Society rescinded Bourne's commission in short order.[113]

Yet the African Civilization Society itself survived, and continued to plan its own settlement in Yorubaland, despite its straitened finances. No emigration agency based in New York could expect an easy time, though. In April 1860, perhaps 1,200 black New Yorkers huddled in Zion Church to hear Garnet defend himself. "We believe the African Civilization Society to be no other than an auxiliary to the negro-hating American Colonization Society," moved George Downing, livid that any abolitionist could support such a scheme even as the slave states made to expel their freepeople. "Canes and fists became very unsteady ... and everything betokened a representation of 'Donnybrook Fair,'" reported one attendee. "There is much work *here* for a Civilization Society."[114]

---

[112] Blackett, "International Support," 312–14.   [113] Miller, *Black Nationality*, 220–6.
[114] "The Colored Citizens of New York and the African Civilization Society," *Liberator*,
   May 4, 1860.

Garnet survived unscathed, and dispatched his own explorer and fellow Presbyterian, Elymas Rogers, whom he tasked with researching the prospects for a church as well as a colony. While missionaries might die at their post, wrote Rogers from Liberia in early 1861, "they may derive consolation from the thought that if they lose their lives they shall find them again."[115] Ten days later, he died of malaria with Alexander Crummell at his side.[116]

Although Garnet and Delany did not yet know it, Rogers would be the last traveler from either of their organizations to explore Africa. Delany had reached Portland, Maine, on Christmas Day, 1860, and went straight to Chatham. To honor the principle of black self-reliance, he would have to select settlers with sufficient means, already a high bar, while appeasing those who remembered that even his own convention had decided against emigration. Delany also distanced himself from his "young brother Campbell," whose dalliances with white sponsors reflected, he alleged, a West Indian naivety about North American race relations.[117] During early 1861, Delany persuaded several Chathamites to emigrate, with even Mary Ann Shadd Cary, as marriage had made her in 1856, intrigued by a spell of mission work. Yet by the summer of 1861, as the fog of war drifted north from the United States, the Yoruba scheme looked ever unlikelier to proceed. In Abeokuta, Henry Townsend, a British missionary who disliked the Campbell–Delany treaty for threatening his own influence, persuaded the alake to deny ever having signed it. The Foreign Office dropped the project through confusion about whether it should support a scheme with plenty of advocates in Britain, but a bewildering mixture of supporters and opponents in the Niger Valley.[118]

On the western side of the Atlantic, Garnet had recruited more settlers than had Delany, but would keep struggling for money unless he looked beyond the United States, a solution that his white collaborators discouraged. If the Niger Valley Exploring Party cherished blacks' independence from whites, then the white officers of the African Civilization Society cherished Americans' independence from the British, warning emigrants not to become a stalking-horse for the empire.[119] Valuing abolition more than nation, however, Garnet broke with his patriotic patrons and sailed

[115] *AR* 37 (1861), 180.   [116] Miller, *Black Nationality*, 229–31.
[117] Delany, *Official Report*, 8, 15.   [118] Miller, *Black Nationality*, 252–8.
[119] J. P. Thompson, "African Civilization and the Cotton Trade," in Thomas J. Stafford, pub., *Constitution of the African Civilization Society* (New Haven, 1861), 37.

for Britain to tap its coffers.[120] And, valuing success more than failure, Delany reviewed his quarrel with Garnet, and merged the remnants of the Exploring Party into the Civilization Society. In return, Delany secured amendments to the society's charter, disavowing mass emigration and espousing racial self-reliance, which sat comfortably with the society's existing image of itself.[121]

Like so many colonization schemes during the Civil War, the Yorubaland project perished with an uncertain time of death. No American would again reach Abeokuta, though a Jamaican, Robert Campbell, got as far as Lagos. Unable to travel farther because of the instability arising from Britain's recent annexation of that port, Campbell settled in Lagos instead and turned his hand to journalism, founding a familiar-sounding title, the *Anglo-African*.[122] As late as summer 1862, Delany still insisted that he too would emigrate, but the next year found him enlisting black Americans to push their way down the Mississippi, not up the Ogun.[123] Although the Emancipation Proclamation instilled a certain ecumenicism in the Rev. Garnet, who also recruited black troops, he never turned against emigration, supporting a scheme in the British West Indies through 1863.[124] Another difference between the two men was that, even while promoting Yorubaland, Garnet had volunteered as an agent for a rival destination, which latterly stole west Africa's limelight: Haiti.

SUPPORTING REGENERATION: HAITI

Like Africa, Haiti, which occupies the western third of the island of Hispaniola, had fascinated emigrationists even prior to the founding of the ACS. Yet the nation's origins lay in piteous, protracted bloodshed. Inspired by the French Revolution, the mixed-race *gens de couleur* of a colony then known as St. Domingue had petitioned Paris for equal rights, which the white planters tried to thwart. As tensions grew, each side armed its slaves, who comprised most of the population of the Caribbean's largest sugar producer. It was a fatal mistake. The slaves rose from 1791, which encouraged France and its enemies to intervene

[120] "Letter from Rev. H. H. Garnet," *WAA*, October 19, 1861.
[121] "The African Civilization Society," *Christian Recorder*, December 7, 1861.
[122] Blackett, "Return to the Motherland," 377–9.
[123] "Dr. M. R. Delany," *Douglass' Monthly*, August 1862.
[124] Martin B. Pasternak, *Rise Now and Fly to Arms: The Life of Henry Highland Garnet* (New York, 1995), 111.

alike. The ensuing morass saw one black insurgent, Toussaint Louverture, gradually draw together an autonomous polity, though he refrained from declaring independence. In 1802, Napoleon's armies invaded in order to regain control of St. Domingue, and captured Louverture, whose troops successfully fought back at the prospect of being reenslaved. In 1804, Louverture's successor, General Jean-Jacques Dessalines, exploited France's defeat to proclaim the state of "Haiti," a native term meaning "mountainous." Thereafter, the second country in the Americas to break free from European rule lit a beacon of black pride and of abolition at its most aggressive.[125] But that achievement came at the cost of internal instability, revolving in no small part around colorist factionalism, and of a dearth of diplomatic recognition from other powers.[126]

No government would acknowledge Haiti until France did, and Paris's saber-rattling forced Port-au-Prince to maintain expensive standing armies. Haiti's leaders were convinced that prosperity could return only with plantation agriculture, but their populace rejected anything redolent of slavery. Another panacea, however, might lie in the immigration of free African American workers. Dessalines, whose reign as Emperor Jacques I (1804–6) would end in his assassination, advertised in the US press for settlers, probably unaware that he had an ally in President Thomas Jefferson (1801–9), who considered sending rebellious slaves to St. Domingue in the wake of Gabriel's Conspiracy (1800). Yet Jefferson changed his mind, wary of empowering a country that could export race war. White support for emigration to Haiti, from that point, would emanate from those of a more antislavery bent. In 1814, one of Dessalines's successors, Henry Christophe, contacted the British abolitionists William Wilberforce and Thomas Clarkson, hoping that they could persuade their own government to extend recognition. Clarkson suggested that Christophe promote African American immigration, which would strengthen his position "at home and in the eyes of foreigners, and of France in particular." Such settlers might bring financial capital, technical expertise, and grounds for recognition by the United States, as well.

---

[125] Leslie M. Alexander, "'The Black Republic': The Influence of the Haitian Revolution on Northern Black Political Consciousness, 1816–1862," in Maurice Jackson and Jacqueline Bacon, eds., *African Americans and the Haitian Revolution* (New York, 2010), 57–79; Claire Bourhis-Mariotti, "'Go to Our Brethren': Haiti as the African Americans' Promised Land in the Antebellum Era," *Revue française d'études américaines* 142 (2015), 6–23.
[126] David Nicholls, *From Dessalines to Duvalier: Race, Colour and National Independence in Haiti* (New Brunswick, NJ, 1996), 33–107.

Christophe turned to Prince Saunders, a Boston schoolteacher who had married Paul Cuffe's daughter and moved to Haiti in 1816. Saunders toured the northern states to some success, but Christophe died in 1820, before the project could bear fruit.[127]

It took until 1824 for the long-awaited movement to materialize, when President Jean-Pierre Boyer (1818–43) appealed to those white Americans frustrated with the poor logistics of the Liberia project, who included Benjamin Lundy and Loring Dewey, a rogue ACS agent.[128] Yet Boyer's breakthrough lay with African Americans themselves, who had been amenable to emigration ever since an economic downturn in 1819, but who had long been averse to the Colonization Society. "When they may be at liberty to come hither, they will find in us brothers," one of Boyer's aides promised an American correspondent. While some black Americans resented Dewey for establishing another white-run society to promote their removal, others embraced Boyer's offer, delivered simultaneously through a Haitian canvasser, Jonathas Granville. By the fall of 1824, Samuel Cornish, Richard Allen, and James Forten had declared their support for a movement that swept New York, Philadelphia, and Baltimore, taking perhaps 6,000 emigrants.[129]

Yet the tide turned the next year, when Boyer upbraided dissatisfied settlers by discontinuing their grants of land. He also effectively bought French recognition by agreeing to a ruinous indemnity, which forced him to impose a rural code in order to boost productivity – an embarrassing turn of events for those abolitionists who had hailed Haiti as an idyll of free labor.[130] Perhaps two-thirds of the Americans returned. Yet the very thought of Haiti never ceased to inspire abolitionists or to send slave-holders a powerful but mixed message: Did the terrible events of its revolution demonstrate the dangers of doubling down on slavery, as colonial St. Domingue had, or of interfering with the institution?[131] Haiti's ideological, even symbolic importance to Americans would not be matched by a further emigration movement until shortly before the Civil War, and black leaders started to overlook it as a destination, just as they did Africa. For their part, proslavery thinkers added the irrefutable

---

[127] Sara Fanning, *Caribbean Crossing: African Americans and the Haitian Emigration Movement* (New York, 2015), 1–10, 29–30, 36–9.
[128] Loring Dewey, *Correspondence Relative to the Emigration to Hayti of the Free People of Colour* (New York, 1824), i.
[129] Miller, *Black Nationality*, 74–82.   [130] Fanning, *Caribbean Crossing*, 100–10.
[131] Bruce Dain, "Haiti and Egypt in Early Black Racial Discourse in the United States," *Slavery and Abolition* 14 (1993), 139–42.

evidence of Haiti's stagnation to their case file against emancipation.[132] "Hereafter, when we speak of Hayti, we shall refer ... to all the movements in behalf of the African – Sierra Leone and Liberia, colonization and abolition," *De Bow's Review* promised its readers in 1848.[133] Yet white reformers kept alive their interest in the only black state in the Americas.[134] Frances Wright, a Scottish-born freethinker who had bought slaves and settled them at Nashoba, Tennessee, to prepare them for freedom, sent them to Haiti when she abandoned that venture in 1829. A handful of more conventional slaveholders also chose to free their chattels in Haiti rather than Liberia, though southern influences in the Department of State prevented US consuls from helping them. Still, enough African Americans had crossed the Caribbean that, in 1835, the General Baptist Convention dispatched William Munroe of Detroit to minister at Port-au-Prince.[135] While US diplomats might shun Haiti, missionaries and merchants maintained the link between the two oldest independent states in the Western Hemisphere.

Black Mission: Holly and Geffrard

The infamous *Appeal* (1829) of David Walker, a Boston clothing merchant and abolitionist, lambasted the United States for its hypocritical institutions while lauding Haiti, except in one particular: the country was "plagued with that scourge of nations, the Catholic religion," to say nothing of Vodou, which Haitians syncretized with Catholicism.[136] It was, accordingly, religious mission that drew the Rev. James Theodore Holly, Haiti's most dogged defender in the United States, to western Hispaniola. "Every colored man should feel binding ... the duty to sustain [Haiti's] national existence," he argued in the call to the Cleveland Convention.[137] Some years later, Holly described how secret sessions at that meeting had tasked Martin Delany with researching the Niger Valley (a claim that would prove useful to Delany, too); James

---

[132] Walter Johnson, *River of Dark Dreams: Slavery and Empire in the Cotton Kingdom* (Cambridge, MA, 2013), 317.
[133] J. D. B. De Bow, "The West India Islands," *De Bow's Review* 5 (1848), 498.
[134] Chris Dixon, *African America and Haiti: Emigration and Black Nationalism in the Nineteenth Century* (Westport, 2000), 49–52.
[135] Alfred N. Hunt, *Haiti's Influence on Antebellum America: Slumbering Volcano in the Caribbean* (Baton Rouge, 2006), 169–73.
[136] David Walker, *Walker's Appeal, in Four Articles* (Boston, 1830), 31.
[137] Newsom, *Arguments*, 32.

Whitfield, a Buffalo barber and poet, with Central America; and Holly himself with Haiti. Yet missions needed money, and Holly had converted from Catholicism to Episcopalianism, a denomination with a minuscule black following and an institutional aversion to antislavery. Backed by private sponsors instead, Holly visited Haiti in the summer of 1855 and found its emperor, Faustin Soulouque (1849–59), interested in immigration but unable to offer privileges without the assembly's assent.[138] Once back in the United States, Holly lectured on what he had seen, defending Haiti's tendency toward autocratic rule by reminding his audience of the iniquities of American republicanism, which permitted "a vagabond set of politicians … to enact such an odious law as the Fugitive Slave bill."[139] Ordained as an Episcopal minister in early 1856 and assigned the parish of St. Luke's, in New Haven, Connecticut, Holly looked forward to the second convention at Cleveland – and was disappointed that it then proved so unhelpful, forcing him to seek assistance elsewhere. "I am not opposed to pressing white men into our service so long as they fulfil the behests of our race," he explained to Delany.[140] During 1856–9, Holly duly cultivated those white Episcopalians prepared to devote dollars to encouraging their black brethren into the fold.

For all Holly's efforts to muster a mission of English-speaking Protestants, it was French-speaking Catholics, fleeing white violence in parts of Louisiana, who reached Haiti first. In 1858, Soulouque appointed Emile Desdunes, a native of New Orleans, to canvass the evacuees, and in May 1859, 150 free people of color cast off from the Crescent City.[141] While Frederick Douglass erred in his prediction that 2,000 would leave by the end of the year, the violence in Louisiana certainly accounted for 500 by the end of the next.[142] "The Government of Hayti holds forth great inducements," hinted the (white) *New Orleans Delta*, while the *Weekly Anglo-African* rued the white inconsistency that would accuse free blacks of indolence and then mourn their industry when they were about to depart.[143] Meanwhile, in Haiti, a mixed-race former army general,

---

[138] Dean, *Defender of the Race*, 19–22.
[139] James Theodore Holly, *A Vindication of the Capacity of the Negro Race for Self-Government, and Civilized Progress* (New Haven, 1857), 42.
[140] J. T. Holly to Delany, January 29, WAA, February 9, 1861.
[141] Caryn Cossé Bell, *Revolution, Romanticism, and the Afro-Creole Protest Tradition in Louisiana, 1718–1868* (Baton Rouge, 1997), 85–6.
[142] "The Free Colored Population of Louisiana…," *Douglass' Monthly*, June 1859.
[143] "Emigration from Louisiana to Hayti," *Pittsburgh Gazette* (reprint), July 2, 1859; "The Free Colored People of Louisiana," WAA, July 30, 1859.

President Fabre Geffrard (1859–67), had just overthrown Soulouque and reestablished a republic of sorts, but expanded his predecessor's American program. "Liberator of the Haitian people ... another kind of glory awaits you, which is the continuation of the path of Louisianan emigration for Haiti," a would-be immigrant wrote one of Geffrard's ministers.[144] Yet Port-au-Prince's ability to even recruit in New Orleans was a testament to the latter's unique urbanity within the South. When, in 1860, a "native Haytien" canvasser appeared in Mobile, the sheriff advised him that the laws of Alabama mandated his speedy departure.[145]

White Appropriation: Redpath

Moreover, for all that Holly had tried to foster African diasporic unity, it was a white immigrant from the Anglo-Scottish borders, James Redpath, who sent something close to Douglass's estimate of 2,000 to Haiti, though mostly from the free states and Canada, and as part of a movement that lasted through the summer of 1862. Redpath was, at once, the most radical abolitionist and cynical colonizationist of his day, even as he rejected the latter label. He had made his name reporting for Horace Greeley's *New-York Tribune* from "Bleeding Kansas," where guerrillas fought to secure that territory for slavery or freedom, and had probably known that one of them, John Brown, meant to launch his ill-fated raid of October 1859 on Harper's Ferry. At least, Redpath eulogized Brown as a martyr in his *Echoes of Harper's Ferry* (1860), and disregarded a US Senate subpoena to divulge what he had known about Brown's conspiracy.

The earlier part of 1859 had found Redpath in Haiti, however, investigating its capacity for recaptives from the coastwise slave trade, whom he proposed to liberate in an act of "philanthropic piracy." He was impressed by Haiti's populace, but troubled by the sway of the army and of the Catholic Church.[146] Returning to his Massachusetts home, Redpath advised African Americans to remain in the United States until

---

[144] P. Laviolette, exposé, April 15, 1860, in François-Élie Dubois, *République haïtienne: deux ans et demi de ministère* (Paris, 1867), 232–3.

[145] C. Labuzan to J. Russell, No. 9, October 5, 1860, Slave Trade and African Department Records, FO84/1112, 168–9, TNA.

[146] John McKivigan, *Forgotten Firebrand: James Redpath and the Making of Nineteenth-Century America* (Ithaca, 2008), 1–2, 47, 54–5, 61–5; Albert J. Von Frank, "John Brown, James Redpath, and the Idea of Revolution," *Civil War History* 52 (2006), 157–60.

Geffrard, whose politics otherwise looked promising, offered more protections. "Although Hayti is nominally a Republic, the Government is in fact a Military Monarchy," he warned. "This [immigration] scheme is calculated to degrade and demoralize."[147] After two further visits to Haiti by the summer of 1860, though, Redpath satisfied himself that the revolution of the "regenerators" was for real. He persuaded Geffrard to improve his government's 1859 offer to emigrants and to promise not only exemption from military service, but also a free passage and five *carreaux* (sixteen acres) of land. "At least two thirds of our lands are fallow lands," President Geffrard told the Legislative Chamber, which approved his changes. "How can it be otherwise, when the labor necessary to cultivation is wanting, in consequence of our deficient population?"[148] In July 1860, Redpath completed the arrangements for a Haitian Emigration Bureau, to be based in Boston with Redpath at its head. He would report to Victorien Plésance, secretary of state for foreign relations, and to Auguste Élie, director-general of immigration. The bureau's budget of $20,000 dwarfed that of any black-led outfit, but Redpath was under instructions to spend part of it persuading US politicians to recognize Haiti.[149]

If Redpath's whiteness allowed him to lobby politicians to acknowledge a black government, then his abolitionism allowed him to recruit a remarkable range of (mostly black) subagents, who would distribute his *Guide to Hayti* and canvass colonists on whichever circuit Redpath assigned them. His payroll included not only emigrationists such as Garnet, Holly, and J. Dennis Harris, a free-born physician who had recently toured the Caribbean (while omitting Haiti, of all places), but also stalwarts of the stay-and-fight brigade, such as William Wells Brown, a novelist and playwright, and William J. Watkins, Douglass's right-hand man.[150] While Brown could claim a lifelong interest in Haiti, the offer of a salary likely influenced all of Redpath's appointees.[151] Since the bureau's operations demanded that Redpath deal in hard numbers, he spoke of a few tens of thousands of

[147] "Black Emigration to Hayti," *Douglass' Monthly*, May 1859.
[148] F. N. Geffrard, address, September 1, 1860, in James Redpath, ed., *A Guide to Hayti* (Boston, 1861), 123.
[149] Dixon, *African America*, 145–6.
[150] J. Dennis Harris, *A Summer on the Borders of the Caribbean Sea* (New York, 1860), 76–7; J. Redpath to V. Plésance, November 3, 1860, Bureau of Emigration Correspondence, Boston Public Library (hereafter, "Redpath-BPL").
[151] William Edward Farrison, *William Wells Brown: Author and Reformer* (Chicago, 1969), 74, 256–8, 333–8.

emigrants over several years – modest enough to assuage black misgivings about mass removal, but ambitious enough that Garnet could simultaneously support a small emigration to Africa and a larger one to Haiti.[152]

Where black Americans were willing to go, their white allies could conscionably follow. James Redpath recruited John Brown, Jr., and Richard Hinton, a fellow Briton and veteran of the "Kansas Crusade." He also won over better-known abolitionists, including William Lloyd Garrison, at least for a time.[153] In a debate that contemporaries were quick to view in terms of personalities (and personal "conversions"), Redpath almost won the greatest prize of all: Frederick Douglass's endorsement. During the crisis of 1860–1, as the bonds of Union sundered and the slave states made to banish their black inhabitants, Douglass at first conceded that Haiti would be a better choice than Liberia, then privately offered Garnet his support, and then publicly accepted Port-au-Prince's offer of a steamer ticket – though only to tour the country.[154]

The first group to emigrate under the bureau's auspices left in December 1860, and the last in August 1862, with departures peaking in late 1861.[155] Knowing of Liberia's woes, Redpath warned settlers about tropical diseases and advised them to learn some French and consult his own glossary of Haitian Creole.[156] Yet Redpath understood, thinking again of Liberia's poor reputation, that it was also for Haiti to make a good first impression. "The views that these emigrants send back will influence, favorably or otherwise, thousands of others," he warned Plésance. "If my advice is seemingly obtrusive, I know that you will overlook it for the sake of the zeal which alone inspires it."[157] If Redpath was prescient in imagining that blacks across North America would debate his scheme with passion, he was positively clairvoyant in predicting that his own collaborators would tire of his self-righteous tone.

Glowing reports from the earliest colonists soon gave way to complaints, though such skepticism did not prevent further sailings, even once the Civil War had begun and the Confederacy had commissioned privateers. Settlers were disillusioned by the profound cultural, linguistic, and

---

[152] "No Change – A Word to My Friends and Foes," *WAA*, December 22, 1860.

[153] Redpath to Plésance, December 1, 1860, Redpath-BPL.

[154] David W. Blight, *Frederick Douglass: Prophet of Freedom* (New York, 2018), 337–9; "Emigration to Hayti," *Douglass' Monthly*, January 1861; Redpath to Plésance, February 9, 1861, Redpath-BPL; Redpath to F. Douglass, April 5, 1861, James Redpath Papers, Duke University.

[155] Dixon, *African America*, 178.   [156] Redpath, *Guide to Hayti*, 131, 162.

[157] Redpath to Plésance, December 23, 1860, Redpath-BPL.

religious differences between Haiti and anglophone North America. Whether they had seen themselves as likely to radiate or absorb superior civilization while in Hispaniola, they could only come away disappointed at their misapprehensions. In an evenhanded survey of the challenges that immigrants would face, a veteran traveler to Haiti, Benjamin Hunt, had thought that its government would "probably" uphold its promise to respect religious diversity, but warned that it had not always done so.[158] William Newman, who had emigrated from Canada to Haiti just prior to Redpath's scheme, regretted his move after a policeman forced him to raise his hat to a Catholic procession in Port-au-Prince.[159] Meanwhile, Sabbatarian immigrants were upset by markets held on a Sunday.[160] And if Redpath had promised his Protestant settlers that Haitians "professed no spiritual allegiance to the Pope," Fabre Geffrard soon signed a concordat with Pope Pius IX (1846–78), which the *Weekly Anglo-African* feared would deliver Haiti into the white hands of the Vatican.[161] Immigrants also had to adapt to different ethical norms, in which house burglary was almost unknown, but theft from allotments quite acceptable.[162]

Settlers might have tolerated the lack of spiritual sustenance had Haiti better met their temporal needs. The government placed more than 1,000 of the Redpath immigrants around the port of St. Marc (Map 2.2), home to the Louisianans who had preceded them. Although Redpath had described the town as "very healthy," the Artibonite River proceeded to burst its banks to a level not seen in forty years, swamping almost a mile either side.[163] From the stagnant water arose yellow fever, causing dozens of deaths and devastating some of the cohesive communities that had transplanted themselves from continental North America. No sooner had Holly guided his Connecticut flock to a newer haven on one of Geffrard's estates, Drouillard, than his own mother and daughter died. Himself prone only to fervor, not fever, Holly called for more colonists, claiming the recent interments as a "triumphant witness in behalf of the noble

---

[158] Benjamin Hunt, *Remarks on Hayti as a Place of Settlement for Afric-Americans* (Philadelphia, 1860), 16.
[159] Redpath to the *Chatham Planet*, March 13, 1861, Redpath-BPL.
[160] Redpath to A. Élie, October 20, 1861, James Redpath Papers, LC (hereafter, "Redpath-LC").
[161] Redpath, *Guide*, 138; "Forlorn Hope for Hayti," *WAA*, November 2, 1861.
[162] Alexandre Bonneau, *Haïti: ses progrès, son avenir* (Paris, 1862), 106–7.
[163] M. Ricard to F. Jean-Joseph, June 11, *Le Moniteur Haïtien*, November 2, 1861.

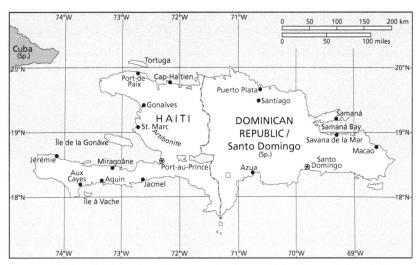

MAP 2.2 In his *Guide to Hayti* (Boston, 1861), on which this map is based, James Redpath endorsed Haitian irredentism by labeling the Dominican Republic the "Eastern Part" of Haiti.

cause of Haytian Emigration."[164] The *Weekly Anglo-African* was appalled: "it does seem a queer way to build up 'colored nationalities' by enriching a soil already the richest in the world."[165] A publicist by profession, Redpath thought it better to acknowledge the suffering around St. Marc, lest the movement lose all credibility.[166] Haiti's own response was to redirect new immigrants to Aquin, on the southern peninsula, and to transfer the flood victims from public to private lands, which would reduce the burden on the treasury, though at the social cost of dispersing the English-speaking communities.[167] Unfortunately, Port-au-Prince overcompensated: in sending later immigrants to well-drained chalk uplands, it left them high and dry when drought struck in 1862.[168]

While pious immigrants might accept such acts of God, the inaction of man was harder to tolerate. Haiti was quick to naturalize the colonists, an

---

[164] "Differences of Opinion," *WAA*, October 5, 1861.
[165] "Hospitable Graves in Hayti!," ibid.
[166] Redpath to Élie, February 12, 1862, James Redpath Correspondence, NYPL.
[167] Redpath to S. Rameau, February 8, 1862, ibid.; "Exposé de la situation de la République," *Le Moniteur Haïtien*, October 26, 1861.
[168] W. Brazier, testimony, December 10, 1863, Letters Received by the Office of the Adjutant General, RG94/M619/201, NARA.

act that many resisted in order to retain consular protection, but slow to survey and distribute the land that it had promised them by contract.[169] "The American immigrants ... are in a pack of trouble at the non-realization of the ... eloquent lies of James Redpath," reported a black compatriot merely visiting Haiti. "It's feared that the bayonet and bullet may be the final argument offered on the part of the Government."[170] Or even a set of black laws: one Representative Midouin, tired of complaints from the foreign ingrates, moved a ban on immigration.[171] A committee rejected his proposal, which would restrain "one of the main agents of the prosperity of our republic," but Midouin had sounded a remarkable echo of the Midwest in the Caribbean.[172] If the Americans were frustrated with the Haitians, the feeling was mutual: officials had told the pioneers in no uncertain terms that their job was to toil, not to demand the political inclusion denied them in the United States.[173] The elevation of the race was to be coterminous with that of the black nation, not that of the black individual.

African American Responses

Distressed dispatches from Haiti emboldened American opponents of emigration, who had been left reeling by the movement's explosive growth.[174] The bureau had been flooded with applications from the interior states and Canada, and not just the Northeast, the burned-over district of many a previous migratory mania. Haiti's offer of homesteads, disseminated in a circular bearing Geffrard's name, had arrived in the febrile atmosphere of a white onslaught against black rights. Moreover, the scheme appealed to those advocates of free produce – Haiti already grew coffee and was diversifying into cotton – who could never accept the

---

[169] H. Byron to J. Russell, No. 13, April 24, 1862, Haiti Correspondence, FO35/57, 59, TNA; Redpath and A. Proctor, contract, June 15, 1861, Alexander Proctor Papers, Duke University; J. W. Duffin to G. Smith, November 15, 1861, Gerrit Smith Papers, Syracuse University.

[170] John Hope Franklin and Loren Schweninger, *In Search of the Promised Land: A Slave Family in the Old South* (New York, 2006), 180–4; J. H. Rapier, Jr., to J. P. Thomas, July 5, 1861, Rapier Family Papers, Howard University.

[171] "Chambre des représentants," *Le Moniteur Haïtien*, August 2, 1862.

[172] "Chambre des représentants," ibid., August 9, 1862.

[173] "Mr. George C. Anderson ...," *Pine and Palm*, August 3, 1861.

[174] John R. McKivigan, "James Redpath and Black Reaction to the Haitian Emigration Bureau," *Mid-America* 69 (1987), 139.

new Africa movement.[175] Over the winter of 1860–1, most opponents of emigration accordingly kept a low profile, except for James McCune Smith. "Your schemes ... have neither the charm of novelty nor the prestige of success," he told Garnet, incredulous that the minister could accept an agency from someone who had so lately advised blacks against going to Haiti.[176] Others also had misgivings, but showed more reserve. "I have nothing to say against Haytian emigration," Delany told Holly, "except that I am surprised that ... the government would appoint a white man, thereby acknowledging negro inferiority."[177] Although Holly countered that Redpath was "the white servant, Geffrard the black master," the scheme's critics sided with Delany.[178]

Deep down, the bureau's agents knew that they had to justify themselves, especially since none of them, bar Holly, would ever move to Haiti. The scheme "does not assume the invincibility of prejudice, ... nor do we by going to Hayti, cease to battle against [prejudice]," tried William J. Watkins.[179] "I have heard colored men say that we cannot rise in this country, but I have never heard any one say so connected with this movement," concurred his colleague, William Wells Brown.[180] Yet skeptics saw parallels between the Emigration Bureau and the Colonization Society. While Frederick Douglass was almost alone in treating the Civil War as a portent of better times – after all, passengers to Haiti would peak several months after the conflict's outbreak – he canceled his trip to gather his thoughts on Redpath's bureau. "Like the old American Colonization Society, ... it has its headquarters, its offices, its numerous Secretaries, its traveling agents," he observed, repudiating the project but reiterating his thanks to Haiti itself for its earlier, uncomplicated offer of a refuge for Louisiana's exiles.[181] Both schemes aimed "to keep the light from us, by preventing discussion," agreed George Downing.[182] He was right: Redpath moved to stifle criticism in the *Weekly Anglo-African* by buying it out and starting a promotional title, the *Pine and Palm*, in its stead. In the summer of 1861, Smith helped finance a revived "Anglo," as its readers called it, and a publication once open to both sides of

---

[175] Robert I. Rotberg and Christopher K. Clague, *Haiti: The Politics of Squalor* (Boston, 1971), 89.
[176] "Emigration," *WAA*, January 12, 1861.
[177] "To the Rev. J. Theodore Holly," *Chatham Planet*, January 21, 1861.
[178] Holly to Delany, January 29, *WAA*, February 9, 1861.
[179] "Mr. Wm. James Watkins," *Pine and Palm*, August 3, 1861.
[180] "Discussion on Emigration," ibid.
[181] "The Haytian Emigration Movement," *Douglass' Monthly*, July 1861.
[182] "Discussion on Emigration."

the debate dedicated itself to fighting emigration.[183] In a letter to its editor, Robert Hamilton, Mary Ann Shadd Cary toasted the newspaper's rebirth. "Who, may I ask, is this James Redpath, in the hollow of whose hand lies trembling the destiny of our people?" she demanded.[184] Her anger turned to fury when it transpired that the Haitian government had been paying Redpath two dollars per immigrant.[185]

But James Redpath's attack on the freedom of the press was only one aspect of his dictatorialism. Despite the unorthodox, colonizationist turn to his abolitionist beliefs, he retained a Garrisonian's absolutism, which revealed itself in his dealings with colleagues. When Richard Hinton suggested changes to the *Pine and Palm*, Redpath rejoined, "I do *not* feel your friendship to be priceless.... I am the leader of the Haytian movement and the editor consequently of the organ of it."[186] When, at Redpath's behest, Port-au-Prince sent a Haitian "gentleman" to assuage intending emigrants, Redpath accused its appointee of being a "self-elected spy" who coveted the bureau's directorship.[187] When Redpath learned that he would have to share his brief for securing US recognition with a Boston merchant, he threatened to resign.[188] Least appealing of all were his racial assumptions. Influenced by his time in Haiti, he projected a Caribbean colorism onto American abolitionism, accusing New York's "*colored* [mixed-race] cliques" of opposing a "*Black* Nationality," and making sure to appoint both dark-skinned agents, such as Garnet and Holly, and light-skinned ones, such as Harris.[189] Like many a reformer, Redpath also found noble words easier than noble deeds. Although he had asked Auguste Élie to repeal the ban on white citizenship (a fundamental law that Haiti shared with Liberia), so that he might "have the honor of being the first white adopted citizen," Redpath also wrote Élie about the "admirable laborers for your landed proprietors" who would surely be freed by the American conflict.[190] Violent in temperament, Redpath hinted at personal instability, in late 1861, by publicly renouncing his former advocacy of violence in politics.[191] "The last wonder is, whether he will slip out quietly from this scheme," wrote Shadd Cary,

---

[183] McKivigan, *Forgotten Firebrand*, 69, 73.
[184] "Haytian Emigration," *WAA*, September 28, 1861.
[185] "The Haytian Fever and Its Diagnostics in Canada," *WAA*, December 14, 1861.
[186] Redpath to R. J. Hinton, May 17, 1861, Redpath Papers, Duke.
[187] Redpath to Plésance, June 8, 1861, Redpath-LC.
[188] Redpath to Plésance, June 15, 1861, Redpath-LC.   [189] Dixon, *African America*, 199.
[190] Redpath to Élie, May 6 and July 15, 1861, Redpath-LC.
[191] "A Preparatory Word," *Pine and Palm*, December 14, 1861.

mystified that the hagiographer of John Brown could disavow bloodshed that presaged freedom for America's slaves.[192]

It took Redpath less than a year to confirm Shadd Cary's conjecture. In February 1862, he had warned Port-au-Prince that he would resign "if all abuses occasioned by neglect [of the immigrants] were not promptly remedied."[193] It is doubtful that the government feared missing out on Redpath's pompous missives, so many of which demanded more money to sustain a project that had, in any case, supplied urban artisans, not the rural laborers that Haiti wanted. That October, Redpath announced that subscribers to the *Pine and Palm* would instead receive the *Liberator*, and left the bureau in the hands of George Lawrence, Jr., his black subeditor, who kept it open into 1865, mostly answering occasional applications by prospective settlers.[194] Where Holly clung to Haiti for the rest of his life, dying at Port-au-Prince in 1911, Redpath reverted to type, becoming a publisher again.[195] Whatever Redpath's belated misgivings about the Haiti scheme, he had also been made redundant by a war that had brought forth better-placed proponents of black resettlement.

Over the course of his life, Redpath threw himself into so many causes that it is unlikely he looked back on his emigrationist phase as at all inconsistent with whatever core beliefs he held. In fact, he would die shortly after ghostwriting Jefferson Davis's *Short History of the Confederate States* (1889), a seminal text in "Lost Cause" apologetics. Yet the South's bid for independence was not the only wartime effort that, however hard its advocates might try, would come to naught.

---

[192] "A Correction," *WAA*, December 28, 1861.
[193] Redpath to I. Carey, February 14, 1862, Redpath Correspondence, NYPL.
[194] "Special Notice," *Liberator*, November 14, 1862; G. Lawrence, Jr., to J. Mitchell, October 14, 1862, George Lawrence Jr. Letter Book, George F. Usher Papers, Yale.
[195] Dean, *Defender of the Race*, 105; McKivigan, *Forgotten Firebrand*, 84.

3

The Republican Party and Resettlement, to 1863

For all that politicians recurred to separatism whenever they debated slavery and expansion, no party adopted colonization as policy until the Civil War. Granted, under the Second Party System, the colonizationist vision of social harmony through racial redemption appealed more to the Whigs than to the Democrats, for the work served God while calling on Mammon, anathema to the adherents of President Jackson. Yet the national footing of both parties meant that neither risked fracture by sponsoring a measure with such emancipationist overtones.

Meanwhile, single-issue antislavery parties remained minor affairs, trampled by the two-horse race over matters that the electorate deemed more important than ending human bondage. Such factions took root in abolitionism, moreover, which remained stony ground for colonization. Neither the Liberty Party (1840) nor its more successful scion, the Free Soil Party (1848), endorsed black expatriation. Although James Birney and his Liberty Party had broken from the nonpartisan Garrisonians in an attempt to enter mainstream politics, both sides continued to agree on the iniquities of the ACS. For the Free Soil Party, such aversion was less of a given. Its origins lay in the "Barnburners'" break from the New York Democratic Party over the latter's refusal to back the Wilmot Proviso (1846), which would have banned slavery in any lands won from Mexico, though the new party came to encompass politicians across the North. In principle, the lowest common denominator of "free soil," that the territories should be preserved for white settlers and protected from the stultifying effects of slavery (and of a black presence altogether), should have appealed to exclusion-minded voters.[1] In practice, most Free Soilers showed their abolitionist colors, protesting the black laws and colonization alike, which precluded any mass appeal to white midwesterners, their natural constituency.[2]

In 1854, the ambitious Illinois Democrat, Senator Stephen Douglas, bowed to southern pressure while pushing through the Kansas–Nebraska Act, which organized the eponymous territories at the cost of permitting slavery within their bounds. Douglas drew on the Compromise of 1850, which had left it to the settlers of the Mexican Cession to determine whether they would seek statehood under slavery or freedom, but northerners objected to his extending that formula of "popular sovereignty" eastward to the Louisiana Purchase (1803), which, since the Missouri Compromise (1820), had been regulated by a 36°30′N line above which territory had to remain free. Until 1860, the Democratic Party would survive the ensuing sectional showdown by parroting Douglas's own answer: leave the decision to local voters. Where dismayed Democrats could simply desert their party, however, the Whigs succumbed to the gash between their evangelical supporters in the North and slaveholding supporters in the South.[3] All of a sudden, there was a vacuum in American politics – and seasoned observers discerned that some new force must fill it.

THE REPUBLICANS AND COLONIZATION, TO 1861

New Party, Old Idea?

The story of the realignment of 1854–60, from the Second to the Third Party System, has been told many times. Suffice it to say that, by the election of 1856, a new alliance, the Republicans, had emerged as the Democrats' main opponents. The Republicans were united on just one point, that slavery not be allowed in the territories, a restriction that most commentators assumed would choke the institution.[4] Since all could see

---

[1] Richard H. Sewell, *Ballots for Freedom: Antislavery Politics in the United States, 1837–1860* (New York, 1976), 99, 185–7.

[2] Eugene H. Berwanger, *The Frontier against Slavery: Western Anti-Negro Prejudice and the Slavery Extension Controversy* (Urbana, 1967), 125.

[3] James M. McPherson, *Battle Cry of Freedom: The Civil War Era* (New York, 1988), 117–30.

[4] Eric Foner, *Free Soil, Free Labor, Free Men: The Ideology of the Republican Party before the Civil War* (New York, 1970), 115–16.

that the black population of the United States would keep growing, one question in particular perplexed the architects of the new party: "if we are to have no more slave states what the devil are we to do with the surplus niggers?"[5] By definition opposed to diffusion, which would have spread African Americans throughout the West, would the not-yet Grand Old Party adopt colonization instead?

Certainly, for a decade from the mid-1850s, the Republican Party strived for the geographic separation of black from white Americans as the obvious solution to a conundrum that it had set itself by imagining a United States without slavery (or the controls under which that institution placed almost nine-tenths of African Americans). Such separation might assume various forms, many of which are treated in Chapter 6. Well into the Civil War, however, most Republican advocates of resettlement supported a policy that they recognized as colonization, even if an improved hybrid on its Liberian rootstock. The "political colonizationists," as the ACS dubbed them, pressed their case within the party from 1858, and saw it adopt the policy in 1862, once the Republicans were in office and fighting a war that looked ever likelier to end slavery.

For the many claims that Republicans made for their colonization program, one has captivated historians even more than it did contemporaries: that touting the idea could counter Democratic accusations that excluding slavery from the territories would somehow bring about the social and political equality of African Americans.[6] "The policy ... would be a complete stopper to all the nonsensical talk about 'wooly heads' etc.," wrote one constituent to his US senator.[7] Another Republican was even blunter: "I believe practically it is a damn humbug. But it will take with the people."[8] It was true that the Democratic machine turned out racial invective incessantly, especially in the lower North. Yet colonization's presumed power did not stop at the Mason–Dixon Line: one promoter thought it "the only point needing ... comprehension by the Southern people to make us as strong at the South as at the North."[9] For the Republican colonizationists believed that their plan would bring out a

---

[5] D. R. Tilden to B. F. Wade, March 27, 1860, B. F. Wade Papers, LC.
[6] Richard Blackett, "Lincoln and Colonization," *OAH Magazine of History* 21 (2007), 21.
[7] H. Wing to L. Trumbull, May 4, 1860, Lyman Trumbull Correspondence, LC.
[8] Tilden to Wade, March 27, 1860, Wade Papers.
[9] M. Blair to J. R. Doolittle, November 11, 1859, in Duane Mowry, ed., "Letters of Edward Bates and the Blairs, from the Private Papers of Senator Doolittle," *Missouri Historical Review* 11 (1917), 137.

latent antislavery from the non-slaveholding majority in the South, and thereby turn a sectional party national.

Burdened with the knowledge that historical actors broadcast a message that they thought would appeal to voters, scholars face an interpretive problem. "When and where does the message change from being what it seems – a report on some policy that the leader obviously wants support for – to an effort to shape the public mind?" as one historian has asked.[10] In other words, it is easy, even tempting in this instance, to posit a false dichotomy between political advocacy and personal sincerity. Since the modern civil rights era, scholars have been embarrassed, even incredulous, that the Republican Party and its first (and greatest) president, Abraham Lincoln (1861–5), could have ended slavery while wasting so much time on the impractical, amoral, and abortive work of sending black Americans overseas.[11] Indeed, they focus almost entirely on Lincoln himself, to the exclusion of other Republicans and to the detriment of a debate that overheats when they dispute how seriously he took the idea. Ironically, it is "Honest Abe" whose earnestness can be ascertained the easiest of all, because, as president, he mostly furthered black resettlement through quiet, even secretive actions, which could not have garnered him any benefit in the eyes of the public.[12]

Nevertheless, analyzing astute historical actors requires the historian to triangulate between three considerations. First, the Republican colonizationists were forthright that they intended to persuade the prejudiced, and so left themselves fully exposed to Democratic accusations of cynicism.[13] In reality, the Republican Party remained putty in the hands of the factions that it loosely clumped together. Far from planning electoral

---

[10] Phillip Shaw Paludan, "Lincoln and Colonization: Policy or Propaganda?," *Journal of the Abraham Lincoln Association* 25 (2004), 23.

[11] For defensive treatments, see Gabor S. Boritt, "The Voyage to the Colony of Linconia: The Sixteenth President, Black Colonization, and the Defense Mechanism of Avoidance," *Historian* 37 (1975), 619–32; McPherson, *Battle Cry*, 507–10; and Michael Vorenberg, "Abraham Lincoln and the Politics of Black Colonization," *Journal of the Abraham Lincoln Association* 14 (1993), 22–45. For recent correctives to the same, see Brian R. Dirck, *Abraham Lincoln and White America* (Lawrence, 2012), 96–106, 126–9; Eric Foner, *The Fiery Trial: Abraham Lincoln and American Slavery* (New York, 2010), xix–xx; and Michael Vorenberg (revising his earlier views), "After Emancipation: Abraham Lincoln's Black Dream," in John Y. Simon et al., eds., *Lincoln Revisited: New Insights from the Lincoln Forum* (New York, 2007), 215–30.

[12] Phillip W. Magness and Sebastian N. Page, *Colonization after Emancipation: Lincoln and the Movement for Black Resettlement* (Columbia, MO, 2011), 118–20.

[13] Frank P. Blair, Jr., *The Destiny of the Races of This Continent* (Washington, DC, 1859), 22.

ruses in some sort of consensual, centralized operation, the political colonizationists had to convince other Republicans to make their party – and country – that of the white man. Second, their Democratic opponents, well aware of the shortcomings of the Liberia project, would not be easily deceived if colonization's neophytes failed to answer crucial questions about timescale, funding, and compulsion.[14] Indeed, it is doubtful that colonization won over many Democrats at all: while the prospect of black removal might have persuaded a few waverers to change their vote, the Third Party System soon settled down to the polarization that defined American politics. For most Democrats, that meant rallying their base with apocalyptic prophecies, eschewing compromise, and spitting out the bitter pill that expatriation could never sweeten: emancipation.[15] Third, Republican proponents of racial separation were quick to admit that, for their own part, they shared the widespread sentiments that they cited to justify their work.[16] If anyone, it was the leaders of the ACS who were prone to playing Pontius Pilate, and to blaming public opinion for their own amorality.

Moreover, politics is not just about winning elections but also about enacting agendas once in power. A substantive colonization policy addressed several concerns of a party fully prepared to expand the federal government to make internal "improvements" of all kinds. Colonization would offer an overseas outlet for African Americans, guaranteeing that the western territories would remain the preserve of the much-valorized white farmer.[17] It would place a cordon of free black settlements in the Caribbean, the primary, even sole target of the Republican colonizationists, to preempt those American expansionists who wished to plant slavery there.[18] And it would boost the commerce of the United States by making better use of the underworked lands of the American tropics, perhaps even by winning the nineteenth century's greatest prize: reliable transit of the Central American isthmus.

---

[14] *CG* 37 Cong., 2 Sess., 2503–5 (June 2), and Appendix, 107–8 (April 16, 1862).
[15] Mark E. Neely, Jr., "Colonization and the Myth That Lincoln Prepared the People for Emancipation," in William A. Blair and Karen Fisher Younger, eds., *Lincoln's Proclamation: Emancipation Reconsidered* (Chapel Hill, 2009), 53–7.
[16] Trumbull, speech, August 7, 1858, in Blair, *Destiny of the Races*, 30; *CG* 35 Cong., 1 Sess., 293 (January 14, 1858).
[17] Foner, *Free Soil*, 11–18.
[18] Robert E. May, *Slavery, Race, and Conquest in the Tropics: Lincoln, Douglas, and the Future of Latin America* (New York, 2013), 181–8.

Colonization schemes always married a grim, "realistic" forecast for US race relations to an unrealistic estimation of the logistical, political, and diplomatic obstacles that such plans would face. On the one hand, by shunning Africa, the Republican Party better addressed the question of distance than had the ACS. The Republicans also grounded colonization, for the first time, in the patronage that only a ruling national party could confer. On the other hand, the Republicans were ambitious indeed in the diplomatic prerequisites of their plan, which involved bypassing polities that invited black immigrants, namely, Liberia and Haiti, in favor of those that had no history of doing so.

However feasible (or not) colonization was, it intrigued a large proportion of the party of Lincoln, including Lincoln himself. Eliminating slavery from the territories might well have been the only buoy by which the inchoate, incoherent Republicans could navigate the choppy waters of change. But colonization was the policy that kept resurfacing amid the party's swirling currents of nationalism and sectionalism, expansionism and exclusionism, and racial egalitarianism and white supremacism.

The Blairs and Their Bedfellows

In 1856, the Republican Party fought its first presidential election, running the "Pathfinder of the West," the explorer John Frémont, against the Democrat James Buchanan, a career politician who, owing to his absence from the United States as minister to Britain, had avoided the taint of the Kansas–Nebraska Act and the battle that followed, on the western plains and in the halls of Washington, to win that land for slavery or freedom. While Frémont lost, his defeat was a heartening one: the Republicans swept the upper North and would win the Electoral College the next time if they gained just Pennsylvania and one other state.[19] Another sign of the changing landscape had manifested itself as the president of the convention that had chosen Frémont: Francis Preston Blair, a veteran political insider and until recently a staunch Democrat (Figure 3.1).[20] He was the latest exponent of an upper South tradition of economic antislavery, which would have abolished a dwindling institution to entice the investment, ingenuity, and (white) immigration that the free states so clearly enjoyed. By the late 1850s, Blair's older son, Montgomery, was involved in the politics of Maryland, while his younger son, Francis, Jr. (Frank),

[19] McPherson, *Battle Cry*, 153–62.
[20] William E. Parrish, *Frank Blair: Lincoln's Conservative* (Columbia, MO, 1998), 60.

FIGURE 3.1 Francis Preston Blair, Sr. (1791–1876). Journalist, colonizationist, and veteran Washington insider.
Brady-Handy Collection, LC

the family's chosen one for a national career, was immersed in those of Missouri.[21]

Maryland and Missouri were the two states where slavery was at its least stable, and where the Blairs were keenest to prove an axiom dear to them and beguiling to their new allies: that the non-slaveholding commoners of the South would readily topple the planter aristocracy *and* its peculiar institution, if only they could be sure that the slaves would be removed once freed.[22] In 1856, Francis Blair, Sr., had touched on colonization in a campaign circular, though admitted that he had not yet identified how slavery would disappear: it "may gradually go out Southward, and an improved race of blacks appear as a colony of our country within the tropics of South America."[23] While Blair awaited the workings of providence, another centrist eager to place nation above section tried to claim colonization for the Democratic Party instead.

---

[21] Foner, *Free Soil*, 150, 156–7, 269–70.
[22] F. P. Blair, Sr., to W. H. Beecher, January 15, 1857, BL.
[23] "Letter from Francis P. Blair," *New York Daily Times*, September 22, 1856.

Like Blair, Robert Walker, a former secretary of the treasury with ties to both North and South, had once put his faith in a "race funnel" to draw blacks to the tropics, which he had outlined in an 1844 plea to northern critics of the US annexation of Texas.[24] He also prefigured Blair in switching to more proactive means, advocating a steamer line to Liberia in 1850, and praising that country to the Pennsylvania Democratic Committee in 1856.[25] With that body's support, he tried to turn the presidential nominee, Buchanan, to a policy that would hold together the party's sectional wings "as the only real antagonist of abolition."[26] Evidently, his proposal went no further. From then on, the Democratic Party ceded colonization to its Republican foil, even as individual Democrats occasionally gestured to the idea. Thanks to Stephen Douglas's miracle cure of popular sovereignty, why dispense more medicine now that the Democracy's wounds were healed – or, at least, stitched back together?

Although they never knew it, the Blairs gained a much-needed breathing space from Walker's failure, getting to hone their thoughts on colonization without being preempted. Taking roughly a year to do so, they then spent the next decade repeating their views to anyone who would listen. Before the Civil War, that included many Republicans, mesmerized by Frank Blair's 1856 election to the US House for St. Louis. Amid the factionalism of the state Democratic Party from whose turbulent ranks he had emerged, he had not actually run as a Republican, but antislavery northerners were inspired nevertheless by a candidate on a free-soil platform having prevailed in a slave state.[27] "It is a good sign, when the member from Missouri can say such things," the Massachusetts abolitionist Theodore Parker told the new congressman.[28] "Frank Blair is the man of the West, of the age," wrote New York's (and the Union's) most prominent Republican, Senator William Seward.[29] While the Blairs promised that the white South awaited only a federal government willing

---

[24] Robert J. Walker, *Letter Relative to the Annexation of Texas* (Washington, DC, 1844), 14.

[25] R. J. Walker to M. S. Clarke, July 23, 1850, in A. H. Brown, pub., *Debates of the Convention of Indiana* (Indianapolis, 1850), 1:606–7; Robert J. Walker, *An Appeal for the Union* (New York, 1856), 9–10.

[26] Walker to J. Buchanan, October 3, 1856, James Buchanan Papers, Historical Society of Pennsylvania.

[27] Parrish, *Frank Blair*, 63–64.

[28] T. Parker to F. P. Blair, Jr., January 26, 1858, in Blair, *Destiny of the Races*, 33.

[29] W. H. Seward to J. W. Webb, October 1, 1858, reel 57, WHS.

to confront the planter "chivalry," for many Republicans, the evidence was there already: the Blairs themselves, minor slaveholders though they were.[30]

In early 1857, Francis Blair brought colonization to his younger son's attention, advising him to make his "maiden speech the exponent of some system which shall deliver the country from this sectional quarrel."[31] For someone who would later describe colonization as the "culminating point" of Republican doctrine, Frank Blair was nonplussed at first.[32] He wondered whether it would be better to simply await the next census, which would reapportion House seats in favor of the free states and so allow the North greater political latitude.[33] Just days later, however, Frank had warmed to his father's idea: "the more I think of it, the better I like it."[34] He decided to avoid Francis's reference to the struggle between North and South, and instead to speak for his own section, the West, and to demand that the public lands be distributed as homesteads "for the purpose of inviting settlers who own no negroes and thus excluding negroes."[35] Through 1860 and beyond, the Blairs duly emphasized that white resettlement in the territories and black resettlement in the tropics would reinforce each other.

The Blairs also weighed up the filibusterers, those US adventurers inclined to invade the unstable Central American states of that era. Despite the infamous deeds of mercenaries such as William Walker, who usurped the presidency of Nicaragua in 1856 and reinstituted slavery to curry favor in the US South, tropical expansionism was never the purely proslavery venture that the Blairs imagined. (In fact, Walker had started out battling Nicaraguan conservatives, to the acclaim of local liberals, before becoming corrupted by the prospect of power.)[36] Many northern Democrats, notably Stephen Douglas and James Buchanan, hoped that Cuba, in particular, might be annexed under the more agreeable auspices of the federal government, to acclaim across the Union –

---

[30] Foner, *Free Soil*, 119–21.
[31] F. P. Blair, Sr., to F. P. Blair, Jr., February 5, 1857, reel 1, BF.
[32] F. P. Blair, Jr., to Doolittle, October 15, 1859, in Mowry, "Letters of Edward Bates and the Blairs," 134.
[33] F. P. Blair, Jr., to F. P. Blair, Sr., February 12, 1857, reel 2, BF.
[34] F. P. Blair, Jr., to F. P. Blair, Sr., February 22, 1857, ibid.
[35] F. P. Blair, Jr., to F. P. Blair, Sr., February 18, 1857, ibid.
[36] Michael Gobat, *Empire by Invitation: William Walker and Manifest Destiny in Central America* (Cambridge, MA, 2018), 1–11.

and at the ballot box, for the party that made it happen.[37] Still, the Blairs could be forgiven for thinking filibusters another machination of the "Slave Power" and for presenting their own plan as the peaceful alternative for extending American influence throughout the region.[38]

In fact, the Blairs' enthusiasm for colonization as a tool of foreign policy was the most novel part of their program. "Every abolitionist would have to ask himself … whether to have [Central America] on Walker's plan, under military rule supplied by slaves," or on the Blairs' own plan, predicted Francis in the spring of 1857.[39] His son added "a thought worth incorporating into the scheme": that Britain's decades-old campaign to stop the Atlantic slave trade had failed because it offered no adequate substitute for unfree African labor. The answer, claimed Frank, was to fill the gap by resettling black Americans, as though an illicit traffic destined only for Brazil and Cuba could somehow justify his hunger for annexing swathes of two continents replete with countries that had long abolished slavery.[40] While Frank admitted hoping to manipulate "men of humane feelings" by evoking the slave trade, the family's enmity for filibustering was quite serious. By late 1857, Francis, Sr.'s self-founding colony of just a year earlier had become, in the Blairs' still-private plans, a mooted US protectorate extending from Central America to the Amazon.[41]

In January 1858, during heated debates in the US House on whether to admit Kansas under a free or a slave constitution, Representative Frank Blair delivered his maiden speech. He moved that a select committee look into acquiring territory in Central or South America, which would be settled with both the already free and those yet to be freed. Their political rights would, moreover, be guaranteed under a US dependency. Blair then launched into a lengthy speech that showed all the signs of his father's assiduous research in the Library of Congress. "We ought to put it out of the power of any body of men to plant slavery anywhere on this continent, by … giv[ing] to all of these countries … the power to sustain free institutions," he announced. Claiming the mantle of Thomas Jefferson, an intellectual forebear of black removal whose name stood safely above the

[37] May, *Slavery, Race, and Conquest,* 59–77, 178–9.
[38] Sharon Hartman Strom, "Labor, Race, and Colonization: Imagining a Post-Slavery World in the Americas," in Steven Mintz and John Stauffer, eds., *The Problem of Evil: Slavery, Freedom, and the Ambiguities of American Reform* (Amherst, 2007), 267.
[39] F. P. Blair, Sr., to F. P. Blair, Jr., March 19, 1857, reel 1, BF.
[40] F. P. Blair, Jr., to F. P. Blair, Sr., June 23, 1857, reel 2, BF.
[41] F. P. Blair, Sr., to F. P. Blair, Jr., October 21, 1857, reel 1, BF.

sectional fray, Blair also avoided the controversial name of the ACS, dismissing Africa on account of its "barbarous state." Yet, like the Liberian colonizationists, he credited a change of scenery with the power to transform a "degraded class" into one that could civilize the natives; in this instance, "reinvigorate the feeble people of the southern Republics."[42] Although pseudo-scientific racism was in its infancy, Blair's claim was a remarkable statement of blacks' ability, when nurtured by US institutions, to improve a mixed-race population.[43] But his argument was risky on two fronts: for espousing a racial equality solid enough to undermine his entire case for colonization and, conversely, for presuming blacks so well suited to the tropics as to justify slavery at those latitudes.

Although Blair's resolution never reached a vote, he had effectively laid out the antebellum colonization program of the Republicans. A Georgia Democrat, Lucius Gartrell, answered the South's apostate with a stark rejoinder: Blair was swimming against the tides of history. The Missourian had misstepped by citing the free Caribbean, whose rulers now admitted that productivity had collapsed since emancipation and who kept importing bonded labor from China and India (Chapter 5). "[The British] Government, satisfied that the experiment has failed, is beginning to throw aside these misguided notions of philanthropy," taunted Gartrell, who announced that he would not keep shadowing Blair's scheme, lest doing so somehow concede that the question of emancipation belonged to Congress and not to the states. His deliberate silence prefigured the response of most proslavery thinkers to the plan.[44] Still, the Blairs were never out to persuade the likes of Gartrell, needing first to convince their own colleagues within the Republican Party. Over the following months, Senators James Doolittle (Wisconsin), Preston King (New York), and Henry Wilson (Massachusetts) spoke up in Congress for the scheme.[45] Doolittle would prove a stalwart, standing in as Capitol Hill's champion of colonization once Blair lost his seat in the 1858 midterms, and resuming their collaboration once Blair regained it in 1860.[46] Like the Blairs, Doolittle was a former Democrat whose sympa-

---

[42] CG 35 Cong., 1 Sess., 293–8 (January 14, 1858).
[43] For notions of "race" by the 1850s, see George M. Fredrickson, *The Black Image in the White Mind: The Debate on Afro-American Character and Destiny, 1817–1914* (New York, 1971), 130–52.
[44] CG 35 Cong., 1 Sess., 391–3 (January 25, 1858).
[45] Ibid., 2207 (May 18), 3034 (June 14), and Appendix, 172–3 (March 20, 1858).
[46] Parrish, *Frank Blair*, 73, 86.

thies lay squarely with his fellow whites. None could doubt his personal commitment to colonization, for his fellow Wisconsinites, not on the frontline of the putative influx of freedpeople that so disturbed Illinoisans, Indianans, and Ohioans, would even accuse their senator of being too enamored of the policy.[47] Yet some northern abolitionists voiced at least a modicum of respect for the Blair project. "I do not see that it traverses any principle of justice," admitted Senator Charles Sumner of Massachusetts, always the first to inveigh against a traversed principle of justice.[48] "We must respect it as coming from an earnest and sincere emancipationist in a slave state," conceded Sumner's fellow Bostonian, Charles Francis Adams.[49] Maybe they saw little point in opposing an idea that might win votes while containing too many defects to ever bear fruit.[50]

Not all abolitionists were willing, however, to allow the South's fifth column to operate as freely in the North. "The theory assumes two propositions which need to be settled," insisted a Massachusetts journalist. "First, that the removal ... of this class is desirable; secondly, that such an enterprise is within the scope of federal authority."[51] Likewise, Joseph Medill's *Chicago Tribune* criticized Blair for "basing all antislavery movements on the superior claims of the white race."[52] Curiously, several black leaders were delighted by a plan at once so complimentary and yet so contemptuous of them. Until 1858, the Blairs seem to have been unaware of the very existence of black emigrationists, who were, however, quick to introduce themselves once Frank had gone public. "The subject has actively occupied the attention of this class of persons themselves since 1854," James Theodore Holly informed Blair, hailing how white colonizationists had finally shaken off their fixation on Liberia. "The Saxon and negro are the only positive races on this continent, and the two are destined to absorb into themselves all the others," wrote James Whitfield in his own letter to Blair, touting Central America

[47] J. M. Burgess to J. F. Potter, April 16, 1862, John F. Potter Papers, Wisconsin Historical Society; D. Noggle to Doolittle, May 30, 1862, James R. Doolittle Papers, Wisconsin Historical Society.
[48] C. Sumner to J. R. Lowell, December 14, 1859, James Russell Lowell Papers, Harvard.
[49] Entry, January 26, 1859, Charles Francis Adams Diary, Massachusetts Historical Society.
[50] David Brown, "William Lloyd Garrison, Transatlantic Abolitionism and Colonisation in the Mid Nineteenth Century: The Revival of the Peculiar Solution?," *Slavery and Abolition* 33 (2012), 233–50; Sewell, *Ballots for Freedom*, 332.
[51] "African Colonization," Lowell *Daily Citizen and News*, July 12, 1859.
[52] Foner, *Fiery Trial*, 125.

with strong echoes of Blair's separatist but egalitarian language. Meanwhile, J. Dennis Harris offered his services as "an agent among our people," be it to disseminate information or direct an expedition.[53]

A confident Frank Blair took to the campaign trail in the summer of 1858 to stump for Republicans fighting close races in the Midwest. Losing his own seat through such complacency, he then rode the lecture circuit, speaking at the Boston Mercantile Library Association in early 1859. The avowed "backwoodsman" stressed the commercial benefits of colonization, since a message dominated by white homesteading would never be as well received in the Northeast as it would have been in the Northwest.[54] Even then, Adams, sitting in the audience, sensed a certain parochialism: "the transfer of four or five millions of souls is probably less in [Blair's] mind than ... the salvation of Missouri in getting rid of her hundred thousand slaves."[55] Later that year, Blair spoke to a similar organization, the Young Men's Mercantile Library Association of Cincinnati, which "begged [him] to avoid as far as possible censuring the administration."[56] Both lectures were bland enough to be reprinted as campaign documents, the first as *The Destiny of the Races* (1859) and the second as *Colonization and Commerce* (1859).

The Program's Problems

Since the Blairs adjusted their appeal as the occasion demanded, they never answered three crucial questions to the satisfaction of Republican colleagues, who would not officially adopt colonization until a year into the Civil War.

First, how did they intend to defeat the filibusterers in what Frank worryingly described as "the vacant regions of Central and South America" without acting as aggressors themselves?[57] Mostly, the Blairs just assumed that their program held a self-evident attraction to Central America, the region that they increasingly emphasized to the exclusion of South America. They contended that only the proslavery tenor of recent US expansionism had propelled the republican isthmians toward the protection of the monarchical British. "The encroachments of our

---

[53] J. T. Holly to F. P. Blair, Jr., January 30, J. M. Whitfield to Blair, February 1, and J. D. Harris to Blair, December 10, 1858, in Blair, *Destiny of the Races*, 34–5, 38.
[54] Ibid., 3; F. P. Blair, Jr., to M. Blair, October 16, 1858, BL.
[55] Entry, January 26, 1859, Adams Diary.
[56] F. P. Blair, Jr., to F. P. Blair, Sr., October 25, 1859, BL.
[57] Blair, *Destiny of the Races*, 23.

transatlantic brethren would never have been attempted, but for the departures manifested in late movements from the principles of the founders," Frank Blair had claimed in his congressional debut.[58] Yet his father hoped that resettling free blacks would commend itself to the Blairs' transatlantic brethren, too, by competing with the slave trade to fulfill the tropics' demand for labor.[59] Hanging precariously over Anglo-American relations in Central America was the Clayton–Bulwer Treaty (1850), in which Britain and the United States had agreed not to occupy, fortify, or colonize the region. The treaty had been ratified under a Whig administration, and the Democrats sought to abrogate it for conceding too much to London, which, during the 1850s, claimed ambiguity over its existing colony of British Honduras (Belize) to cling onto prior holdings. In his first term in Congress, Frank would vote with the Democrats to repudiate the treaty, as befitted an overt annexationist.[60]

But tropical expansion was a volatile issue in antebellum politics, since whites struggled to predict how African American migration southward, a racial "destiny" that they took as axiomatic (Chapter 6), would affect the delicate balance between slavery and freedom in the United States. In principle, Republicans could unite in resisting conquest undertaken in the name of slavery. "Shall we give niggers to the niggerless, or land to the landless?" asked Ohio's Senator Benjamin Wade, exasperated at how debates over annexing Cuba kept stalling a homestead bill.[61] Yet they could not agree on the alternative for a region that they could hardly ignore. For Doolittle, the best check to filibusters was, of course, colonization, which would involve "outflanking them [and] posting a strong and faithful force in their rear."[62] He was even more enthusiastic than the Blairs on colonization's foreign implications, probably because any resettlement treaties would have to be submitted to the Senate – and to his stewardship.

Politicians of all stripes struggled, however, to divine how putative changes to the map of the Americas would, in practice, help or hinder the causes of proslavery, antislavery, colonization, and everything in between. In 1857, Francis Blair had been right to mourn the failure of a further Anglo-American agreement, the Dallas–Clarendon Treaty, which

---

[58] CG 35 Cong., 1 Sess., 297 (January 14, 1858).
[59] F. P. Blair, Sr., to F. P. Blair, Jr., February 14, 1857, reel 1, BF.
[60] William E. Smith, *The Francis Preston Blair Family in Politics* (New York, 1933), 1:405–6.
[61] CG 35 Cong., 2 Sess., 1354 (February 25, 1859).
[62] Doolittle to Potter, July 25, 1859, Potter Papers.

collapsed when the Senate balked at Britain agreeing to yield territory to Nicaragua and Honduras on condition that slavery never be permitted in its cession.[63] But when the (US-Mexican) McLane–Ocampo Treaty came up for debate in 1860, tendering the United States a right of transit across Mexico's Isthmus of Tehuantepec, the Senate voted it down on sectionally mixed lines.[64] Despite the best efforts of a New York businessman, Edward Dunbar, to claim that the treaty would force white southerners to adopt colonization by bottling them up with their slaves (through placing antislavery settlers to the south), not even Doolittle took the bait. For Dunbar had suggested that *white* emigrants to Mexico, from "the slave hating North and slave hating Europe," provide the cordon that he envisioned.[65] In that respect, Dunbar echoed Representative Eli Thayer of Massachusetts, who had organized the free-state emigration to Kansas and who had offered, shortly before Frank Blair's maiden speech, to reprise that act in Central America. In short, the Blairs and Doolittle were frustrated to find that they did not hold a monopoly on plans for antislavery colonization in the tropics, even within their own party.[66]

Second, what constitutional status did the Republican colonizationists imagine for their black settlements, such as would placate the United States, Britain, and the concessionary government itself? The political veteran Francis Blair, Sr., had predicted this problem as early as 1857, when he had looked to the precedents set by a recent Anglo-Honduran treaty as a "substitute for a colonization code on the part of Congress," which would "give ultimate control in a [US] quasi-protectorate."[67] In June 1858, Doolittle moved that the Senate Committee on Foreign Relations investigate acquiring land for black settlers "under the laws of the State or States to which they emigrate," though Washington would make further arrangements to uphold the settlers' rights.[68] The senator's resolution contained room for misunderstanding as well as for maneuver,

[63] F. P. Blair, Sr., to F. P. Blair, Jr., February 14, 1857, reel 1, BF.

[64] Pearl T. Ponce, "'As Dead as Julius Caesar': The Rejection of the McLane-Ocampo Treaty," *Civil War History* 53 (2007), 342–78.

[65] E. E. Dunbar to Doolittle, January 5, "1859" [i.e., 1860], and J. D. Andrews to Doolittle, January 5, 1860, Doolittle Papers.

[66] William W. Freehling, *The Road to Disunion* (New York, 1990–2007), 2:72, 239–40; May, *Slavery, Race, and Conquest*, 182; CG 35 Cong., 1 Sess., 227–31 (January 7, 1858).

[67] F. P. Blair, Sr., to F. P. Blair, Jr., August 27, 1857, reel 1, BF.

[68] CG 35 Cong., 1 Sess., 3034 (June 14, 1858).

and portended the complications that would befall the one isthmian colony that the Lincoln administration attempted.

Before even approaching foreign diplomats, though, the Blairs would have to appease American critics who demanded to know whether a black colony would ever find itself on the path to statehood. In 1858, Francis Blair had told Gerrit Smith, a receptive abolitionist, that the scheme would not "incapacitate" such dependencies from entering the Union – but added that he would rather not "raise manifold objections besides ... that of making the black race participants with the white in the political power."[69] Privately, Frank Blair told Francis that "we should avoid incorporating into the Government the colored races to the south of us, but simply extend our influence over them"; publicly, he invoked Native American reservations as the apposite precedent.[70] Whenever coloniza- tion came up in Congress, though, the scheme's defenders struggled to dissemble. One supporter of the Blairs, Senator Lyman Trumbull of Illinois, confessed that he would not "endanger the peace of the Union" by admitting a black state.[71] "That is, offend the slaveholders," admon- ished a New Englander.[72] In 1860, the junior senator for Ohio, a Democrat, George Pugh, pointedly asked his senior counterpart, Benjamin Wade, whether black colonies would be "equal participants" in the federal government.[73] Perhaps Frank Blair, who by that point deemed his own scheme "somewhat threadbare," was quietly glad to miss out on the Thirty-Sixth Congress (1859–61), when others' adulation turned into audit.[74]

Third, would the migration require the colonists' consent? On the one hand, black voluntarism was nonnegotiable for other Republicans, most of whom already opposed state laws banning blacks' immigration, let alone any federal scheme that might exile them.[75] "I will consent to no form of compulsion," warned Gerrit Smith, who could not quite bring himself to join the Republican Party.[76] Certainly, the first phase of the

---

[69] F. P. Blair, Sr., to G. Smith, April 19, 1858, Gerrit Smith Papers, Syracuse University.
[70] F. P. Blair, Jr., to F. P. Blair, Sr., September 10, 1858, BL; F. P. Blair, Jr., *Colonization and Commerce* (n.p., 1859), 2.
[71] CG 36 Cong., 1 Sess., 102 (December 12, 1859).
[72] C. Taintor, Jr., to Trumbull, December 1859, Lyman Trumbull Family Papers, Abraham Lincoln Presidential Library.
[73] CG 36 Cong., 2 Sess., Appendix, 30 (December 20, 1860).
[74] F. P. Blair, Jr., to F. P. Blair, Sr., November 29, 1860, BL.
[75] Foner, *Free Soil*, 286–90.
[76] Smith to F. P. Blair, Sr., April 13, 1858, in Blair, *Destiny of the Races*, 32.

Blairs' scheme at least dovetailed with voluntarism. They sought pioneers, which accorded with blacks' own belief in selective emigration, and hoped to avoid premature controversy. On the other hand, the Republicans would have to transport slaves at some point if they were to whiten America, and then they would face the old dilemma about premising emancipation on emigration. In an 1860 speech at New York's Cooper Union, Frank Blair laid out "a process of probation, leading to liberation," under which planters and state legislators would choose whether to expatriate their slaves.[77] The same year, his brother, Montgomery, chaired the Maryland Republican Convention, which endorsed the state's recent ban on manumission without removal.[78] "I can never join a party, the leaders of which conspire to expel us from the country," announced black Philadelphian Robert Purvis. "It is true they talk of doing it with our 'own consent.' But ... it will not be long before measures are taken to compel us."[79] Fundamentally, colonization always rested on a disquieting imbalance: while a deportationist audience would never be alienated, only disappointed, by a voluntarist message, the reverse could never be true. So even ostensible advocates of consent could quietly contemplate expulsive measures, or harbor ominous intent in using near-synonyms such as "expatriation," "removal," and "transportation" – historically, the term for sending convicts to penal colonies.

Yet the many cracks running through the scheme might prove fractures rather than fault lines if the Blairs handled such questions carefully. After all, their plan did not have to hold together; people just had to vote for it. Accordingly, they prepared to hammer the appropriate plank into the national Republican platform for 1860. "Party workers are the most timid of men and will never risk themselves," Frank Blair advised James Doolittle. "We can never get the members of Congress at Washington to go forward ... until the Legislatures at home ... declar[e] in favor of the measure."[80] On cue, in their inaugural messages of early 1860, Governors William Dennison (Ohio), Samuel Kirkwood (Iowa), and Alexander Randall (Wisconsin), Republicans all, asked their assemblies to pass

---

[77] F. P. Blair, Jr., *Speech at the Cooper Institute* (Washington, DC, 1860), 11.
[78] Montgomery Blair, *Address before the Maryland State Republican Convention* (Washington, DC, 1860), 7.
[79] "Speech of Robert Purvis," *Liberator*, May 18, 1860.
[80] F. P. Blair, Jr., to Doolittle, November 3, 1859, in Mowry, "Letters of Edward Bates and the Blairs," 135.

resolutions supporting Central American colonization.[81] None obliged, the relevant committee of the Ohio legislature feeling too much loyalty to the senior scheme of the ACS.[82]

Undeterred, the Blairs continued trying to write colonization into the manifesto for 1860. Obsessed with winning the lower northern states that had eluded Frémont in 1856, Doolittle asked the chairman of the national committee, Governor Edwin Morgan of New York (1859–62), whether he might encourage his own legislature to back colonization.[83] Despite the growing group of midwestern Republicans lobbying for the scheme, it was unclear whether they would manage to persuade the authors of the convention's platform. Assuming that its drafters discussed the plank at adequate length, "there might be general if not universal concurrence," predicted one of Lyman Trumbull's friends.[84] In fact, despite all three Blairs turning up to parley at Chicago's "Wigwam," the wooden edifice hosting the convention, they failed in their mission. While a sheepish Francis would claim that the colonization plank had involved "too many details to be introduced," he had actually stayed up all night trying to sway the committee's members.[85] Although amenable in principle, they had obsessed too much with countering the Democratic Party on its own terms to take such an initiative.[86]

Yet the Chicago Convention had not only to construct a platform but also to choose a man to stand on it. The prominent candidates held strong opinions on colonization. The frontrunner, Seward, was averse: "I am always for bringing men and States *into* this Union, never for taking any *out*."[87] Uncharacteristically, he had told Montgomery Blair earlier that year that he "rejoice[d] in the Colonization Scheme coming as it does from Missouri."[88] Given that Seward would subsequently offer Frank the

---

[81] W. Dennison, message, January 9, 1860, in Richard Nevins, pub., *Messages and Reports of Ohio* (Columbus, 1860), 2:179–80; S. J. Kirkwood, message, January 11, 1860, in Benjamin F. Shambaugh, ed., *Messages of the Governors of Iowa* (Iowa City, 1903), 2:243–6; A. W. Randall, message, January 12, 1860, in James Ross, pub., *Journal of the Assembly of Wisconsin* (Madison, 1860), 39–40.

[82] J. Orcutt to R. R. Gurley, March 1, 1860, reel 88, ACS.

[83] Doolittle to E. D. Morgan, January 29, 1860, Thurlow Weed Papers, University of Rochester.

[84] Wing to Trumbull, May 4, 1860, Trumbull Correspondence.

[85] F. P. Blair, Sr., to A. Lincoln, May 26, 1860, AL.

[86] M. Blair to J. A. Andrew, February 19, 1861, John A. Andrew Papers, Massachusetts Historical Society.

[87] Sebastian N. Page, "'A Knife Sharp Enough to Divide Us': William H. Seward, Abraham Lincoln, and Black Colonization," *Diplomatic History* 41 (2017), 362–91; Frederick W. Seward, ed., *Seward at Washington* (New York, 1891), 227.

[88] M. Blair to F. P. Blair, Sr., January 17, 1860, BL.

role of running mate, however, his sincerity on that occasion had been suspect.[89] Meanwhile, Salmon Chase, a founder of the Free Soil Party and Dennison's predecessor as governor of Ohio, had kept his distance from the Blairs. Recently, Chase had drafted a valedictory message acknowledging that most white Ohioans "would gladly see ... provision made for the colored race in more congenial latitudes," only to delete that passage from the final version following objections from critical readers.[90] With friends like these, the Blairs needed Edward Bates of Missouri. A one-time Whig, Bates had endorsed Liberia since the 1820s, switching his allegiance to the American tropics in 1860, and vouched to Frank Blair for the black emigrationist J. Dennis Harris.[91] Yet father and sons suffered a second setback at Chicago when they failed to excite the delegates over the elderly, conservative Bates.[92]

Fortunately, the convention chose another midwesterner the Blairs knew well: Abraham Lincoln. "I find ... all Republicans rejoicing in the Chicago nomination, and all content with the platform," Francis Blair told Lincoln. "The great point however ... is not developed in it – how are we to get deliverance from 'the irrepressible conflict'?"[93] They agreed on the answer. Out of office between 1849 and 1861, Lincoln had had time to sharpen his thinking on black resettlement. He addressed the Illinois State Colonization Society in 1855, became one of its managers by 1857, and donated at least $10 to the ACS.[94] Unlike the Blairs, Lincoln never abandoned Africa, even as he joined them in supporting other destinations. "My first impulse would be to free all the slaves, and send them to Liberia," he announced in an 1854 speech protesting the Kansas–Nebraska Act. "But a moment's reflection would convince me, that whatever of high hope ... there may be in this, in the long run, its sudden execution is impossible."[95] As such, the greater viability of the Blairs' Central American alternative rescued Lincoln from a maze of his own hedging. He probably conferred with Frank twice in early 1857 when the

---

[89] M. Blair to C. M. Clay, December 31, 1881, reel 27, BF.   [90] Foner, *Free Soil*, 293–4.
[91] Entry, March 17, 1860, in Howard K. Beale, ed., *The Diary of Edward Bates, 1859–1866* (Washington, DC, 1933), 113; Harris to F. P. Blair, Jr., January 29, 1860, BL.
[92] Marvin R. Cain, *Lincoln's Attorney General: Edward Bates of Missouri* (Columbia, MO, 1965), 110–15.
[93] F. P. Blair, Sr., to Lincoln, May 26, 1860, AL.
[94] "Outline for Speech to the Colonization Society," January 4, 1855, *CWAL*, 2:298–9; "State Colonization Society," *Daily Illinois State Journal*, January 28, 1857; J. C. Finley to W. McLain, August 14, 1856, reel 80, ACS.
[95] "Speech at Peoria, Illinois," October 16, 1854, *CWAL*, 2:255.

latter visited Springfield.[96] By June, Lincoln publicly intimated that colonization might become Republican policy and, from 1858, followed
Blair's progress avidly.[97] Having made his own name in senatorial campaign debates with Stephen Douglas the same year, Lincoln spoke
approvingly to a New York audience in 1860 of Thomas Jefferson's
vision of gradualism and colonization.[98]

The long-rumbling rupture of the Democratic Party over the increasingly bankrupt panacea of popular sovereignty made the presidential
election of November 1860 a complicated, four-way race. By the most
credible counterfactuals, however, Abraham Lincoln would still have
won the Electoral College in a traditional, two-candidate contest. The
tyranny of the (sectional) majority that had so troubled the progenitor of
nullification, the late John Calhoun, had come to pass. His native state of
South Carolina promptly seceded, drawing in the other six of the lower
South by February 1861. Believing disunion a conspiracy of the planters,
and black removal the ideal way to call their bluff, the Republican
colonizationists assumed that their moment had come. "I hope that
Lincoln will say something in his inaugural favorable to the separation
of the Races," William Dennison told Francis Blair. "I shall be surprised if
we do not see prompt movements in nearly all the slave states to organize
a Republican party."[99] In turn, Blair wrote his daughter, Lizzie, that he
"really believe[d] that the South Carolina phrenzy will ultimately give
success to Frank's scheme of deliverance."[100] Doolittle thought that
colonization would do less, privately accepting that the lower South had
forever forsaken the policy, and could only pray to God to bring about
the separation of the races, not the sections.[101]

Over the winter of 1860–1, politicians dredged up colonization amid a
flurry of mooted concessions.[102] Although Kentucky's Senator John
Crittenden, of the conciliatory but ineffectual Constitutional Unionist
Party, did not include colonization in the compromise package that came

---

[96] Joseph Fort Newton, *Lincoln and Herndon* (Cedar Rapids, 1910), 114; F. P. Blair, Jr., to
    F. P. Blair, Sr., February 18, 1857, reel 2, BF.
[97] "Speech at Springfield, Illinois," June 26, 1857, *CWAL*, 2:409–10; F. P. Blair, Jr., to
    Lincoln, October 18, 1859, AL.
[98] "Address at Cooper Institute, New York City," February 27, 1860, *CWAL*, 3:541.
[99] Dennison to F. P. Blair, Sr., November 10, 1860, BL.
[100] F. P. Blair, Sr., to E. B. Lee, November 14, 1860, BL.
[101] Doolittle to M. Doolittle, December 2, 1860, Doolittle Papers.
[102] C. B. Sedgwick to D. Sedgwick, December 6, 1860, in Earle Field, ed., "Charles
    B. Sedgwick's Letters from Washington, 1859–1861," *Mid-America* 49 (1967), 136;
    A. I. Wynkoop to H. Greeley, January 1861, Horace Greeley Papers, LC.

to bear his name, Douglas appropriated Crittenden's proposed amendments to the US Constitution and added the federal colonization of free
African Americans, as the states might mandate.[103] "If the Northern
States want to get rid of their free negroes, let them do so," replied one
southerner. "We can get rid of ours without it costing a cent. We can
reduce them to slavery."[104] From the other pole, the abolitionist Senator
Henry Wilson, though favorable to allowing the United States to annex
territory for colonization, criticized Douglas's measure, whose restriction
to the already free was "not intended to encourage emancipation, but to
perpetuate slavery."[105] At the Peace Conference, a February 1861 meeting
of moderates, the modified Crittenden amendments came up again,
Douglas's colonization clause included. They failed on a 5-14 vote, the
ayes coming from the delegations of Kentucky, Missouri, North Carolina,
Tennessee, and Virginia.[106] The other states preferred to leave colonization to the ACS, believing it a more efficient agency than the US government.[107] There ended any chance that colonization might save the Union.

Meanwhile, in Montgomery, delegates from the seceded South
founded the Confederate States of America with alarming alacrity.
Loath to alienate the upper South, which had yet to secede (*if* it did),
the Confederate Convention virtually copied the US Constitution, including its ban on the slave trade. That immediately landed the Confederate
Congress with the dilemma, so lately familiar to its US counterpart, of
how to dispose of recaptives while endorsing neither emancipation nor
enslavement. In February, the Confederate president, Jefferson Davis,
refused to sign a bill that would have allowed "foreign states or
Societies" – less euphemistically, Liberia or the ACS – the right to bid to
remove imported Africans, failing which the latter would be sold as
slaves. (To his credit, it was the second part that troubled Davis.) The
problem found its solution only in the failure of another *Echo* to reach
southern shores, and in the higher priorities of war.[108]

---

[103] S. A. Douglas, joint resolution, December 24, 1860, S. Rep. 288, 36 Cong., 2 Sess.
(1860), 9.
[104] J. H. Smith to A. H. Stephens, December 26, 1860, Alexander Hamilton Stephens
Papers, LC.
[105] *CG* 36 Cong., 2 Sess., 1093 (February 21, 1861).
[106] L. E. Chittenden, *The Debates and Proceedings in the Secret Sessions of the Conference
Convention* (New York, 1864), 423-4.
[107] J. B. Major, pub., *Report of the Kentucky Commissioners to the Late Peace Conference*
(Frankfort, 1861), 10.
[108] S. Doc. 234, 58 Cong., 2 Sess. (1904), 1:83-4, 95.

War also meant that one delegate, the South Carolina secessionist William Porcher Miles, had to hold his peace when the Confederacy adopted the Stars and Bars, a flag based on Old Glory. As his committee had argued, another new government, the Republic of Liberia, had once chosen to mimic the US flag. And when, during the early hours of April 12, 1861, Confederate guns opened fire on Fort Sumter, Charleston, what could have been more tragic than doing so under a banner inspired by one already "pilfered ... by a free negro community"?[109]

CONFISCATION, COLONIZATION, AND CONTRABANDS, APRIL 1861–JULY 1862

From the outbreak of war, it was ever more obvious, to ever more Americans, that the conflict would free ever more slaves. And whenever black freedom beckoned, black removal was sure to follow. How emancipation and colonization affected each other was a matter of furious debate among Republicans, whom secession had left with a majority that made differences within the party more important than those with the opposition. War propelled an old circular argument, about whether colonization hastened or slowed emancipation, from the realm of abstraction into that of reality. During the Thirty-Seventh Congress (1861–3), most Republicans not already committed to the Blair–Doolittle plan weighed up bills for black resettlement in terms of their immediate relationship to slave emancipation. As such, it would be simplistic to view wartime colonization as inherently radical *or* conservative.[110]

It is safe to say, however, that white Americans lagged behind their black compatriots in grasping the speed at which the struggle would become one of liberation. In a famous precedent of May 1861, US Major General Benjamin Butler refused to return three slaves who had escaped to Union lines at Fort Monroe, Virginia, claiming that their masters had forfeited them through rebellion. At such an early juncture, the army's material provisions for the "contrabands," as Unionists dubbed the refugees, were no better than its legal ones. In mid-1861, there was just one agency – country, rather – that might solve the problem at a stroke. "I am in favor of sending them straight to Hayti," now-Postmaster General Montgomery Blair wrote Butler. "Congress could

---

[109] Ibid., 1:102.
[110] "Speech of General Jim Lane," *Douglass' Monthly*, December 1861; M. F. Conway to F. P. Blair, Sr., November 28, 1861, BL.

afterwards adjust the matter either by paying for them or confiscating them."[111] The expediency of the Haitian Emigration Bureau would earn its director, James Redpath, easy audiences in Washington through mid-1862, with Doolittle and Lincoln both willing to let him recruit from Union footholds within the Confederacy.[112] In a portent of a common diplomatic concern, however, Port-au-Prince itself worried about entanglement with the Confederate government, now located at Richmond, over accepting what amounted to stolen property in people.[113]

Preparation: Lincoln's First Annual Message

While Congress retroactively approved the logic of "contraband" status in its (First) Confiscation Act of August 1861, the president set the agenda in his annual message that December. Reviewing the black refugee crisis, and prophesying that the loyal slave states of Delaware, Kentucky, Maryland, and Missouri would emancipate their own slaves, Lincoln asked lawmakers to provide for colonization and to extend their offer to all free black Americans. "To carry out the plan may involve the acquiring of territory," he admitted, citing the Louisiana Purchase as a precedent. Lincoln also recommended that the federal government recognize Haiti and Liberia, but left the decision to congressmen, asking them to appropriate money for a chargé d'affaires to each government.[114] Some commentators thought the two proposals connected, but Postmaster General Blair and Secretary of State William Seward, the former a supporter of colonization and the latter an opponent, would each claim credit for Lincoln's appeal for recognition.[115] Although the Haitian Emigration Bureau and American Colonization Society took the president's message as a signal to lobby lawmakers, congressmen needed no encouragement.[116] Both defenders and detractors of the two black governments would see the diplomatic revolution as the acknowledgment of Haiti; they feted, or feared, Liberia rather less.[117]

---

[111] M. Blair to B. F. Butler, June 8, 1861, in Jessie A. Marshall, ed., *Private and Official Correspondence of Gen. Benjamin F. Butler* (Norwood, MA, 1917), 1:130.
[112] Redpath to V. Plésance, April 29, 1862, James Redpath Correspondence, NYPL.
[113] Redpath to J. Jay, September 9, 1861, Jay Family Papers, Columbia University.
[114] "Annual Message to Congress," December 3, 1861, *CWAL*, 5:39, 48.
[115] "Army Correspondence," *WAA*, December 21, 1861; F. P. Blair, Sr., to Andrew, March 11, 1862, Andrew Papers; Seward, *Seward at Washington*, 22.
[116] *CG* 37 Cong., 2 Sess., 18–19 (December 5, 1861).   [117] Ibid., 1806 (April 24, 1862).

Diplomatic recognition aside, politicians were unsure whether to treat colonization as a foreign or a domestic policy. Either designation raised its own problems. But from December 1861 to July 1862, bills touching on colonization inevitably wended their way across the snare-ridden terrain of confiscation, a measure that forced Republicans to confront each other over the rightful limits of seizure.[118] Lyman Trumbull, who chaired the Senate Committee on the Judiciary, wasted no time in introducing the more stringent confiscation bill that the public already demanded, and made sure to include a colonization clause.[119] Yet the policy came before other committees, too. James Harlan of Iowa offered a bill authorizing Lincoln to acquire any needful territory, which went to Charles Sumner's Senate Committee on Foreign Relations.[120] James Doolittle produced a bill of his own, "for the collection of direct taxes in insurrectionary districts," which would sell rebel-owned land and place the proceeds in a frozen account. The southern states could thaw those funds, one-third of which would be reserved for colonizing their black residents, once they had again sworn loyalty to the Union. The bill covered so many points that Doolittle confessed that at least three committees might lay claim to it.[121]

Meanwhile, in the House, John Gurley of Ohio offered his own confiscation bill in December 1861 after consulting Lincoln; it would transport slaves to Florida and apprentice them to loyal masters.[122] Gurley steered the bill toward the Committee on Military Affairs, chaired by Frank Blair.[123] "He may change it somewhat, leaving the place of colonization open," thought Gurley.[124] In fact, by January 1862, Blair had commandeered the House confiscation bill, which echoed Doolittle's by funding resettlement with taxes on rebel-owned land.[125] Several abolitionists now admitted misgivings about the incipient legislation. "There was great merit in the plan submitted by Mr. Blair a few years ago," Gerrit Smith

---

[118] Patricia M. L. Lucie, "Confiscation: Constitutional Crossroads," *Civil War History* 23 (1977), 307–21; John Syrett, *The Civil War Confiscation Acts: Failing to Reconstruct the South* (New York, 2005), 20–1.

[119] CG 37 Cong., 2 Sess., 25–6 (December 5, 1861).   [120] Ibid., 36 (December 10, 1861).

[121] Ibid., 125 (December 18, 1861).

[122] William H. Smith, *A Political History of Slavery* (New York, 1903), 2:64; A Bill to Confiscate the Property of Rebels (December 9, 1861), U.S. House Records, RG233/37A-B1/HR121, NARA.

[123] CG 37 Cong., 2 Sess., 35–6 (December 10, 1861).

[124] J. A. Gurley to R. Carter, December 10, 1861, Letters to Robert Carter, Harvard.

[125] A Bill to Enforce the Collection of the Direct and Other Taxes (January 15, 1862), RG233/37A-B1/HR217, NARA.

chided Gurley. "It contemplated, if I recollect, no less than full civil and political rights for the colonists."[126] One of Trumbull's correspondents congratulated him on the confiscation clauses of his own bill, which were a "bold step forward," but decried those on colonization as a "wedge for dividing the anti-slavery sentiment of the country."[127] Such disquiet also permeated Congress itself. "Mr. Thad Stevens [of Pennsylvania] stumped it up to Frank (who now sits on the Democratic side) – said bitterly – 'you have deserted the Republican Party,'" reported Lizzie Blair Lee to her husband. "'Well says Frank if so – I go with the majority … who vowed with me to support the Constitution Union about which we care more than the niggers.'"[128] Frank Blair was perplexed that Republicans accused him of conservatism when they had so recently praised his radicalism. But he did know the reason, as he told one New York Republican: "colonization is the only thing in regard to slavery which will divide us."[129] Blair's divergence from his erstwhile allies or, as he would see it, their divergence from him reached its bitter climax two years later.

Over the winter of 1861–2, while confiscation and colonization worked their inextricable way through committee, President Lincoln proselytized for two beliefs that he had affirmed in his annual message. One was gradual emancipation, to be undertaken by the border states, and the other was compensation to the slaveowners for the same, to be underwritten by the federal government. He had identified Delaware, with fewer than 2,000 slaves, as the obvious starting point for a movement that could forever separate the loyal South from the disloyal. In November 1861, he met the First State's Representative George Fisher and handed him an emancipation bill for Dover to debate, but by February 1862, Lincoln could see that his disciple had proved no fisher of assemblymen.[130] In March, an undaunted president advised Congress to pass a joint resolution to compensate any state that adopted gradual emancipation.[131] Despite Montgomery Blair's warning that "the great

[126] "Gerrit Smith to John A. Gurley," *Liberator*, January 3, 1862.
[127] W. G. Snethen to Trumbull, December 8, 1861, Trumbull Correspondence.
[128] E. B. Lee to S. P. Lee, December 15, 1861, in Virginia Jean Laas, ed., *Wartime Washington: The Civil War Letters of Elizabeth Blair Lee* (Urbana, 1991), 91.
[129] F. P. Blair, Jr., to I. Sherman, January 16, 1862, Isaac Sherman Collection, Huntington Library.
[130] Patience Essah, *A House Divided: Slavery and Emancipation in Delaware, 1638–1865* (Charlottesville, 1996), 162.
[131] "Message to Congress," March 6, 1862, *CWAL*, 5:144–6.

objection to emancipation in [Delaware] was that the free negroes would remain," Lincoln did not mention colonization on this occasion.[132] His omission mystified the Senate, where John Sherman, an Ohio Republican, worried about departing from Lincoln's exact brief, lest doing so somehow infringe states' rights. Doolittle countered that colonization must have been implicit in Lincoln's message, since the states would infringe *federal* rights if they assumed diplomatic powers to expatriate their black inhabitants.[133] But colonization caused its first standoff not over confiscation or gradualism but over immediate abolition in a place under the Capitol's undisputed remit: Washington, DC.[134]

Abolition: The District of Columbia

In December 1861, Henry Wilson had introduced what would become the District of Columbia Compensated Emancipation Act, which resurfaced in the Senate in March 1862. From then on, debates over colonization fell largely to the upper house, and those over confiscation to the lower. A Kentucky Unionist, Senator Garrett Davis, set the tone by adding a $100,000 appropriation to the bill for colonizing those who would be emancipated. Doolittle spotted the lack of voluntarism in Davis's terse wording, and Davis proudly admitted it. "I am better acquainted with negro nature than the honorable Senator from Wisconsin, [who will] never find one slave in a hundred that will consent," explained Davis.[135] A kindred spirit, the Delaware Democrat Willard Saulsbury, moved an amendment of his own to scatter Washington's freedpeople over the free states.[136]

The Senate's leading colonizationist, James Doolittle, had to perform a balancing act between the predictable prejudices of senators from the loyal South and the disappointing dissension of his colleagues from the North. An abolitionist, John Hale of New Hampshire, scorned the logistics of mass resettlement, driving Doolittle to the Senate blackboard, where he drew up charts attributing the certain success of colonization to slated decreases in the black population.[137] For his part, James Harlan shrugged at the dangers of "amalgamation," arguing that Washington's

---

[132] M. Blair to Lincoln, March 5, 1862, AL.
[133] CG 37 Cong., 2 Sess., 1371 (March 26, 1862).
[134] Michael J. Kurtz, "Emancipation in the Federal City," *Civil War History* 24 (1978), 250.
[135] CG 37 Cong., 2 Sess., 1191–2 (March 12, 1862).   [136] Ibid., 1356 (March 25, 1862).
[137] Ibid., 1319 (March 21, 1862), and Appendix, 95 (April 11, 1862).

3,000 slaves would remain in domestic service, "in the bosom of the families of this metropolis."[138] From the Republican Party's other wing, one of Abraham Lincoln's Illinois friends, Orville Browning, even doubted that "while the races do continue together, that it is not better ... in the relation of master and slave."[139] On March 24, Doolittle faced two crucial votes in the Senate. He won the first, 23-16, but lost the second on a 19-19 tie. First, he succeeded in amending Garrett Davis's own amendment, with the effect of returning colonization to a voluntary basis. Concerned, for diametric reasons, about the overall credibility of the colonization clause, Davis himself voted for the change, while Hale, Sumner, and Wilson voted against it. Not even voluntarism, however, could save the final version of the clause from the ensuing tie, which the vice president (and president of the Senate), Hannibal Hamlin of Maine, broke in the negative.[140]

The colonization clause received a second chance, however, when credible reports began to circulate that President Lincoln would veto any emancipation bill without one. "Although the proposition of the Senator from Wisconsin was voted down ... I yet hope that he will see that that provision is ingrafted," announced Sherman, leader of the senatorial about-face.[141] Doolittle, who magnanimously replied that colleagues must have confused his amendment with Davis's, got to rerun the vote, which went 27-10 in his favor. The bill itself passed 29-14.[142] A signally unchastened Doolittle described the triumph of the "life giving policy" in an ecstatic letter home.[143] In the House, the bill passed with less fanfare, though Frank Blair undermined Doolittle by declaring that "compulsory colonization is [not] necessary ... but neither do I regard it with any abhorrence."[144] (In an open letter that fall, Blair would deny that he had ever supported coercion, claiming that his "votes and speeches in Congress give the lie to this statement.")[145] Despite his own misgivings about the District Emancipation Act, which had not, after all, solicited local slaveholders' consent or adhered to gradualism, Lincoln appended his signature. "I am gratified that the two principles of compensation, and colonization, are both recognized," he told Congress.[146] One black

---

[138] *CG* 37 Cong., 2 Sess., 1357 (March 25, 1862).   [139] Ibid., 1520 (April 3, 1862).
[140] Ibid., 1333–4 (March 24, 1862).   [141] Ibid., 1492 (April 2, 1862).
[142] Ibid., 1522–3 (April 3, 1862).
[143] J. R. Doolittle to M. Doolittle, April 4, 1862, Doolittle Papers.
[144] *CG* 37 Cong., 2 Sess., 1634 (April 11, 1862).
[145] "Hon. F. P. Blair to His Constituents," *New York Times*, October 18, 1862.
[146] "Message to Congress," April 16, 1862, *CWAL*, 5:192.

commentator remarked how, after decades of antagonism, immediatists and colonizationists had been vindicated in the same law.[147]

In April 1862, then, the United States formally adopted African American colonization for the first time. It did so over less than seventy square miles of its domains, but, per the Act, it did include all 15,000 black inhabitants of the District of Columbia, not just its 3,000 slaves. With a colonization fund of $100,000 at $100 per head, it could resettle 1,000 of them.[148] "You must know that as emancipation progresses this infernal scheme, expatriation, dies," wrote one James Gloucester to the *Weekly Anglo-African.* He could not have been more wrong. The capital now attracted even more speculators, whom Gloucester had derided as those "so very benevolent gentlemen ... that have been hanging around Congress this winter pushing their very benevolent schemes." For the new law not only created a fund for the putative emigrants, but left their destination wide open.[149]

For one agency, being able to canvass the District of Columbia provided the only reason not to suspend its operations altogether. The ACS had spent its entire life hoping to make common cause with the federal government (and, at times, doing so), only to hesitate now that unprecedented opportunities presented themselves. "There is a school of party politicians, who would be glad to drag us into their scheme of forcible expulsion," suspected Joseph Tracy, overestimating Africa's appeal to the likes of Frank Blair.[150] In May 1862, recalling years of legal wrangles in southern courts over manumittees, the society's executive committee ruled that contrabands did not count as the free people of color specified in its constitution.[151] For the rest of the war, the ACS would not change its stance on escapees from Confederate slavery. True to the split sovereignty on which the organization was based, such forbearance at the center could not prevent independent initiatives by the state societies, or by Liberia itself, which could negotiate directly with the United States – should the United States deign to recognize it.[152]

---

[147] "Sketches from Washington," *Christian Recorder,* April 26, 1862.
[148] An Act for the Release of Certain Persons Held to Service or Labor in the District of Columbia (April 16, 1862), 12 Stat. 378.
[149] "Washington – Alexandria – Colonization," *WAA,* April 19, 1862.
[150] J. Tracy to W. Coppinger, March 15, 1862, reel 236, ACS.
[151] Entry, May 9, 1862, Journal of the Executive Committee, reel 292, ACS.
[152] Sebastian N. Page, "The American Colonization Society and the Civil War," in Beverly C. Tomek and Matthew J. Hetrick, eds., *New Directions in the Study of African American Recolonization* (Gainesville, 2017), 211.

Recognition: Haiti and Liberia

At such a propitious time, Monrovia and Port-au-Prince made sure to send agents to Washington, who might not only promote emigration, but also mold any recognition law in ways favorable to that end. While Haiti already had a local operative in James Redpath, Liberia had taken Lincoln's first annual message as a signal to appoint three black commissioners: Edward Wilmot Blyden, J. D. Johnson, and Alexander Crummell, the last of whom had been in the United States on unrelated business since early 1861.[153] A handful of white Americans, office-seekers hoping to secure the impending vacancies in the foreign service, also offered to treat colonization as part of the resultant posts' brief.[154] Yet anything touching on diplomacy had first to go through the good offices of Charles Sumner, chairman of the Senate Committee on Foreign Relations, who was as keen to decouple colonization and recognition as he was to ensure that Liberia and Haiti were acknowledged in the same bill.[155] Six weeks of conflict in committee with Garrett Davis and James Doolittle, who had each tried to overlay recognition with resettlement, had persuaded Sumner that he should pause before submitting any bill to Congress. By late April, he was confident that "the Colonization question and the social question have both been discussed on the District Bill, thus clearing the way for the Hayti Bill on its own exclusive merits."[156] It was time to expose recognition to the taunts of the policy's inevitable opponents in Congress.

Although Sumner had successfully circumvented the prejudices of the Senate, he could not legislate for the House, where brief but lowbrow debate ensued. As the ACS had long predicted, the specter of black diplomats loomed large. "How fine it will look, after emancipating the slaves in this District, to welcome here at the White House an African, full-blooded, all gilded and belaced," mocked a notorious Ohio Democrat, Samuel "Sunset" Cox.[157] Yet one of the bill's supporters managed to rise above the prejudices of his own section. "The question before us seems to me to be simply one of fact. Is Liberia a nation?" asked

[153] Wilson Jeremiah Moses, *Alexander Crummell: A Study of Civilization and Discontent* (Amherst, 1992), 134–45; "Intelligence from Liberia," *WAA*, April 5, 1862.
[154] C. V. Dyer to Trumbull, January 16, 1862, Trumbull Correspondence; H. R. Smith to Chase, January 29, 1862, Salmon P. Chase Papers, LC.
[155] Tracy to J. H. B. Latrobe, January 15, 1862, reel 236, ACS.
[156] Sumner to Andrew, April 22, 1862, in Beverly Wilson Palmer, ed., *The Selected Letters of Charles Sumner* (Boston, 1990), 2:109.
[157] *CG* 37 Cong., 2 Sess., 2503 (June 2, 1862).

a Tennessee Unionist, Horace Maynard. Another southerner was uneasy, though. "I have always been ... [a] supporter of the Colonization Society," explained now-Representative John Crittenden, "but can I not be permitted to feel this kindness ... without being required to acknowledge [Liberians] as our equals?" Debate moved to the rank of the impending diplomats, which would determine the degree of ceremony accorded them, but Cox lost an amendment to demote the slated commissioners to consuls general. The House then passed the bill, 86-37.[158]

Thus began the scramble for posts that the White House itself had accepted should not be set at ministerial rank.[159] For their part, the American Colonization Society and Haitian Emigration Bureau aspired to Monrovia and Port-au-Prince's own vacancies in Washington more than the US missions to those capitals. Diplomatic norms permitted governments to appoint foreign nationals to represent them, and more readily than they allowed those governments to send bona fide citizens whose color would offend the receiving state.[160] "Geffrard would never send any one to Washington who could be told from a white man," thought a US agent in Port-au-Prince, Seth Webb, Jr.[161] It "was never the intention of the Liberian government" to send a black diplomat to Washington, concurred the US agent in Monrovia, John Seys.[162] But no commentator predicted just how far patronage, not expertise, would drive the White House's appointments – or how little the problem of prejudice would obstruct their opposite numbers.[163] To Liberia, Lincoln sent Abraham Hanson of Wisconsin, at Doolittle's behest, and to Haiti, Benjamin Whidden of New Hampshire, at Hale's.[164] *From* Liberia, which already had friends enough in Washington, came an eventual commission for the New York colonizationist, John Pinney, and from Haiti came Fabre Geffrard's aide-de-camp, the light-skinned Ernest Roumain.[165] "You can tell the President of Haiti that I shan't tear my shirt if he does send a nigger here," Lincoln had assured Redpath, who had self-

[158] Ibid., 2533–6 (June 3, 1862).   [159] McLain to J. Seys, June 12, 1862, reel 203, ACS.
[160] McLain to J. Hall, May 3, 1862, ibid.
[161] S. Webb, Jr., to F. W. Bird, January 14, 1862, Francis William Bird Papers, Harvard.
[162] Seys to C. B. Smith, December 23, 1861, H. Exec. Doc. 28, 37 Cong., 3 Sess. (1863), 19.
[163] McLain to Seys, June 12, 1862, reel 203, ACS.
[164] Doolittle to W. H. Seward, June 24, 1862, reel 70, WHS; J. Leavitt to J. R. Giddings, June 26, 1862, Joshua R. Giddings Papers, Ohio Historical Society.
[165] "Arrival of the Haytian Minister," *New York Times*, February 18, 1863.

interestedly hoped to hear the opposite.[166] Although whites' racial anxieties had long delayed recognition, it was the substance and not the semantics of Lincoln's sentiments that now settled the question.

Legislation: The Direct Taxes and Second Confiscation Acts

In June 1862, the Direct Taxes Act, which ultimately assigned one-fourth (rather than one-third) of rebel land-sale revenues to colonization, passed virtually unnoticed.[167] With the second session of the Thirty-Seventh Congress ending in July, however, the clock ticked for two items of business: compensation, for the loyal South, and confiscation, for the disloyal.

Confiscation unleashed a storm over Capitol Hill, as politicians disputed the legal limits of forfeiture, the rightful redistribution of confiscated land, and the needful provisions for the freedpeople. Inevitably, they also asked where former slaves might *go*, since few congressmen believed that the freedpeople would win acceptance from their former masters.[168] Colonization was the House's all too predictable response to several of the confiscation bill's many deficiencies: if Frank Blair spoke up for resettlement because he thought that the states would react by passing further black laws (which he deemed their right), Rhode Island's William Sheffield feared that the contrabands' newfound freedom would come to an untimely end unless they were placed beyond slaveholders' reach.[169] Congressmen from the upper South had a fair grievance against those from the lower North, whose black laws blocked a safety valve that could be replicated only with a credible colonization policy. "There is a very great aversion in the West – I know it to be so in my State – against having free negroes come among us," admitted Illinois's Senator Lyman Trumbull.[170] But other Republicans were dismayed at their colleagues' distraction from the task in hand: confiscation. "The prejudice of race lies at the bottom of all our difficulty," lamented Representative Samuel Blair, of Pennsylvania. "We cannot get an effectual confiscation of property . . . lest the black population of the North may be increased."[171] Meanwhile, Representative Thomas Eliot of Massachusetts disliked the ever-growing

---

[166] John McKivigan, *Forgotten Firebrand: James Redpath and the Making of Nineteenth-Century America* (Ithaca, 2008), 78.
[167] An Act for the Collection of Direct Taxes in Insurrectionary Districts (June 7, 1862), 12 Stat. 425.
[168] Syrett, *Confiscation Acts*, 30–1.
[169] CG 37 Cong., 2 Sess., Appendix, 170–2 (May 23, 1862).
[170] CG 37 Cong., 2 Sess., 944 (February 25, 1862).   [171] Ibid., 2301 (May 22, 1862).

scope of Frank Blair's colonization clause, which Eliot had assumed was meant only to help those forbidden, if freed, from remaining in their own state.[172] Yet congressmen could see that a confiscation bill would pass in one form or another, and its opponents, that they would do better to try tweaking its specifics.

In the Senate, legislators' final thoughts on colonization dominated a day of debates at the end of June. Late in the bill's development, Senator Morton Wilkinson of Minnesota proposed that Congress actually provide some funds to help African Americans emigrate, suggesting $500,000. His amendment proved strangely contentious: even as enthusiastic a colonizationist as Trumbull had asked to keep appropriations out of the bill, lest they disrupt its passage.[173] Colleagues warned Wilkinson not to jeopardize the legislation through editing a text thrashed out in joint committee, but he insisted that, since the army already had to feed the freedpeople, $500,000 to remove them would represent a saving.[174] Although Wilkinson's amendment failed, Senator James Harlan and Representative Thaddeus Stevens, who chaired the House Committee on Ways and Means, each asked the administration to recommend a sum for general colonization purposes, above and beyond the $100,000 earmarked for the District.[175] They received the answer of $500,000, just as Wilkinson had floated.[176] The House was so pressed for time that it approved the appropriation ahead of the law whose needs it addressed.[177] On July 17, 1862, the final day of its second session, the Thirty-Seventh Congress passed the Second Confiscation Act, which, among other things, allowed the president to resettle such freedpeople "as may be willing to emigrate, having first obtained the consent of the government of said country to their protection and settlement within the same, with all the rights and privileges of free-men."[178] Those words marked a moral victory for the principle of black consent, and a mortal defeat for the prospects of mass removal. Ironically, the Act guaranteed the freedpeople rights abroad that Republicans were not yet willing to grant them in the United States.[179]

[172] Ibid., 2357–8 (May 26), 2792 (June 18, 1862).   [173] Ibid., 1628 (April 11, 1862).
[174] Ibid., 2997 (June 28, 1862).   [175] J. Mitchell to Lincoln, July 1 and 3, 1862, AL.
[176] C. B. Smith to T. Stevens, July 3, 1862, Caleb Blood Smith and Charles William Spooner Papers, Huntington Library.
[177] CG 37 Cong., 2 Sess., 3328–9 (July 14, 1862).
[178] An Act to Suppress Insurrection, to Punish Treason and Rebellion, [and] to Seize and Confiscate the Property of Rebels (July 17, 1862), 12 Stat. 592.
[179] Herman Belz, *A New Birth of Freedom: The Republican Party and Freedmen's Rights, 1861 to 1866* (New York, 2000), 13.

Yet legislators did not manage to tie up all their loose ends. At the eleventh hour, James Doolittle had reported a bill from the Senate Committee on Foreign Relations for a bureau of migration (to superintend black resettlement), an idea that Eli Thayer, too, had proposed to Lincoln. (In Thayer's version, it would have organized white immigration as well as black emigration.)[180] But the sands of the hourglass buried that item.[181] The president had also launched a last-minute initiative of his own, summoning the representatives of the border states to beg them to accept compensated emancipation before the inevitable effects of war destroyed slavery anyway. "Room in South America for colonization, can be obtained cheaply, and in abundance," he promised.[182] The majority of the attendees rejected his overtures.[183] Should they change their minds, *while* they could, the House Select Committee on Emancipation submitted a report that proposed $20,000,000 for colonization. "The retention of the negro among us with half privileges is but a bitter mockery to him," claimed the committee, headed by an Indiana Republican, Representative Albert White, though heavily influenced by another of its members, Frank Blair.[184] A month later, Lincoln would express similar thoughts – and in unforgettable words.

EMANCIPATION, EMIGRATION, AND ENLISTMENT, AUGUST 1862–MARCH 1863

Delegations

For all the Democratic doom-mongering that had plagued the passage of the Second Confiscation Act, the law ended up a feeble hodgepodge of compromises, and one that Abraham Lincoln was reluctant to enforce.[185] Since he doubted the Act's validity, he was uneasy about colonizing the contrabands, at least until he, as the executive, had affirmed their freedom.[186] Military reversals in the eastern theater persuaded him, however, that it was time for the commander-in-chief of the US armed forces

---

[180] CG 37 Cong., 2 Sess., 3335 (July 15, 1862); E. Thayer to Lincoln, November 28, 1861, AL.

[181] CG 37 Cong., 2 Sess., 3401 (July 17, 1862).

[182] "Appeal to Border State Representatives to Favor Compensated Emancipation," July 12, 1862, CWAL, 5:318.

[183] C. A. Wickliffe et al. to Lincoln, July 14, 1862, AL.

[184] H. Rep. 148, 37 Cong., 2 Sess. (1862), 13–14.   [185] Syrett, *Confiscation Acts*, 55.

[186] R. R. Gurley to Coppinger, October 18, 1862, reel 235, ACS; AR 57 (1881), 69.

to attack the rebels by seizing their slaves. The president convened his cabinet in late July to announce that he had decided to issue an emancipation proclamation when the right moment came. He also proposed several military orders, one of which provided for black colonization in an unspecified tropical country. The attendees did not get around to discussing the order, and agreed to drop it.[187] Yet, in the inner sanctum of Lincoln's virtual bureau of migration (to which he had hitherto admitted few but the Blairs), other figures started to appear.

One was the secretary of the interior, Indianapolis lawyer Caleb Smith. Although Lincoln would charge him as late as September with executing the colonization laws, Smith's office had in fact administered them for some time.[188] The Department of the Interior had been the best fit for what Seward called "questions relating to Negroes" ever since President Buchanan tasked it with returning the recaptives to Africa.[189] The sickly Smith relied on his assistant secretary, a fellow Hoosier and lawyer, John Usher, who would succeed him at the New Year of 1863.[190] Yet colonization was uncharted territory for the federal government, and Lincoln was unlikely to refuse any offer of help exploring it, especially if that offer came from an old friend: the Rev. James Mitchell. Indeed, in the fall of 1861, Lincoln had secured the US agency at Gaboon for Mitchell's brother-in-law, George Savitz, who, however, rejected the appointment.[191] Seemingly present in Washington since, it was Mitchell who had fielded Thaddeus Stevens's request for a figure to put in the end-of-session appropriations bill. Mitchell's name also came up as possible director of Doolittle's mooted bureau of migration, where he would have operated under the Department of the Interior, to which Lincoln now appointed him in any case, with an ad hoc commission of early August 1862.[192] Duly empowered, the minister exhorted the capital's African

---

[187] Entries, July 21 and 22, 1862, in John Niven et al., eds., *The Salmon P. Chase Papers* (Kent, 1993–8), 1:349–51.

[188] Lincoln to Smith, September 12, 1862, *CWAL*, 5:418–19.

[189] W. Stuart to J. Russell, No. 203, September 4, 1862, in James J. Barnes and Patience P. Barnes, eds., *The American Civil War through British Eyes: Dispatches from British Diplomats* (Kent, 2003–5), 2:169.

[190] Elmo R. Richardson and Alan W. Farley, *John Palmer Usher: Lincoln's Secretary of the Interior* (Lawrence, 1960), 18–19.

[191] Lincoln to Seward, October 3, 1861, *CWAL*, 4:547; G. F. Savitz to Seward, November 9, 1861, Despatches from U.S. Consuls in Gaboon, RG59/T466/1, NARA II.

[192] W. T. Willey, letter of recommendation, July 16, 1862, Letters Received by the Commissioner of the Bureau of Refugees, Freedmen, and Abandoned Lands, RG105/M752/16, NARA; Lincoln, letter of commission, August 4, 1862, Miscellaneous

Americans to add the missing ingredient to Lincoln's emigration schemes: emigrants.

Since the spring, black northerners had taken growing umbrage at the colonizationists on Capitol Hill and the promoters who courted them. In April 1862, Senator Henry Lane, an Indiana Republican, presented the memorial of Joseph Williams and other African Americans, "for themselves, their relatives, and friends," praying for Congress's help in moving to Central America.[193] "The 'petition' does not represent the wishes of any intelligent community that we know of in this country," one Philadelphian warned Charles Sumner.[194] (Another memorial, submitted to Congress in January 1862 by James Whitfield and 240 other black residents of his new home, California, must qualify that claim.)[195] Sure enough, the petition of Joseph Williams, one of Redpath's former agents, had actually come from the pen of another white man, Ambrose Thompson, an entrepreneur who was lobbying the administration to send black Americans to his concession on the Isthmus of Chiriquí (Chapter 4).[196] Between the blandishments of James Redpath, Joseph Williams, Alexander Crummell, and J. D. Johnson, it would be a miracle, thought the ACS's William McLain, if the District's African Americans did "not come to think they are the most magnificent people in the world."[197] In fact, they thought themselves the most burdened, forever worrying that white politicians would scrutinize their responses for vicarious permission to deport up to 4,000,000 of their "fellow" African Americans.

In late July, the Social, Civil, and Statistical Association, a mutual aid society of the capital's most-educated black men, ordered Redpath and Johnson to leave town.[198] Two of them assaulted Johnson, who had

---

Contracts, Records Relating to the Suppression of the African Slave Trade and Negro Colonization, RG48/M160/8, NARA II.

[193] *CG* 37 Cong., 2 Sess., 1730–1 (April 21, 1862).

[194] J. Underdue to Sumner, April 22, 1862, Charles Sumner Papers, Harvard; J. C. Davis et al., *An Appeal from the Colored Men of Philadelphia* (Philadelphia, 1862), 8.

[195] Robert S. Levine and Ivy G. Wilson, eds., *The Works of James M. Whitfield: "America" and Other Writings by a Nineteenth-Century African American Poet* (Chapel Hill, 2011), 11–12; Joan R. Sherman, "James Monroe Whitfield, Poet and Emigrationist: A Voice of Protest and Despair," *Journal of Negro History* 57 (1972), 174–5; H. Misc. Doc. 31, 37 Cong., 2 Sess. (1862), 4.

[196] "Memorial Written for Joseph E. Williams," April 18, 1862, Richard Wigginton Thompson Papers, Rutherford B. Hayes Presidential Library and Museums.

[197] McLain to Coppinger, April 29, 1862, reel 203, ACS.

[198] McLain to Hall, July 30, 1862, ibid.

unwisely told an abolitionist, Indiana's Representative George Julian, that he would like to see the contrabands forcibly removed to Liberia.[199] With perfect timing, James Mitchell then arranged to speak to local black worthies at the AME Union Bethel Church in order to select a deputation to discuss colonization with Lincoln. Directed by the meeting to reject emigration and to refuse to speak for any other group, Edward Thomas and four other delegates came forward.[200]

On August 14, 1862, Mitchell ushered them into a room at the White House, where, rather than getting to engage in a dialogue, they heard a presidential monologue infamous to this day. "Without the institution of Slavery and the colored race as a basis, the war could not have an existence," Lincoln told his audience. "It is better for us both, therefore, to be separated." Reviewing the pros and cons of Liberia, Lincoln acknowledged that "you would rather remain within reach of the country of your nativity," and proceeded to advocate Chiriquí instead. In a figure hardly calculated to appease deportationists, he suggested that as few as twenty-five families might make a successful start on the isthmus.[201]

In fact, the president's address appeased nobody. The ACS was livid that Lincoln had, just moments earlier, met Joseph Jenkins Roberts, on tour in the United States, only then to damn Liberia with faint praise. It also groaned at seeing its old antagonist, James Mitchell, promoted to the highest councils of the nation.[202] Abolitionists were appalled that the president had chosen to blame the victims of racism rather its instigators, even as a wave of antiblack riots swept the lower North.[203] "Pray tell us, is our right to a home in this country less than your own, Mr. Lincoln?" demanded a black New Jerseyite.[204] "What will foreign nations, on whose good or ill will so much is supposed now to depend, think of this project?" worried Robert Purvis.[205] Global diplomats, already poised to

---

[199] "Important Meeting of the Colored People of Boston," *Liberator*, August 1, 1862; McLain to Gurley, August 4, 1862, reel 203, ACS.

[200] Kate Masur, "The African American Delegation to Abraham Lincoln: A Reappraisal," *Civil War History* 56 (2010), 128–30.

[201] "Address on Colonization to a Deputation of Negroes," August 14, 1862, CWAL, 5:370–5.

[202] McLain to Gurley, August 26, 1862, reel 93, ACS.

[203] V. Jacque Voegeli, *Free but Not Equal: The Midwest and the Negro during the Civil War* (Chicago, 1967), 34–5.

[204] "A Colored Man's Reply to President Lincoln on Colonization," *Liberator*, September 5, 1862.

[205] William Wells Brown, *The Black Man, His Antecedents, His Genius, and His Achievements* (New York, 1863), 256.

recognize the Confederacy, indeed doubted the Union's purported anti-slavery, with the London *Times* mocking Lincoln's "scheme of philanthropic expatriation."[206] Meanwhile, the Union Bethel meeting watched aghast as Thomas betrayed his brief by heading out to recruit pioneers for the president's project.[207] Yet one influential white man had also changed his mind after thinking about what Lincoln had said: the Kansas Republican and abolitionist, Senator Samuel Pomeroy, who was enthralled by Lincoln's own thrall to colonization. Later that August, Pomeroy volunteered as expedition leader in order to tease out the emancipation proclamation that rumor had as sitting in Lincoln's desk drawer.[208] The president accepted Pomeroy's offer, saddling colonization with a second bureaucrat of unclear connection to the Department of the Interior.

Interpreting a favorable draw at the Battle of Antietam as a good enough omen, Abraham Lincoln convened the cabinet on September 22 and told it that he would now issue the Preliminary Emancipation Proclamation. The document would announce that, if the rebels did not surrender and return to the Union by January 1, 1863, all slaves behind their lines would be declared free. It would also promise to continue the colonization effort. According to Salmon Chase, the secretary of the treasury and one of three diarists within the cabinet, Seward persuaded Lincoln to specify that colonization would happen only "with the consent of the colonists, and the consent of the States in which colonies might be attempted."[209] The secretary of state's advice reflected complications emerging from the Chiriquí scheme, as well as the diplomatic implications of recent offers from Britain and the Netherlands to accept African Americans in their West Indian colonies (Chapter 5). Not two weeks after officially assigning colonization to the Department of the Interior, Lincoln was about to turn to the Department of State, Seward's dislike for the policy notwithstanding.[210]

Amendments

In two further meetings, of September 24 and 26, Lincoln asked the cabinet's opinion about reaching immigration treaties with amenable

[206] Blackett, "Lincoln and Colonization," 21.
[207] Masur, "African American Delegation," 135–9.
[208] A. S. Hill to S. H. Gay, August 25, 1862, Sydney Howard Gay Papers, Columbia University.
[209] Entry, September 22, 1862, in Niven, *Chase Papers*, 1:395.
[210] Jacob W. Schuckers, *The Life and Public Services of Salmon Portland Chase* (New York, 1874), 454n.

governments. Chase preferred "simple arrangements, under the legislation of Congress," to guarantee such privileges as host countries might offer settlers. Perceiving that the treaty-making process would slow colonization, Seward backed formal agreements, "but evidently did not think much of the wisdom of ... sending out of the country laborers needed here."[211] Another of Lincoln's former rivals and current colleagues, Attorney General Edward Bates, wrote a paper advocating tightly framed treaties with as many states as possible, but advised that blacks "should go as emigrants, not colonists."[212] In other words, the settlers should not expect to request US assistance once they had committed to a new nationality. The conversation then turned to coercion. According to the former Democrat and secretary of the navy, Connecticut's Gideon Welles, Postmaster General Blair was for "deportation" and Attorney General Bates for "compulsory deportation," while President Lincoln "objected unequivocally to compulsion." Lincoln ended the third and final meeting convinced, moreover, that colonization should proceed only by treaty.[213]

To put it another way, the administration had taken until the fall of 1862 to accept that resettling African Americans would require the consent of host polities. Before the year was out, it would prove all too adept at forgetting that epiphany. But on September 30, Seward sent a circular to his ministers to Britain, France, Denmark, and the Netherlands, laying out the terms on which the United States would seek treaties for black emigration to those powers' tropical American colonies.[214] Although he did not state as much, Seward's instructions would provide the template for all foreign proposals thereafter, including those tendered on behalf of Colombia, within whose borders the province of Chiriquí fell. Pending favorable responses, the White House considered its next move.

The stakes were high indeed: years later, George Julian, Gideon Welles, and Henry Wilson would each disclose his impression that Abraham Lincoln would never have issued the Preliminary Emancipation Proclamation had he known that colonization would fail.[215] As the

---

[211] Entry, September 24, 1862, in Niven, *Chase Papers*, 1:399.
[212] Entry, September 25, 1862, in Beale, *Diary of Bates*, 262–4.
[213] Entry, September 26, 1862, in Howard K. Beale, ed., *Diary of Gideon Welles, Secretary of the Navy under Lincoln and Johnson* (New York, 1960), 1:152.
[214] Seward to C. F. Adams et al., No. 360, September 30, 1862, PRFA 37 Cong., 3 Sess. (1862), 202–4.
[215] Allen Thorndike Rice, ed., *Reminiscences of Abraham Lincoln by Distinguished Men of His Time* (New York, 1886), 61–2; Gideon Welles, "Administration of Abraham

Chiriquí project ran into further problems, the ACS swooped to redirect the expedition, which comprised the legally free residents of the District and so could not incur litigation by any former owners. "'I am perfectly willing that these colored people should be sent to Liberia, provided they are willing to go,'" admitted Lincoln. "'But there's the rub. I cannot coerce them.'"[216] In late November, a clerk found the president in fatalistic mood: "what troubles him is to provide for the blacks – he still thinks that many of them will colonize."[217] James Mitchell, who hailed the treaty policy for placing colonization on a firmer footing, now decided to make common cause with John Pinney, whose New York auxiliary was more open than the parent ACS to recruiting from the black population at large.[218]

On December 1, 1862, Abraham Lincoln opened the final session of the Thirty-Seventh Congress with his second annual message. It was a confusing, closely argued affair, though it stopped short of the self-contradiction that some critics alleged.[219] The president outlined colonization's mixed fortunes to date, reporting that African Americans were unwilling to leave – and the Central American states, to take them. He then called for three amendments to the US Constitution, shoring up compensation, colonization, and gradual emancipation, which might, he suggested, be allowed to unfold until 1900. He proposed federal funds for *any* slave state, not just the loyal states, that passed a law at least initiating emancipation. Those Confederate states that promptly returned to the Union and accepted his offer, therefore, would exempt themselves from the working of the Emancipation Proclamation. The colonization scheme found Lincoln in similarly convoluted mode. "I cannot make it better known than it already is, that I strongly favor colonization," he reiterated. "And yet I wish to say there is an objection urged against free

Lincoln," *Galaxy* 24 (1877), 444; Henry Wilson, *History of the Rise and Fall of the Slave Power in America* (Boston, 1872–7), 3:381.

[216] Entry, October 23, 1862, in Donald MacLeod Diary, Virginia Museum of History and Culture.

[217] T. J. Barnett to S. L. M. Barlow, November 30, 1862, Samuel L. M. Barlow Papers, Huntington Library.

[218] James Mitchell, *Report on Colonization and Emigration* (Washington, DC, 1862), 27–8; CG 37 Cong., 3 Sess., 269 (January 12, 1863); Mitchell to M. Simpson, October 13, 1862, Matthew Simpson Papers, LC.

[219] Paludan, "Lincoln and Colonization," 30; Barry Schwartz, "The Emancipation Proclamation: Lincoln's Many Second Thoughts," *Society* 52 (2015), 594; Bjørn F. Stillion Southard, "Abraham Lincoln's Second Annual Message to Congress and Public Policy Advocacy for African Colonization," *Rhetoric and Public Affairs* 21 (2018), 389, 409.

colored persons remaining in the country, which is largely imaginary."[220] Lincoln proceeded to argue that freed African Americans would not swarm northward, though qualified that claim, too, by hinting that the free states might wish to pass further black laws.[221] His second annual message would be the last time that he mentioned colonization in public. But once he had called to write the policy into the very charter of the nation, what more could he say?[222]

While Lincoln angered abolitionists with his untimely reversion to the old Clay formula for emancipation, he confused just about everybody by invoking changes to the Constitution, which two-thirds of Congress and three-fourths of the states would have to ratify.[223] "It would probably require years.... In the meantime what becomes of the Emancipation Proclamation?" worried one editor.[224] In fact, the president meant to press ahead with the proclamation and colonization alike, since his scheme of gradual emancipation had represented an offer to the rebellious states to reenter the Union and preempt a worse outcome for slavery. "The operative part is the last paragraph, where the President announces and vindicates emancipation," Charles Sumner reassured a friend; the rest was "surplusage."[225] Behind the closed doors of the White House, a long-brewing conflict between the cabinet's preeminent egotists, William Seward and Salmon Chase, hindered the executive's own progress on colonization for much of December.[226]

Enlistment

On January 1, 1863, as scheduled, Abraham Lincoln issued the Emancipation Proclamation. Gone were the preliminary version's

[220] "Annual Message to Congress," December 1, 1862, *CWAL*, 5:520–1, 529–37.
[221] George M. Fredrickson, *Big Enough to Be Inconsistent: Abraham Lincoln Confronts Slavery and Race* (Cambridge, MA, 2008), 110.
[222] Kevin R. C. Gutzman, "Abraham Lincoln, Jeffersonian: The Colonization Chimera," in Brian R. Dirck, ed., *Lincoln Emancipated: The President and the Politics of Race* (DeKalb, 2007), 71.
[223] Entry, December 1, 1862, in Theodore Calvin Pease and James G. Randall, eds., *The Diary of Orville Hickman Browning* (Springfield, IL, 1925–33), 1:591; "Lincoln's Message," *Richmond Daily Enquirer*, December 8, 1862; H. L. Dawes to E. Dawes, December 2, 1862, Henry L. Dawes Papers, LC.
[224] "The President's Message," *New York Evangelist*, December 4, 1862.
[225] Sumner to E. L. Pierce, December 3, 1862, in Edward L. Pierce, *Memoir and Letters of Charles Sumner* (London, 1877–93), 4:113.
[226] "Washington, ca. 22 December 1862," in Michael Burlingame, ed., *Dispatches from Lincoln's White House: The Anonymous Civil War Journalism of Presidential Secretary William O. Stoddard* (Lincoln, 2002), 128.

references to compensation and colonization, which he had included only as a preview of his then-forthcoming annual message, and which could hereafter only weaken an edict premised on military necessity. Otherwise, the omission betokened nothing: "That statesman will be ... benevolent who begins now to ... solve the problem of an eventual exodus," wrote one of Lincoln's private secretaries in an anonymous article for the press.[227] The Emancipation Proclamation also announced that freed slaves would "be received into the armed service of the United States."[228] Historians have echoed abolitionists in treating black recruitment as an automatic death sentence for colonization: to ask the obvious question, why exile potential soldiers?[229] Yet scholars should not treat abstraction as attestation, or transgress into racial tokenism. For reasons of age, gender, physical condition, and proximity to US forces, only a minority of African Americans could ever be put in uniform – and even then, only for as long as war lasted.

In truth, few contemporaries saw emigration and enlistment as mutually exclusive. In December 1862, a Pennsylvania Republican, Representative John Hickman, floated an omnibus bill to raise 100 black regiments, provide race-blind education in the southern states, and establish a steamer line to Africa to remove black dependents on the United States. While the *Liberator* rued the last of Hickman's suggestions, the *Evening Bulletin* discerned that the first two betrayed a lame-duck abolitionist, "using the brief time remaining to him ... to 'out-Herod Herod' in the way of radicalism."[230] Moreover, a New York Republican, Representative Alexander Diven, tried to add a proviso to the eventual enlistment act (sponsored by Thaddeus Stevens) for the federal government to colonize black soldiers and their families once surplus to US requirements.[231] Even Lincoln's commissioner of colonization, James Mitchell, was willing to place African Americans in arms as well as on ships, preferring to delay the major resettlement effort to peacetime.[232]

Once the Thirty-Seventh Congress had ratified black enlistment, it faced one last item of racially charged business: bills for compensated

---

[227] "The Proclamation," in Michael Burlingame, ed., *With Lincoln in the White House: Letters, Memoranda, and Other Writings of John G. Nicolay* (Carbondale, 2000), 101.
[228] "Emancipation Proclamation," January 1, 1863, *CWAL*, 6:30.
[229] Foner, *Fiery Trial*, 244; Vorenberg, "Politics of Black Colonization," 43.
[230] "Congress," *Liberator*, December 26, 1862; "Hickman and Negro Regiments," San Francisco *Evening Bulletin*, January 10, 1863.
[231] *CG* 37 Cong., 3 Sess., 631 (January 30), 688–9 (February 2, 1863).
[232] Mitchell to Lincoln, July 1, 1862, AL.

emancipation, with colonization, in Maryland and Missouri. Introduced by Representative Francis Thomas, a Maryland Unionist, and Representative John Noell, a Missouri Democrat, Thomas's bill died for want of support from the rest of the Maryland delegation, but Noell's failed only when the House ran out of time to reconcile its version with the Senate's, introduced by another Missourian, John Henderson.[233] Colonization stalked the ultimately fruitless debates that Noell and Henderson initiated. "I am not willing to appropriate any money ... for the purpose of taking these people out of the country," announced a Maine Republican, Senator William Fessenden, in January 1863.[234] John Henderson was dismayed that his fellow senators now struck colonization from the bill, flouting the report of the House Select Committee on Emancipation.[235] Another Missouri Unionist, Senator Robert Wilson, doubted that his constituents would accept emancipation without colonization.[236] In the House, one of the state's Democrats, Representative Elijah Norton, accused Henderson himself of sabotaging the colonization clause, and questioned the legitimacy of the recent state elections that had decided for emancipation.[237] Conspicuous by his absence from the debate was Frank Blair, who had entered the army in 1862. Controversially, he had not relinquished his House seat to do so, though his support for colonization had almost cost him it anyway at the fall elections, St. Louis having become a hotbed of radical emancipationism.[238]

Bereft of Blair's presence on Capitol Hill, Lincoln and Mitchell conferred with Henderson instead, but to no avail: Congress expired in March, which thwarted the Missouri bill.[239] Nonetheless, the spring of 1863 revealed the green shoots of a viable colonization policy. The president could draw on appropriations totaling $600,000, a respectable sum in the mid-nineteenth century, especially for a task that Lincoln understood as the mere "commencement" of a self-sustaining migration.[240] With that money, he might colonize any rebel-owned slaves or

---

[233] William W. Freehling, "'Absurd' Issues and the Causes of the Civil War: Colonization as a Test Case," in his *The Reintegration of American History* (New York, 1994), 143; Walter B. Stevens, *Lincoln and Missouri* (Columbia, MO, 1916), 85.
[234] CG 37 Cong., 3 Sess., 589 (January 29, 1863).
[235] Ibid., 613–14 (January 30, 1863).   [236] Ibid., 780 (February 7, 1863).
[237] Ibid., Appendix, 150 (February 28, 1863).   [238] Parrish, *Frank Blair*, 147–53.
[239] Mitchell to Lincoln, March 5, 1863, William E. Barton Collection, University of Chicago.
[240] "Address on Colonization to a Deputation of Negroes," August 14, 1862, CWAL, 5:370–5.

black Washingtonians who chose to leave the United States. Naturally, the latter were closer to hand. In November 1862, and again in January 1863, Lincoln met with Chauncey Leonard, a local pastor who wished to investigate Liberia on behalf of his flock, happily issuing Leonard a draft on the fund.[241] Yet the colonization laws did not extend to the next nearest groups, the freepeople of the North and the slaves of the loyal South, even though Lincoln himself would have seen them all included.[242] While black voluntarism would always provide the limiting factor (as Lincoln himself acknowledged), he was still stung by legislators' tepid response to his second annual message, describing Montgomery Blair as the "only friend who supported him in his project."[243] Until other Republicans saw sense, the president would avoid further embarrassment by pursuing colonization on a need-to-know basis.

In October 1854, Lincoln had told a crowd at Peoria, Illinois, that he did not know how whites might right the wrong done slaves. "What next? Free them, and make them politically and socially, our equals? My own feelings will not admit of this; and if mine would, we well know that those of the great mass of white people will not."[244] In February 1863, Lincoln told a politician in Washington, DC, Representative William Cutler of Ohio, "that he was troubled to know what we should do with these people – Negroes – after peace came," conceding, "'whatever you and me may think on these matters peoples opinions were every thing.'"[245] The same fatalism that had always haunted Lincoln, that haunted *all* colonizationists, was as strong as ever. As the Emancipation Proclamation went into effect, black soldiers would, ideally, end up not only free from their masters, but triumphant in arms over them. Anyone who had ever feared for racial harmony after emancipation now had grounds for despair, even if – *especially* if – the Union emerged victorious.

---

[241] Magness, *Colonization after Emancipation*, 27; G. W. Samson to Gurley, November 1, 1862, reel 93, ACS.
[242] Mitchell to Willey, January 10, 1863, Waitman T. Willey Papers, West Virginia University.
[243] T. H. Hicks to M. Blair, April 9, 1863, box 72, BF.
[244] "Speech at Peoria, Illinois," October 16, 1854, *CWAL*, 2:256.
[245] Entry, February 9, 1863, in Allan G. Bogue, ed., "William Parker Cutler's Congressional Diary of 1862–63," *Civil War History* 33 (1987), 330.

As president of the United States, and commander-in-chief of its colonization campaign, Abraham Lincoln had another set of worries: the expeditions that he had spent so long planning kept collapsing. For, believe it or not, it turned out that he just could not trust private contractors.

4

Resettlement in Latin America, to 1864

Over the winter of 1860–1, while compromisers such as Senator John Crittenden contemplated continuing to permit slavery in the southern territories of the United States, President-Elect Abraham Lincoln issued a stark warning. "The Missouri [Compromise] line extended ... would lose us everything we gained by the election," he told Thurlow Weed, an intimate of William Seward. "Filibustering for all South of us, and making slave states of it, would follow."[1] In any case, the Crittenden Compromise failed, and the sections of the late Union directed their martial energies at each other instead.

Yet Lincoln's prediction, of resurgent schemes for settling blacks throughout the Americas, came true – or, at least, half-true. For such projects envisioned African Americans, not Africans, and as freepeople, not slaves. From the Rio Grande to Tierra del Fuego, only Uruguay, Paraguay, and Chile would elude proposals, whether floated by consuls, caudillos, or concessionaires, for colonizing black Americans.[2] Away from the contiguous continent, only the Spanish colonies of Cuba and Puerto Rico, among the major Caribbean polities, failed to inspire such moves, while plans for African American immigration emanated from several of the minor islands, too.

---

[1] A. Lincoln to T. Weed, December 17, 1860, CWAL, 4:154.
[2] For the more abortive projects, which this book does not cover, see "South America," New York Times, November 21, 1863 (Argentina); "Sud America," Gaceta del Salvador, October 1, 1862, and "News from Washington," New York Times, January 5, 1863 (Bolivia); A. P. Hovey to W. H. Seward, No. 40, November 28, 1866, PRFA 39 Cong., 2 Sess. (1867), 2:653 (Peru); and E. D. Culver to Seward, No. 18, March 25, 1863, Despatches from U.S. Ministers to Venezuela, RG59/M79/14, NARA II (Venezuela).

Unlike the filibusterers, US politicians were in no position to impose themselves on the Americas, and their Confederate counterparts even less so.[3] Unionists lacked the resources to fight additional wars, feared driving neutrals into the arms of the Confederacy, and viewed the consent of the policy's foreign beneficiaries as essential (even if *who* could offer that consent would prove a complicated matter). Moreover, the indispensable Department of State was headed by William Seward, an opponent of colonization. Without ever disobeying a direct order from Lincoln, Seward repeatedly stalled, stifled, and sabotaged the policy.[4]

Yet for many would-be host countries, the prospect of African American resettlement was intriguing, even inviting. From Mexico southward, there was no government that did not wish to increase its population, sometimes at the cost of generous concessions to promoters of immigration, in order to exploit its own resources and better defend itself against its enemies. Following the wars of independence from France, Spain, and Portugal, there was also no state that had not abolished slavery and at least ended up with a republican form of government – with the important exception, in both respects, of the Empire of Brazil (1822–89), which would seal its own fate in 1888 by forcing emancipation on the slaveholders.[5] But there was also no state in Latin America that preferred (poorer) African Americans to (richer) Europeans, dark-skinned to light-skinned immigrants (save Haiti, in certain phases of its unending cycle of colorism), or concessions that arrogated host-state sovereignty to those that did not.[6] Moreover, few of the Latin American republics had escaped periods of instability, usually a cycle of constitutional government, followed by dictatorship, followed by civil war. Even outside Brazil, Latin America had its homegrown monarchists, who would have readily made common cause with Europeans to end the republican experiment in the only hemisphere where it had survived counterrevolution.[7] Within these political, cultural, and demographic

---

[3] Patrick J. Kelly, "The Cat's-Paw: Confederate Ambitions in Latin America," in Don H. Doyle, ed., *American Civil Wars: The United States, Latin America, Europe, and the Crisis of the 1860s* (Chapel Hill, 2017), 59–60.

[4] Sebastian N. Page, "'A Knife Sharp Enough to Divide Us': William H. Seward, Abraham Lincoln, and Black Colonization," *Diplomatic History* 41 (2017), 366.

[5] Don H. Doyle, *The Cause of All Nations: An International History of the American Civil War* (New York, 2014), 88–9.

[6] Magnus Mörner, *Adventurers and Proletarians: The Story of Migrants in Latin America* (Pittsburgh, 1985), 20–6; José C. Moya, "A Continent of Immigrants: Postcolonial Shifts in the Western Hemisphere," *Hispanic American Historical Review* 86 (2006), 3.

[7] Doyle, *Cause of All Nations*, 93–4.

parameters lay the multilateral debate about the terms on which African Americans might acquire the "tropical homesteads" beloved of Republican colonizationists.[8]

While host governments, labor recruiters, and third parties could request, revise, or resist black resettlement schemes, it was Americans who, given the mooted settlers' provenance, set the agenda. Among those "United Statians," however, diplomats, politicians, and investors often disagreed, even as the Lincoln administration reflexively turned to contractors rather than approaching foreign states through its own ministers. Partly, the White House adhered to the old Jacksonian aversion to the direct involvement of government in matters of money, which was typical of wartime procurement practices at home as well as abroad. Yet its deference to contractors also reflected instability in several countries other than the United States, which allowed concessionaires to claim (often hotly disputed) official permission to cede certain territories and privileges.[9]

Colonization projects in Latin America can be considered under four rubrics – artificial ones, of course, but useful all the same. The first was using black colonists to counter military interventions by those European empires that saw an opportunity in the prostration of the United States, namely, France, which invaded Mexico, and Spain, which annexed the Dominican Republic. The second was using colonists to toil on underworked plantations, the basis of one plan for Brazil and another two for Ecuador. The third was using colonists to open up the transit routes of the Central American isthmus, the outstanding appeal of the Chiriquí site, in Panama, then an outlying province of Colombia. The fourth, which implicitly admitted the failure of the first three, was sending colonists to whichever country would accept them. By 1863, that meant Haiti, though under the auspices of the US government this time, not those of the Haitian Emigration Bureau. That expedition, to one of Haiti's satellite islands, the Île à Vache, confirmed the catastrophe, portended by the earlier projects, of when one sovereign state interacts with another through intermediaries.

---

[8] Thomas D. Schoonover, "Misconstrued Mission: Expansionism and Black Colonization in Mexico and Central America," *Pacific Historical Review* 49 (1980), 617–20.
[9] Sharon Hartman Strom, "Labor, Race, and Colonization: Imagining a Post-Slavery World in the Americas," in Steven Mintz and John Stauffer, eds., *The Problem of Evil: Slavery, Freedom, and the Ambiguities of American Reform* (Amherst, 2007), 264.

REPELLING INTERVENTION: MEXICO AND THE
DOMINICAN REPUBLIC

Although both were monarchies, the France of Napoleon III (1852–70) and the Spain of Isabella II (1833–68) each made sure to secure ostensibly democratic mandates from conservative elements in Mexico and the Dominican Republic to annex those states. But specious plebiscites could not mask the scale of the pair's ambitions: while Spain hoped to restore its old colonies, and proceeded to provoke war with Peru and Chile once it had annexed the Dominican Republic, France planned a new empire that would impose a cordon of "Latin" influence against the "Anglo-Saxon" expansionism of the United States.[10] Indeed, it was in this era that the catchall term "Latin America" first became common in describing what was really Ibero-America, except for Haiti.[11]

Having exploited the weakness of the United States, Napoleon and Isabella would each suffer reverses in their American adventures, and so contribute to their own fall a few years later. And having hoped that a Spanish revival in the Caribbean would better protect slavery in its colonies of Cuba and Puerto Rico (especially from filibusters), Madrid would actually hasten abolition by driving both islands to rebellion from 1868. Still, in 1861, few observers could have foreseen that the French and Spanish ventures would backfire so badly. After all, the war-ravaged United States could spare few resources to project its power beyond its own borders – except, perhaps, for its black population.

Mexico

The slaves of the US Southwest had long enjoyed an obvious refuge: Mexico, immediately to the south, and, until the massive transfer of territory confirmed in the Treaty of Guadalupe Hidalgo (1848), to the west as well.

For their part, Mexican politicians had, since the 1830s, assessed the benefits and drawbacks of African American immigration for its likely

---

[10] Doyle, "The Atlantic World and the Crisis of the 1860s," in his *American Civil Wars*, 6–10.

[11] Nicholas Guyatt, "Tocqueville's Prophecy: The United States and the Caribbean, 1850–1871," in Jörg Nagler et al., eds., *The Transnational Significance of the American Civil War* (New York, 2016), 215; José C. Moya, ed., *The Oxford Handbook of Latin American History* (Oxford, 2010), 5.

effect on their attempts to populate the sparse northern provinces. They had already invited white Americans to the frontier state of Texas, who had accepted their offer, only to import slaves and secessionism – a factor in Mexico City's 1829 decree abolishing slavery. And if Mexico accepted fugitive bondspeople, it might invite incursions by US expeditions sent to reclaim them. But in 1831, a senator, Francisco Manuel Sánchez de Tagle, argued that black refugees would form a barrier against invasion, since they would always fight for freedom under Mexico rather than slavery under the United States. For the same reason, abolitionists also took an interest in black resettlement across the border, notably, Benjamin Lundy, a colonizationist critical of the Liberia project, who made three journeys to Texas, in 1830–1, 1833–4, and 1834–5. Delegates to Philadelphia's 1833 national black convention also considered emigration to Mexico, which prompted the consul at New Orleans, Pizarro Martínez, to warn Mexico City that free African Americans in Texas would attract white settlers keen to exploit their labor.[12]

A change in Mexico's government in 1833 tipped the balance toward the liberal approach to immigration. "If [African Americans] would like to come, we will offer them land for cultivation ... under the obligation [that they] obey the laws of the country," Mexico's vice president announced to its chargé in the United States.[13] On his later travels, Lundy encountered several expatriates who had accepted Mexico's offer, including Henry Powell, "a very intelligent and respectable coloured man, who migrated hither from Louisiana." Lundy was pleased to learn from one Colonel Almonte that Mexico meant to impose emancipation on white settlers in Texas, who had previously secured an exemption from the 1829 abolition act. "No person from a foreign country will be permitted to touch a slave who escapes and takes refuge in Mexico," noted Lundy, who planned a fugitive settlement that he compared to a second Canada. While on the road, he heard of James Birney's (original) repudiation of the ACS, hailing that "noble" act, but had the perspicacity to forecast opposition from those who might equate his own project with African colonization. It was a moot point. No sooner had the state of Tamaulipas granted him land than the American colonists in Texas rose

---

[12] Steven Hahn, *A Nation without Borders: The United States and Its World in an Age of Civil Wars, 1830–1910* (New York, 2016), 44–5; Rosalie Schwartz, *Across the Rio to Freedom: U.S. Negroes in Mexico* (El Paso, 1975), 18–21.

[13] Schwartz, *Across the Rio*, 21–2.

(1835–6), wrested that region from Mexican control, and discredited all American-run immigration schemes.[14]

Yet Mexico still appealed to proponents of black colonization, inspiring far more concrete plans than Robert Walker's famous "race funnel." "Would not the free blacks of the slave states rush thither in crowds? ... Would not the slaveholder be completely hemmed in?" exulted a northern abolitionist.[15] "Ten thousand can be sent to Mexico more readily than a single hundred to Africa," noted a logistics-minded southerner.[16] Even Mary Ann Shadd, loyal to Canada though she was, backed emigration to Mexico if Britain could somehow unify that country with a black-dominated southern United States.[17] In 1860, a Tennessee assemblyman tried to impart substance to black expulsion by moving to instruct the state's US senators to press for the annexation of a further portion of Mexico. Yet his fellow legislators refused to offer even indirect support to a program that they now associated with the "Black Republicans."[18]

While whites dallied with colonization in Mexico, blacks voted with their feet. In 1851, fugitive slaves settled in Coahuila and joined forces with Seminole Indians fleeing the Creek. Although Mexican officials were distrustful at first, having just watched their country lose half its territory to the United States, the colonists won their spurs by repulsing Comanche raiders and Mexican separatists alike.[19] So many refugees fled over the border that Texan planters begged the United States to reach an extradition treaty covering slaves, which Mexico always refused. Defeat in the Mexican-American War had ended the recent hegemony of the conservatives and begun that of the liberals, who espoused a free-soilism in which smallholders would be the source of national regeneration. Having founded a ministry of *fomento* (development) in 1853, the Mexican government rekindled the spirit of the mid-1830s by inviting free black immigrants as well as fugitive slaves. In 1857, officials granted land in Veracruz to a Louisianan, Louis Fouché, and offered his colonists citizenship with exemption from military service. The same year, forty former

---

[14] Thomas Earle, ed., *The Life, Travels and Opinions of Benjamin Lundy* (Philadelphia, 1847), 129, 145, 149, 184, 186–9.

[15] "Letter from Ohio," *American and Foreign Anti-Slavery Reporter*, November 1, 1842.

[16] J. Catron to D. Webster, June 2, 1851, in Charles M. Wiltse et al., eds., *The Papers of Daniel Webster* (Hanover, 1974–86), 7:253.

[17] Mary A. Shadd, *A Plea for Emigration, or Notes of Canada West* (Detroit, 1852), 37–8.

[18] E. G. Eastman, pub., *House Journal of Tennessee* (Nashville, 1859), 661, 966.

[19] Ricardo Herrera, "Transnational Immigration Politics in Mexico, 1850–1920," dissertation, University of Arizona (2013), 41–7.

residents of New Orleans founded another settlement in Veracruz, at Tlacotalpán.[20] An English-language newspaper, the *Mexican Extraordinary*, evoked the horrors of Haiti at the mere mention of black settlers, while a liberal publication, *El Siglo XIX*, vaunted "the immigration of such an unfortunate race that is enslaved in some parts of our continent."[21] In Louisiana, as white militias preyed on residents of color, a black committee of vigilance could only mourn several Mexico-bound "deserters from their native soil" as the wheat rather than chaff of local society.[22]

No sooner had Mexico's president, Ignacio Comonfort (1855–7), granted the Fouché allotment than he was ousted by resurgent conservatives, who resented the secular constitution that he had promulgated.[23] The country descended into the War of the Reform (1857–60), from which the liberal government, now in the hands of Benito Juárez (1858–72), emerged triumphant but impoverished. The ill-fated McLane–Ocampo Treaty (1859), between the United States and Mexico, tried to deliver Juárez dollars in return for transit rights, but in late 1861, Britain, Spain, and France dispatched a debt-collecting expedition. Britain and Spain withdrew once France's Napoleon III started subduing Mexico in an attempt to make it a client state. Having failed to defeat the liberals at the ballot box and on the battlefield, Mexican conservatives collaborated with the invaders. So began the War of the French Intervention (1861–7), which would end in the execution of Napoleon's puppet ruler, the Emperor Maximilian (1864–7).[24] Although US politicians prioritized their own civil war, they wondered how they might help Juárez, counter Confederate designs, and bolster the Union's influence in Mexico. They also worried about domestic emancipation, which led many of them, at one point or another, to a single answer to these vexed questions: black colonization in Mexico.[25]

---

[20] Schwartz, *Across the Rio*, 31–42.
[21] "Free Negro Emigrants to Mexico," *Daily Picayune*, August 12, 1857; Schwartz, *Across the Rio*, 42.
[22] Alexandre Barde, *Histoire des comités de vigilance aux Attakapas* (Saint-Jean-Baptiste, LA, 1861), 337–8.
[23] Méridier, pub., *Documens (traduits) relatifs à la colonie d'Eureka* (New Orleans, 1857), 9.
[24] Doyle, *Cause of All Nations*, 114–18.
[25] For Mexican schemes, see Nicholas Guyatt, "'The Future Empire of Our Freedmen': Republican Colonization Schemes in Texas and Mexico, 1861–1865," in Adam Arenson and Andrew R. Graybill, eds., *Civil War Wests: Testing the Limits of the United States* (Oakland, 2015), 95–117.

In June 1861, Postmaster General Montgomery Blair duly approached Juarez's minister to the United States, Matías Romero. "Negroes live in hot climates," explained Blair. "Mexico has these hot climates. It would be as advantageous for the Mexicans as for the Negroes that the latter should be established on those lands." Romero replied that, while Mexicans did not *need* black labor, "we believe all human beings are endowed with the same rights without distinctions about … the color which nature painted their faces with."[26] Recalling this encounter with Blair, Romero warned his superiors that December about the contents of Abraham Lincoln's first annual message, especially its appeal for the United States to acquire more territory.

Yet Romero himself invited trouble by directing Domingo de Goicouria, a member of a Mexican financial mission, to Blair, whom Romero named as a potential source of 1,000 African American laborers for Goicouria's proposed railroad from Veracruz to Mexico City.[27] By February 1862, Romero's suggestion had somehow mutated into a quiet offer from Goicouria to Blair to sell the United States the island of Cozumel, off the eastern coast of Yucatán, for black colonization. Blair delivered the news to Romero, who reminded him that "Mexico [was] firmly decided against alienating another inch of national territory." The minister added that his government would likely consent to black immigration itself, as long as Mexico did not forfeit sovereignty over the island. "The Negroes do not wish to go anywhere, except under the protection of the United States flag," countered Blair. Unwilling to alienate his closest contact in Lincoln's cabinet, Romero politely replied that the administration "must begin by persuading us that the ancient policy of constant aggressions against our territory has been abandoned." He also made a point prefigured by John Calhoun's opposition to the "All Mexico" movement of 1846–8: if the United States annexed even more territory, it would just exacerbate the racial heterogeneity that had already plunged it into crisis.

Blair appeared to accept Romero's argument, and Romero, Blair's retreat – but the minister was still worried. Other conversations with James Doolittle and William Seward, in conjunction with Lincoln's first

---

[26] M. Romero to Minister of Foreign Relations, No. 156, June 6, 1861, in Thomas D. Schoonover, ed., *Mexican Lobby: Matías Romero in Washington, 1861–1867* (Lexington, 1986), 5.
[27] Romero to Minister, Nos. 348 and 355, December 3 and 6, 1861, in Matías Romero, ed., *Correspondencia de la legación mexicana en Washington durante la intervención extranjera, 1860–1868* (Mexico City, 1870–92), 1:619–20, 626–7.

annual message and Representative Frank Blair's colonization bill, had left Romero fearful for the Mexican mainland itself, especially the Yucatán Peninsula. Romero also distrusted Goicouria, a Cuban who had admitted that he would happily sell out Mexican interests for personal gain.[28] As such, the Cozumel affair already contained the same ingredients as the later, better-known Chiriquí episode: a Latin American state wracked by its own civil war and simultaneously hungry for US support, jealous of its own sovereignty, and dogged by venal parties purporting to speak in its name. Mexicans would view the encounter as a near-miss: even today, a plaque in Cozumel's museum commemorates the time that the United States tried to purchase the island.[29]

However worried Romero had been, he could always disabuse peaceful Yanqui expansionists of their optimism as long as they went through the proper channels. By contrast, US Secretary of State William Seward, forced to be the first port of call for a policy not of his choosing, had to stanch a deluge of American diplomats sending him colonization proposals that were usually self-interested and yet expectant of nothing but praise for doing the president's will. Sometimes, such solicitors were not even full diplomats, or their plans had gone well beyond the proposal stage. As French troops neared Mexico City in early 1862, the US consul at Havana, Robert Shufeldt, sailed to Veracruz and traveled to the capital to influence the negotiations between the US minister, Thomas Corwin, and the Mexican minister of foreign affairs, Manuel Doblado. Corwin and Doblado had been thrashing out a loan treaty when Shufeldt appeared and persuaded Corwin to submit a colonization agreement alongside the main document.[30]

Prior to the civil wars that now tormented Mexico and the United States alike, Robert Shufeldt had captained steamers from New Orleans to Tehuantepec, the narrowest part of the transoceanic isthmus in Mexico. Posted to Cuba by the Lincoln administration, Shufeldt kept gazing westward and, in November 1861, warned Seward that the Confederacy likely had designs on Tehuantepec. Ironically, in view of subsequent events, he also lectured the secretary of state on "the fallacy ... that negro labor is indispensable to the proper development of tropical resources."[31] Then in January 1862, he received his copy of

---

[28] Romero to Minister, No. 32, February 1, 1862, in Schoonover, *Mexican Lobby*, 16–19.
[29] P. W. Magness to S. N. Page, email, November 29, 2010.
[30] Guyatt, "Future Empire," 95–6.
[31] R. W. Shufeldt to Seward, November 21, 1861, Despatches from U.S. Consuls in Havana, RG59/M899/41, NARA II.

Lincoln's first annual message, reversed his course, and wrote Charles Sumner, chairman of the Senate Committee on Foreign Relations, to tender Tehuantepec for black resettlement.[32] Granted two months' leave by Seward for what was supposed to be a fact-finding mission to Mexico, it was only on the eve of sailing that Shufeldt wrote the secretary of his real plan: recruiting 3,000–5,000 men to hold Tehuantepec under the Mexican flag.[33]

While Seward himself ordered Shufeldt to stop as soon as he heard of the consul's initiative, Shufeldt at least managed to convince Corwin. In April 1862, the minister had reached a treaty lending Mexico $11,000,000 in return for creating a land board that would sell parts of the national domain until Mexico had repaid its loan.[34] The treaty's very design readily allowed Shufeldt to add his own scheme to it. "If our treaty is ratified, we have a hold in the future of Mexico ... and room enough in the tierra Caliente for two millions of free negroes," agreed Corwin.[35] In his own draft, Shufeldt emphasized Tehuantepec where Corwin had been less specific about location. Endorsing Shufeldt's plan, Corwin promised Doblado that "those who are proposed as colonists ... [are] a patient and laborious people."[36] But Doblado discerned worrying ambiguities: while Shufeldt's text conceded that land should be sold under private title, it also required Mexico to accept US forces on the isthmus, "for the proper protection of said immigrants," until all other foreign powers had withdrawn.[37]

As desperate as he was for a loan, Manuel Doblado could exert leverage of his own. He insisted that the US Senate ratify the treaty before his government would even consider the colonization deal. He answered ambiguity with ambiguity, accepting Robert Shufeldt's conditions save those "incompatible with the ... Sovereignty of the Constitutional Government" – whichever those were.[38] "Experience shews that the want

---

[32] Shufeldt to C. Sumner, January 17, 1862, Charles Sumner Papers, Harvard.
[33] Shufeldt to Seward, May 1, 1862, RG59/M899/45.
[34] N. Andrew N. Cleven, "The Corwin-Doblado Treaty, April 6, 1862," *Hispanic American Historical Review* 17 (1937), 499–506.
[35] T. Corwin to A. C. Allen, May 18, 1862, AL.
[36] Corwin to Doblado, May 17, in Corwin to Seward, No. 24, May 20, 1862, Despatches from U.S. Ministers to Mexico, RG59/M97/30, NARA II.
[37] Shufeldt to Doblado, May 16, in Shufeldt to Seward, June 5, 1862, RG59/M899/45.
[38] Doblado to Shufeldt, May 19, 1862, in Shufeldt to Seward, June 5, 1862, RG59/M899/45.

of population is one of the principal causes of the general bad condition of the country," admitted Doblado. "But the Mexican Government does not wish to enter into contracts ... [that] affect the national sovereignty." He also warned Thomas Corwin that, should the Senate fail to ratify their treaty, Mexico had come to a rival agreement with Britain, whose delegates would get to sit on the land board instead of Americans.[39]

Hoping to proceed to Washington to promote his project, Shufeldt called at Havana, where he found new instructions from the Department of State. "You seem to suppose yourself clothed with diplomatic powers," Seward had warned him. "This was not the purpose of the government when it sanctioned your visit."[40] Shufeldt wrote a sarcastic reply, which did not deserve the patience that Seward accorded it.[41] "The present difficulties in Mexico are ... a consequence of our own civil war," the secretary explained. "They add to the seductions held out to foreign states to make excuses for intervention here before we shall have completely closed the breach at home."[42] Sure enough, the Confederate secretary of state, Judah Benjamin, would learn of Shufeldt's movements, and alert Napoleon III to the fact of US intrigues; it was as well that Benjamin never established Shufeldt's *purpose*.[43] Foolishly, Shufeldt refused to accept Seward's second admonition as well. "A proper disposition of these unfortunate people in accordance with ... the published suggestions of the President, is a subject in which every citizen of the U.S. has a right," insisted the consul, forwarding the text of a new colonization treaty, which he had drafted alone this time.[44]

Seward now spurned subtlety. He reminded Shufeldt that it was illegal for citizens to enter into unauthorized diplomacy, warning him that he had "incurred the President's very decided disapprobation." The Senate having just rejected the Corwin–Doblado Treaty, Shufeldt had, Seward alleged, also raised expectations that the United States could not meet.[45] Seward's man in Havana could only lick his wounds, though Corwin soothed Shufeldt by reassuring him that "no place on earth is equal to the

[39] Doblado to Corwin, May 19, 1862, Records of Foreign Service Posts, RG84/Mexico/13, NARA II.
[40] Seward to Shufeldt, May 23, 1862, Consular Instructions, RG59/59/31, NARA II.
[41] Shufeldt to Seward, June 5, 1862, RG59/M899/45.
[42] Seward to Shufeldt, June 24, 1862, RG59/59/31.
[43] Frederick C. Drake, *The Empire of the Seas: A Biography of Rear Admiral Robert Wilson Shufeldt, USN* (Honolulu, 1984), 68–9.
[44] Shufeldt to Seward, July 4, 1862, RG59/M899/45.
[45] Seward to Shufeldt, July 14, 1862, Robert Wilson Shufeldt Papers, LC.

Tierra caliente" for black colonization.[46] Years later, in an unpublished autobiography, Shufeldt chose to remember how "Seward sent me to Mexico ... to ascertain from that Government the practicality of settling our southern negroes on the isthmus of Tehuantepec." He had the temerity to add, "the scheme was quixotic."[47] His account was a travesty – and yet, in 1862, the White House did hint at its disappointment that the Senate had undermined black colonization by rejecting the Corwin– Doblado Treaty.[48]

From 1863, the enlistment of African Americans helped other commentators make the obvious connection between ejecting French soldiers from Mexico, and, when the time came, black soldiers from the United States. "Would not an armed force of 400,000 well disciplined colored Troops ... soon settle ... these difficult questions, on the soil of Mexico itself?" asked a lieutenant colonel in the Illinois volunteers.[49] "Doubtless an effort will be made to have the Southern States return, with slavery in full bloom," predicted a reader of the *Liberator*, who suggested preempting racial strife by sending all blacks in uniform at war's end to topple "the throne constructed by the upstart Emperor."[50] Strikingly, Lincoln himself was unenthused by such schemes. In December 1862, one of his Illinois friends, Major General John Palmer, had offered to lead an expedition of African Americans to Mexico.[51] While Lincoln had appreciated the gesture, he deemed force unnecessary to evict the French.[52] The Blairs thought otherwise, and Matías Romero watched the family closely from 1865, when Confederate defeat freed up Union forces for foreign service.[53] For Unionists continued to discern how easily African Americans might cross the border from Texas, itself a location that white northerners proposed for black resettlement. Although such plans belong more properly to Chapter 6, which covers black resettlement within the United

---

[46] Corwin to Shufeldt, July 11, 1862, ibid.

[47] Shufeldt, "Through Mexico to the Pacific," ibid.

[48] "Washington Correspondence, 13 July 1862," in Michael Burlingame, ed., *Lincoln's Journalist: John Hay's Anonymous Writings for the Press, 1860–1864* (Carbondale, 1998), 280.

[49] G. R. Clark to Lincoln, April 4, 1864, Miscellaneous Letters Received, Records Relating to the Suppression of the African Slave Trade and Negro Colonization, RG48/M160/8, NARA II.

[50] "Letter to a California Senator," *Liberator*, November 25, 1864.

[51] J. M. Palmer to L. Trumbull, December 11, 1862, Lyman Trumbull Correspondence, LC.

[52] "Master Spirit of the Union," *Omaha Daily Bee*, October 29, 1893.

[53] Romero to Minister, No. 284, June 18, 1865, in Schoonover, *Mexican Lobby*, 69; Romero to Minister, No. 512, October 20, 1865, in his *Correspondencia*, 5:711–13.

States, nothing did more to strain the distinction between foreign and domestic colonization than did the narrow, shifting course of the Rio Grande, or the fluid sovereignty of the borderlands through which it flowed.

The Dominican Republic

Mexico was not the only theater of European aggression during the American Civil War. The Dominican Republic, formerly the Spanish colony of Santo Domingo, had long been the object of intrigue by Britain, France, the United States, and Haiti, which, as the Dominican Republic's neighbor on the island of Hispaniola, had occupied it once before (1822–44) and forever hoped to do so again. In fact, it was under the immigration scheme of Haiti's Jean-Pierre Boyer that African Americans had settled at Puerto Plata and Samaná. The outstanding harbor at Samaná was so widely coveted by the powers that it took a combination of rumblings from Haiti, war in the United States, and a worried Dominican President Pedro Santana's (1858–61) request for a Spanish protectorate (granted in 1861) for Madrid to steal a march on its rivals. Yet the United States had had energetic agents in the Dominican Republic since 1853, in the shape of William and Jane Cazneau, fervent believers in American penetration of the entire Caribbean.[54] For US expatriates in the Dominican Republic, black and white, the Spanish occupation posed a grave problem.

Most Dominicans saw themselves as white, though they were of mixed race by Anglo-American standards. Despite vaunting their supposed lack of prejudice, they also saw blackness and *haitianismo*, the quality of being Haitian, as at once inextricable and undesirable.[55] Accordingly, in 1849, a US special agent, Benjamin Green, had reported that the Dominican Republic had banned black immigration.[56] A decade later, J. Dennis Harris, an African American visiting the country as part of a Caribbean tour, noted a recent ordinance permitting the immigration of "the agricultural class, or those following some craft," which made no reference to color.[57] During the American Civil War, the improbability of any US

[54] Rayford W. Logan, *Haiti and the Dominican Republic* (London, 1968), 34–40.
[55] Ernesto Sagás, *Race and Politics in the Dominican Republic* (Gainesville, 2000), 2–3.
[56] B. E. Green to J. M. Clayton, No. 2, September 27, 1849, in William R. Manning, ed., *Diplomatic Correspondence of the United States: Inter-American Affairs, 1831–1860* (Washington, DC, 1932–9), 6:51.
[57] J. Dennis Harris, *A Summer on the Borders of the Caribbean Sea* (New York, 1860), 60.

move on the Dominican Republic meant that colonization projects would have to come from third parties. More than anyone, that meant Jane Cazneau. In the 1850s, she had encouraged American planters to transfer their slaves to the more promising soil of Cuba and Nicaragua, and their manumittees to the Dominican Republic.[58] Hoping to harness some of the publicity garnered by James Redpath's Haiti scheme, she then proposed that white Americans move to the Dominican Republic, as part of a parallel migration to that of black Americans to Haiti, but added that the harmonious coexistence of different groups in eastern Hispaniola precluded hard and fast rules on such matters.[59]

In April 1862, an associate of the Cazneaus, Joseph Fabens, discussed colonization with Secretary of the Interior Caleb Smith.[60] The next year, Hiram Ketchum, president of a new outfit, the American West Indies Company, submitted a proposal to Smith's successor, John Usher, for recruiting contrabands at Hilton Head, a US foothold in South Carolina. Usher told Ketchum to tour the District of Columbia instead, and to avoid troubling military commandants elsewhere for a pass.[61] Thinking of Spain's occupation of the Dominican Republic, William Seward informed Usher that, despite his own diplomatic circular of September 30, 1862, he would not pursue an emigration treaty on behalf of Ketchum.[62]

In the end, the United States needed neither to engage further with the American West Indies Company nor to eject Spain from the Dominican Republic. The African American expatriates of the Samaná Peninsula, who in 1854 had marched to the country's eponymous capital, Santo Domingo, to oppose any treaty with the United States, were already reeling from Spain's reimposition of state Catholicism when, in early 1863, a revolt broke out against Spanish rule.[63] "When Mr. Fabens was ... attempting to get up a colony of American negroes for Santo Domingo, he pledged himself that religious liberty ... was guaranteed by

---

[58] Linda S. Hudson, "Jane McManus Storm Cazneau (1807–1878): A Biography," dissertation, University of North Texas (1999), 249–50.
[59] Gerald Horne, *Confronting Black Jacobins: The United States, the Haitian Revolution, and the Origins of the Dominican Republic* (New York, 2015), 261.
[60] C. B. Smith to J. W. Fabens, May 1, 1862, S. Exec. Doc. 55, 39 Cong., 1 Sess. (1866), 6–7 (hereafter, "S. Exec. Doc. 55").
[61] J. P. Usher to H. Ketchum, April 24, 1863, ibid., 30–1.
[62] Seward to Usher, April 25, 1863, Domestic Letters of the Department of State, RG59/ M40/55, NARA II.
[63] Anne Eller, "Dominican Civil War, Slavery, and Spanish Annexation, 1844–1865," in Doyle, *American Civil Wars*, 148–54.

the Spanish Crown," charged a US commentator. "Already has Popery resumed its sway ... and the attempt will be made to re-enslave the unfortunate negroes."[64] As Catholic in his methods as in his personal faith, William Cazneau also switched to asking Spain for permission to import white refugees from the Confederacy, a group that, it is fair to surmise, would not have coexisted harmoniously with African Americans.[65] Yet, as this book's Epilogue shows, Hispaniola never lost its multicultural allure in the eyes of those Americans troubled by race relations in their own land. From 1865, once Spain had withdrawn, the Dominican Republic would regain its prominent billing among the would-be annexations of the United States.

REPOPULATING PLANTATIONS: BRAZIL AND ECUADOR

The Cazneaus had seen African Americans as one possible immigrant group among many, even for the menial work of tilling the soil. By contrast, the only mature proposals to emerge from the independent states of the South American continent, one for Brazil and two for Ecuador, envisioned black labor specifically, to restock depleted planta-tions.[66] Yet there was a crucial difference between them: while Ecuador had abolished slavery in 1851, Brazil would not do so until 1888. Even as half the landmass of South America had become free soil, the court of Dom Pedro II (1841–89) quietly supported the institution of slavery, the Atlantic slave trade (until 1850, when London forced Rio de Janeiro to close it), and, now, despite Brazil's proclamation of neutrality, the Confederate cause.[67]

---

[64] "Persecution in Santo Domingo," *Independent*, July 23, 1863.
[65] Wayne H. Bowen, *Spain and the American Civil War* (Columbia, MO, 2011), 96.
[66] For the Brazil scheme, see James L. Crouthamel, *James Watson Webb: A Biography* (Middletown, 1969), 173–5; Gerald Horne, *The Deepest South: The United States, Brazil, and the African Slave Trade* (New York, 2007), 172–83; Nícia Villela Luz, *A Amazônia para os negros americanos (as origens de uma controvérsia internacional)* (Rio de Janeiro, 1968), 10–16; and Maria Clara Carneiro Sampaio, "'Não diga que não somos brancos': os projetos de colonização para afro-americanos do governo Lincoln na perspectiva do Caribe, América Latina e Brasil dos 1860," dissertation, University of São Paulo (2013), 94–133. For the Ecuadorian schemes, see Robert L. Gold, "Negro Colonization Schemes in Ecuador, 1861–1864," *Phylon* 30 (1969), 306–16.
[67] Rafael Marquese, "The Civil War in the United States and the Crisis of Slavery in Brazil," in Doyle, *American Civil Wars*, 225.

Brazil

The mass removal of African Americans to the Brazilian interior might have been an ambitious plan, but it was also an old idea. In 1852, the Virginia oceanographer Matthew Fontaine Maury had proposed that the southern states sell their slaves to Brazil, which would no longer have to import fresh Africans.[68] He saw such an outflow as the next step in a process that had started with the northern US states selling their surplus slaves southward. "Suppose [the slave] had been sent to South America instead of to South Carolina, – it would have still been the same to him, but how different to the country!" claimed Maury.[69] He had the support of a former minister to Brazil, his fellow Virginian Henry Wise, who held similarly lucrative views about how the Old Dominion might export its excess slaves.[70]

In 1862, Abraham Lincoln's minister to Brazil, the Whig-turned-Republican newspaperman James Watson Webb, took up Maury's mantle (knowingly or not) with an ebullient dispatch to William Seward. Although formerly an advocate of Liberia, Webb now thought that "the finger of God . . . point[ed] to the northern provinces of Brazil as the future home of the manumitted negro." He did not envision black Americans directly supplying the wants of the booming coffee growers of the south, around Rio de Janeiro, but, rather, filling the northern vacuum left by the movement of Amazonian slaves toward Rio for that purpose. While the draft treaty that Webb enclosed foresaw eventual Brazilian citizenship for the hundreds of thousands who might be transported, he also knew that Brazilian law forbade the immigration of free blacks. Echoing Frank Blair's prewar suggestion of "probation," Webb's solution was simple: colonize the contrabands while still slaves. "Freedom being the object in view, the true philanthropist does not insist that it shall be immediate," he told Seward. The US government's outlay would be repaid by three years' apprenticeship, administered by a joint stock company. Yet Webb also called on Washington "to separate the government from all duties not legitimately or necessarily within its sphere, and to get rid of the jobbing and patronage which would grow out of this enormous

---

[68] Walter Johnson, *River of Dark Dreams: Slavery and Empire in the Cotton Kingdom* (Cambridge, MA, 2013), 299–302.
[69] Matthew Fontaine Maury, *Commercial Conventions: Direct Trade, a Chance for the South* (Lynchburg, 1852), 25–6.
[70] Horne, *Deepest South*, 108.

undertaking."[71] He then sent Seward a separate, unofficial letter outlining the patronage necessary to the venture, which, happily, the Brazilian government was about to bestow on Webb, and all but nominating himself for the job of project manager.[72] Seward sighed. Although Webb's draft treaty foreshadowed the secretary's own circular that fall, the minister had asked for too much, too soon. "Whether [freedpeople's] consent shall be required . . . whether they shall be colonized within our own jurisdiction . . . or whether in some Central or South American country, with the consent of their government . . . remain[s] a subject of earnest but as yet very confused discussion," Seward told Webb.[73] By the time that Webb's colleague, the US consul at Rio, Richard Parsons, arrived in Washington to promote Webb's plan, their moment had passed: "the President is ardently for a Central American colonization, as near at hand, and more likely to take with the blacks," reported Parsons.[74] The wounded Webb now claimed indifference all along to his own proposal. "I based all I wrote upon the recommendation of the President to colonize. If this matter were left to me . . . I would place [freedpeople] all along the Mexican Frontier," he informed Seward.[75] As his tone of overcorrection hinted, Webb would still think it necessary, as late as 1864, to defend his original proposal before Seward as more selflessly patriotic than its profitmaking element might have implied.[76] Meanwhile, that January, Dom Pedro II admitted to one of Brazil's senators that "the successes of the American Union force us to think about the future of slavery in Brazil."[77] Unlike in the United States, a small number of blacks had already reached the highest levels of society, so white Brazilians did not view the cultural consequences of emancipation with the same horror that white Americans did.[78] But even

---

[71] Richard Graham, "Another Middle Passage? The Internal Slave Trade in Brazil," in Walter Johnson, ed., *The Chattel Principle: Internal Slave Trades in the Americas* (New Haven, 2004), 292; J. W. Webb to Seward, No. 17, May 20, 1862, *PRFA* 37 Cong., 3 Sess. (1862), 704–12. Hereafter, "*PRFA*" (without elaboration) refers to that volume unless stated otherwise.

[72] Webb to Seward, June 6, 1862, reel 70, WHS.

[73] Seward to Webb, No. 33, July 21, 1862, *PRFA*, 712–15.

[74] R. C. Parsons to Webb, August 24, 1862, James Watson Webb Papers, Yale.

[75] Webb to Seward, September 23, 1862, reel 72, WHS.

[76] Webb to Seward, No. 76½ (*sic*), March 9, 1864, Despatches from U.S. Ministers to Brazil, RG59/M121/32, NARA II.

[77] Doyle, *Cause of All Nations*, 301.

[78] Thomas E. Skidmore, "Racial Ideas and Social Policy in Brazil, 1870–1940," in Richard Graham, ed., *The Idea of Race in Latin America, 1870–1940* (Austin, 1990), 8.

in the 1920s, more than three decades after abolishing slavery, Brazil still hesitated to fill vacancies on its coffee plantations with African American immigrants.[79]

Ecuador

Where James Watson Webb would have seen his compatriots remain slaves for the sake of his own interest, the US minister to Ecuador, Friedrich Hassaurek, remained above suspicion when he endorsed local planters' request for black Americans, since he was merely asserting the latter's right to immigrate. In October 1862, Hassaurek told Seward that one Benigno Malo had offered to sell the United States 50,000 acres on the Suya River. "I do not want negroes for my own use. I want to make them proprietors of the soil," Malo had assured Hassaurek, who forwarded the plan to the Department of State without comment.[80] Seward had just issued his circular of September 30, 1862, mandating the approval of host governments, so rejected the (private) arrangement outright.[81] Having in the meantime sought parallel permission from President Gabriel García Moreno (1861–5), an economic modernizer of otherwise conservative tendencies, Hassaurek found him possessed of such "strong antipathies against the Negro race" that he dared not mention Malo's project.[82] (By contrast, Webb's scheme had found favor with Brazil's executive, Pedro II, whose cabinet, however, had resisted repealing Brazil's black law.[83]) Seward approved Hassaurek's course of (in)action with a note whose very brevity betrayed his pleasure at striking another destination off the list.[84]

There the story might have ended but for a New York businessman, E. P. Larkin, who, along with several owners of estates around Guayaquil, revived the idea of importing African Americans. At the end of 1863, Larkin made two inquiries of Hassaurek: whether any part of the

---

[79] Teresa Meade and Gregory Alonso Pirio, "In Search of the Afro-American 'Eldorado': Attempts by North American Blacks to Enter Brazil in the 1920s," *Luso-Brazilian Review* 25 (1988), 87.

[80] F. Hassaurek to Seward, No. 42, October 2, 1862, *PRFA*, 909.

[81] Seward to Hassaurek, No. 23, November 6, 1862, *PRFA*, 910.

[82] Hassaurek to Seward, No. 55, January 16, 1863, Despatches from U.S. Ministers to Ecuador, RG59/T50/6, NARA II.

[83] Webb to Seward, July 7, 1862, reel 70, WHS.

[84] Seward to Hassaurek, No. 31, February 9, 1863, Diplomatic Instructions of the Department of State, RG59/M77/52, NARA II.

1839 treaty between Ecuador and the United States prevented "free coloured citizens of the United States ... hir[ing] out their own services," and whether they would enjoy exemption from military service, as that treaty stipulated.[85] Those were basic, but contentious questions: since the *Dred Scott* ruling (1857), the corpus of US treaties had been largely inadequate to the needs of black colonization, such agreements usually being framed around the reciprocal rights of "citizens." "Every nation has an original right to prohibit the immigration ... of certain classes of foreigners," Hassaurek informed Larkin. Nevertheless, through treaty, precedent, and downright decency, Ecuador had surrendered that right. Moreover, "persons of African descent are citizens of the United States according to a late opinion of Attorney-General Bates," added the minister, who approved Larkin's plan.[86] Hassaurek had proceeded from a simplistic, unduly optimistic, and yet common enough reading of an 1862 opinion by Edward Bates, who had indeed shown freepeople to be US citizens – while keeping quiet about the slaves, as behooved a supporter of their compulsory colonization.

Accordingly, it was a nasty surprise for Hassaurek, a liberal who had fled Austria after Europe's failed uprisings of 1848, to belatedly discover that President Moreno had, in July 1863, banned African American immigration, "partly because similar measures have been adopted in the other South American States, and partly because it is in the interest of the Republic."[87] It was the kind of nonexplanation that a Hoosier might have given for the Indiana black laws. Hassaurek denounced Moreno's actions to Seward as a "direct contravention of the constitution, laws, and traditionary policy of Ecuador." While Quito had done well, Hassaurek continued, to reject the Malo scheme, which would have forfeited title to a foreign government and created a distinct cluster of blacks, requests from the scattered planters whom Larkin represented would diffuse (and so defuse) such settlers, and asked only that Americans be allowed due freedom of movement.[88]

In a further meeting with Moreno, Hassaurek was delighted to appease the president's misgivings about former slaves, citing reports from the Union frontline that "they had thus far behaved exceedingly well, both as

---

[85] E. P. Larkin to Hassaurek, December 3, 1863, in Hassaurek to Seward, No. 109, February 3, 1864, RG59/T50/7.

[86] Hassaurek to Larkin, December 21, 1863, in Hassaurek to Seward, No. 109, February 3, 1864, RG59/T50/7; Hassaurek to Seward, December 26, 1863, reel 81, WHS.

[87] P. Herrera to Hassaurek, February 1, in Hassaurek to Seward, No. 109, February 3, 1864, RG59/T50/7.

[88] Hassaurek to Seward, No. 109, February 3, 1864, RG59/T50/7.

laborers and as soldiers."[89] Ecuador's secretary of the interior, Rafael Carvajal, modified the earlier decree by permitting entry to all North Americans who knew a useful trade or held a contract to labor. Carvajal reiterated that immigrants would not be allowed to gather in one place, "because all projects of colonization remain prohibited."[90] Friedrich Hassaurek reported these dealings to William Seward, who, though complimentary of his minister's "interesting criticisms upon the abstract principles involved," told him not to trouble himself further about an expedition that existed only on paper.[91]

CROSSING THE ISTHMUS: CHIRIQUÍ AND CENTRAL AMERICA

Chiriquí (Colombia)

While the distance involved in transporting African Americans to Brazil and Ecuador made those schemes uncompetitive, a different expedition, though ultimately abortive, came so close to sailing that a crowd of black Washingtonians who had already disposed of their property besieged the White House, demanding to be sent forthwith to an isthmian province of Colombia, Chiriquí.[92]

What made the pan-American plethora of colonization proposals so tiresome for Seward was that Lincoln had quietly favored the Chiriquí site since the fall of 1861, months before Congress had passed a single colonization law. The scheme was a holdover from the previous administration, and the relevant leaseholder a Philadelphia shipbuilder, Ambrose Thompson, who had approached President James Buchanan to offer what had then been a potential naval base and coaling station. Opponents alleged that the scheme was a swindle, based on poor title, poor coal deposits, and poor terrain for any railroad. In early 1861, Congress rejected the contract.[93]

---

[89] Hassaurek to Seward, No. 112, February 17, 1864, RG59/T50/7.
[90] R. Carvajal to Governor of Guayas, March 3, in Hassaurek to Seward, No. 117, March 14, 1864, RG59/T50/7.
[91] Seward to Hassaurek, No. 66, March 10, 1864, RG59/M77/52.
[92] For the Chiriquí scheme, see Warren A. Beck, "Lincoln and Negro Colonization in Central America," *Abraham Lincoln Quarterly* 6 (1950), 162–83; Sebastian N. Page, "Lincoln and Chiriquí Colonization Revisited," *American Nineteenth Century History* 12 (2011), 289–325; and Paul J. Scheips, "Lincoln and the Chiriqui Colonization Project," *Journal of Negro History* 37 (1952), 418–53.
[93] Paul J. Scheips, "Buchanan and the Chiriqui Naval Station Sites," *Military Affairs* 18 (1954), 64–80.

Undeterred, Thompson met with the new administration and resumed his offer, to which Lincoln and the Blairs appended colonization plans for recaptives and, in short order, contrabands.[94] Gideon Welles and Salmon Chase each declined to investigate the proposal, which accordingly fell into the clutches of Caleb Smith and John Usher.[95] Yet the Department of the Interior, jocularly known as "the Department of Everything Else," did not assume the task of colonizing African Americans just because of its experience in resettling recaptives. Its wartime heads were personally vested in the success of the Chiriquí scheme: Smith probably held a stake in any payout to Thompson, while Usher certainly did.[96]

One complication was destined, however, to draw the Chiriquí project toward the Department of State, much to the chagrin of Smith, Usher, *and* Seward: Colombia was emerging from a civil war of its own, and had sent rival representatives to the United States. In 1860, former president Tomás de Mosquera (1845–9) had instigated a rebellion of liberals disaffected by one of his conservative successors, Mariano Ospina (1857–61). By 1862, Mosquera had triumphed, but Seward remained wary, understandably, of recognizing a regime born of insurrection. In Washington, the agents of the de facto "United States of Colombia," Manuel Murillo and Francisco Párraga, angled to supplant those of the de jure "Granadine Confederation" (until 1858, "New Granada," the name that its adherents tended still to use), Pedro Herrán and José María Hurtado. Awkwardly, Herrán was Mosquera's son-in-law, and had been his appointee before switching sides.[97]

The old regime was not *so* keen to cling onto accreditation, however, as to accept American affronts to Colombian – or, indeed, to Granadian – sovereignty. In May 1862, Ambrose Thompson had admitted to Caleb Smith that the United States could not expect to obtain jurisdiction over the Chiriquí site.[98] The next month, Lincoln summoned Herrán to pore over a map of the Chiriqui Improvement Company's (CIC's) concession,

[94] Lincoln to Smith, October 23, 1861, *CWAL*, 4:561–2; F. P. Blair, Sr., to Lincoln, November 16, 1861, AL.
[95] Lincoln to Smith, October 24, 1861, *CWAL*, 5:2–3; S. P. Chase to Lincoln, November 27, 1861, AL.
[96] Page, "Chiriquí Colonization," 299–300.
[97] Stephen J. Randall, *Colombia and the United States: Hegemony and Interdependence* (Athens, GA, 1992), 47–9.
[98] A. W. Thompson to Smith, May 14, 1862, Richard Wigginton Thompson Papers, Rutherford B. Hayes Presidential Library and Museums; Smith to Lincoln, May 16, 1862, S. Exec. Doc. 55, 10–11.

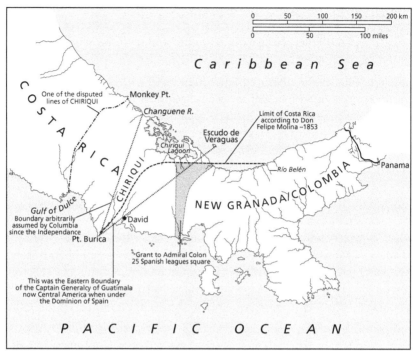

MAP 4.1 In his only major contribution to the Chiriquí project after assembling
the black deputation, James Mitchell researched the territorial dispute between
Costa Rica and Colombia, submitting this map to advise Caleb Smith against
dispatching the expedition.

Based on a manuscript map enclosed in J. Mitchell to C. B. Smith, October 14, 1862,
Richard Wigginton Thompson Papers, Rutherford B. Hayes Presidential Library and
Museums

and Herrán confirmed that New Granada would still object to a coal-
mining venture that made no claims to sovereignty.[99] The Costa Rican
minister, Luis Molina, also announced that his own government had a
long-running boundary dispute with New Granada/Colombia over
Chiriquí, and could never consent to a colony approved by Bogotá, which
San José saw as an occupying power (Map 4.1).[100] For good measure, the
secretary of the Smithsonian Institution, Joseph Henry, analyzed a sample

[99] Seward to Lincoln, June 5, 1862, AL; P. A. Herrán to Lincoln, June 14, 1862, R. W.
Thompson Papers.
[100] L. Molina to Seward, September 19, 1862, *PRFA*, 899–900.

of Chiriquí coal and found it a friable, inferior specimen as likely to catch fire while stored in a ship's bunker as when shoveled into its boiler.[101]

Despite these auguries, Abraham Lincoln convened his infamous meeting of August 1862 with the deputation of black Washingtonians, a full transcript of which was disseminated in newspapers worldwide. Historians have been so fixated on the president's frankness about race relations that they have overlooked his comparable candor about the Chiriquí concession itself. "A speculation is intended by gentlemen, who have an interest in the country," admitted Lincoln, reminding the delegates that "whites as well as blacks look to their self-interest." He also alluded to the Colombian Civil War, sounding a note of desperation in his assurances that "all the factions are agreed alike on the subject of colonization, and want it."[102] However misplaced Lincoln's hopes that the stench of corruption and fog of isthmian war would somehow disperse, he had evidently researched the regional situation. Unfortunately, he had also become so engrossed in its details that he forgot to tell his (global) audience which part of "Central America" he had just described, failing to refer to Colombia or Chiriquí by name.

Even before his botched announcement of the Chiriquí project, Lincoln had, according to Usher, "become very apprehensive that it is a scheme to enrich political hacks." Whatever agreement Lincoln drafted with Ambrose Thompson would not offer an immediate windfall, but would instead stagger payments on evidence of results.[103] Even so, at the end of August, Lincoln almost canceled the negotiations once he discovered the identity of one of the company's stakeholders: Richard Thompson (no relation to Ambrose Thompson). A Hoosier and former Whig like Smith and Usher, Dick Thompson had befriended Abraham Lincoln during their common term in the US House (1847–9). The president admitted that he was "willing to do anything personal to serve [Thompson] . . . yet he could not go before the people, admitting that he had so applied public money."[104] For Lincoln to close the contract and appeal for black pioneers, the expedition would require more disinterested leadership, which

[101] J. Henry to J. P. Lesley, May 28, 1862, in Nathan Reingold et al., eds., *The Papers of Joseph Henry* (Washington, DC, 1972–2008), 10:268–9; Lesley to Henry, May 30, 1862, J. Peter Lesley Papers, American Philosophical Society.
[102] "Address on Colonization to a Deputation of Negroes," August 14, 1862, *CWAL*, 5:374.
[103] Usher to M. P. Usher, August 10, 1862, John P. Usher Papers, Kansas Historical Society.
[104] A. W. Thompson to R. W. Thompson, October 6, 1862, box 43, Ambrose W. Thompson Papers, LC.

emerged in the form of Samuel Pomeroy. At first, the US senator for Kansas hoped to do nothing more than hasten Lincoln's announcement of the Emancipation Proclamation, but easy access to the colonization fund would corrupt him, and he would never account for the better part of $25,000 advanced by Smith.[105] Aside from that exceptional draft to Pomeroy, however, the administration's final contract with Ambrose Thompson, of September 12, 1862, limited any single payment to $10,000, to be disbursed as settlers moved into CIC lands. Going by the acreage of the company's holdings and the stipulated size of settlers' allotments, the agreement provided for up to 250,000 colonists.[106] With the venture under way, Pomeroy advertised in the press for the free blacks of the United States to join him for an October 1 sailing.[107]

Scholars usually ascribe Abraham Lincoln's eventual suspension of the Chiriquí expedition, early that October, to the outcry that resounded across Central America, every part of which imagined itself, thanks to the president's poor wording, the receptacle for an unwanted torrent of African Americans.[108] In fact, the real cause for pause was the unresolved question of which regime, if either, could offer consent on behalf of Colombia. Ambrose Thompson's response was to obtain it from both. It helped that one of the new regime's representatives was also an employee of the CIC. "Our cause is your cause," Francisco Párraga told Thompson, hoping that his patron might secure Colombia's unrecognized mission an interview with the secretary of state.[109] Still, not even Párraga would authorize a scheme that offended his sensibilities. "We have no hatred or prejudice against the negro race already existing among us, but an increase of African population by immigration is not permitted," he warned Pomeroy. Párraga explained that Colombians blamed the Jamaican workers who had stayed in the country after laying Panama's transisthmian railroad for stoking the racial tensions that had led to the "Watermelon War" of 1856, a riot that had killed several US travelers and landed Bogotá with an indemnity to Washington.[110] To appease Párraga, Ambrose Thompson promised that the black settlers would adhere to the laws of Colombia, and had Caleb Smith add an article to their own contract, stipulating that the United States remove colonists for

---

[105] Page, "Chiriquí Colonization," 301–3.
[106] Smith and A. W. Thompson, contract, September 12, 1862, S. Exec. Doc. 55, 13–14.
[107] "Important from Washington," *New York Herald*, August 26, 1862.
[108] "Colonization of Negroes in Central America," *New York Times*, August 22, 1862.
[109] F. Párraga to A. W. Thompson, October 24, 1862, R. W. Thompson Papers.
[110] Párraga to S. C. Pomeroy, August 26, 1862, ibid.

bad behavior.[111] That placated Párraga, who added that Thompson might land 50,000 further settlers on the Magdalena River – who should not, however, then expect to call on the assistance of the United States. "The principle 'where a Roman is, there is Rome' which Europe has pretended to make prevail in its intercourse with the growing states of Spanish America ... has been very expensive," Párraga explained.[112] Manuel Murillo echoed his junior diplomat's offer, though back in Colombia, at least one commentator thought them presumptuous to have offered settlers yet more land.[113]

Strangely, the expedition had not looked quite so alive in some time as just after its postponement.[114] Suddenly, the agents of the old regime also approved resettlement in some form, even if they did not recognize the CIC's concession. José María Hurtado told John Usher that New Granada, as Hurtado continued to deem Colombia, would not object to a colony on the Pacific coast, far from the maddened Costa Ricans. He also hinted that he might offer "unconditional assent ... for some small personal consideration," which, one month later, the ever-vigilant Mexican minister, Matías Romero, suspected had transformed into a request for a $2,000,000 US loan to the de jure government.[115] Predicting payday for himself no less than for Hurtado, Usher took the good news to Seward, who appeared to accept that the assent of both regimes would suffice to release the expedition. A veteran of the Senate's withering debates over the earlier, Buchanan–Thompson contract, Seward had expressed doubts the previous winter about the concessionaire's title.[116] Now that the project had resurfaced with colonization attached, Seward advised Lincoln against spending money as long as the European empires offered to take African Americans for free (Chapter 5). Having commissioned Joseph Henry's damning report, Seward also scoffed at Chiriquí's coal.[117]

---

[111] A. W. Thompson to Párraga, August 30, 1862, ibid.
[112] Párraga to A. W. Thompson, September 26, 1862, box 43, A. W. Thompson Papers.
[113] Randall, *Colombia and the United States*, 53; "Al pié de estas líneas ...," *La Estrella de Panamá*, October 30, 1862.
[114] J. P. Usher to Pomeroy, October 7, 1862, S. Exec. Doc. 55, 21.
[115] Usher to R. W. Thompson, October 12, 1862, Usher Papers; Romero to Minister, No. 358, November 12, 1862, in his *Correspondencia*, 2:581–2.
[116] Usher to R. W. Thompson, December 26, 1861, Richard W. Thompson Papers, Allen County Public Library.
[117] Usher to Pomeroy, October 13, 1862, Usher Papers.

Little wonder, then, that the secretary of state produced further reasons why the expedition should not sail. "Now I am told by Mr. Seward that the 'Representatives of a Government *are not the Government*' and 'nothing short of a Treaty will be satisfactory,'" reported Pomeroy in late October.[118] Two weeks later, Lincoln met Pomeroy to confirm that the administration would insist on treaties, as the cabinet had decided that September. The president then offered the senator a preview, in effect, of his second annual message. Referring to Colombia's instability, Lincoln told Pomeroy that "this colony might become obnoxious and the present residents might object to carry[ing] out the principles of government now established." Lincoln hoped to ensure that the United States had the legal means to defend its expatriates, by reaching a bespoke treaty before dispatching the expedition.[119] Yet it was that prospect, of US intervention in defense of an incongruous, non-Catholic, non-Hispanic enclave, that so worried Central America.[120] Maybe the proviso was the idea of that internal saboteur, William Seward, whose reading of regional responses to black colonization had told him that such a prerequisite would prevent a treaty ever being reached.

For those settlers ready to depart, the wait was insufferable. The first wave, of 500, comprised mostly residents of the District of Columbia, even though Samuel Pomeroy had broadcast his appeal to free African Americans across the United States. The authorities made no effort to check whether would-be emigrants had resided in Washington at the time of the District Emancipation Act: a black petition to Lincoln, to order Pomeroy to weigh anchor, was signed by applicants from Washington, Maryland, New York, and Illinois, the last being one of James Mitchell's black assistants, the poet and emigrationist John Willis Menard.[121] Although some of the pioneers had lived in the District since at least April (and therefore qualified under the Act), others had resided elsewhere more recently than that. While the relevant records have long been lost, there is little reason to doubt Samuel Pomeroy's claim of more than 13,000 enrollments. At the headquarters of the American Colonization Society, two black Pennsylvanians called on William McLain, asking where they might find Pomeroy, whom they assumed an agent of the

---

[118] Pomeroy to O. H. Browning, October 27, 1862, Orville H. Browning Papers, Abraham Lincoln Presidential Library.
[119] C. S. Dyer to A. W. Thompson, November 11, 1862, box 7, A. W. Thompson Papers.
[120] Schoonover, "Misconstrued Mission," 620.
[121] "The Negroes Anxious to Emigrate," Springfield *Daily Republican*, November 3, 1862.

ACS. Their mistake stung McLain all the more when Lincoln and Usher reminded him, shortly afterward, that the administration could not reimburse the society for any classes of emigrant not covered by the appropriations, a rule that it had brazenly disregarded for the Chiriquí project.[122]

The passenger manifest for Chiriquí included some unlikely names. "Events stronger than any power I can oppose to them have convinced my son that the chances here are all against him, and he desires to join your colony," mourned Frederick Douglass in an open letter to Pomeroy.[123] With white rioters throughout the lower North attacking African Americans, and the Confederates encircling Washington, expatriation appealed to black northerners more than ever. While Pomeroy's colonists surrounded the White House, demanding the order to set sail, one of Ambrose Thompson's spies in the Department of the Interior, a clerk named Charles Dyer, found Lincoln bereft at the setbacks to his scheme. "Like Micawber [he] is waiting for something to 'turn up,'" Dyer thought.[124] From early November until late December, the president hoped that that "something" would be a trio of amendments to the Constitution, but even as congressmen refused to indulge his dreams of compensated emancipation and colonization, the Chiriquí scheme collapsed. Shortly after the New Year of 1863, the president belatedly discovered that Ambrose Thompson's cabal extended as far as the new secretary of the interior, John Usher. Lincoln's source was a German-American businessman, Bernard Kock, who, as this chapter will show, ended up embarrassing Lincoln more than Usher ever could have done.[125]

Unfortunately, in the meantime, the Chiriquí controversy had gone much farther than the District of Columbia and a district of Colombia. Indeed, the summer of 1862 had spared the Department of State on just one front: the remarkably equanimous response of the British government to the scheme. Despite the Clayton–Bulwer Treaty (1850), which stipulated mutual Anglo-American restraint in Central America, London had agreed, once Washington had conceded that the "emigrants would have to look solely to the local government for protection," that the Chiriquí

---

[122] W. McLain to J. B. Pinney, October 11, and McLain to Hall, October 13, 1862, reel 204, ACS.

[123] David W. Blight, *Keeping Faith in Jubilee: Frederick Douglass' Civil War* (Baton Rouge, 1989), 143n34; "Fred. Douglass' Views of Colonization," Philadelphia *Press*, September 5, 1862.

[124] Dyer to A. W. Thompson, November 11, 1862, box 7, A. W. Thompson Papers.

[125] B. Kock to F. P. Blair, Sr., January 16, reel 11, and Blair to Kock, January 18, 1863, reel 22, BF.

project did not constitute colonization of the forbidden kind.[126] The foreign ministries of Central America were not so easily appeased, being unfamiliar with Lincoln's idiomatic usage of "colonization" – and at far greater risk than Britain from US expansionism. Although those versed in Yankee peculiarities, such as Manuel Murillo, might try to explain to their fellow Latin Americans that the policy was "only about removing people of the African race," isthmians were horrified at a word that evoked filibustering.[127] Unaware of the specifically Colombian context to the Chiriquí scheme's plodding progress during late 1862, historians have always attributed the White House's indefinite suspension of the expedition to the wider regional backlash against the United States. In fact, since the administration harbored no designs on the rest of Central America, William Seward was quick to reassure regional governments, with the significant exception of Costa Rica, that the United States would send no settlers where they were not wanted. But for those American investors who had spent a long time cultivating schemes with skeptical authorities, recovering from the adverse effects of the press's coverage of Lincoln's meeting with the black deputation would prove a protracted process.

Central America

To survey Central American responses from north to south is to start with Guatemala. In 1859, the US minister, a proslavery Kentuckian, Beverly Clarke, had warned Guatemala's foreign minister that southerners would object to any award of land made to "philanthropists" out to resettle African Americans.[128] Ironically, it was also Guatemala where the incoming Lincoln administration tried to contain the contagion of secession by sending its own minister, Elisha Crosby, to secure a site quickly enough to win over those southerners who might be inspired to remain in the Union if they could believe that the federal government was about to implement a colonization scheme. Years later, Crosby recalled that the Republicans Francis Blair, Preston King, Benjamin Wade, Charles Sumner, and

---

[126] W. Stuart to J. Russell, No. 301, October 18, 1862, in James J. Barnes and Patience P. Barnes, eds., *The American Civil War through British Eyes: Dispatches from British Diplomats* (Kent, 2003–5), 2:212–13.

[127] "Inmigración de libertos norte-americanos a Chiriquí," *La Estrella de Panamá*, November 29, 1862.

[128] B. L. Clarke to L. Cass, No. 11, July 22, 1859, Despatches from U.S. Ministers to Central America, RG59/M219/6, NARA II.

William Seward had hatched the plan – noteworthy in itself, if accurate of the last two. Crosby approached President Rafael Carrera (1851–65) and his Honduran counterpart, José Santos Guardiola (1856–62). As Crosby recalled, "they put the question to me, 'If the U.S. want to colonize the free blacks ... why don't they appropriate some of their own sparsely populated territory to this purpose?'" In the best tradition of Robert Shufeldt, Crosby's autobiography would minimize his own enthusiasm for the venture, which he described as having collapsed with the Civil War's outbreak.[129]

In fact, Crosby pushed the idea into 1862, with the support of Carrera and other planters, though one observer thought that Crosby had pestered *them* more than vice-versa.[130] But that August, Antonio José de Irisarri, the minister to the United States for Guatemala and El Salvador, was just as surprised as his compatriots to read the sloppy semantics of Lincoln's monologue to the black Washingtonians. "Central America is nothing more than the union ... of Guatemala, Salvador, Honduras, Nicaragua, and Costa Rica," Irisarri told Seward, not imagining for a moment that Lincoln had meant Chiriquí, on the fringes of a *South* American nation.[131] Seward replied by sniffing that it was "unusual to base diplomatic communications upon informal conversations ... reported in public journals," disavowing a conference to which the White House itself had invited a stenographer from the Associated Press. Seward did as Irisarri asked, however, and ruled out both governments that the minister represented.[132] Still concerned, Irisarri wrote home, warning that any such colonists might call in "auxiliaries from the vagabonds who will be available after the war," and evoking the fate of Mexico once it had settled Texas with Americans.[133]

Having resisted Elisha Crosby's initial entreaties, Guatemala's neighbor, Honduras, attracted concessionaires only from 1862. That March, the US consul at Tegucigalpa, William Burchard, had written Seward to recommend African American emigration to the Bay Islands and Atlantic coast at large. In August, the US minister, James Partridge, established

---

[129] Charles A. Barker, ed., *Memoirs of Elisha Oscar Crosby: Reminiscences of California and Guatemala from 1849 to 1864* (San Marino, CA, 1945), 87–91.

[130] Walter A. Payne, "Lincoln's Caribbean Colonization Plan," *Pacific Historian* 7 (1963), 68–9; E. O. Crosby to Seward, No. 12, May 6, 1862, *PRFA*, 881–2.

[131] A. J. de Irisarri to Seward, August 26, 1862, *PRFA*, 883.

[132] Seward to Irisarri, September 5, 1862, *PRFA*, 883–4.

[133] Mary Patricia Chapman, "The Mission of Elisha O. Crosby to Guatemala, 1861–1864," *Pacific Historical Review* 24 (1955), 278.

from Santos Guardiola's successor that, while the "government was anxious for an immigration of industrious *whites*," it viewed the coast as already awash with unruly black communities.[134] For his part, Seward took those remarks as enough to strike Honduras from the list, but in November, a New York businessman, William Coombs, asked Luis Molina, who represented Honduras and Nicaragua as well as Costa Rica, whether he might be allowed to introduce 500 African Americans.[135] Molina, while announcing no personal "opposition to the importation of colored laborers," refused to disobey his government's instructions.[136] A week later, Elisha Crosby once more approached the Department of State, though this time with respect to Honduras alone, and reported that one of his contacts favorable to black colonization, León Alvarado, would be that government's next minister to the United States.[137] Seward reminded Crosby that, whatever Alvarado's preferences, the government that, moreover, he only *might* come to represent had not changed its stance.[138] Yet Alvarado was also acquainted with the era's outstanding US expert on isthmian affairs, the New York archaeologist and journalist Ephraim Squier, who met Lincoln in March 1863 to discuss colonization on the Bay Islands.[139] "Let us have a map, for I am not very strong on the geographics," laughed the president. Wary of backing another Central American adventurer, though, Lincoln took the matter no further.[140]

To the south of Honduras lay Nicaragua, which most contemporaries assumed the likeliest location for an isthmian canal on account of its easier terrain than the narrower but hillier Panama. Having read Squier's *Nicaragua* (1852), the black abolitionist James McCune Smith hailed the country's ethnic diversity as a rejoinder to racial separatism:

---

[134] W. C. Burchard to Seward, March 15, 1862, Despatches from U.S. Consuls in Tegucigalpa, RG59/T352/1, NARA II; J. R. Partridge to Seward, No. 11, August 26, 1862, *PRFA*, 891–2.

[135] Seward to Partridge, No. 8, September 18, 1862, *PRFA*, 892; W. J. Coombs to Molina, November 12, 1862, E. G. Squier Papers, LC.

[136] Molina to Coombs, November 13, 1862, Squier Papers.

[137] Crosby to Seward, No. 27, November 21, 1862, RG59/M219/7.

[138] Seward to Crosby, No. 36, January 19, 1863, RG59/M77/28.

[139] W. D. Giles to E. G. Squier, March 11, 1863, Squier Family Papers, New-York Historical Society; J. S. Mackie to R. D. Owen, May 13, 1863, American Freedmen's Inquiry Commission Records, Harvard; G. Mathew to R. B. P. Lyons, August 30, 1863, Correspondence of the Legation in the United States, FO115/389, 267–8, TNA.

[140] "A Little Story," *Frank Leslie's Illustrated Newspaper*, July 29, 1865. The article is anonymous, but betrays the firsthand knowledge of the newspaper's editor, Squier.

"hear that, American Colonizationism! Where is the barrier which the Almighty has placed between the admixture of the negro and the white man?"[141] That year, Martin Delany was elected mayor of Greytown (San Juan del Norte), Nicaragua, in his absence (and without his foreknowledge), a result engineered by a friend and recent immigrant, David Peck. Like William Walker, whose own filibuster lay in the future, Peck had dethroned unpopular local conservatives in the process; again like Walker, Peck had also won that election on the strength of a powerful minority, not the local majority – which, in this case, meant the Miskito Indians, happy nonetheless to see the white elite displaced.[142] Thereafter, Nicaragua attracted little interest from African Americans until 1861, when 150 exiles from Louisiana made their way to Greytown.[143] They cannot have attracted much attention, because in 1862, it took an open letter from a Confederate provocateur, John Heiss, to apprise Nicaraguans of the North's own expulsive whims.[144] Walker's successor, President Tomás Martínez (1857–67), was so shocked that he started planning concerted resistance by the Central American republics.[145]

The US minister, Andrew Dickinson, explained to his counterpart in Costa Rica, Charles Riotte, why Nicaraguans were so averse to colonization. First, they abhorred being considered the equals of emancipated slaves; "paradoxical as it may seem, the colored population are the most exercised."[146] Second, news had already leaked that an agent of the Accessory Transit Company, an isthmian firm owned by the transportation magnate Cornelius Vanderbilt, had broached importing black American labor into the country. Third, a handful of southern secessionists had moved to Nicaragua even before the Walker filibuster and had wisely kept their distance from it (though not Heiss himself): having, therefore, retained "the esteem of this government, . . . they have seized upon this colonization scheme from its inception."[147] Dickinson understood that he needed to visibly respond to even groundless accusations against the United States, and sent a messenger to Washington to secure dispatches reassuring the region.[148] As the panic subsided, thanks in part to

[141] "Nicaragua," *FDP*, January 8, 1852.
[142] Robert S. Levine, *Martin Delany, Frederick Douglass, and the Politics of Representative Identity* (Chapel Hill, 1997), 62–3.
[143] "The Haytian Movement," *WAA*, May 4, 1861.
[144] "Inserciones," *Gaceta oficial de Honduras*, August 10, 1862.
[145] P. Zeledon to Irisarri, July 29, 1862, *PRFA*, 885–6.
[146] A. B. Dickinson to Seward, No. 27, September 12, 1862, *PRFA*, 893–4.
[147] Dickinson to C. N. Riotte, September 10, 1862, *PRFA*, 895–6.
[148] McLain to Pinney, October 11, 1862, reel 204, ACS.

a government decree banning the immigration of "freed negroes or other degraded caste[s] of people," Dickinson reported that he had rekindled Nicaragua's latent sympathies for the Union, while Heiss claimed to his own government that he had directed them forever Dixieward.[149] By 1863, the US consul at San Juan del Sur wondered whether Nicaragua might now accept African Americans, but acknowledged that "rebel sympathizers" remained an obstacle.[150]

It was Costa Rica that had the most compelling grievance against the Chiriquí project, if it was an accurate one: the expedition would actually land on Costa Rican soil.[151] Besides, William Seward stalled Luis Molina with hollow words whenever the minister protested Pomeroy's expedition. To Molina's claims that Chiriquí comprised only a Costa Rican and a contested part, Seward replied that the expedition would go nowhere but the Colombian part; to Molina's claims that Pomeroy was still canvassing settlers, Seward replied that the United States would "take no step in the matter contrary to the expressed wishes ... of Central America," whatever that meant.[152] The diplomats could not know that the dictates of their role had forced both of them to take a stance contrary to their personal beliefs: while Seward privately opposed the transfer of African Americans to Central America, Molina in fact supported it, under the right constraints – as did his superior, the foreign minister, Francisco María Iglesias. Through mid-1862, the US minister to Costa Rica, Charles Riotte, had successfully softened local prejudices against a colony that he had long been planning. Like his colleague in Ecuador, Friedrich Hassaurek, Riotte had cited promising "information on the behavior of freed slaves contained in northern and English papers," which had been enough to persuade Iglesias to ask the Costa Rican congress to set aside some territory for them.[153]

When news of Lincoln's August address reached Costa Rica, Iglesias recoiled. "At first, I thought that the establishment of colonies of freed blacks in our deserted and unhealthy coast would be beneficial," he

---

[149] Zeledon to Molina, September 11, 1862, *PRFA*, 906–7; Dickinson to Seward, No. 30, November 12, 1862, RG59/M219/13; A. D. Mann to J. P. Benjamin, No. 31, November 2, 1862, reel 4, Confederate States of America Records, LC.

[150] B. L. Hill to Z. Chandler, November 10, 1863, Zacariah Chandler Papers, LC.

[151] Michael D. Olien, "United States Colonization Programs for Blacks in Latin America during the 19th Century," *Contributions of the Latin American Anthropology Group* 1 (1976), 12.

[152] Seward to Molina, September 24 and October 1, 1862, *PRFA*, 903–6.

[153] Riotte to Seward, No. 33, May 15, 1862, *PRFA*, 887.

admitted to Molina, while advocating an immediate ban on all North American immigrants.[154] Yet Riotte, knowing Iglesias's true feelings, handled him with a mixture of flattery and firmness. How poorly it would reflect on "the sagacity of Costa-Rican Statesmen," oozed Riotte, "if the artificial excitement, fostered in the neighboring republics, should really prove contagious."[155] In early November 1862, Costa Rica passed a law banning black and Chinese immigration – and infringing its treaty with the United States, as Riotte reminded Iglesias.[156] They agreed to hold a convention to discuss immigration, which came to naught after Seward signally failed to send his minister the necessary guidelines.[157] But by 1866, Riotte had given up on the sagacity of Costa Rican statesmen. "All their protestations of a desire for immigration are sham and hypocrisy," he told Seward, listing their prejudices against different nationalities. As to Americans, Riotte claimed that Costa Ricans believed that "negroes from the United States are dangerous because of their being spoiled by a spirit of independence."[158]

INVITING FAILURE: HAITI

If there was one country that just might accept black Americans of independent spirit, then it was Haiti. At the end of 1862, with the Emancipation Proclamation looming and no emigration project in sight, a desperate Lincoln turned to the black republic.[159] Rather, he turned to another middleman clutching another lease, breaking the rules that he had set himself a month earlier in his second annual message.

---

[154] Schoonover, "Misconstrued Mission," 617.
[155] Riotte to F. M Iglesias, No. 27, September 20, in Riotte to Seward, No. 51, November 27, 1862, RG59/M219/18.
[156] Riotte to Iglesias, No. 36, November 27, in Riotte to Seward, No. 51, November 27, 1862, RG59/M219/18; Decreto XXXVII, in de la Paz (pub.), *Colección de las leyes de Costa Rica* (San José, 1872), 17:158–60.
[157] Riotte to Seward, No. 60, February 14, 1863, RG59/M219/18.
[158] Riotte to Seward, No. 161, December 25, 1866, RG59/M219/20.
[159] For the Île à Vache scheme, see Frederic Bancroft, "The Ile à Vache Experiment in Colonization," in Jacob E. Cooke, ed., *Frederic Bancroft, Historian* (Norman, 1957), 228–58; Willis D. Boyd, "The Île a Vache Colonization Venture, 1862–1864," *Americas* 16 (1959), 45–62; and James D. Lockett, "Abraham Lincoln and Colonization: An Episode that Ends in Tragedy at L'Ile a Vache, Haiti, 1863–1864," *Journal of Black Studies* 21 (1991), 428–44.

Disaster Avoided

In early 1862, a New Orleans trader, Bernard Kock, had been so impressed by the Haitian cotton displayed at London's International Exhibition that he decided to investigate the country at once. That August, in Port-au-Prince, he signed an agreement with President Geffrard for the Île à Vache, an uninhabited island off Haiti's southwestern coast.[160] The next month found Kock in Washington, outlining his proposition for cotton cultivation to Caleb Smith, Abraham Lincoln, James Mitchell, and Edward Bates, but having to compete with the Chiriquí contract. Lincoln was too preoccupied with Ambrose Thompson's scheme to pay attention to Kock's; Mitchell, by contrast, had barely been involved in the former after convening the black delegation, and switched his support to the latter; and Bates denounced Kock as a "charlatan adventurer."[161] Nonetheless, Lincoln forwarded Kock's proposal to Samuel Pomeroy, whose interest in Chiriquí had likely become unethical by this point. "The papers submitted for my consideration contain very large promises . . . rarely if ever offered to the settlers of any new country," warned the senator.[162]

On New Year's Eve, 1862, as black northerners gathered in churches to await confirmation of the Emancipation Proclamation, Abraham Lincoln hastily drew up a contract with Bernard Kock. Helped by James Doolittle and the Blairs, who, like Mitchell, had turned against the Chiriquí scheme because of its blatant flaws, Lincoln and Kock reached an agreement for colonizing 5,000 contrabands. It was dated December 31, 1862, though they actually signed it in the early hours of January 1, 1863, before the president issued the Emancipation Proclamation.[163] The contract marked "the beginning of the second great Exodus," effused Francis Blair.[164] But Lincoln asked Kock to tell nobody about the

---

[160] Bernard Kock, *Statement of Facts in Relation to the Settlement on the Island of A'Vache* (New York, 1864), 1–2.
[161] Kock to Smith, September 6, and Mitchell to Lincoln, November 6, 1862, Documents Pertaining to Bernard Kock's Proposal, RG48/M160/9; Kock to Lincoln, October 4, 1862, AL; entry, November 29, 1862, in Howard K. Beale, ed., *The Diary of Edward Bates, 1859–1866* (Washington, DC, 1933), 268.
[162] Pomeroy to Lincoln, December 1, 1862, Communications Relating to S. C. Pomeroy, RG48/M160/8.
[163] Entry, September 26, 1862, in Howard K. Beale, ed., *Diary of Gideon Welles, Secretary of the Navy under Lincoln and Johnson* (New York, 1960), 1:151; Kock, *Statement*, 4.
[164] E. B. Lee to S. P. Lee, December 31, 1862, in Virginia Jean Laas, ed., *Wartime Washington: The Civil War Letters of Elizabeth Blair Lee* (Urbana, 1991), 223.

contract, not even members of the cabinet, except for the indispensable William Seward and supportive Montgomery Blair.[165]

No sooner had Lincoln signed the agreement than Seward refused to certify it.[166] The secretary's misgivings were prescient. "Prevent the consummation of a fraud upon the Interior Department to the amount of twenty five thousand dollars," wired Robert Murray, the US marshal at New York. He had gathered evidence that Kock had a slew of debts and even planned to sell his passengers into Cuban slavery.[167] The contractor offered to demonstrate his good faith by taking only 1,500 settlers and by accepting payment in supplies rather than cash, but Mitchell, for one, now excused himself from the scheme.[168] The Blairs divulged to Kock, for Lincoln's ear, the fact of Usher's stake in the Chiriquí project, to prevent the revival of that rival venture.[169] As was the case for Mitchell, however, that marked the Blairs' last dealing with Kock.

Yet Kock had (literally) closer competition than Thompson: James De Long, US consul at Aux Cayes, a port on the Haitian mainland across the bay from Kock's new island. In early 1863, De Long came to Washington to request 500 contrabands to fulfill his own lease from Port-au-Prince.[170] He won the support of Mitchell, Usher, Menard (who wished to leave as soon as possible for the "limits of a Negro Nationality"), and, strangely enough, Seward. The secretary of state might have thought that, if colonization *had* to happen, it would be better kept within the Department of State.[171] Yet Seward would not relent on his circular, telling De Long to return to Haiti to obtain clearance from its government.[172] By April 1863, James De Long's expedition had collapsed, probably because Bernard Kock managed to rekindle his own, which evidently held Lincoln's favor.[173] While it was awkward enough for a consul to double up as a

[165] John T. Doyle, "An Episode of the Civil War," *Overland Monthly and Out West Magazine* 9 (1887), 540–1.

[166] Seward to Lincoln, January 3, 1863, AL.

[167] R. Murray to Usher, January 13, 1863, Kock Documents.

[168] Kock to Lincoln, January 17, 1863, AL; Mitchell to Usher, January 19, 1863, Kock Documents.

[169] F. P. Blair, Sr., to Kock, January 18, 1863, reel 22, BF.

[170] J. De Long, proposition, February 25, 1863, reel 183, WHS.

[171] Seward to Usher, February 9, 1863, Communications Relating to the Claim of James De Long, RG48/M160/9; De Long to F. W. Seward, February 20, 1863, reel 76, WHS; J. W. Menard to Usher, April 11, 1863, Miscellaneous Letters.

[172] De Long to Usher, April 3, 1863, De Long Communications.

[173] Menard to E. Roumain, April 5, 1863, reel 37, Maximilien Collection, NYPL.

concessionaire, De Long's new role, that of sore loser to a competitor whose own venture fell under his consular jurisdiction, was egregious. To relieve the stigma attached to his own name, Bernard Kock had mustered two New York associates, Paul Forbes and Charles Tuckerman, whose syndicate included two further, silent partners: Leonard Jerome, a financier who had already lost several fortunes (and who would become grandfather to Winston Churchill), and Henry Raymond, who had cofounded the Union's most influential newspaper, the *New York Times*.[174] The four entrepreneurs invested $70,000 in return for a half-share between them, and Bernard Kock started fitting out the *Ocean Ranger*.[175] On the eve of its departure, the partners learned that the White House refused to recognize a contract that they had assumed they were fulfilling with its blessing. Later that year, Kock, on the one side, and Forbes and Tuckerman, on the other, would make conflicting claims about the administration's objections at that juncture. The former argued that Lincoln had turned against the entire agreement, and the latter, that he was willing to renew it with parties other than Kock.[176] Wherever the truth lay, contractor and contract now changed alike. Bernard Kock surrendered his lease to the syndicate (nominally, he believed), while Charles Tuckerman was on the cusp of signing its own agreement with Lincoln when he noticed a change from the version that Kock had shown him.

The president had already insisted that the syndicate forgo payment until it presented a consular certificate showing that the emigrants had landed, lest they be "tampered with by evil disposed persons while on the voyage" – that is to say, sold into slavery.[177] Seward now told Tuckerman, whose modest means always made him the most plaintive of the partners, to obtain Haiti's assent to the September 30 circular, which stipulated that settlers not come to want.[178] Protesting that the *Ocean Ranger* was incurring demurrage, Tuckerman threatened to

---

[174] Usher to L. W. Jerome, December 14, 1863, S. Exec. Doc. 55, 41; Usher to H. J. Raymond, September 18, 1863, Letters Sent, RG48/M160/1.

[175] Kock, *Statement*, 6–7; Paul S. Forbes and Charles K. Tuckerman, *Statement of Circumstances Attending the Experiment of Colonizing Free Negroes at the Island of A'Vache* (New York, 1864), 5–6.

[176] Kock, *Statement*, 9; Forbes, *Statement*, 6.

[177] Charles Eames, *Papers Relating to the Colonization Experiment at A'Vache* (n.p., 1865), 2, in Tuckerman to W. H. Seward, October 2, 1865, Correspondence Concerning the Claim of Paul S. Forbes and Charles K. Tuckerman, RG48/M160/9.

[178] E. D. Smith to Usher, April 9, 1863, Forbes Correspondence.

abandon the venture unless the administration backed down.[179] Usher and Seward met him halfway, drafting a certificate for President Geffrard to retroactively approve Seward's provisions.[180]

It was an awkward, even awful compromise, to which Charles Tuckerman assented "because *time* was of such vital importance."[181] Like Abraham Lincoln (in making the original contract with Bernard Kock), William Seward had broken his own rules; like Lincoln, he would rue his mistake. Meanwhile, John Usher resented the triumph of Kock's scheme over Ambrose Thompson's, telling Tuckerman that he was "making a good thing" out of a contract that awarded $50 per settler where $12 would have sufficed.[182] Nonetheless, Usher likely spoke for Lincoln's genuine buyer's remorse when he warned Tuckerman, just days after the president had signed the agreement, that the New Yorkers should not expect further emigrants.[183] In conjunction with Seward's own interventions, Usher's words sealed the fate of a colony run by capitalists who faced the stark choice between doubling down and cutting their losses.

Disaster Assured

For more than 400 settlers (it is impossible to ascertain the exact number), the ship had already sailed.[184] In the original negotiations, President Lincoln had asked Kock to relieve the "embarrassment of the administration" by recruiting from the contraband camps, so Tuckerman had turned to Fort Monroe, canvassing its inhabitants alongside James Redpath's former agent, William J. Watkins. Their passenger manifest comprised mostly Tidewater Virginians, but also more than twenty North Carolinians and an Alabamian. Almost all were in their twenties, though the oldest was sixty-two, and men outnumbered women threefold.[185] An expedition slanted toward young men was ideal for the toils of a first wave of pioneers, but, despite Lincoln's express hopes for a rounded demographic mix, it hardly contained the makings of a permanent settlement. All that historians can identify of the colonists' own motives comes

---

[179] Tuckerman to Lincoln, March 31, 1863, AL.
[180] Usher to P. S. Forbes and Tuckerman, April 3, 1863, S. Exec. Doc. 55, 24–5.
[181] Tuckerman to Seward, April 2, 1863, reel 77, WHS.
[182] Tuckerman to Usher, April 18, 1864, Forbes Correspondence.
[183] Usher to Tuckerman, April 17, 1863, S. Exec. Doc. 55, 29–30.
[184] Robert Bray, "Abraham Lincoln and the Colony on Ile-a-Vache" (online, 2012), 3n2.
[185] Doyle, "An Episode," 540–1; Boyd, "Île a Vache Colonization Venture," 51.

FIGURE 4.1 Scrip for the settlers of the Île à Vache, signed by Bernard Kock and Andrew Ripka.
Enclosed in B. F. Whidden to W. H. Seward, No. 31, July 30, 1863, Abraham Lincoln Papers, LC

from the testimony of white agents bent on discrediting each other. According to Charles Tuckerman, one "old and respectable negro," when asked whether he fully understood the choice before him, called upon God "to witness that [the settlers] left ... with the knowledge that they were going to a strange and new land." According to James De Long, though, who avidly gathered evidence of the contractors' misdeeds, Watkins had told the settlers that they would sail to Washington, to meet the president.[186]

Events took an unpleasant turn on board ship, which had been contaminated by a smallpox epidemic raging near Fort Monroe. Allegedly, Watkins and Kock charged their passengers for food and water, forcing them to change their US dollars for a scrip that the leaseholder had issued in his own name (Figure 4.1).[187] In early May, the *Ocean Ranger* anchored in Ferret Bay, on the northwestern tip of the Île à Vache, and Kock immediately isolated the smallpox sufferers on a different beach. Although he found three houses that his overseer had already erected, Kock discovered that the New Yorkers had refused to send supplies until they heard of the expedition's arrival. A letter awaited him from

[186] Tuckerman to Usher, April 18, 1864, Forbes Correspondence.
[187] A. Scott et al., affidavit, January 28, 1864, Correspondence and Reports Relating to D. C. Donnohue, RG48/M160/9.

Tuckerman, which admonished Kock, as the latter bitterly protested, "to properly clothe, shoe, and shelter [his] negroes, while [Tuckerman] was sitting in New York in possession of all the goods purchased ... for that purpose."[188] Although Kock, the self-appointed "governor" of the island, had dreamed of a large settlement in its interior, the colonists would never get to move from pitiful palmetto huts on the shore. While the settlers largely managed to avoid the crocodiles that guarded the island's fresh-water pools, they could not escape the chigoe fleas that constantly burrowed into their feet, reports of which reached Lincoln himself.[189] Lord Lyons, the British minister to Washington, found the matter of the settlers' suffering "so painful" for the administration that he could not elicit any information about the project.[190] Even the US commissioner to Haiti, Benjamin Whidden, never heard from his own government about a venture whose death throes he dutifully reported nonetheless.[191]

In July 1863, Paul Forbes and Charles Tuckerman requested payment from John Usher for fulfilling all conditions asked of them bar one: obtaining Fabre Geffrard's signature to the terms of William Seward's circular. Instead, Port-au-Prince had naturalized the settlers, the only solution possible "without awakening jealousy between the native population and the Emigrants."[192] That compromise did not appease Secretary Usher. "It is to be regretted that you entered upon the removal of these persons until you had first obtained the guarantees from the Haytien government," he told Forbes and Tuckerman. Usher asked how, exactly, he had just read a report in the Confederate press crowing, albeit hyperbolically, that half of the settlers had already died.[193]

For its part, Haiti had not rejected Seward's demands without careful reflection, but its government had always found itself in two minds about the opportunities presented by the Civil War. On the one hand, the conflict had brought about US recognition as well as a gap in the global cotton market that Haiti might still plug with the field-hand expertise that

[188] Kock, *Statement*, 12–14.
[189] W. S. Skinner, affidavit, September 24, in B. F. Whidden to Seward, No. 39, October 3, 1863, Despatches from U.S. Ministers to Haiti, RG59/M82/1, NARA II; John Eaton, *Grant, Lincoln, and the Freedmen* (New York, 1907), 91–2.
[190] Lyons to E. M. Archibald, July 18, 1863, Slave Trade and African Department Records, FO84/1202, 187–9, TNA.
[191] Whidden to De Long, No. 4, October 17, 1863, RG59/M82/1.
[192] Forbes and Tuckerman to Usher, July 7, 1863, Forbes Correspondence.
[193] Usher to Forbes and Tuckerman, July 7, and Usher to Tuckerman, July 8, 1863, S. Exec. Doc. 55, 33–4.

Redpath's scheme had failed to deliver.[194] On the other, even the nation that had repelled Napoleon Bonaparte's finest feared entanglement with Jefferson Davis's, and so preferred to recruit northern immigrants, however unfamiliar they were with cash crops.[195] Whatever course it charted, though, Haiti could always trust one well-placed American to help it. No sooner had its envoy to the United States, Ernest Roumain, arrived in Washington than the commissioner of colonization, James Mitchell, obtained him a coveted copy of the recent US treaty with Liberia.[196] Mitchell assured Roumain that he now spurned "the Spanish American States" and contractors such as Kock, preferring direct arrangements with Haiti, Liberia, and the British colonies, which, their "white nationality" aside, at least offered "unity of language, civil laws, and religious faith."[197]

Independently of Mitchell, Charles Tuckerman importuned Roumain for Port-au-Prince's blessing on the Île à Vache project, to fulfill the one remaining technicality of his contract with Lincoln.[198] In June 1863, Roumain heard back from his superiors, who had decided that, since as strong a power as Britain had decided against alienating the Confederacy with formal arrangements for black colonization (Chapter 5), Haiti could hardly do less. "We must, therefore, avoid dealing with the question of emigration as one government to another," explained Haiti's foreign minister.[199] While the council of state had now approved Kock's earlier transfer of his lease to Forbes and Tuckerman, it refused to underwrite the settlement itself.[200] Roumain broke the news to Tuckerman, and Tuckerman conveyed it to John Usher. If one of Bernard Kock's allegations was correct, that Seward had meant his own circular to thwart colonization altogether by setting terms that no host state could accept, then the secretary of state's gamble had somehow failed *and* succeeded – ominously, in that order.[201]

Marooned more than 1,300 miles from Fort Monroe, the inhabitants of the Île à Vache had every reason to think that their erstwhile compatriots had forgotten all about them. When a supply ship finally arrived, on

---

[194] Eller, "Dominican Civil War," 155; H. Byron to J. Russell, No. 10, November 8, 1862, Haiti Correspondence, FO35/56, 44–5, TNA.
[195] G. Lawrence, Jr., to Roumain, No. 6, March 12, 1863, reel 37, Maximilien Collection.
[196] Mitchell to Roumain, March 24, 1863, ibid.
[197] Mitchell to Roumain, March 20, 1863, ibid.
[198] Tuckerman to Roumain, April 15, 1863, ibid.
[199] A. Dupuy to Roumain, June 3, 1863, ibid.
[200] J. Damier to Roumain, June 11, 1863, ibid.   [201] Kock, *Statement*, 3.

July 1, without the lumber for their long-awaited houses, they rebelled. Under the watchful eye of Andrew Ripka, a Philadelphia cotton merchant and agent reporting directly to Forbes and Tuckerman, Kock called in Haitian troops to quell the disorder. By the middle of July, Kock stopped distributing rations to his workers, "in order to avoid their shirking work with a full stomach." The smallpox having run its course, with about thirty casualties, Kock prayed that the colony would finally flourish.[202]

In August, Ripka left for the United States to hand the administration its first eyewitness report not to have come from the pen of Kock, De Long, or anyone else heavily vested in the business. Although an appointee of the New Yorkers, Ripka's account was so evenhanded that Usher offered to extend his role under an official commission, which Ripka thought proper to decline.[203] The secretary instead chose his own law partner, Dillard Donnohue, who sailed to the island that November.[204] In the meantime, a shipper familiar with Haiti, Allston Wilson, appeared from nowhere to echo some of the administration's prior concerns, while concluding on a more optimistic note. It was true, admitted Wilson, that Bernard Kock had not kept several promises, prioritizing his own accommodation over the settlers'. But he also planned a new village for the salubrious savannah of the interior, while recent rains had revived failing corn and cotton. "I heard many [settlers] express a wish to be back to old Virginia, whilst the experience of others caused them to be thankful that they were free and out of harm's way," reported Wilson. "The colony depends entirely upon the future good or bad management ... in the course of the next six months there would be an important change manifested."[205] In other words, prosperity was just around the corner.

Stopping at Port-au-Prince on his way to the Île à Vache, Donnohue met Ripka, who confessed that the investors had instructed him to either sell their interest or abandon the colony altogether.[206] Back in New York, the partners even asked Hiram Ketchum's American West Indies Company whether it could transfer the settlers to Santo Domingo, but that firm had since recommitted itself to encouraging strictly white immigration to eastern Hispaniola.[207] Andrew Ripka, Dillard Donnohue, and

---

[202] Ibid., 18–21.   [203] Tuckerman to Usher, October 20, 1863, Forbes Correspondence.
[204] Usher to D. C. Donnohue, October 17, October 20, and November 16, 1863, S. Exec. Doc. 55, 36–7, 38, 39.
[205] A. Wilson to Usher, October 31, 1863, Donnohue Correspondence.
[206] Donnohue to Usher, December 5, 1863, ibid.
[207] Archibald to Stuart, September 14, 1863, FO84/1202, 192–3.

Benjamin Whidden conferred to determine the fate of a highly anomalous group of people, who had, after all, taken Haitian citizenship and who came closest to US jurisdiction as commodities in a private concern's contract – the very chattel status that they had tried to escape.[208] Ripka reported that Haiti would not let him send the settlers to the mainland or keep them on the island under continued white management, though Geffrard had intimated that he would accept settlers for his own estate.[209] Ripka agreed with Donnohue that the partners had "no right to sell a people who had already received great injustice," and transferred his powers to that investigator, whose official status would carry greater weight with Port-au-Prince.[210] Writing Usher as soon as he could, Donnohue reported that Allston Wilson's statement had been "a well devised tissue of falshoods," meant to hasten payment by attributing teething troubles to the now-deposed Kock, who was, however, also in Port-au-Prince at that moment, asking the authorities to restore him to power. "He is not without influence here," warned Donnohue. "He speaks their language and has the assurance of the devil."[211] Without having even visited the Île à Vache, Donnohue advised Usher to recall the expedition.

Once he reached the island, Donnohue tried to count the colonists. He found only 292 on site and another 73 scattered around the port of Aux Cayes, while other inquiries persuaded him that no more than 420 had ever left Fort Monroe.[212] Kock must have enjoyed some success lobbying the Haitian government, because he showed up on the island once more, managing to walk not 150 yards among "his people" before they surrounded him. Kock shrieked that the colonists wanted to kill him, and Donnohue, joking that they wanted merely to embrace him, booked him a berth on the next steamer.[213] Harder for Donnohue to pack off on a boat was James De Long, who, though pleased to meet the impartial official whom the settlers had long needed, was too mindful of his own plantations to squander any chance to transfer the colonists from penury to peonage.[214] "He does not deserve any credit for the information furnished the Government," reported Donnohue, attributing De Long's

---

[208] Whidden to De Long, No. 8, November 18, 1863, RG59/M82/1.
[209] Tuckerman to Usher, January 9, 1864, Forbes Correspondence.
[210] Donnohue to Usher, December 5, 1863, Donnohue Correspondence.
[211] Donnohue to Usher, December 6, 1863, ibid.
[212] Donnohue to Usher, January 3, 1864, ibid.
[213] Donnohue to Usher, January 5, 1864, ibid.
[214] De Long to Usher, December 28, 1863, De Long Communications.

accurate but acerbic dispatches to his bitterness at his own venture's failure.[215]

In early 1864, General Fabre, the local governor, and Ernest Roumain, back from the United States, visited the island to persuade the settlers to move to farms on the Haitian mainland.[216] The two officials' request reflected their urgent desire to (literally) remove any grounds for US intervention – a prescient concern, as it turned out. Invoking the same American need for a Caribbean coaling station that had spawned the Chiriquí project, Donnohue boasted to Usher that he could establish one on the island with a single man-of-war. He was in part motivated by revenge, especially for Haiti's attempts to bind the settlers to labor: "a score of such islands would not compensate for the outrages they have perpetrated on our contrabands."[217] Yet Donnohue was also angrier than he was consistent: he variously advised the settlers to return to the United States, but also to accept work in Haiti, and dismissed the Île à Vache as infertile, but noted that twenty acres of cotton had begun to mature.[218]

It was just as well that the tight turnaround of the steamer that ran between Port-au-Prince and New York forced the administration to act quickly on Donnohue's early, negative reports, otherwise the president might have mirrored his agent's vacillations. On February 1, 1864, Lincoln asked Secretary of War Edwin Stanton to order a transport vessel, and Stanton in turn asked Quartermaster General Montgomery Meigs to name a reliable man.[219] Meigs instructed one of his assistants, Edward Hartz, to navigate the *Marcia C. Day* as though for Aspinwall (Colón), Panama, and to open his sealed orders, which were to change course for the Île à Vache, only on reaching 20°N.[220] Hartz was accompanied by men of the Invalid Corps, reserves mustered out of combat through injury, who invalided themselves even more by cooking with infectious tropical seawater.[221] On anchoring, they were met by Donnohue and De Long, who asked Hartz to accept forty destitute Redpath-era emigrants

---

[215] Donnohue to Usher, February 2, 1864, Usher Papers.
[216] Donnohue to Usher, January 5, 1864 (second letter), Donnohue Correspondence.
[217] Donnohue to Usher, January 3, 1864, ibid.
[218] Donnohue to Usher, January 16 (both letters), and February 2, 1864, ibid.; De Long to Whidden, No. 9, January 18, 1864, RG59/M82/1.
[219] E. M. Stanton to M. C. Meigs, February 3, 1864, Edward L. Hartz Papers, Duke University.
[220] Meigs to E. L. Hartz, February 4, 1864, ibid.
[221] Entry, February 20, 1864, Edward L. Hartz Diary, LC.

who had clustered around Aux Cayes.[222] Those settlers' "experimental voluntary expatriation had not yet rendered them the less citizens of our country," agreed Hartz.[223] On departing, he counted aboard 364 Île à Vache and 28 Redpath returnees, a total of 392.[224] The *Marcia C. Day* left behind the handful who had gone to the mainland and found work, some of whom were imprisoned shortly afterward for theft.[225]

On March 20, 1864, the ship moored at Alexandria, Virginia. The passengers disembarked for a contraband camp, Arlington's Freedmen's Village, where they had several choices. Some joined the army, as a Massachusetts recruiter swooped on the "best looking lot of 'darks' he ha[d] ever seen."[226] Others went to work for the Union Pacific Railway Company.[227] "The returned Haytian Colonists are on just the same footing as other Freedmen," decreed a quartermaster. "If they labor, they will be classed with laborers, – if not, they will be classed with dependent Freedmen."[228] The returnees did receive some special attention, though. Over the winter of 1863–4, William Seward visited Freedmen's Village several times. He evidently confided his major point of disagreement with the president to the camp's superintendent, Danforth Nichols, for in 1872, Nichols would thank Seward for his service to the nation, "knowing that it was through you that the scheme of Colonization . . . was prevented even though strongly advocated by the lamented Lincoln."[229] As the afterlife of the Île à Vache venture showed, Seward also felt guilty, however, about his own part in its demise.

Since the summer of 1863, the investors, especially Charles Tuckerman, had disputed with John Usher the likely contents of the colony's postmortem report, even as the colonists themselves continued to die on the island. All that we know of the settlers' suffering comes from the adversarial accounts of white antagonists. As the unwinnable argument showed, however, there was blame enough to go around. At first, Forbes and Tuckerman claimed that they had tried to fulfill what any businessman would have thought a valid contract, albeit one under another's name.[230] Secretary Usher countered that the only agreement

[222] De Long to Hartz, March 1, 1864, Hartz Papers.
[223] Entry, February 29, 1864, Hartz Diary.   [224] Entry, March 6, 1864, ibid.
[225] R. Loring to Whidden, No. 20, March 15, 1864, RG59/M82/1.
[226] T. Drew to J. A. Andrew, March 24, 1864, John A. Andrew Papers, Massachusetts Historical Society.
[227] E. M. Greene to D. B. Nichols, April 1, 1864, D. B. Nichols Scrapbooks, LC.
[228] E. M. Greene to D. B. Nichols, April 4, 1864, ibid.
[229] Nichols to Seward, April 5, 1872, reel 110, WHS.
[230] Tuckerman to Seward, October 17, 1863, Forbes Correspondence.

that should have concerned them was their own.[231] Then, tried Tuckerman, Seward's blank guarantee, for Geffrard to sign, had been unworkable, the kind of promise "which our own Government with regard to Irish or Chinese emigrants would never agree."[232] Had the administration "not clung to the literal carrying out of the clause," then the contractors would have received the money needed to make the enterprise a success.[233] Awkwardly, Donnohue's mercurial reports had seen Usher reverse position on whether the island was forlorn or fertile, and the United States therefore responsible (or not) for a venture doomed (or not) from the start.[234] Eventually, Tuckerman realized that he should concentrate his fire on James De Long, whom all acknowledged as a problematic party.[235] In 1865, following Usher's resignation and Lincoln's death, Tuckerman's case ended up with Seward, who offered what compensation he could: a diplomatic vacancy. In 1868, Charles Tuckerman became the first US minister to Greece.[236]

On the Île à Vache itself, the remains of the only African American colony officially backed by the federal government have long disappeared. The few, flimsy structures washed into the waves, as did the bones of the smallpox victims, buried in shallow, sandy graves.[237] The island's main settlement, Madame Bernard, had been called "Habitation Bernard" in an earlier, populated phase of its history, so reflects no link to Bernard Kock.[238] Yet the name of a town on Ferret Bay itself, Cacor, is but a variant of KaKock in Creole – and "Kock's Place," that deathtrap for his colonists, now contains a luxury resort.[239] In 2013, Haiti's prime minister proposed building an airport on an island once so densely wooded that the settlers could barely penetrate it on foot.[240]

The tragedy of the "Cow Island" project was that, from an early day, Abraham Lincoln was aware that he should not proceed – and yet

[231] Usher to Tuckerman, October 19, 1863, S. Exec. Doc. 55, 37.
[232] Tuckerman to Usher, July 29, 1863, Forbes Correspondence.
[233] Tuckerman to Usher, October 20, 1863, ibid.
[234] Tuckerman to Usher, April 18, 1864, ibid.
[235] Tuckerman to Seward, September 7, 1864, and Tuckerman to J. Harlan, December 27, 1865, ibid.
[236] Tuckerman to Seward, July 10, 1868, reel 104, WHS.
[237] R. Henry, affidavit, September 23, in Whidden to Seward, No. 39, October 3, 1863, RG59/M82/1.
[238] Kock, *Statement*, xvi.
[239] Ian Thomson, *Bonjour Blanc: A Journey through Haiti* (London, 2004), 154.
[240] "Haiti Set to Break Ground on New Airport in Ile a Vache," *Caribbean Journal* (online), August 10, 2013.

proceed he did. After all, he had known since the summer of 1862 that he would do better to shun private contractors, who had a questionable knack of making themselves all too readily available. From the moment that John Usher informed Charles Tuckerman that the first wave of colonists would also be the last, the settlement had descended into a vicious cycle of underinvestment by all parties concerned – except for the settlers themselves, who had vested their lives in it.

The president had another reason, though, for being so equivocal about seeing through his second attempted "contract colony" in Latin America. In the spring of 1863, even as he closed the deal with Forbes and Tuckerman, Lincoln shored up a superior substitute: the tropical American colonies of the British Empire, which preferred an ongoing harvest of immigrant labor to a one-time windfall of federal funds. What neither Lincoln nor Seward nor Usher knew was that they had stumbled on a solution that the colonies themselves had proposed ever since the emancipation of their own slaves, three decades earlier.

5

Resettlement in the European West Indies, to 1865

In the fall of 1917, the "father of black history," Carter Woodson, received a letter from an elderly Marylander, Stansbury Boyce, telling him of a long-forgotten episode of African American emigration. "Owing to the rapid decadence of the sugar industries of the British West Indies on the Abolition of Slavery," explained Boyce, "business men from England were sent to Baltimore to try to get free colored people to go to Trinidad." Boyce duly found himself, "an infant in arms," on a ship bound for the island. In his fifteen years abroad, he attended school and worked as a bookkeeper, estate overseer, and sign-painter.[1] Woodson was fascinated by the wider implications of Boyce's story and, in his *Century of Negro Migration* (1918), suggested that historians investigate African American emigration to the British Caribbean.[2] A century later still, this chapter follows his advice.

From the abolition of slavery in the British West Indies (1834) to the same milestone in the United States (1865), the metropolitan and colonial governments of the British Empire sought immigrants to compensate for the natives' newfound freedom from plantation discipline. Recruiters turned to Africa, China, and India, the last of which would prove the most fruitful source of labor.[3] During the middle third of the nineteenth century, however, canvassers wondered whether the answer lay right in front of them: the United States. "Why we should go to the other end of

---

[1] S. Boyce to C. G. Woodson, November 1, 1917, Carter Godwin Woodson Papers, LC.
[2] Carter G. Woodson, *A Century of Negro Migration* (Washington, DC, 1918), 69–74.
[3] K. O. Laurence, *Immigration into the West Indies in the 19th Century* (St. Lawrence, Barbados, 1971), 7–9, 45.

the world to procure the labour we require, when an ample supply is close at hand, I can hardly say," admitted one Belizean administrator.[4] Despite three waves of colonial interest in American immigration, peaking in 1839–41, 1850–1, and 1862–4, the republic of slavery never provided the empire of (questionable) liberty with more than a handful of the laborers that it needed to demonstrate the (downright doubtful) economic success of emancipation.[5] Yet Americans kept emitting so many favorable signals that imperial planners could not help reaching for their croupier rakes and shunting black counters from continental North America to the Caribbean.

That said, in a black Atlantic crisscrossed by migrations, permanent and temporary, West Indians and African Americans met each other in all directions.[6] In the early 1840s, Jamaican and Guyanese agents visited Liberia to try to recruit dissatisfied colonists, among them a future secretary of state, Hilary Teage, by offering them a voluntary middle passage.[7] A Trinidadian commentator even predicted that the American Colonization Society's ungodly experiment in taking black laborers from the New World to the Old would soon come to a well-deserved end.[8] Conversely, black Barbadian artisans, excluded from economic opportunities by the island's swollen population, looked to Liberia, first in 1847–8 and then again in 1864–5. The second time, an otherwise idle ACS obliged them, ignoring its own charter by funding the transportation of non-American blacks.[9] In 1861, one of James Redpath's agents persuaded forty inhabitants of the subtropical British island of Bermuda to move to Haiti, while in 1862, one of Monrovia's commissioners to the United States, Edward Wilmot Blyden, parted from his

---

[4] F. Seymour to E. J. Eyre, No. 134, December 14, 1862, in Colonial Office, pub., *Correspondence Respecting the Emigration of Free Negroes from the United States to the West Indies* (London, 1863), 8.

[5] For the economic results of abolition, see Seymour Drescher, *The Mighty Experiment: Free Labor versus Slavery in British Emancipation* (New York, 2002), 158–237.

[6] R. J. M. Blackett, "The Hamic Connection: African-Americans and the Caribbean, 1820–65," in Brian L. Moore and Swithin R. Wilmot, eds., *Before and after 1865: Education, Politics, and Regionalism in the Caribbean* (Kingston, 1998), 318.

[7] W. Fergusson to J. Russell, October 8, 1841, Sierra Leone Correspondence, CO267/166, 64–5, TNA; R. G. Butts to H. E. F. Young, January 7, 1845, HCPP 1847–8 (732), 18–19.

[8] "We subjoin below . . .," Port of Spain *Gazette*, February 7, 1843.

[9] Caree A. Banton, *More Auspicious Shores: Barbadian Migration to Liberia, Blackness, and the Making of an African Republic* (New York, 2019), 29–73; Melanie J. Newton, *The Children of Africa in the Colonies: Free People of Color in Barbados in the Age of Emancipation* (Baton Rouge, 2008), 274–6.

colleagues to recruit for Liberia in his native St. Thomas, a Danish possession.[10]

As Blyden's background showed, not all colonies in the Caribbean were British, either. In 1785, a veteran of the American Revolutionary War, the Marquis de Lafayette, had bought a tract in Cayenne (French Guiana) precisely because of its distance from St. Domingue (Haiti) and the major slave societies. Unlike the British recruiters of the following century, Lafayette was no crude capitalist, but a reformer who envisioned an experimental colony for phasing US slaves into freedom. He sent 12,000 French volunteers to prepare the site, all but 1,000 of whom had died two years later, only for French revolutionaries to confiscate his grant anyway.[11] In 1821, following France's restoration of slavery (1802) and of the monarchy (1814), its minister to the United States, Baron Hyde de Neuville, asked the ACS whether it might direct emigrants to French Guiana instead of Africa. "The King of *the Franks* has no desire to introduce new slaves into one of his most valuable colonies," punned the diplomat, whose French-language letter played on the dual meaning of "Franc" as "Frenchman" and "freeman."[12] The society evidently contained itself at de Neuville's wit. Once the Second Republic abolished slavery again (1848), this time for good, French officials sporadically revisited the idea.[13] During the American Civil War, they were joined by their counterparts in Denmark, which had seen slavery collapse in its colonies during the revolutionary year of 1848, as well as by those in the Netherlands, which resisted emancipation until 1863.

For African Americans, though, non-British options did not even register. Not only had Britain moved for emancipation earlier, but its colonies offered a common language, similar institutions, and, for the most part, a shared Protestantism. Moreover, African Americans left in significant numbers for only three of the British dependencies: Guiana, Jamaica, and Trinidad, the largest sugar colonies, whose planters had met emancipation (1834) and the termination of the transitional period known as "apprenticeship" (1838) with despair. While Jamaica's ensuing

---

[10] "We understand that ...," Bermuda *Royal Gazette*, August 6, 1861; Hollis R. Lynch, *Edward Wilmot Blyden: Pan-Negro Patriot, 1832–1912* (New York, 1970), 33; "To Persons of African Descent in St. Thomas and Other West India Islands," *Saint Christopher Gazette*, September 5, 1862.

[11] Nicholas Guyatt, *Bind Us Apart: How Enlightened Americans Invented Racial Segregation* (New York, 2016), 207–9.

[12] H. de Neuville to ACS, March 2, 1821, H. Rep. 348, 21 Cong., 1 Sess. (1830), 253–5.

[13] "Immigration coloniale," *Revue coloniale* 8 (1852), 293–9.

underproduction of sugar boiled down to freedpeople leaving the plantations, Trinidad and Guiana, which were more recent conquests (from Spain and the Netherlands), had never obtained enough labor, having been in the process of economic and demographic expansion when Westminster had passed the Slavery Abolition Act.[14] Indeed, Guiana, the one British colony on the South American continent, was barely settled beyond the coast.[15] But from one colony to another, the answer was always the same: find more nonwhite hands to work the fields.

Recruiters thought hard, and presumed harder, about the merits of the various ethnicities available to them. Yet African Americans represented the obvious choice, if experienced in plantation agriculture – and still a tempting one, even if not. After all, their white rulers were keen to eject them from their native land, and to find somewhere better suited to that task than Liberia.[16] Moreover, if African Americans immigrated to the British Empire, its own freedpeople would get to learn from those already familiar with life outside of slavery.[17] Promoters of such schemes highlighted black Americans' skill with tools and livestock, their physical muscularity, and the Protestant work ethic that they would instill in a heterodox populace (or, in Trinidad, a mostly Catholic one).[18]

Themselves prone to thinking in transactional terms, imperial canvassers knew that they would have to offer black Americans something in return. It could never be money: wages in the colonies were, notoriously, one-fourth to one-half their levels in the United States. While some British publicists countered that North Americans would enjoy heightened earning power in a region with a gentler climate than the United States (and with a more relaxed, "Creole" attitude to work), most recruiters thought it better to move the conversation to a higher plane.[19] The British

---

[14] Laurence, *Immigration*, 22.

[15] Alan H. Adamson, "The Reconstruction of Plantation Labor after Emancipation: The Case of British Guiana," in Stanley L. Engerman and Eugene D. Genovese, eds., *Race and Slavery in the Western Hemisphere: Quantitative Studies* (Princeton, 1975), 457; Herbert S. Klein, *African Slavery in Latin America and the Caribbean* (New York, 1986), 136.

[16] W. H. Burnley, remarks, July 4, 1836, HCPP 1836 (512), 164.

[17] Henry Morson, *The Present Condition of the British West Indies* (London, 1841), 23.

[18] C. H. Darling to Elgin, No. 95, August 8, 1845, HCPP 1846 (322), 80; R. Bushe, remarks, June 10, 1842, HCPP 1842 (479), 280; N. W. Pollard to G. F. R. Harris, September 17, 1851, Trinidad Correspondence, CO295/174, 492, TNA.

[19] "We understand it has been said ...," *Guiana Chronicle*, February 3, 1840; Peter Gallego, *Remarks on Emigration to the Coloured Class of the United States*, in Alexander Barclay, *An Address to Philanthropists Generally* (Montreal, 1844), 26; "Labour in the West Indies," *Antigua Herald and Gazette*, November 16, 1850.

consul at Baltimore put it best when, in 1840, he reported that local African Americans were leaving for Trinidad "not so much in the hope of obtaining higher wages for their labour, or of otherwise promoting their physical comfort, but under a firm conviction that their moral and political condition will be at once improved."[20] From an early date, then, African Americans made clear what they expected to hear from colonial recruiters: that life under the empire of liberty would also be one of social and political equality.

"The spirit of British legislation no less than the force of public opinion forbids the establishment of invidious distinctions," promised a Guyanese agent in 1840.[21] "There are certain barriers here which a colored man cannot step over," a Jamaican abolitionist reminded black New Yorkers in 1851.[22] The same year, another canvasser assured a potential settler that, in Trinidad, "not only *may* Coloured men hold offices of trust and emolument ... but they actually *do* hold them."[23] Did such claims accurately represent a world that sounded, at once, so similar and yet so different from the United States?

At the turn of the 1840s, almost 2,000 African Americans left the United States and Canada to take that gamble.

THE FIRST WAVE: TRINIDAD, GUIANA, AND JAMAICA, 1839–1845

Trinidad and Guiana

It was a Trinidadian recruiter who reached America first, though a Guyanese competitor came hot on his heels. In fact, Columbus's "Island of the Trinity" had a history of accepting African Americans – just without their masters' consent. In 1815, Trinidad had received almost 1,000 fugitive slaves who had taken Britain's side in the War of 1812. Allocated lands in Naparima, they soon gained a reputation for hard work.[24] Trinidad also tried to import black veterans in a less direct

---

[20] J. MacTavish to Palmerston, No. 6, May 29, 1840, United States Correspondence, FO5/352, 32–3, TNA.

[21] "Immigration Society," Guiana *Royal Gazette*, March 21, 1840.

[22] "Colonization in Jamaica," New York *Evening Post*, October 17, 1851.

[23] Pollard to J. M. Brown, October 3, 1851, West Indies Correspondence, CO318/193, 151–2, TNA.

[24] Gerald Horne, *Negro Comrades of the Crown: African Americans and the British Empire Fight the U.S. before Emancipation* (New York, 2012), 72–3.

way, by coaxing toward more salubrious climes those who had escaped to Nova Scotia, just as Sierra Leone had done for the African American refugees who had accumulated in the colony after the Revolutionary War. In 1821, Trinidadian and Nova Scotian officials persuaded nearly 100 black veterans to move to the Caribbean. Like the earlier, direct immigrants from the United States to Trinidad, the Nova Scotian "Maroons" flourished, but, being illiterate, they could not send back word to their families, which sowed the rumor that they had been reenslaved. White Nova Scotians would never succeed in scotching that myth, which choked further emigration from the province.[25]

As the passions of war cooled in the United States, and the debates over labor became heated in the colonies, some white Americans hinted that they would tolerate, even welcome, recruiters out to remove legally free African Americans. In 1839, the Trinidad council commissioned the island's preeminent planter, William Burnley, to canvass North America. It was a visit home for the New York native, whose family had taken Britain's side in the Revolutionary War.[26] Predictably, black New Brunswickers and Nova Scotians rebuffed Burnley, who swiftly proceeded south, to the eastern United States.[27] In September 1839, he reached Philadelphia, the birthplace of black opposition to colonization – if "colonization" was what he was offering. Certainly, he could expect a more respectful hearing than, say, the ACS's Ralph Gurley, for Burnley represented the British Empire, whose August 1 anniversary of abolition in the West Indies had already become a fixture in the African American calendar.[28] A committee comprising Robert Purvis and Robert Forten, one of James Forten's sons, duly invited Burnley to distribute 5,000 pamphlets.[29]

While Burnley's brochure dutifully surveyed Trinidad's climate and crops, he knew full well what to stress: "the political and social advantages which the coloured inhabitants of Trinidad enjoy."[30] He seems to

---

[25] Robin W. Winks, *The Blacks in Canada: A History* (New Haven, 1971), 123–4.

[26] Selwyn R. Cudjoe, *The Slave Master of Trinidad: William Hardin Burnley and the Nineteenth-Century Atlantic World* (Amherst, 2018), 143–9; Norman Lamont, *Burnley of Orange Grove* (Port of Spain, 1947), 1–2; J. A. Mein to Normanby, No. 24, April 25, 1839, CO295/125, 259.

[27] Winks, *Blacks in Canada*, 124.

[28] Van Gosse, "'As a Nation, the English Are Our Friends': The Emergence of African American Politics in the British Atlantic World, 1772–1861," *American Historical Review* 113 (2008), 1005.

[29] Julie Winch, *Philadelphia's Black Elite: Activism, Accommodation, and the Struggle for Autonomy, 1787–1848* (Philadelphia, 1988), 63–4.

[30] William Hardin Burnley, *Description of the Island of Trinidad* (New York, 1839), 5.

have succeeded in concealing his past as the island's largest slaveholder and, worse yet, as the emissary that his fellow planters had sent to London in a last-ditch effort to thwart the Abolition Act.[31] Nevertheless, African Americans across the Northeast were skeptical. "Trinidad wants *laborers* with capacity and willingness to work *in the field*," noted New York's Samuel Cornish.[32] William Whipper, though a close friend of Forten and Purvis, compared the scheme to that of the ACS, and urged "the good people of Trinidad" to ask for Americans of all colors if sincere about immigration. Yet Burnley acquired a luster of legitimacy by appointing as his agent a black Philadelphian, Frederick Hinton, who had been more involved than Whipper in the futile campaign to prevent Pennsylvania's 1838 disfranchisement of black men. The disaffected Hinton was accordingly amenable to emigration.[33]

While rancor raged in the City of Brotherly Love, a monumental migration to Trinidad took place from Baltimore, a slave-state city whose black inhabitants faced a higher risk of legal expulsion than did their free-state peers. Bizarrely, black Baltimoreans had already been canvassed by an agent from Guiana (and Burnley's rival), Edward Carbery, who had invited two delegates to his colony and watched them declare in its favor.[34] In November 1839, local African Americans had gathered at the Bethel AME Church to listen to Carbery's promises that immigrants to Guiana would be free to choose their employer.[35] The meeting had elected two painters, Nathaniel Peck and Thomas Price, to report on the colony. At Annapolis, the statehouse hastily expanded its existing right of return for black residents who wished to investigate Liberia, adding Trinidad and Guiana by name. Duly protected, Peck and Price departed.[36]

Arriving in the Guyanese capital, Georgetown, in January 1840, the explorers were greeted by Governor Henry Light (1838–48), who "assured us if we or any of our brethren should feel disposed to emigrate

---

[31] Cudjoe, *Slave Master of Trinidad*, 73–9.
[32] "Trinidad – An Explanation," *Colored American*, October 12, 1839.
[33] Winch, *Philadelphia's Black Elite*, 64; Robert Buchanan et al., *To Coloured Emigrants: Sure and Profitable Speculation in Trinidad* (New York, 1840), 8.
[34] Christopher Phillips, *Freedom's Port: The African American Community of Baltimore, 1790–1860* (Urbana, 1997), 215–17.
[35] Edward Carbery, *Inducements to the Colored People of the United States to Emigrate to British Guiana* (Boston, 1840), 9.
[36] Martha S. Jones, *Birthright Citizens: A History of Race and Rights in Antebellum America* (New York, 2018), 59–61; Chap. 5 (January 27, 1840), in William McNeir, pub., *Laws of Maryland* (Annapolis, 1840), unpaginated.

to Guiana, we might rely upon his protection." They experienced similar kindness from the US consul, Moses Benjamin, who offered to host them. Even the planters, who, in their impatience, had poured personal funds into an organization to promote the presumptive influx, the Voluntary Subscription Immigration Society, allowed Peck and Price to ask *them* the questions. While impressed by Guiana, the two companions noted that, as in all the British colonies, the law denied office to those not born under the Union Jack. That March, they made the short voyage to Trinidad, where they met three or four black Americans who had already immigrated, but to considerable disappointment. "As they were mechanics, they no doubt went out with … high-wrought expectations," surmised Peck and Price. In April 1840, the pair returned to Baltimore, convened another meeting, and declared for Guiana. While either colony would be preferable to the United States, Trinidad's agriculture was cruder and its workers' lodgings smaller.[37]

Unbeknown to Peck and Price, however, more than 100 black Baltimoreans had already enrolled for that inferior location, Trinidad. For also present at the meeting were some recent visitors to the island, who had sailed out the previous fall and now returned with stories of high wages on the sugar estates for an easy quota of daily tasks. Peck and Price could not match that promise, because they had been altogether less ambitious: they had asked Guiana's planters whether they would be willing to pay immigrants not with money, but with a share of the crop. (Unsurprisingly, their answer had been "yes.")[38] Within days, a wave of Baltimoreans, mostly families rather than individuals, initiated a movement that, for about a year from late 1839, saw roughly 1,300 free African Americans from the eastern seaboard leave for Trinidad, 200 for Jamaica, and fewer than 100 for Guiana.[39]

The move to Trinidad conferred mixed results on both settler and planter, though emigrants continued to sail even as the first negative reports filtered back. "There is no employment for women but field labour," warned one American, adding that many settlers had been located in a sickly part of the island accessible only by boat.[40] Others noted that estate managers reveled in divide-and-rule: "jealousy exists on

---

[37] Woods and Crane, pub., *Report of Messrs. Peck and Price* (Baltimore, 1840), 4, 14, 22.
[38] Phillips, *Freedom's Port*, 217–19.
[39] Harris to H. G. Grey, No. 17, February 21, 1848, HCPP 1847–8 (245), 275; H. Light to J. Russell, No. 79, June 6, 1840, HCPP 1841, 1 Sess. (321), 136–7; H. Spalding, remarks, June 24, 1842, HCPP 1842 (479), 402.
[40] "American Emigrants to Demerara and Trinidad," *Anti-Slavery Reporter*, May 20, 1840.

the part of the native laborers toward the emigrants, and ... is cherished by the planters."[41] One American admitted that he had struggled to adjust to the tropical climate of alternate wet and dry seasons, but was otherwise satisfied; another, the Rev. Hamilton, participated in the island's antislavery society; and yet another was delighted to receive official permission to found his own church.[42]

For their part, the planters had already lowered their expectations, since William Burnley had manifestly failed to deliver the coveted field hands of America's lower South. "The emigration can only proceed from the free blacks," Burnley explained to the British House of Commons in 1840. "The great majority are to be found in the northern states, as they will not allow a slave to be freed in the slave states unless he be sent immediately out of the country."[43] Evidently, Burnley was aware of the black laws, but unaware of just how many freedpeople flouted them. Yet black northerners were no mere consolation prize. If such immigrants tended to abandon the estates in favor of short-term contract labor, that also meant that they repaired the colony's notorious roads for a fair price.[44] Outside the world of work, a Trinidadian minister was impressed at how the Americans raised the moral tone of the island, while a physician observed that their initial sickness was due less to innate mortality and more to their lack of local contacts to look after them while they acclimated.[45]

During 1840–1, three Pennsylvania Quakers visited the West Indies to witness the effects of emancipation. While in Trinidad, they toured those plantations that had acquired black Americans. At one estate, the Friends found the women keener to return to the United States than the men, while those immigrants of 1815 who also lived there were not as advanced as the recent arrivals, having suffered the ill effects of planters' erstwhile prejudice against free settlements. It was William Burnley's pleasure to host the traveling trio at Mon Plaisir, a plantation where workers lived rent-free in return for doing five tasks per week. "The benevolent proprietor of this estate manifests a great desire to improve their condition," noted the tourists, probably ignorant of his checkered past. They were impressed, as well, by Trinidad's Governor Henry

---

[41] "Trinidad Emigration," *Liberator*, October 9, 1840.
[42] "Meeting of the Colored Population of Baltimore," *Trinidad Standard*, February 4, 1841.
[43] Burnley, remarks, June 26, 1840, HCPP 1840 (527), 381.
[44] T. F. Elliot and E. E. Villiers to G. W. Hope, December 3, 1841, HCPP 1842 (379), 110.
[45] A. David, report, June 30, and S. Philip, J. H. Hamilton, and J. Butler, remarks, March 22, May 6, and July 19, 1841, respectively, ibid., 57, 67, 72, 100.

MacLeod (1840–6), whose "partiality" for the Americans was obvious. A second wave of Baltimorean interest in Trinidad a decade later suggested that the Quakers were not alone in their favorable opinion of the colony.[46] Of Guiana there was less to say, since there were fewer immigrants to say it. There was nothing *wrong* as such with the colony, for those minded to go *somewhere*. But William Burnley and Edward Carbery had been competitors more than collaborators, and the former's superior timing had come at the latter's expense. When, in 1839, Carbery had landed in the United States, he had been disappointed to learn that an agent from Trinidad had gotten there first. Lacking clear instructions from Guiana's government, Carbery hastily offered black Baltimoreans a free passage, purely because he heard that Burnley had made such an offer.[47] Since he could not hope to persuade them of Guiana's merits until Peck and Price returned with their report, Carbery headed north, to the curiously warm reception of a wintry Boston, where a black founder of the American Anti-Slavery Society, James Barbadoes, volunteered as his agent.[48] Still, New England could never provide emigrants in large numbers, and Edward Carbery returned to Baltimore, only to discover that, in his absence, the Trinidad mania had taken hold.[49]

In Guiana, one commentator, hearing only of Nathaniel Peck and Thomas Price's adjudication in that colony's favor, feared that its immigration budget would prove too small.[50] He need not have worried. The few Baltimoreans who disembarked from the *Porpoise* did, however, record their reactions in letters home. "This is a fine country, but I am afraid to say come, for there may be ... some disappointed persons," reported a brickmaker.[51] "Sorry I am that I ever left my native country, at the instance of Mr. Carbery's false allurements," rued a tanner. His companions agreed that Carbery should have at least been forthright about the high cost of fresh produce.[52] In late 1840, the *Guiana Chronicle* reviewed the colony's efforts to date. It was true, the editor admitted, that the middle states of the Union wanted rid of their free black

---

[46] George Truman et al., *Narrative of a Visit to the West Indies, in 1840 and 1841* (Philadelphia, 1844), 89–90, 96–7, 101, 106.
[47] "Public Meeting," *Guiana Chronicle*, December 14, 1839.
[48] "Letter to Edward Carbery," *Liberator*, February 21, 1840.
[49] "Causes of the Ill Success of Attempts, Hitherto, to Obtain Emigrants from America," *Guiana Chronicle*, December 1, 1840.
[50] "We have before us ...," ibid., April 27, 1840.
[51] "British Guiana," *Liberator*, October 2, 1840.
[52] "American Immigrants," *Royal Gazette of British Guiana*, September 24, 1840.

residents. But that class gathered in cities, where it could stand firm against oppression, while rural laborers probably had never even heard of Guiana. It was pointless, then, for the planters to "form societies and hold public meetings without number."[53] When the colonial government looked back on the failure three decades later, it had become more willing to assign blame, singling out the quarrelsome members of the Voluntary Subscription Immigration Society.[54]

Jamaica

The laggard of the "big three," Jamaica, heard in April 1840 of the doings of Guiana and Trinidad. A Mr. Whitmarsh, who ran a silk company in the north-coast town of St. Ann's, claimed to know of hundreds of free African Americans who would readily immigrate. Since the government at Spanish Town had already instructed its agent, Alexander Barclay, to travel to London for a meeting with the Colonial Office, it simply added an American leg to his impending mission.[55] "Avoid any negotiations that can possibly lead to the imputation that emancipated slaves have been removed to Jamaica without their consent," the colony's secretary warned Barclay.[56] When he arrived in Baltimore that June, Alexander Barclay immediately looked for William Burnley and Edward Carbery. A "respectable colored person" told him that local blacks had ultimately taken so strongly against Guiana because, the scheme being funded by a planter syndicate, they had doubted Carbery's promises of a free choice of employer, whereas Trinidad sponsored immigrants "perfectly unfettered."[57] In July, Barclay, Carbery, and Burnley finally met, in New York. The first two agreed that "no efficient number of people can be procured from this Country"; the last begged to differ. Although Barclay made sure to appoint a US subagent and publish a pamphlet promoting Jamaica, he proceeded to Britain a skeptic.[58]

[53] "Immigration from America," *Guiana Chronicle*, November 28, 1840.
[54] HCPP 1871 (C. 393), 38.
[55] Thomas C. Holt, *The Problem of Freedom: Race, Labor, and Politics in Jamaica and Britain, 1832–1938* (Baltimore, 1992), 197–8; Monica Schuler, *"Alas, Alas, Kongo": A Social History of Indentured African Immigration into Jamaica* (Baltimore, 1980), 3; "When the house ...," Kingston *Morning Journal*, April 4, 1840.
[56] J. M. Higginson to A. Barclay, April 28, 1840, FO5/356, 283–4.
[57] Barclay to Higginson, June 28, 1840, Jamaica Correspondence, CO137/249, 274–5, TNA.
[58] Barclay to Higginson, July 31, 1840, CO137/249, 280–3.

How it must have galled Carbery, then, that more emigrants *still* went to Jamaica than to Guiana. They even included his own subagent, James Barbadoes, who would pay for his change of destination by promptly dying of malaria.[59] The first arrivals disembarked in Jamaica in November 1840. One was a mother of eight, who had thought that their education would prove cheaper than in the United States.[60] In April 1841, a black American missionary, Nancy Prince, discussed the immigrants' plight with the US consul at Kingston, who declared it "a folly for the Americans to come to the island to better their condition." The settlers agreed, lamenting how their children would "starve in foreign lands."[61] By 1842, a local coffee planter reported that many of the Americans had returned home through unemployment, as they made only goods that Jamaica was bound to keep importing from Britain.[62] With that fizzle ended the last significant emigration of black people to the British West Indies from the United States, even if not from Canada. Going by the debate that resettlement in the Caribbean continued to inspire, observers could have been forgiven for thinking otherwise.

Antislavery, Proslavery, and Diplomacy

The three colonies' initiatives had caught America at the end of a decade of intellectual realignment over slavery. "The bulk of the population ... is anxious to get rid of the colored people," reported Carbery from the United States. "At the same time, three parties ... must be conciliated – the Abolitionist, the Colonizationist, and the Southern people."[63] Yet the second constituency was a lost cause for the imperial canvassers. In the summer of 1839, a Liverpool-based correspondent asked the ACS's president of the board (and former mayor of Buffalo), Samuel Wilkeson, whether the society might send emigrants to Guiana rather than Liberia. Although Wilkeson offered his regrets that the workings of British abolition should have forced colonial planters to look abroad for laborers, his answer was "no." Supplanting native laborers with American immigrants

---

[59] Blackett, "Hamic Connection," 319.
[60] "Colored Emigrants from the United States," Kingston *Morning Journal*, November 14, 1840.
[61] Nancy G. Prince, *A Narrative of the Life and Travels of Mrs. Nancy Prince* (Boston, 1853), 48, 51.
[62] H. Spalding, remarks, June 24, 1842, HCPP 1842 (479), 402–3.
[63] "Delegates from America," *Guiana Chronicle*, January 22, 1840.

would drive the former to poverty, while the latter would remain under the same white rule that had demeaned them all their lives.[64]

From Philadelphia, the Quaker colonizationist Benjamin Coates applauded Samuel Wilkeson, having struggled to get a black acquaintance to explain how he could, at once, support West Indian emigration and oppose African colonization: "I cannot sir, I agree with you, it is very inconsistent," Coates's interlocutor had replied.[65] Colonizationists were incredulous that the British abolitionist Thomas Fowell Buxton, head of the (original) African Civilization Society, could have recently proposed sending black West Indian missionaries to Africa even as he criticized the work of the Colonization Society, and even as other British abolitionists encouraged white West Indian canvassers in the United States to lambast Liberia for *their* own purposes. "Why prejudice the American colored man against the land of his forefathers, while every effort is made to qualify the same class of men in the West Indies to emigrate thither?" asked the *African Repository*.[66] The ACS might have taken cold comfort in learning that there was another group that thought Buxton's plan nonsense: the West India lobby, which, however, thought much the same of the ACS's.

By contrast, the first group that Carbery had named, the abolitionists, were never united against black emigration to the West Indies, which, they hoped, would bolster the free Caribbean against the flourishing slave economies of Cuba and Brazil.[67] As in 1817, African Americans were quicker than their white compatriots to turn against a new project for black resettlement; as in 1817, many African Americans initially supported it nonetheless, and would deny their early interest in due course. In 1841, William Burnley reviewed his recent trip to the United States, describing the abolitionists as, at first, his allies: "they could not assist me openly and directly, having ... committed themselves deeply against expatriation in any shape; but ... they were too shrewd not to perceive that any failure in the great experiment of free labor in the British Islands would inevitably rivet the chains of slavery in the United States." Abolitionists opened the columns of their journals to Burnley, enabling

---

[64] S. Wilkeson to anon., September 9, 1839, *AR* 16 (1840), 22–4.
[65] B. Coates to Wilkeson, November 27, 1839, reel 33A, ACS.
[66] Bronwen Everill, "British West Africa or 'the United States of Africa'? Imperial Pressures on the Transatlantic Anti-slavery Movement, 1839–1842," *Journal of Transatlantic Studies* 9 (2011), 140; *AR* 16 (1840), 283–4.
[67] Edward Bartlett Rugemer, *The Problem of Emancipation: The Caribbean Roots of the American Civil War* (Baton Rouge, 2008), 259.

him to disseminate information about sailings to Trinidad.[68] Edward Carbery, too, noticed some strange (and strained) differences within American abolitionism. Blaming his lack of success on those black pastors who had turned against emigration once they realized that it would empty their pews, Carbery (accurately) observed that the *Colored American*, "after playing fast and loose for some time, came out at length very decidedly against the scheme." Within William Lloyd Garrison's American Anti-Slavery Society, "certain of the New York abolitionists," almost certainly those about to break away to found the American and Foreign Anti-Slavery Society, denounced the West Indies movement in order to defy Garrison, who had endorsed Guiana, though Trinidad less so.[69]

The currents running through Atlantic abolitionism reached high tide on the banks of the River Thames, at the World Anti-Slavery Convention of June 1840. From the lectern at Exeter Hall, Thomas Fowell Buxton announced that nobody should confuse the work of his Civilization Society with that of the Colonization Society, a claim that he did not deign to substantiate. Yet delegates were unsure how to interpret black American emigration to the West Indies. Reporting for the Committee on Free Labor, John Sturge, a Birmingham manufacturer (and brother of the better-known Joseph Sturge), briefly reviewed the alternative sources of labor and came out in favor of the scheme. Compared with the immigration "of ignorant and helpless beings from another hemisphere," that of free African Americans might confer "immense advantages," as long as equal rights were extended them. But a delegate from New York, James Fuller, persuaded the Convention not to endorse any form of black emigration, given how quick the ACS had been to claim vindication at the founding of Buxton's own society.[70] In July, after spending a few months in Britain, William Burnley returned to the United States. While he had not attended the convention, he knew of its ruling and blamed it for the newfound coldness that he experienced. "With every abolition press in America now closed against me, it was hopeless . . . to expect any further emigration from the Northern ports," he recalled. He headed to the southern states, where, he hoped, free blacks would act more

---

[68] "Meeting of the Agricultural Society," *Trinidad Standard*, February 15, 1841.
[69] "Causes of the Ill Success"; "Emigration to British Guiana," *Liberator*, February 14, 1840.
[70] British and Foreign Anti-Slavery Society, pub., *Proceedings of the General Anti-Slavery Convention* (London, 1841), 360–1, 395–6.

independently of whites.[71] In a similar vein, Edward Carbery criticized American abolitionists for deferring to their British allies, who suddenly decried all West Indian immigration schemes.[72]

Since colonial recruiters made no more efforts on US soil for the rest of the 1840s, abolitionists gave them little thought. Yet boosting the free West Indies, while getting to provoke slaveholders *and* colonizationists, continued to appeal to many reformers, who had thought the recruitment drive of 1839–41 *premature*, more than anything, in that the colonies were still groping for a stable free-labor basis. "After a few years shall have ... given character to the legislation of the island, it might be a happy home," reported an American missionary to Jamaica, urging black would-be immigrants to delay, rather than cancel, their plans.[73] Moreover, since most white Americans believed that blacks would eventually gravitate to the tropics (Chapter 6), the English-speaking Caribbean had much to recommend it: "the British West Indies offer a most inviting field for colored enterprise," Ohio abolitionist Salmon Chase advised Frederick Douglass.[74] From 1850, even opponents of emigration had to admit that fugitive slaves needed a refuge somewhere and that it might as well be those British colonies to the south as to the north.[75] But indenture, a common type of contract binding laborers to employers, would be an inescapable part of any immigration scheme funded by planters, a fact that bothered American and British abolitionists alike.[76]

Although not directly involved in the colonies' recruitment campaign, the metropolitan government in Britain had to adjust to its ramifications. First, that meant the political rights that black Americans craved so dearly – and that colonial recruiters promised so laxly. Absent adequate laws of naturalization, "the permanent occupation of land should ... be followed by the possession of the privileges of British subjects," Trinidad's Governor MacLeod wrote Lord John Russell, the secretary

[71] John Hope Franklin, *The Free Negro in North Carolina, 1790–1860* (Chapel Hill, 1943), 203; "Meeting of the Agricultural Society."

[72] "Causes of the Ill Success."

[73] "Letter from Rev. C. S. Renshaw," *Colored American*, July 18, 1840.

[74] S. P. Chase to F. Douglass, May 4, 1850, Salmon P. Chase Papers, Historical Society of Pennsylvania.

[75] S. J. Wolcott to G. Whipple, June 6, 1851, American Missionary Association Archives, Tulane.

[76] "We have before us ...," *Anti-Slavery Reporter*, April 1, 1851; "Colored Laborers in Jamaica," *National Era*, September 22, 1859.

of state for the colonies.[77] The Colonial Office replied that it was not minded to allow immigrants to acquire land, since they had been imported to repopulate the old estates.[78] Second, the current rules on immigration favored single women (to increase the future population), whereas the entire families likely to emigrate from the United States would be balanced for gender.[79] The Colonial Office offered no relief there, either. But it did waive a third rule on the assumption that African Americans would be better informed than most immigrants.[80] In 1843, London repealed, for North America only, a ban of 1838 on laborers entering into contracts without first seeing the colony, which it had passed as a safeguard against deceptive recruitment practices.[81]

Just as, during the American Civil War, the diplomatic complications arising from the US Department of the Interior's colonization schemes would drag in the Department of State, so the British Colonial Office's immigration projects now dragged in the Foreign Office. Some other agent than the interested parties would have to certify any contracts to labor: realistically, that meant the British consuls at New York, Baltimore, Charleston, and New Orleans. In late 1842, the foreign secretary, the earl of Aberdeen, had broached the matter with his minister to the United States, Henry Fox. In turn, Fox spoke to the secretary of state, the Whig Daniel Webster, whose "incurable constitutional indolence in all things not belonging to the higher order of political questions" stymied progress. An answer appeared in the offing, though, from Webster's successor, Abel Upshur, a Virginia slaveholder. "Upshur tells me that he is quite sensible of the advantages ... [of] being relieved of as large a number as possible of the free men of colour," Fox told Aberdeen. If Upshur worried, at the same time, that the scheme might enable slaves to escape, the British minister reassured him that consular certification would filter out any fugitives.[82]

Alas, Fox had been foxed. His mundane request for US assistance in recruiting black laborers had contained an explosive, if inadvertent admission: the "great experiment" of free labor had failed, and Britain needed to fill the gap left by abolition. Secretary Upshur rattled off a

---

[77] H. MacLeod to Russell, No. 26, June 8, 1840, HCPP 1840 (613), 153.
[78] Elliot and Villiers to J. Stephen, August 4, 1840, ibid., 154.
[79] MacLeod to Russell, No. 77, August 3, 1841, HCPP 1842 (301), 423.
[80] Madhavi Kale, *Fragments of Empire: Capital, Slavery, and Indian Indentured Labor Migration in the British Caribbean* (Philadelphia, 1998), 110–11.
[81] G. W. Hope to C. J. Canning, January 27, 1843, FO5/399, 163–5.
[82] H. S. Fox to Aberdeen, No. 98, July 29, 1843, FO5/392, 333–9.

number of questions about the effects of emancipation for Robert Harrison, the US consul at Kingston, Jamaica, but did not even wait for Harrison's reply before summoning Fox to reject his proposal.[83] Although Upshur might not, according to Fox, subscribe to "exaggerated and impracticable doctrines, on the subject of slavery," he did share his fellow planters' fear of abolitionists spiriting away human property under false papers. To assuage Fox, Upshur reminded him that no laws in the United States forbade black emigration (black *im*migration being another matter entirely) and that the federal government had to avoid falling foul of state black laws by supporting a scheme that enticed African Americans to certain ports. Citing the pointless pains to which Alexander Barclay, William Burnley, and Edward Carbery had gone, Fox asked Aberdeen whether the desired field hands had ever been within reach anyway.[84] Belatedly, Britain had its answer on the third constituency that Carbery had identified: "the Southern people." In an ugly mirror image of abolitionist ambivalence about the West Indies, however, some slaveholding colonizationists still saw the region as an easier outlet than Liberia for those bothersome freepeople.

Canada

There was somewhere, however, where the British Empire could canvass African Americans without causing a contretemps. During the 1840s and 1850s, Canada West witnessed several schemes to transfer its black inhabitants to Trinidad and Jamaica. Such projects were part of a broader Anglo-American impulse to reserve North America for people of European extraction, for the empire was solidifying around a distinction between white settler colonies, in Canada and Oceania, and nonwhite extractive colonies, in the tropics.[85] Ostensibly redolent of earlier efforts in Nova Scotia, the antebellum impetus started with Thomas Rolph, a white abolitionist troubled by fugitive slaves' vulnerability to vexatious extradition warrants.[86] Rolph cast his – rather, their – lot with Trinidad, and contacted Governor MacLeod in the summer of 1840. "I find on

---

[83] Steven Heath Mitton, "The Upshur Inquiry: Lost Lessons of the Great Experiment," *Slavery and Abolition* 27 (2006), 89–93.

[84] Fox to Aberdeen, No. 115, August 27, 1843, FO5/393, 172–80.

[85] Ikuko Asaka, *Tropical Freedom: Climate, Settler Colonialism, and Black Exclusion in the Age of Emancipation* (Durham, 2017), 9.

[86] Allen P. Stouffer, *The Light of Nature and the Law of God: Antislavery in Ontario, 1833–1877* (Baton Rouge, 1992), 59–63.

consultation with the coloured people of Canada, that from 300 to 500 will be happy to proceed to Trinidad to settle there permanently, provided I accompany them in the capacity of surgeon," Rolph reported, thereby claiming medical credentials that he had not earned.[87]

In writing the governor of another colony, Thomas Rolph had bypassed his own, Lord Sydenham, who, finding no evidence that his office had ever heard from Rolph, warned Russell that the Ancaster apothecary might have just dispensed a pack of lies. Sydenham thought the fugitives unwilling to leave, and admitted that he, too, would rather they remained.[88] If an apologia that Rolph wrote in 1844 is to be believed, the black residents of Colchester, Sandwich, and Amherstberg "assembled in throngs" to hear him disavow any motive but their welfare.[89] Although briefly salaried by the government of Trinidad, Rolph would make a loss from a venture that never went beyond the planning stage, whether because of an attempted deception that had backfired or a personal delusion that had cost him dear. Refused reimbursement by the Colonial Office for his failure to furnish the human goods that only he had promised, Thomas Rolph disappears from the historical record.[90]

At the same time as working for Trinidad, Rolph had cooperated with Peter Gallego, a black inhabitant of Ancaster, whose own preference was for Jamaica. His color conferring a credibility unavailable to Rolph, Gallego enjoyed greater, though still limited, success.[91] A native of Canada, Gallego was tired of prejudice – and of Britons' complacency that no such sentiment stalked their dominions.[92] He investigated Jamaica at the behest of a black convention, eventually becoming a teacher in Kingston. He also reprinted the pamphlet that Alexander Barclay had issued in the United States four years earlier, approving it with "the *fair* side of [Jamaica] is here more particularly represented ... the *dark side* [having been] described to us by our abolition friends."[93] Between 1842 and 1843, Gallego brought 110 black Canadians to Jamaica, whose government hoped for even more.[94] But in 1844, London advised Spanish Town that the failure of Rolph's Trinidad

---

[87] T. Rolph to MacLeod, August 31, 1840, HCPP 1842 (301), 416.
[88] Sydenham to Russell, No. 51, April 23, 1841, Canada Correspondence, CO42/478, 367–8, TNA.
[89] Thomas Rolph, *Emigration and Colonization* (London, 1844), 314.
[90] Stouffer, *Light of Nature*, 65.   [91] Asaka, *Tropical Freedom*, 97.
[92] "American Prejudice against Colour in Canada," *Patriot*, August 22, 1842.
[93] Barclay, *Address*, 7, 25.
[94] Asaka, *Tropical Freedom*, 98; Darling to Elgin, October 24, 1843, HCPP 1844 (530), 36.

movement might bode ill for its own.[95] Disappointed by the low numbers to step off the *Countess of Durham*, the Jamaican government closed its Canadian agency in 1845. It had been tempted to keep it open, however, because of the sterling work already undertaken by one of Gallego's collaborators, Stephen Virginia, to counter rumors detrimental to the project.[96]

Although the increase in African American immigration from 1850 strained race relations in Canada, only the province's governors general, Charles Metcalfe (1843–5), the earl of Elgin (1847–54), and Edmund Head (1854–61), harbored an imperial vision expansive enough to vest serious hopes in black emigration to the West Indies.[97] (It helped that Metcalfe and Elgin had first acted as governor of Jamaica.) Furthermore, the white abolitionists of Toronto took a firm stance against any whiff of colonization by another name.[98] Black immigrants to Canada thought more carefully, though, before dismissing plans for their own transfer to the tropics. After all, the Toronto Convention (1851) had supported a North American League between Canada and Jamaica, to trade free produce with the other (to the exclusion of the United States) and to assert universal black rights to landownership. While the journalist Henry Bibb devoted himself to the league, its very ambition prevented it ever leaving the drawing-board.[99] He was not the only African American in Canada to embrace the British Lion wherever it extended its protecting paw, but in 1854, Samuel Ringgold Ward, who, fifteen years earlier, had almost left the United States for Trinidad, joined Mary Ann Shadd in ruling out emigration to the West Indies.[100] They argued that the plan "promulgat[ed] the dangerous doctrine that God's children ... cannot live together ... unless those of darker hue, become 'hewers of wood and drawers of water.'"[101] Although Governor General Head *was* an advocate of that doctrine, he ended his plans to transfer black Americans to the

---

[95] Elliot and C. A. Wood to Stephen, May 24, 1844, Land and Emigration Commission Records, CO386/48, 386, TNA.

[96] J. W. Dunscomb to Darling, No. 7, October 24, 1844, and Darling to Dunscomb, No. 6, January 27, 1845, HCPP 1846 (322), 76–8.

[97] Asaka, *Tropical Freedom*, 96; Elgin to F. Peel, April 10, 1854, CO318/208, 208–10; E. Head to Darling, October 5, 1858, HCPP 1859, 2 Sess. (31), 273.

[98] "The following interesting ...," *Anti-Slavery Reporter*, November 1, 1851.

[99] Roger W. Hite, "Voice of a Fugitive: Henry Bibb and Ante-Bellum Black Separatism," *Journal of Black Studies* 4 (1974), 276–82; Floyd J. Miller, *The Search for a Black Nationality: Black Emigration and Colonization, 1787–1863* (Urbana, 1975), 111–13.

[100] Samuel Ringgold Ward, *Autobiography of a Fugitive Negro* (London, 1855), 51.

[101] "Constitution of the Provincial Union," *Provincial Freeman*, August 19, 1854.

West Indies when, in 1860, the Foreign Office realized that such travelers, if forced into any southern port in a storm, would be liable not only to imprisonment, but now to enslavement.[102] That situation, however hypothetical it might have sounded, would have been the opposite of a very real one that had caused Anglo-American tension during the 1830s and 1840s, when a number of American coastwise slavers had beached in the Bahamas, only for the British authorities to liberate those on board.[103]

THE SECOND WAVE: FREE LABOR, FREE PRODUCE, AND FREEPEOPLE, 1850–1860

Despite the eleventh-hour timing of the Foreign Office's epiphany about black expeditions that sailed from Canada, Britain had long known of the American South's aversion to its black inhabitants, immigrants, and itinerants. Notably, South Carolina's Negro Seamen Act (1822), in ordering the detention of Her Majesty's subjects of color until their ship weighed anchor, had opened a running sore in Anglo-American relations.[104] From 1850, white Americans' redoubled drive to expel their free black neighbors made white Antilleans wonder once more whether they might acquire them. The early 1850s brought forth three missions proceeding from that premise: one by the British consul at Havana, David Turnbull, for the Caribbean colonies at large; another by a recruiter in the Burnley mold, Nathaniel Pollard, for Trinidad; and another by two abolitionists, William Wemyss Anderson and John Scoble, for Jamaica. Although Guiana appointed one J. W. Sandiford, his agency was abortive.[105]

Turnbull and the Slave Trade

Of the three ventures, David Turnbull's was the most remarkable, both in itself and in the response that American slaveholders accorded it. A fiery

[102] C. Fortescue to Head, No. 101, October 20, 1860, Canada Entry Books, CO43/152, 420–1, TNA.

[103] Don E. Fehrenbacher, *The Slaveholding Republic: An Account of the United States Government's Relations to Slavery* (New York, 2001), 104–11.

[104] Michael Schoeppner, *Moral Contagion: Black Atlantic Sailors, Citizenship, and Diplomacy in Antebellum America* (New York, 2019), 1–13.

[105] "Emigration from the United States," *Antigua Herald and Gazette*, November 15, 1851; H. Barkly to Grey, January 6, 1851, British Guiana Correspondence, CO111/280, 26–8, TNA.

abolitionist who, during his term as consul at Havana, had investigated slave imports into Cuba with undiplomatic gusto, Turnbull knew that, once Britain's Sugar Duties Act (1846) had equalized tariffs on free- and slave-grown sugar, the former would never prove competitive with the latter.[106] The British Empire could only deprive unfree soil of labor by attacking the slave trade, and deliver free soil as much labor as possible.[107] It occurred to Turnbull that Britain might seek a partner in the shape of the United States, which had outlawed the slave *trade*, at least, and might agree to send black exiles to the Caribbean rather than to Africa. "The manifest impossibility of transferring more than three millions of slaves to the other side of the Atlantic appears to have engendered the idea that ... the thinly-peopled islands of this Archipelago might form a convenient outlet," ran Turnbull's assessment of American sentiment.[108] In the spring of 1850, he called at Washington on his way to London, checking in with the British minister, Henry Bulwer, before taking his idea to the US government.

With the Capitol still fumbling for a grand compromise between the sections, Turnbull easily gained the ear of Senators Daniel Webster, William Seward, and Henry Clay. Despite Clay's presidency of the ACS, "it was not very difficult to convince [him] ... that some nearer and more desirable point must be sought for than Cape Palmas." Nor did Turnbull struggle to persuade those sugar planters he met, whose viability would be vitiated if America's own sugar tariffs were ever repealed, of the sweet delights of Anglo-American cooperation.[109] A Monsieur Sigur of Louisiana, "perfectly aware ... that the removal of his slaves to Jamaica would work their emancipation," thought the US sugar sector so depressed that he would rather transfer his slaves to free but fertile soil, as long as he could secure five years' apprenticeship from them.[110] Once Turnbull reached London, he convinced the secretary of state for the colonies, Earl Grey, as well as the members of the West India Association, "whose want of coherence has been proverbial."[111] Better yet, Turnbull won over the US ministers to Britain and France, Abbott

---

[106] David R. Murray, *Odious Commerce: Britain, Spain, and the Abolition of the Cuban Slave Trade* (Cambridge, UK, 1980), 133–58.
[107] D. Turnbull to Palmerston, July 16, 1850, CO318/188, unpaginated.
[108] David Turnbull, *The Jamaica Movement* (London, 1850), 32.
[109] Turnbull to Palmerston, March 30, 1850, CO318/187, unpaginated.
[110] Turnbull to Grey, June 17, 1850, CO318/188.
[111] Turnbull to Grey, October 14, 1850, CO318/188.

Lawrence of Massachusetts and William Rives of Virginia, sectional peacemakers who had recently discussed colonization with each other.[112] Diplomats on the eastern side of the Atlantic agreed so very much on the broad merits of Britain's impending offer to the United States that they worried only about its details. Although Grey made sure to ask the opinions of the colonies' governors before proceeding, he would have to secure the assent of US administrators at some point.[113] An under-secretary at the Colonial Office asked Lawrence and Rives how to broach such a delicate matter, but the ministers differed: "Lawrence thought that it would be prudent to leave as much as might be, to be done by the Americans themselves. Rives's opinion ... [was] that the initiative should be taken in the British Colonies, as any project ... originated by Slave owners is viewed by the Abolitionist Party with so evil an eye."[114] In October 1850, Earl Grey duly issued his circular to the colonies, permitting them to offer African American settlers a financial bounty and swift naturalization. By stressing the benefits available to the immigrants, Grey had almost avoided misconstruction. But one of his further suggestions, that the colonies allow those "in a state of slavery" to indenture themselves (he surely meant manumission conditional on emigration), was freighted with ambiguity.[115]

At the New Year, 1851, one of Antigua's absentee proprietors spotted the danger. He warned Grey that US commentators would interpret the circular as "enticing away the American Planters' Slaves," a violation of southern state law.[116] Yet when news of the circular reached America, sectional responses, north and south, were nothing but complimentary. The antislavery *National Era* lamented how African Americans were unlikely to show enough enterprise to accept Grey's kind offer, while the *Richmond Enquirer* advocated reassigning Virginia's Liberian colonization fund to the West Indian scheme.[117] Shortly afterward, Turnbull died, but his brainchild lived on – and got itself into trouble. A native of Georgia, resident in Britain, called on Abbott Lawrence, protesting the

---

[112] Turnbull to Grey, June 11, 1850, CO318/188; Paul Quigley, *Shifting Grounds: Nationalism and the American South, 1848–1865* (New York, 2011), 93.
[113] B. Hawes to Turnbull, August 14, 1850, West Indies Entry Books, CO319/50, 5–6, TNA.
[114] Elliot, memorandum, August 28, 1850, CO318/188.
[115] Grey, circular, October 16, 1850, H. Exec. Doc. 29, 32 Cong., 1 Sess. (1852), 3.
[116] O. Pell to Grey, January 2, 1851, CO318/193, 76–7.
[117] "Improvement of the Colored People," *National Era*, March 13, 1851; "Jamaica and the Free Negroes," *Daily Richmond Enquirer*, March 5, 1851.

circular in the very terms that Grey's friendly critic had foreseen. All too aware, unlike his visitor, of his own enthusiasm for the scheme, Lawrence wrote a dispatch to the equally complicit Daniel Webster, who had just reassumed the Department of State, assuring Webster that Grey had meant no harm.[118] The US House demanded to see their correspondence, forcing Grey to clarify that he had meant only to act with masters' consent.[119] In 1860, a New York lawyer, John Bigelow, recounted the episode to Frank Blair, opining that congressmen had been "saucy" in their overreaction to Grey.[120]

Pollard and the Black Laws

Congressmen might have been saucier still had more of them known that, in 1851, a recruiter from Trinidad had also come to the United States and colluded with the most important colonizationists in American politics. Like David Turnbull, Nathaniel Pollard, the superintendent of public works for Trinidad, cleared his mission with the British Legation, whose secretary, John Crampton, made an ignominious (and ignorant) request: Could Pollard avoid canvassing Canada, where virtually any African Americans had to be the self-stolen property of southern slaveholders?[121] Unwittingly, Crampton had done Pollard a favor. "The States have been remodelling their constitutions this year, and the Southern Section ... [has] put this class of people in a still worse position," Pollard told the Trinidadian government.[122] Moreover, he would not have to stray far from Washington to mine the richest seams of black distress, for the 1850 census had counted high numbers of free African Americans in Maryland and Virginia, where they were "political nonentities."[123] Pollard had placed himself perfectly.

Coincidentally, Henry Clay had just written an open letter to colonizationists to consider the Caribbean as well as Africa.[124] Pollard wrote Clay to seek his counsel. "The city of Baltimore has been well chosen by you as

---

[118] A. Lawrence to D. Webster, November 8, 1851, H. Exec. Doc. 29, 32 Cong., 1 Sess. (1852), 3–4.
[119] Grey to Lawrence, February 20, 1852, H. Exec. Doc. 99, 32 Cong., 1 Sess. (1852), 2.
[120] J. Bigelow to F. P. Blair, Jr., March 8, 1860, BL.
[121] Pollard to Harris, June 14, 1851, CO295/174, 199.
[122] Pollard to T. F. Johnston, July 2, 1851, CO295/174, 242.
[123] Pollard to Harris, July 9, 1851, CO295/174, 234–5.
[124] H. Clay to T. Hankey, Jr., May 10, 1851, in Melba Porter Hay, ed., *The Papers of Henry Clay* (Lexington, 1959–92), 10:890–1.

the theatre of your operations," replied Clay, advising Pollard that his own state, Kentucky, did not feel the "pressure" of its free black population as acutely as the eastern states did.[125] From Indiana, Governor Joseph Wright also replied to Pollard's inquiries, telling him that, while the legislature had not yet enacted Article XIII, it would soon "take some efficient steps to get rid of the Colored population."[126] Wright enclosed the minutes of the state's recent black convention, which had ruled against Liberia but endorsed Grey's circular for offering "a home upon the soil of … Brittania's Isle, on terms of equality."[127] By contrast, Trinidad's commercial agent in Canada, Henry Stewart, assured Pollard that local African Americans showed little interest in emigrating.[128]

So it *was* the Chesapeake region, if any, that would deliver laborers. But Pollard recalled the mixed blessings of William Burnley's human haul, asking a black go-between from Baltimore, one Scott, not to offer bounties to anyone but farmers or artisans with skills in shortage.[129] When Scott replied, however, that those locals "who had intended to migrate to Africa [now] talk[ed] very strongly of going to Trinidad," Pollard changed his mind.[130] Inspired by an emigrationist meeting that ruled for Canada and the Dominican Republic (for offering "the 'sine qua non' of their leaving – a homestead"), Pollard widened his offer to all applicants, whatever their profession. Even Baltimore's industrial workers, in demanding land and a homestead, at least aspired to agriculture, while Pollard also acknowledged that Burnley's urban recruits had hardly burdened Trinidad.[131] Although local returnees from the migration of 1839–41 reciprocated Pollard's favorable impression of them with their own fond memories of Trinidad, they also recalled Burnley's broken promises, so Pollard was relieved to receive permission from Governor George Harris (1846–54) to offer them crown lands.[132] Prompted by that reminder of the discretion that governors could exercise, Pollard then buttonholed Maryland's own, a Democrat, Enoch Lowe (1851–4), but

---

[125] Clay to Pollard, September 6, 1851, in Mary Elizabeth Thomas, ed., "Henry Clay Replies to a Labor Recruiter from Trinidad," *Register of the Kentucky Historical Society* 77 (1979), 263–5.
[126] J. A. Wright to Pollard, September 3, 1851, CO295/174, 359–60.
[127] Anon., pub., *The Minutes of the State Convention of the People of Color* (Indianapolis, 1851), 10, in CO295/174, 394–9.
[128] H. Stewart to Pollard, June 17, 1851, CO295/174, 239–40.
[129] Pollard to S. Scott, June 16, 1851, CO295/174, 218.
[130] Scott to Pollard, June 18, 1851, CO295/174, 220.
[131] Pollard to Harris, August 1 and 8, 1851, CO295/174, 264, 280–1, 285–6.
[132] Harris to Pollard, August 19, 1851, CO295/174, 252–3.

found him loyal to Liberia. Yet Pollard remained confident that Maryland's legislators, whenever they next assembled, would readily reassign their colonization appropriations to the lowest bidder.[133]

Retrenchment certainly actuated the governor of Virginia, whom Pollard visited from his Maryland base. Like a later occupant of the office, Henry Wise (1856–60), the Democrat John B. Floyd (1849–52) wished to abandon Africa for the Americas, having already discussed West Indian colonization with one of the Commonwealth's US senators, Robert Hunter.[134] They thought black Virginians resigned to leaving, as long as homesteads awaited them at their destination.[135] In July 1851, in a warm conversation lasting two hours, John Floyd and Nathaniel Pollard agreed that Trinidad would pay to transport all those laborers who had indentured themselves and that Virginia would pay for the unindentured. In a foretaste of a more famous episode, Floyd then summoned a deputation of local African Americans, reminded them of their "anomalous position," and warned them that "he could not answer for the moment when a majority of the State would insist on their compulsory removal."[136] One of them, a barber, Richard Henderson, asked Pollard whether the colony would pay for local delegates to visit the island.[137] Bound by his narrow commission, Pollard replied that Trinidad just might fund a group of farmers drawn from throughout the state.[138] By returning to Baltimore, however, Pollard stalled whatever momentum he had mustered in Richmond. In September, Henderson warned him that volunteers had dried up for want of information, which came as no surprise to Pollard, whose budget did not extend to advertisements in the press.[139] Amid ambiguity whether Trinidad would offer two or five acres per settler, the former being too miserly for Floyd to conscionably draw on state funds, the Virginian branch of Pollard's plan snapped.[140]

The scheme's Maryland mainstay soon dissolved as well. In Baltimore, Pollard convened another meeting, where one or two attendees gave a "flattering account" of Trinidad.[141] But some of the Burnley-era

---

[133] Pollard to Harris, October 10, 1851, CO318/193, 149–50.
[134] R. M. T. Hunter to W. H. L. E. Bulwer, October 9, 1850, Dalling and Bulwer Papers, Duke University.
[135] Pollard to Harris, July 9, 1851, CO295/174, 238.
[136] Pollard to Johnston, July 22, 1851, CO295/174, 267–76.
[137] R. W. Henderson to Pollard, July 16, 1851, CO295/174, 266–7.
[138] Pollard to Henderson, July 21, 1851, CO295/174, 267.
[139] Henderson to Pollard, September 12, and Pollard to Johnston, August 11, 1851, CO295/174, 361, 312–14.
[140] Pollard to Harris, September 17, 1851, CO295/174, 266–7.
[141] Pollard to Henderson, September 16, 1851, CO295/174, 362–3.

immigrants who had remained on the island had written to warn their Maryland kin to place no weight in Pollard's promises, the council having just overruled Governor Harris's offer of crown lands. In the colony itself, the councilors' decision sparked fierce debate. "The views of the Proprietary Body extend no further than to overstock the labor market," wrote one columnist, accusing the planters of short-sightedness.[142] In November 1851, the *Comet* landed in Trinidad with all of fifteen immigrants, among them, in all likelihood, a young Stansbury Boyce.[143] One editor wondered why the colony had ever pursued Americans, whose lust for land was notorious, when Indian "Coolies" were content with wages.[144] Another thought that Pollard's southern base of operations had forced him to fawn over slaveholding politicians so much as to stifle his appeal to would-be migrants.[145]

Anderson, Scoble, and the Jamaican Mystique

Trinidadians were quick to criticize Pollard's insensitivity toward African Americans because they had just learned that two abolitionists were touring the North and Canada, espousing the cause of Jamaica. One, William Wemyss Anderson, was a Scot who had lived in Jamaica for decades and involved himself in liberal politics.[146] He had long promoted American immigration to the colony, white and black.[147] The other was John Scoble, of the British and Foreign Anti-Slavery Society, on his way to superintend Canada's strife-ridden Dawn settlement. During the 1840s, Scoble had supported Thomas Rolph's scheme, but had also campaigned against abuses by the West Indian planters.[148] Anderson and Scoble's antislavery credentials earned them the rostrum at the Toronto Convention and, shortly afterward, at the Liberty Party's Buffalo Convention. "Were I a coloured man, with my family of helpless boys

---

[142] "Sometime ago …," *Trinidadian*, November 1, 1851.
[143] "An American vessel …," *Trinidadian*, November 19, 1851.
[144] "Our contemporary …," Port of Spain *Gazette*, December 19, 1851.
[145] "Demerara," *Trinidadian*, November 29, 1851.
[146] R. J. M. Blackett, *The Captive's Quest for Freedom: Fugitive Slaves, the 1850 Fugitive Slave Law, and the Politics of Slavery* (New York, 2018), 99–102.
[147] William Wemyss Anderson, *A Description and History of the Island of Jamaica* (Kingston, 1851), 5–16, and *Jamaica and the Americans* (New York, 1851), 30; John Bigelow, *Jamaica in 1850* (New York, 1851), 175.
[148] Asaka, *Tropical Freedom*, 91–4; Gale L. Kenny, "Manliness and Manifest Racial Destiny: Jamaica and African American Emigration in the 1850s," *Journal of the Civil War Era* 2 (2012), 155–6, 163.

and girls about me ... I should deem it my duty not to continue a struggle," said Anderson at Buffalo, invoking the states' latest round of black laws. Scoble, who had joined forces with Anderson after they met by happenstance, did not share that colonist's hunger for hands.[149] He pleased the attendees by proclaiming that "God has given the entire world, for the entire race," but added that those contemplating emigration might at least consider the West Indies. Thanking the Britons for their kind motives, Frederick Douglass reminded them that their logic was nonetheless that of the ACS.[150] John Scoble did not himself move to the Caribbean, ending his days in Canada, while William Wemyss Anderson returned to Jamaica in due course, briefing its assembly that black Americans still feared indenture.[151]

Although Anderson and Scoble might have failed in their mission, the same rationale that allowed them to advocate emigration to the West Indies with a clear conscience fired many an abolitionist's imagination. Like no other colony, Jamaica, the former jewel in the British crown, captivated Americans, even though it was quite the outlier in its inability to resurrect even a shadow of its former sugar industry. Jamaica, whether the island itself or the principle of emancipation that it represented, became the stage for what one book dubbed the "ordeal of free labor," an ideological drama that drew an audience with the widest possible range of views on slavery.[152]

When abolitionists plotted tropical refuges for fugitive slaves, they usually had Jamaica in mind. Worried that his former master might reclaim him, James Pennington made a timely visit to the island in the mid-1840s and saw great potential in its freedpeople.[153] He called for African American missionaries to come and elevate a populace that, though not as degraded as proslavery polemicists might claim, would still benefit from an education by black brethren who had spent longer in

[149] Annie Heloise Abel and Frank J. Klingberg, eds., *A Side-Light on Anglo-American Relations, 1839–1858* (Lancaster, PA, 1927), 274–5n261.
[150] "Emigration of the Free People of Colour of the United States," *Anti-Slavery Reporter*, November 1, 1851.
[151] W. W. Anderson, report, February 24, 1852, in Alexander Manford, pub., *Votes of the Honorable House of Assembly of Jamaica* (St. Jago de la Vega, 1852), 540–3.
[152] Nichola Clayton, "Managing the Transition to a Free Labor Society: American Interpretations of the British West Indies during the Civil War and Reconstruction," *American Nineteenth Century History* 7 (2006), 91–2; William G. Sewell, *Ordeal of Free Labor in the British West Indies* (New York, 1861).
[153] Blackett, "Hamic Connection," 323–4.

freedom.[154] To that end, he encouraged the Kingston-based Jamaica Hamic Association to open a correspondence with the American black convention.[155] He also persuaded the earl of Elgin, then serving as governor of Jamaica (1842–6), to support a scheme to introduce black settlers of independent means, though Pennington was worryingly vague about such colonists' background.[156] Recalling the Upshur upset, Foreign Secretary Aberdeen thought Pennington's plan a ruse to rehome refugees, and ordered Elgin to shelve it. But the idea itself could not be so easily suppressed.[157] In 1851, while in Europe to avoid the effects of the Fugitive Slave Act, William Wells Brown advised his fellow refugees to seek work in the West Indies rather than come to Britain.[158] Strangely, he then excoriated the Dawn settlement's Josiah Henson for making the same suggestion, probably because he just disliked him.[159]

Most black Americans who looked to Jamaica saw it as more than a convenient haven, however. Pennington's proposal had contained the whisper of a campaign that breathed new life from 1850: the free produce movement, which took the flagging cause of sugar and wove it a new banner of cotton. Jamaica was perfect for the second attempt at the "great experiment," since its abandoned plantations offered space for smallholders as well as laborers.[160] Inspired by religious and economic evangelism, three noteworthy African Americans made the island their home for at least part of the 1850s: Henry Highland Garnet, his cousin, Samuel Ringgold Ward, and the lesser-known John Wesley Harrison.[161]

Sailing from Britain in 1852 as a missionary of the United Presbyterian Church of Scotland, Garnet arrived in Jamaica only to learn from his wife, Julia, that a son he had never met had just died. He channeled his grief into parochial work, founding a Sunday school at his Westmoreland church. In 1853, he advertised in the US press, on behalf of two planters, for seventy laborers; he might have held a stake in the business. Frederick Douglass was unimpressed at Garnet's

---

[154] "Intelligence from Jamaica," *Union Missionary*, June 1846.
[155] J. C. Kneeland, pub., *Proceedings of the National Convention of Colored People* (Troy, 1847), 23–5.
[156] Elgin to W. E. Gladstone, No. 33, February 21, 1846, CO137/288, 94–7.
[157] H. U. Addington to Stephen, June 13, 1846, CO137/290, 104–6.
[158] "Fugitive Slaves in England," *Liberator*, July 25, 1851.
[159] R. J. M. Blackett, *Building an Antislavery Wall: Black Americans in the Atlantic Abolitionist Movement, 1830–1860* (Baton Rouge, 1983), 137–8.
[160] Kenny, "Manliness and Manifest Destiny," 158.
[161] Blackett, "Hamic Connection," 324–7.

commercialism, and publicly told him to return to the United States, which illness forced him to do anyway in 1856.[162] But Douglass could only mourn the loss of Ward, who, having opposed emigration to the West Indies as recently as 1854, quietly slipped away the next year – like Garnet, while riding the British antislavery circuit, and unlike Garnet, with his financial probity already in doubt.[163] "While we all deeply regret that [Ward] has seen fit to leave us for other fields of usefulness, we will here and now tender him our best wishes," announced Douglass.[164] Once in Jamaica, Ward broke with his Kingston congregation in 1860, moving to a farm at St. Thomas in the East.[165] Nearby was the parish of St. David, where, in 1853, John Wesley Harrison had immigrated from South Carolina, armed with a lease for a well-equipped plantation that he could enjoy rent-free if he committed to improving it for five years.[166] At one point, he had 250 applicants ready to join him from Canada and the northern states, but the list shrank until it included only Pennington, and the expedition collapsed.[167]

However much Garnet, Ward, and Harrison had hoped to refute white slanders against black ability, or slaveholders' taunts about the failure of free labor, the task that they set themselves, of elevating a people who, logically, must be "backward" in at least some respects, brought out prejudices of their own. "The laboring population [is] indolent, and inefficient beyond anything I have ever seen," Harrison told William Wemyss Anderson.[168] "Emancipation found the negroes, as a whole … as ignorant, and almost as much heathens, as when they were first stolen from Africa," claimed Ward.[169] Criticism turned to contempt whenever colorism reared its head. "A person of mixed blood will not work in the field, although he may be suffering for the commonest necessaries of life," complained the dark-skinned Garnet.[170] A fourth African American in Jamaica, who, unlike the other three, stayed only a short time while traveling throughout the Caribbean, offered a contrary opinion,

---

[162] Martin B. Pasternak, *Rise Now and Fly to Arms: The Life of Henry Highland Garnet* (New York, 1995), 73–7.
[163] Ronald K. Burke, *Samuel Ringgold Ward: Christian Abolitionist* (New York, 1995), 56–8.
[164] C. P. Dewey, pub., *Two Speeches by Frederick Douglass* (Rochester, 1857), 7.
[165] Burke, *Samuel Ringgold Ward*, 58.
[166] "Colored Emigration to Jamaica," *Friends' Review*, July 9, 1853.
[167] Asaka, *Tropical Freedom*, 155–6.
[168] "Emigration of People of Color," *FDP*, August 20, 1852.
[169] "Samuel R. Ward's Letters from Jamaica," *WAA*, August 20, 1859.
[170] "Letter from H. H. Garnet," *FDP*, September 2, 1853.

influenced by his own, lighter skin. Agreeing with a white Jamaican that the island should not import black Americans, John Rapier, Jr., admitted that "the solemn fact is, the negro is not an intellectual creature."[171] But if Frederick Douglass could support black emigration to the Caribbean for how it would undermine slaveholders, and if slaveholders could support black emigration to the Caribbean for how it would make the case for reintroducing slavery, then surely the region lent itself to sweeping generalizations all around?[172]

THE THIRD WAVE: RECAPTIVES, REBELS, AND CONTRABANDS, 1860–1865

From Recaptives to Contrabands: St. Croix

By 1860, imperial canvassers no longer dared turn up in the US South to recruit African Americans. By contrast, they redoubled their efforts to obtain African recaptives, whose disposal had become such a contentious matter for the United States. Although the British minister duly sounded out the Buchanan and Lincoln administrations, it was his Danish counterpart who persuaded American officials to betray Liberia in favor of a closer destination.[173] In the fall of 1860, the vice-governor of the Danish West Indies island of St. Croix (from 1917, one of the US Virgin Islands), Louis Rothe, wrote Secretary of State Lewis Cass of Michigan, offering to take 2,000 recaptives. Cass's assistant secretary, William Trescot of South Carolina, informed Rothe that the law stipulated Liberia. A year later, a change of administration (not to say a revolution in politics) meant that Cass's near-successor, William Seward, listened attentively as the Danish chargé to the United States, Waldemar Raasløff, renewed Copenhagen's offer – but for contrabands, this time.[174]

---

[171] J. H. Rapier, Jr., to J. P. Thomas, February 3, 1862, Rapier Family Papers, Howard University.

[172] "A Wise Forecast," *FDP*, February 19, 1852; "Jamaica," *Daily Picayune*, March 15, 1851.

[173] W. D. Irvine to Russell, No. 5, October 23, 1860, Slave Trade and African Department Records, FO84/1110, 122–5, TNA; R. B. P. Lyons to Russell, No. 4, May 10, 1861, FO84/1137, 131–2.

[174] Michael J. Douma and Anders Bo Rasmussen, "The Danish St. Croix Project: Revisiting the Lincoln Colonization Program with Foreign-Language Sources," *American Nineteenth Century History* 15 (2014), 319–20.

While Seward's subsequent support for Raaslöff's plan would not mark the only occasion that he deviated from his underlying opposition to colonization, the exception that he made here was clearly born of exigency. That early in the war, the Union's provision for black refugees was pitiful. Moreover, Seward could appease his conscience with the "hands-off" approach of simply authorizing a Danish agent to canvass settlers, who might even return to the United States once their indenture had expired. In a further proviso that he would overlook just once thereafter (to stall the Chiriquí scheme), Seward told Raaslöff not to ask for an emigration treaty between Denmark and the United States, which could only embarrass the administration by falling short of the two-thirds Senate majority needed to ratify it.[175]

In February 1862, St. Croix appointed a recruiter, George Walker of New York, who held investments in the island. Being based in the United States, Walker entertained more realistic notions than most canvassers of African Americans' propensity to emigrate. "I can get the consent of Mr. Seward to go to Fort Monroe, Hatteras, or Port Royal," claimed Walker (naming Union contraband camps near Confederate lines), "but when I go to the negroes themselves . . . all the satisfaction I shall get will be 'no want to go Massa.'" Thanks to St. Croix's prematurity in pursuing contrabands, Walker looked likely to get no satisfaction in Washington, either. While the colonial council had instructed its agent to seek field hands, the sole US colonization law to date covered only the residents of the District of Columbia. That impasse redirected the business from George Walker (and Caleb Smith) to Waldemar Raaslöff and William Seward, since the chargé would have to renew Copenhagen's offer to take recaptives if he wanted the matter brought under federal purview.[176]

In May 1862, Seward notified Raaslöff that the Department of State was powerless to help as long as the law prescribed Liberia, but added that Congress might modify its legislation.[177] It would indeed do so, pushed along, in secret, by Seward himself. With the end of session looming, congressional debate was desultory. In spite of Senator Preston King's concerns about "a sort of apprenticeship system," the bill passed the Senate, 30-7.[178] On July 17, 1862, President Lincoln signed it into

---

[175] Sebastian N. Page, "'A Knife Sharp Enough to Divide Us': William H. Seward, Abraham Lincoln, and Black Colonization," *Diplomatic History* 41 (2017), 373.

[176] Douma, "St. Croix Project," 321–3.

[177] W. H. Seward to W. R. Raaslöff, May 29, 1862, H. Misc. Doc. 80, 37 Cong., 2 Sess. (1862), 11–12.

[178] CG 37 Cong., 2 Sess., 3358–9 (July 15, 1862).

law, thereby allowing the executive to enter into arrangements with any foreign government possessing tropical lands where recaptives might be landed. Naval commanders could, moreover, now sail directly to such colonies with their prizes.[179]

Behind the scenes, the key actors sighed with relief. "It is completely impossible to predict which discussions even a[n] ... inconsequential precaution regarding Negroes can cause," noted Raaslöff, explaining to his government why Seward had wanted congressmen to appear the bill's instigators.[180] Other agencies were willing, however, to scrutinize the agreement where Capitol Hill had not. "The course of the Government now bears the aspect ... of simply 'getting rid' of the negroes," protested a Vermont member of the ACS. "The Danish authorities will take the recaptives off our hands without expense! Ergo – make arrangements."[181] In fairness, given the mortality of those recaptives sent all the way to Liberia, the administration had acted with at least a degree of enlightened self-interest. Moreover, the Department of the Interior rejected a second, similar offer from the Spanish minister, in respect of Spain's west African island of Fernando Po (which would have accepted slavers captured in the *eastern* Atlantic), because it failed to address recaptives' welfare as thoroughly as had the St. Croix tender. Yet Secretary of the Navy Gideon Welles refused to update his orders to the commanders of vessels, (incorrectly) deeming the Danish-American agreement an illegal, unratified treaty. It was a moot point, because another treaty of 1862 – the genuine article, this time – that Seward reached with the British minister, Lord Lyons, ceded the Royal Navy its long-desired mutual right of search, allowing it to finally choke off the Atlantic slave trade.[182]

Yet the change in legislation had unforeseen consequences: the vigilant William Trescot, a proslavery ideologue, informed the Confederate Secretary of State Judah Benjamin, a native of St. Croix, of his dealings with Louis Rothe not two years earlier.[183] Observing that Abraham

---

[179] An Act to Amend an Act Entitled "An Act to Amend an Act Entitled 'An Act in Addition to Acts Prohibiting the Slave Trade'" (*sic*) (July 17, 1862), 12 Stat. 592–3.

[180] Page, "A Knife Sharp Enough," 374. The source that that article quotes is courtesy of Douma and Rasmussen.

[181] F. Butler to R. R. Gurley, August 18, 1862, reel 93, ACS.

[182] D. Hunter Miller, ed., *Treaties and Other International Acts of the United States of America* (Washington, DC, 1931–48), 8:852–8.

[183] Don H. Doyle, *The Cause of All Nations: An International History of the American Civil War* (New York, 2014), 188; Quigley, *Shifting Grounds*, 52.

Lincoln had approved the Second Confiscation Act the same day as the Slave Trade Act, Trescot suspected that the deceitful Yankees meant the two laws to act in concert: "nothing would be more desirable for those Islands than just such an importation of labour as would be furnished by the confiscated [American] negroes."[184] Heeding Trescot's warning, Benjamin instructed Richmond's emissary to northern Europe, A. Dudley Mann, to bring the matter before Copenhagen. Mann's subsequent meeting with Carl Christian Hall, serving as both prime minister and foreign minister, satisfied him, if unduly, that Denmark had never intended to steal slaveowners' property.[185] Yet as Waldemar Raaslöff's failure to acquire contrabands had shown, Denmark had, in any case, acted prematurely. The US Congress passed no legislation helpful to colonial canvassers until July 1862, and the administration was thereafter fixated on the Chiriquí contract until September. If West Indian recruiters had interpreted Lincoln's August 14 remarks as a sign to prepare for African American immigration, they still did not receive an invitation until Seward's circular of September 30. Moreover, the secretary of state did not convey his offer to the colonies themselves, but to their metropolitan governments, proffering it through the US ministers to the European governments (and not the European ministers to the US government), who could broach the matter at an ocean's remove from the major stakeholders, the colonies' own canvassers.

Speaking for Britain, now–Foreign Secretary Russell initially rejected the overtures of the US minister, Charles Francis Adams, and that to no regret from William Seward.[186] London would shortly change its mind, however. The Hague, busily preparing to free its own American slaves in 1863 (most of whom were concentrated in Surinam, also known as Dutch Guiana), would respond bullishly, but belatedly.[187] Paris ultimately heeded the advice of its pro-Confederate minister to Washington, Henri Mercier, to avoid all collusion in US emancipation policy. (Incredibly, the

[184] W. H. Trescot to J. P. Benjamin, August 5, 1862, reel 34, Confederate States of America Records, LC.

[185] A. D. Mann to Benjamin, No. 28, October 24, 1862, reel 4, ibid.

[186] C. F. Adams to Seward, No. 253, October 30, and Seward to Adams, No. 404, November 18, 1862, *PRFA* 37 Cong., 3 Sess. (1862), 227–8, 236.

[187] Michael J. Douma, "The Lincoln Administration's Negotiations to Colonize African Americans in Dutch Suriname," *Civil War History* 61 (2015), 116, and *The Colonization of Freed African Americans in Suriname: Archival Sources Relating to the U.S.-Dutch Negotiations, 1860–1866* (Leiden, 2019), 16–17.

foreign minister, Édouard Drouyn de Lhuys, had at first considered Seward's offer with a view to enlisting African Americans into the French armies in Mexico.)[188] Meanwhile, whatever debate Seward's circular might have inspired in Copenhagen, Mann was soon to issue his veiled threat, preempting any Danish response to the United States. Skeptics in the foreign offices of the Old World found kindred spirits in the US ministers accredited to them, abolitionists all, whom Seward had selected to reflect prevailing European opinion.[189] In his public dispatches, the minister to Copenhagen, Bradford Wood, maintained that "we have certainly gained nothing abroad by our offer to expatriate the negroes"; in private letters, he scorned Frank Blair's "impracticality" in pursuing colonization.[190]

Faces Old and New: Guiana and British Honduras

While Seward might have hoped that his circular would die a quiet death on the far side of the Atlantic, his optimism was misplaced. After all, he had issued it not only to address defects in the Chiriquí contract but also to regulate the recruiters that the British colonies had a penchant for sending straight to the United States. Of the big three, Trinidad, remembering Nathaniel Pollard's failure, made few efforts beyond brief inquiries from the governor and the US consul to their respective superiors.[191] Despite its stronger show of interest, Jamaica, whose immigration agencies were then in disarray, likewise failed to hatch a plan.[192] In fact, the island's most dogged lobbyist was the US vice-consul, John Camp, whom James Mitchell would commend to Abraham Lincoln for his efforts.[193] But the planters of Guiana, for whom the Carbery disappointment had become a distant memory, had roused themselves even before Lincoln's

[188] Daniel B. Carroll, *Henri Mercier and the American Civil War* (Princeton, 1971), 245–8.
[189] Kinley J. Brauer, "The Slavery Problem in the Diplomacy of the American Civil War," *Pacific Historical Review* 46 (1977), 447; Doyle, *Cause of All Nations*, 58–9.
[190] B. R. Wood to Seward, No. 100, January 27, 1863, PRFA 38 Cong., 1 Sess. (1864), 2:1098; Wood to Chase, November 10, 1863, Salmon P. Chase Papers, LC.
[191] R. W. Keate to Newcastle, No. 153, August 7, 1862, CO295/218, 425–6; G. Hogg to Seward, No. 30, November 11, 1862, Records of Foreign Service Posts, RG84/Port of Spain/33, NARA II.
[192] Eyre to Newcastle, No. 81, September 20, 1862, and No. 2, January 1, 1863, in Colonial Office, *Correspondence*, 2–3.
[193] J. Mitchell to A. Lincoln, June 16, 1864, Appointment Records for Public Office, RG59/760, NARA II; J. N. Camp to F. H. Pierpont, August 7, 1865, Francis H. Pierpont Papers, Library of Virginia.

August address.[194] Governor Francis Hincks (1861–9) tasked Guiana's secretary, William Walker, with importing black laborers into the Caribbean under happier circumstances than those envisioned by his filibustering namesake. During the voyage to the United States, Walker stopped at St. Thomas, where he learned that Denmark had just made its contract for the recaptives.[195]

Landing at New York that September, William Walker discovered that he faced further competitors. He asked the advice of the British consul, Edward Archibald, who suggested that Walker employ a "coloured clergyman possessing great influence over his brethren." Unfortunately, at a meeting of black Brooklynites, Walker showed little tact: "he appeared to have an idea that colored people were to be picked up here like hogs and transported wherever their captors chose," reported one attendee.[196] While in New York, he encountered Senator Samuel Pomeroy, who promised to consider Guiana should the Chiriquí project fail. Walker then went to Washington, where the British chargé, William Stuart, was managing the legation in Lyons's absence. Stuart told Walker that "the matter was not ripe for active proceedings," an allusion to Seward having disparaged colonization in a recent conversation with him. Next, Walker met Caleb Smith, who informed him that, while Lincoln and Seward deemed emigration a matter for the metropolitan government and not the colonies to arrange, they in fact favored the British Caribbean over Chiriquí. Poignantly, Smith also predicted that the then-tentative Île à Vache tender would come to nothing. Lincoln's commissioner of colonization, James Mitchell, offered Walker "his most cordial cooperation," but, for now, Walker could do little more than appoint a US-based subagent, Samuel Dickson of New York, circulate the obligatory brochure lauding Guiana, and return to the colony.[197]

Meanwhile, in London and Washington, the prospects of an Anglo-American black emigration treaty looked poor at first. Seward had given Stuart two days' notice that he intended to issue his circular, and Stuart swiftly wrote Foreign Secretary Russell to remind him that accepting Seward's offer would align Britain with the Union and its policy of

---

[194] T. D. Edwards to Seward, No. 11, August 16, 1862, Despatches from U.S. Consuls in Demerara, RG59/T336/7, NARA II.
[195] W. Walker to F. Hincks, December 8, 1862, CO111/337, unpaginated.
[196] "The Colored People of Brooklyn," *New York Times*, October 3, 1862.
[197] W. Walker to F. Hincks, December 8, 1862, CO111/337.

confiscation.[198] Elements within the British government were inclined to accept the US invitation, though, as long as all parties proceeded with caution. In mid-October 1862, the secretary of state for the colonies, the duke of Newcastle, permitted the governors of Jamaica, Guiana, and Trinidad to send canvassers to the United States, who were to defer to Lyons.[199] For his part, William Stuart also reconsidered Seward's offer, wondering whether Britain might preserve its neutrality by confining African Americans' embarkation to Boston, New York, and Philadelphia. "This would throw upon the United States Government the burden of their land journey to those ports," Stuart told Russell.[200] The thaw in Britain's initial frostiness was the work of one John Hodge, then in London, who represented a new entrant to the dangerous game of trafficking African Americans: British Honduras (Belize), London's one Central American colony, which the metropole had clung onto for little more than the isthmian foothold that it conferred.[201]

Since the Colonial Office had always exercised impartiality toward the colonies' competing claims on foreign labor, Hodge's unusual provenance did not trouble it. His was not the only proposal circulating for British Honduras, either, though the other one never came to London's attention. For more than a year, a New York merchant, Aaron Columbus Burr, and a Maryland pamphleteer, Anna Ella Carroll, had advertised a concession in British Honduras offering little more than mahogany, the colony's main export, which had furnished only dark prospects since the 1850s.[202] Despite lobbying Washington, Carroll found herself eclipsed by Ambrose Thompson and his Chiriquí scheme.[203] But by contrast with Burr and Carroll (and their small fry), John Hodge was manager of the quasi-monopolistic British Honduras Company (BHC), which aimed to

---

[198] W. Stuart to Russell, No. 255, September 28, 1862, in James J. Barnes and Patience P. Barnes, eds., *The American Civil War through British Eyes: Dispatches from British Diplomats* (Kent, 2003–5), 2:190–1.

[199] Newcastle to Eyre et al., No. 13, October 16, 1862, in Colonial Office, *Correspondence*, 19.

[200] Stuart to Russell, No. 302, October 18, 1862, in Barnes, *Through British Eyes*, 2:213.

[201] For the British Honduras scheme, see Phillip W. Magness and Sebastian N. Page, *Colonization after Emancipation: Lincoln and the Movement for Black Resettlement* (Columbia, MO, 2011).

[202] O. Nigel Bolland, "Systems of Domination after Slavery: The Control of Land and Labor in the British West Indies after 1838," *Comparative Studies in Society and History* 23 (1981), 600–2.

[203] Janet L. Coryell, "'The Lincoln Colony': Aaron Columbus Burr's Proposed Colonization of British Honduras," *Civil War History* 43 (1997), 11.

switch its major output from lumber to sugar.[204] Briefed by the Colonial Office that haste had availed Walker nothing, Hodge prepared his tender to the US authorities with diligence. He arrived at Washington no earlier than April 1863, whereupon he was sucked into the happy vacuum left by the collapse of the Chiriquí contract and the administration's reluctance to send further settlers to the Île à Vache.

While the BHC felled trees in Belize to make room for the putative immigrants, the British minister in Washington cleared obstacles of his own. In January 1863, President Lincoln had summoned Lord Lyons, telling him that "he had been for some time anxious to speak . . . on the subject of promoting the emigration of coloured people." The president admitted that, in Britain's position, he too would avoid taking contrabands, but asked the minister whether his government might accept the unambiguously free. Lyons was willing, but thought a treaty unnecessary, since James Mitchell had offered to supervise any colonial recruiters.[205] Fully restored to anti-colonizationist form, William Seward "begged" Lyons, who shared the secretary of state's skepticism about the scheme's chances of success, to delay any formal offer until Congress's March adjournment, by which time it should have passed laws enlisting African Americans into the army.[206] Meanwhile, Caleb Smith's successor at the Department of the Interior, John Usher, praised the immigration laws of British Honduras, observing, with some audacity, that his department "had been beset by speculators who, while pretending to be friends of the Negro, in reality sought only their own interest."[207] When John Hodge arrived in Washington, Lincoln initially cajoled him to secure a treaty from Lyons, but yielded, authorizing Hodge to visit the contraband camps around Washington and Alexandria, where he received the help of Danforth Nichols, future guardian of the Île à Vache returnees.[208]

While confident of acquiring contrabands, Hodge solicited black northerners as well, deploying a colonist who, unlike William Walker, knew how to address black audiences respectfully. Hodge's collaborator was William Wemyss Anderson, who hastened to New York to reacquaint himself with an old friend, Henry Highland Garnet.[209] Back

---

[204] O. Nigel Bolland, *The Formation of a Colonial Society: Belize, from Conquest to Crown Colony* (Baltimore, 1977), 141.
[205] Lyons to Russell, No. 78, January 27, 1863, in Barnes, *Through British Eyes*, 2:306–8.
[206] Lyons to Russell, No. 177, February 24, 1863, in ibid., 3:7.
[207] Lyons to Russell, No. 277, March 30, 1863, in ibid., 3:29–30.
[208] Magness, *Colonization after Emancipation*, 30.
[209] Phillip W. Magness, "The British Honduras Colony: Black Emigrationist Support for Colonization in the Lincoln Presidency," *Slavery and Abolition* 34 (2013), 44.

in Washington, Hodge's negotiations went well, Usher showing none of the envy that had blighted his dealings with Charles Tuckerman. Then, on May 11, Usher abruptly informed Hodge that he would no longer be allowed to visit the contraband camps, "because, in the opinion of the Secretary of War, it is inexpedient to allow any persons to visit that vicinity for that purpose."[210] In a literal sense, Usher's claim was true: Edwin Stanton had recently denied a similar pass, for Fort Monroe, to John Pinney and J. D. Johnson, who were acting for the New-York State Colonization Society. (Having barely considered Liberia from the late 1850s until the end of 1862, Lincoln had become so frustrated with speculators that he had turned to Africa once more.[211] At the same time, Seward made sure to excise two emigration articles from the US-Liberian treaty that Charles Francis Adams had agreed in London with President Stephen Benson.[212]) What Hodge could not have known was that there was bad blood between Usher and Mitchell, festering since antebellum times in Indiana and now poisoning the workings of the administration. John Usher resented James Mitchell's anomalous office and stubborn streak, and Mitchell, Usher's corruption and inexperience in administering a policy that had long been the minister's vocation.[213]

Despite the skepticism about British benevolence that a Scotch-Irish upbringing had sowed in Mitchell's mind, he had embraced the empire since 1862 for the same reason that he had favored Haiti and Liberia, whenever their governments recruited directly: all three valued the immigrants themselves, and not the federal dollars that came with them. Mitchell now pled the British brief with Seward, having already persuaded Hodge to present a joint proposal with Samuel Dickson, the agent for Guiana, and to accept passengers for free. Yet even at his most businesslike, Mitchell could never resist filling his memorandums with tedious musings on racial destiny. He told Seward of his pride at winning Britain to the conjoined causes of colonization and emancipation, and outlined ethno-nationalist visions of how republics suited whites, and monarchies, mixed races – and of how the British and American "empires" (Mitchell's word) would "bring by united effort a third into

---

[210] J. P. Usher to J. Hodge, May 11, 1863, S. Exec. Doc. 55, 39 Cong., 1 Sess. (1866), 32.

[211] Sebastian N. Page, "The American Colonization Society and the Civil War," in Beverly C. Tomek and Matthew J. Hetrick, eds., *New Directions in the Study of African American Recolonization* (Gainesville, 2017), 215–17.

[212] Seward to Adams, September 23, 1862, in Miller, *Treaties*, 8:867.

[213] Magness, *Colonization after Emancipation*, 34, 82–95.

position."[214] Although his thoughts made heavy reading for anyone, he could not have known that he had lost *Seward* at "colonization."

Yet Mitchell could at least count on one of Seward's cabinet colleagues, Montgomery Blair. Whatever Anglophobia the Blair family had evinced in its prewar vision of filling the Caribbean with US protectorates, that sentiment evaporated now that Britain offered the last, best hope of racial separation. In May 1863, Blair announced in a speech at Cleveland that setting freedpeople to work in the occupied South was but to train them for the tropics, "aided with the capital and intelligence of the great commercial powers."[215] That Blair had alluded to Britain became clear when he met Hodge and Mitchell, told them to strip their proposal of all encumbrance except the right to access the contraband camps, and arranged for Lincoln himself to sign it. In a warm meeting of June 13 with Hodge and Mitchell, Lincoln overruled Usher, informing them that "what he had told [Hodge] at first was his honest desire." He authorized Hodge and Dickson, acting for British Honduras and Guiana, to roam everywhere without hindrance.[216] Even a simple canvassing pass was subject to the approval of Secretary of War Stanton, though, who angered Lincoln by countermanding him once more.[217] If there was just one respect in which the administration's policies of black enlistment and black emigration clashed, it was that recruiters of both kinds competed for the contraband camps nearest Washington.

Unwittingly, Lord Lyons now handed Lincoln's saboteurs another opportunity to impede Hodge's progress. As in 1843, the British minister had to ask the approval of the US secretary of state before he could permit the governors of the relevant colonies to proclaim American ports of embarkation.[218] At the same time, Lyons wrote Russell to check whether he really meant to include contrabands in Britain's offer, warning him that the administration might not speak with one voice. "The President's plan of approving Papers submitted by subordinates, without coming to an understanding with his Cabinet, is not always successful," Lyons explained.[219] A frustrated Hodge asked Mitchell for his help, and Mitchell in turn asked Edward Bates for his, receiving the attorney

---

[214] Mitchell to Seward, May 19, 1863, reel 78, WHS.
[215] Montgomery Blair, *Comments on the Policy Inaugurated by the President* (New York, 1863), 11–12.
[216] Hodge to Lyons, July 9, 1863, CO318/239, 200–1.
[217] "Lincoln and the Negro," *St. Louis Daily Globe-Democrat*, August 26, 1894.
[218] Lyons to Seward, June 17, 1863, PRFA 38 Cong., 1 Sess. (1864), 1:582–3.
[219] Lyons to Russell, June 19, 1863, John Russell Papers, PRO30/22/37, 84–5, TNA.

general's assurance that contrabands were included in the "free persons of color" specified in Lincoln's certificate.[220] Still, Hodge and Dickson would need London's explicit permission as well as Washington's. And at first, Earl Russell approved Lord Lyons's refusal to authorize a ports proclamation, only later capitulating to Newcastle's argument that, beyond restricting embarkation to ports well behind Union lines, Britain owed the Confederacy no duty of care.[221] Meanwhile, in Washington, for two months, Seward stalled Lyons's request for the parallel permission of the United States, presenting Lincoln with a memorandum opposing the scheme. Jolted by the Draft Riots of July 1863, a timely reminder of the murderous depths of white racism, the president insisted that "it would have been better to separate the races than to have such scenes as those in New York the other day, where negroes were hanged to lamp posts."[222] In August, at Lincoln's prodding, Seward duly allowed Lyons to authorize the West Indian colonies to proclaim ports of embarkation.[223]

But Seward's delaying tactics had succeeded in forcing Hodge to leave for British Honduras, ending his chances of obtaining contrabands. He had sailed out, however, with a delegation of free African Americans, including Mitchell's assistant, John Willis Menard (Figure 5.1), who, over the course of six months, had tried to leave for Chiriquí, then Haiti, then Liberia (he had barely missed the departure of the *Mary Caroline Stevens*), and who had now made it to British Honduras. It was worth the wait. "The Negro, the Indian, the Spaniard, the Carib, the Creole, are all blended.... These are truly *Colored People*," enthused Menard in a report to Lincoln.[224] If the colony's franchise struck Menard as narrow, then that would just allow an influx of qualified African Americans to wield serious power. Another of the visitors was smitten. "All able-bodied, energetic, industrious colored men with their families, and a small capital ... cannot fail of success," declared Charles Babcock, a Massachusetts Garrisonian.[225] Menard returned to the United States and presented his findings at Garnet's New York church, where the late riots had left the congregation receptive to Menard's gospel of separatism.[226]

[220] Hodge to Lyons, June 23, 1863, CO318/239, 307.
[221] A. H. Layard to Fortescue, August 8, 1863, CO318/239, 181–2.
[222] "Lincoln and the Negro," *St. Louis Daily Globe-Democrat*, August 26, 1894.
[223] Seward to Lyons, August 10, 1863, *PRFA* 38 Cong., 1 Sess. (1864), 1:620.
[224] "Report of J. Willis Menard," *Anglo-African*, October 24, 1863.
[225] Charles Babcock, *British Honduras, Central America: A Plain Statement to the Colored People of the U.S. Who Contemplate Emigration* (Boston, 1863), 16.
[226] Magness, "British Honduras Colony," 51–2.

FIGURE 5.1 John Willis Menard (1838–1893). Poet, politician, and emigrationist.
Emily Howland Photograph Album, LC

Although Garnet's African Civilization Society had, in more recent times, emphasized the domestic elevation of African Americans, James Mitchell exploited its swing back toward emigration to arrange a little-known sequel to the president's meeting with the black Washingtonians.[227] In November 1863, Lincoln met a delegation from the society, including Garnet's successor as president, George LeVere. No record survives of their conversation, though the attendees evidently requested $5,000. Their stated purpose of elevating "African ancestors in any portion of the earth" reveals little in itself, but William McLain of the ACS recorded that they intended to charter a ship.[228] In that the Civilization Society rebuffed McLain's offer of a free passage to Liberia, the organization was seemingly as keen as ever to keep its distance from the Colonization Society.[229] But the expedition never happened, probably

[227] Mitchell to Lincoln, November 5, 1863, AL.
[228] African Civilization Society to Lincoln, November 5, 1863, AL.
[229] W. McLain to J. Tracy, November 13, 1863, reel 204, ACS.

because John Usher cited his (selective) scruples over misusing the colonization fund for northerners.[230] And with that whimper ended the last of the major nineteenth-century projects for African American emigration to the British West Indies. Despite discerning no further evidence of black interest in immigration, Guiana's Governor Hincks vainly proclaimed US ports of embarkation in 1864. In British Honduras, the BHC changed its annual immigration order from African Americans to Chinese, even as an influx of white emigres from the faltering Confederacy heralded an altogether different class of American immigrant.[231]

Degrees of Freedom: Surinam and Jamaica

Since Abraham Lincoln never provided an epitaph for a scheme that he likely hoped to revive, it fell to the secretary of state, William Seward, to deliver the last rites for black resettlement in the European Caribbean. Seward's cue was a December 1863 dispatch from the US minister to the Netherlands, James Shepherd Pike, containing an emigration treaty that the minister had taken a year to negotiate with The Hague.[232] Pike's opposite number, the Dutch minister to Washington, Roest van Limburg, had in fact asked Seward as early as July 1862 whether the United States might send freedpeople to Surinam, though Limburg himself inclined to the advice of his father-in-law, Lewis Cass, to avoid all involvement in US emancipation policy.[233] Thereafter, negotiations centered on the Netherlands, proceeding slowly because of the contemporaneous abolition of slavery in the Dutch West Indies. As such, the self-destruct mechanism that Seward had embedded in his circular had worked: the one government to call his bluff, and to commit itself by treaty to the Union's war for black freedom, had taken so long in the matter that its moment had passed. "It is not now expected that the treaty in regard to negro emigration will be ratified," Seward wrote Pike in February 1864, informing him that he would not even place the document before the Senate. "The American people have advanced to a new position ... since the President, in obedience to their prevailing wishes,

---

[230] Mitchell to Usher, November 5, 1863, AL.
[231] Wayne M. Clegern, *British Honduras: Colonial Dead End, 1859–1900* (Baton Rouge, 1967), 37–46; Zach Sell, "Asian Indentured Labor in the Age of African American Emancipation," *International Labor and Working-Class History* 91 (2017), 18–20.
[232] J. S. Pike et al., treaty, December 15, 1863, in Miller, *Treaties*, 8:856–7.
[233] Douma, "African Americans in Suriname," 123.

accepted the policy of colonization." Going by that version of events, Seward was evidently keener to spare Lincoln's blushes than to leave historians the slightest trace of the frank conversations that must have passed between the secretary of state and president that winter.[234]

If 1865 represented the beginning of an illusory black freedom in the United States, it marked the end of another in the heart of the West Indies, Jamaica. That October, a Baptist preacher, Paul Bogle, led a protest of disfranchised peasants in Morant Bay, on the island's southeastern tip. The militia shot several demonstrators, whose comrades retaliated by burning the courthouse, an act that left the wider populace liable to the martial law of Governor Edward Eyre (1862–5).[235] His brutal response polarized the British public, sparking a debate, redolent of that unfolding in the United States, about the appropriate governance of lands with large numbers of freedpeople. It also divided two Americans who had immigrated to Jamaica.[236] On the one side was Samuel Ringgold Ward, who directed the blame at a ringleader of mixed race, George William Gordon, whom Eyre would execute out of hand. "The rebellion was evidently planned by a Mulatto, and a few whites were accessories, while by their too great ductility too many negroes were … made cat's paws," lamented Ward. Fealty to the regime was, for Ward, the price of white respect, for "the whole mass of negroes are too commonly classed and generalized, with any portion who do wrong."[237] On the other side was one of Ward's neighbors: John Willis Menard. Despite his praise for British Honduras, Menard had chosen to emigrate to Jamaica, where he soon met with disillusion. He had already alienated the authorities by founding a debating society when they cited the Morant Bay disturbance to search his personal papers, in which they found confessions of his "deep hatred to the ruling class" of the United States, and of his desire for "separation from the white race." The clerk of the peace deemed such statements sufficient to deport Menard, who, probably, was spared the firing squad only because of the same US nationality that he had tried to transcend.[238] In a further twist for a devoted emigrationist, Menard would become the

---

[234] Seward to Pike, No. 142, February 15, 1864, *PRFA* 38 Cong., 2 Sess. (1865), 3:310.
[235] Holt, *Problem of Freedom*, 263–309.
[236] Tim Watson, *Caribbean Culture and British Fiction in the Atlantic World, 1780–1870* (Cambridge, UK, 2008), 187–200, and "The Caribbean Career of John Willis Menard," *Journal of Caribbean History* 50 (2016), 175–6.
[237] Samuel R. Ward, *Reflections upon the Gordon Rebellion* (n.p., 1866), 3, 7.
[238] H. J. Kemble to W. R. Myers, November 2, 1865, CO137/424, 414–16.

first black American elected to the US Congress, but was refused his seat after a white opponent challenged the result.[239]

What, if anything, had united those two Americans in Jamaica? Ostensibly, little: Menard stressed rights, and Ward, obligations; Menard was a republican, and Ward, a monarchist; Menard would achieve a measure of fame, but Ward fell into such obscurity that scholars do not even know when he died. Yet both men had emigrated because they thought the struggle for black rights a global one, even if in a different way from each other.[240]

By 1865, white Americans wondered whether the struggle for black resettlement would, conversely, have to remain a domestic one. Liberia was a long-term letdown; Latin America, a cauldron of corrupt contractors and gainsaying governments; and the European West Indies, a dead-end of diplomatic dithering. The one minister to pursue William Seward's circular to its logical conclusion, James Shepherd Pike, had been no happier at his handiwork than was Seward. "I made [a treaty] here a while ago on negro emigration to Surinam which I hope you will *not* ratify, should it come before you," wrote Pike to his friend and fellow Mainer, Senator William Fessenden. "I think the principle on which it is based, a vicious one."[241] But a year earlier, Pike had also told Fessenden that he would have "no tears to shed over the making of a negro pen" of the entire Confederacy east of the Mississippi, even if it meant forfeiting US jurisdiction forever.[242]

The most persistent, because most proximate, form of racial separation, internal colonization, is at the core of the next chapter.

---

[239] Forrest G. Wood, *Black Scare: The Racist Response to Emancipation and Reconstruction* (Berkeley, 1968), 90.
[240] Jeffrey R. Kerr-Ritchie, "Samuel Ward and the Making of an Imperial Subject," *Slavery and Abolition* 33 (2012), 205–19, and "Samuel Ward and the Gordon Rebellion," *Journal of Caribbean History* 50 (2016), 36–51.
[241] Pike to W. P. Fessenden, April 6, 1864, James Shepherd Pike Papers, LC.
[242] Pike to W. P. Fessenden, January 13, 1863, ibid.

6

Alternatives to Foreign Resettlement, to 1868

From the Revolution through the Civil War, white Americans had imagined that emancipation would send their black compatriots out of sight and out of mind. The Other would, somehow, end up Elsewhere. Yet before Abraham Lincoln had even issued the Emancipation Proclamation, whites had started to wonder whether foreign resettlement schemes would ever answer the perennial, now pressing, "negro question." Promoters, politicians, and the public looked to the peripheries of the contiguous United States – to marginalization in its most literal sense. In so doing, they joined an intellectual tradition that predated even the American Colonization Society.

Yet internal colonization had receded from whites' imagination during the antebellum period, along with the frontier itself. For they had found it easier to consider forfeiting territory to a black colony when the "far West" had meant Ohio, not Oregon, and before the ACS had emerged, with its tempting offer to remove blacks from the United States altogether. Moreover, the Mexican Cession (1848), which made white northerners question the place of slavery in the US territories, bolstered their belief that *freedom* out west should be the preserve of white settlers and that black immigrants should be outlawed. During the 1850s, the prospect of a black district in the West accordingly diminished. It was not until 1861, when secession left the South liable to federal fiat, that northerners would reconsider plans for internal resettlement, to be imposed on that section instead. The utopianism of the would-be black colonies of the early republic, itself a by-product of their distance from the white population, also evaporated. In its place came strategies to help the Union prosecute a civil war and perpetuate a civil peace.

Yet every settlement that whites might propose raised burning questions: whether it could earn statehood, or whether its very existence could justify restricting blacks' rights elsewhere – coerced migration having lost, by war's end, what credibility it had had. As final freedom loomed for 4,000,000 slaves, and white radicals began to speak of black civic equality, advocates of racial separation would have to produce answers with some haste. As one abolitionist put it, "we have got to decide pretty soon … whether [African Americans] shall have a nation of their *own* or a fair share in ours."[1] A US senator was even blunter: "you must kill them, colonize them, or ultimately give them a part of your political power."[2] Remarkably, the earliest proponents of internal colonization had known that their descendants, one day, would face that very quandary.

WESTWARD THE COURSE OF EMPIRE: INTERNAL
COLONIZATION THROUGH 1860

White Antecedents

Like the schemes for black colonization in west Africa, those for North America originated with the reformers and slaveholders of the late eighteenth and early nineteenth centuries. Their projects were explicitly anti-slavery, allowing gradual emancipation a propitious place to unfold, and ameliorative, allowing African Americans space (and, therefore, time) to catch up with white levels of education. And why go to unnecessary pains by locating such settlements any farther away than the presumably abundant wilds of North America? Why let black muscle atrophy in some insalubrious clime, when it could exert itself expanding the contiguous United States? In 1783, the Marquis de Lafayette, prior to settling on Cayenne for his experimental plantation, had asked America's own hero of the Revolutionary War, George Washington, whether they might join forces to buy an American estate for such a venture, but he gave up at Washington's indifference.[3] Other Virginians proved keener than Washington on a domestic colony. A magistrate, William Craighead, proposed a settlement in the Northwest Territory (organized in 1787), then largely under the control of hostile Native Americans. Awkwardly,

---

[1] E. Wright to C. Sumner, March 6, 1865, Charles Sumner Papers, Harvard.
[2] *CG* 39 Cong., 1 Sess., 3035 (June 8, 1866).
[3] Nicholas Guyatt, *Bind Us Apart: How Enlightened Americans Invented Racial Segregation* (New York, 2016), 207–8.

in view of those tribes' own claims to sovereignty over the region, the Craighead settlement's "relation to the government of the United States was to be something analogous to that in which the Indians now stand."[4]

Meanwhile, a future president of the ACS, James Madison, thought that the "interior wilderness of America" might lend itself to a black colony, as did St. George Tucker, a professor of law at the College of William and Mary. In 1795, Tucker had argued that, while "deep-rooted prejudices" would inflame tension between blacks and whites after emancipation, the ostensibly obvious answer of internal colonies might provoke a race war between them (or between blacks and Indians).[5] Unwilling to see slavery survive, however, Tucker thought again. The next year found him contemplating "an immense unsettled territory on this continent more congenial to [black] constitutions than ours," even if it meant African Americans becoming Spanish subjects by moving to Louisiana or the Floridas. Although opposed to blacks' "banishment," Tucker thought that "denying them the most valuable privileges [would] . . . render it their interest to seek [them] in some other climate."[6] By 1801, while still hopeful for a settlement west of the Mississippi, Tucker wondered whether expediency pointed to using the sizable Indian territory extant within Georgia. He also proposed awarding further political rights to those African Americans wise enough to migrate, though stopped short of threatening to remove any existing rights from those who were not.[7] Taken together, Tucker's thoughts on innate racial suitability to certain climates, the appropriate mixture of carrots and sticks, and the dilemma between choosing an easy, proximate location and one less accessible to white settlers anticipated future debates over internal colonization.

Already, though, proposals from northern intellectuals differed in emphasis from those of their southern counterparts. Two pioneers of Philadelphia's fertile culture of antislavery, which blended abolition and colonization down to the Civil War, suggested settlements that would allow African Americans to reach the caliber of citizenship, the only true rebuttal to prejudice. As early as 1763, a French immigrant and Quaker, Anthony Benezet, had suggested the eastern banks of the Mississippi for

---

[4] Archibald Alexander, *A History of African Colonization on the Western Coast of Africa* (Philadelphia, 1846), 61–2.
[5] Guyatt, *Bind Us Apart*, 218.
[6] St. George Tucker, *A Dissertation on Slavery* (Philadelphia, 1796), 94–6.
[7] St. George Tucker, *Letter to a Member of the General Assembly of Virginia* (Baltimore, 1801), 18.

"an advantageous opportunity of beneficial employment for the negroes."[8] He repeated the idea in a 1771 pamphlet: improving tracts of land "would encourage them to exert their abilities and become industrious subjects."[9] Unlike St. George Tucker, Benezet envisioned not a remote, racially homogeneous community, but one in which blacks and whites would work their way toward integration, away from the social pressures of the densely populated seaboard. In 1794, Benezet's mentee, the physician and reformer Benjamin Rush, acquired 20,000 acres in sparsely settled south-central Pennsylvania and submitted a colonization plan to the Pennsylvania Abolition Society. Rush lamented how black Philadelphians were prone to perpetuating "vices ... contracted in slavery" by tending, in freedom, toward domestic service, and how they struggled to acquire land, the prerequisite of republican virtue. But Rush hoped to set a good example to black northerners and white southerners alike, for slaveholders would see his colony in action and draw inspiration for their own. Unlike Benezet, though, Rush meant his settlement to separate the races forever.[10]

Where Benjamin Rush had treated planters as sincere in their denunciations of slavery, a New Englander, Dartmouth College's Moses Fiske, hinted in a 1795 pamphlet, *Tyrannical Libertymen*, that an internal colony, which would elevate African Americans in "arts and learning" and earn statehood in due course, was so self-evidently unobjectionable that any opposition from the slaveholders must expose their hesitation about emancipation as handwringing.[11] But most northern thinkers charted a more tortuous journey than did Benezet and Fiske between their egalitarian beliefs about blacks and their social concerns for their fellow whites. In 1805, an Irish immigrant, Thomas Branagan, argued that a western colony at least 2,000 miles from his adoptive Philadelphia would still honor "the rights of man" while preventing the South from corrupting the North with the free blacks that it emitted.[12]

[8] Guyatt, *Bind Us Apart*, 221.
[9] Anthony Benezet, *Some Historical Account of Guinea* (Philadelphia, 1771), 140.
[10] Guyatt, *Bind Us Apart*, 222–4.
[11] Moses Fiske, *Tyrannical Libertymen: A Discourse upon Negro-Slavery in the United States* (Hanover, 1795), 7–11.
[12] Joanne Pope Melish, *Disowning Slavery: Gradual Emancipation and "Race" in New England, 1780–1860* (Ithaca, 1998), 225–7; Beverly Tomek, "'From Motives of Generosity, as Well as Self-Preservation': Thomas Branagan, Colonization, and the Gradual Emancipation Movement," *American Nineteenth Century History* 6 (2005), 130–6.

Inevitably nationalist in outlook, insofar as the "race question" affected the entire Union, proponents of internal colonization contemplated a crucial role for the federal government, which had jurisdiction over the territories. When, in 1800, the United States moved its capital from Philadelphia to Washington, the proponents of such schemes moved south with it. Samuel Harrison Smith, founder of the *National Intelligencer*, collaborated with another Philadelphian (and architect of the Capitol), William Thornton, to publicize a range of locations for black resettlement, which did not, however, include Africa. In 1802, Thornton advised President Thomas Jefferson to buy Puerto Rico from Spain as a black refuge, but Napoleon's unexpected offer of Louisiana the next year instead drew the president's gaze westward – as did the supplications of his fellow Virginians.[13] For Gabriel's Conspiracy (1800) had galvanized the Virginia legislature into pursuing secret schemes to remove the state's slaves. Requested by Governor James Monroe (1799–1802) to supply land in the West, President Jefferson had replied that he had variously considered the Northwest Territory, which raised the specter of the eventual admission of a black state; the European colonies of the Americas, which their owners were unlikely to cede; and Africa, which, for reasons that Jefferson did not specify, should remain a "last resort." That left Haiti, whose freedom-loving leaders had gained the president's (short-lived) admiration.[14] Monroe took Jefferson's ideas to the legislature, which continued to badger him for an internal colony.

In 1804, Monroe's successor as governor, John Page, sent Jefferson a secret resolution of the legislature requesting part of the previous year's Louisiana Purchase as "the desired asylum for the free negroes and mulattoes and such as may be emancipated hereafter."[15] Surely Page's old friend could not refuse what was barely a show of largesse, given that the Louisiana Territory had almost doubled the size of the United States? Page did not propose statehood for the settlement and agreed with Jefferson that "insurgent negroes" might still be sent to Haiti.[16] Just as he would avoid the embrace of the ACS after 1817, however, Jefferson, who had once written that "when freed, [the slave] is to be removed beyond the reach of mixture," now dismissed black colonization for the

---

[13] Guyatt, *Bind Us Apart*, 249–51.
[14] T. Jefferson to J. Monroe, November 24, 1801, in Paul Leicester Ford, ed., *The Works of Thomas Jefferson* (New York, 1904–5), 9:315–19.
[15] J. Page to Jefferson, October 29, 1804, Thomas Jefferson Papers, Rotunda Collections (online).
[16] Guyatt, *Bind Us Apart*, 255.

danger it posed to the institution of slavery.[17] Having himself suggested Louisiana to Page just one year earlier, Jefferson claimed that he could do nothing without consulting the region's white inhabitants – presumably, the citizens of New Orleans.

Jefferson never explained why he had backtracked. He might have worried about a potential alliance (or, conversely, conflict) between blacks and Indians, about the encroachment of white settlers onto black lands, or about the near-certain opposition of South Carolina and Georgia to the scheme. Nominally a supporter of racial separation until his death, Jefferson would always smother the idea with implacable, even inconsistent qualifications whenever a correspondent approached him with a concrete plan. Slaveholders must initiate the process themselves, Jefferson maintained, and receive fair compensation; all slaves must be freed and resettled in one fell swoop (or none freed at all), though never, he added, in one *location*; white settlers must not encounter the "blot" of black colonies in the West, but the federal government must, for its part, permit the diffusion of slavery into the territories. Whether conscious or not, such self-contradiction made for a lifetime of inaction from Jefferson.[18]

It had taken less than a decade to vindicate Moses Fiske: a slaveholder of radical words had proved conservative in deed. In 1806, Virginia's frustrated assembly banned manumission without removal, which was effectively to ban manumission. In 1816, one of its members, a Federalist lawyer, Charles Mercer, consulted the journals of its secret sessions after hearing a colleague denounce Jefferson as a hypocrite. At some point that fall, Mercer met his soon-to-be cofounder of the ACS, Robert Finley, who, having dismissed internal settlements for how they might harbor fugitive slaves, had trudged his own path to colonization in Africa.[19] The rest was history – almost. That year, Virginia's legislators asked now-President Madison to consider adding a site in the Pacific West to the new, Liberia-focused scheme, but Madison did not oblige them. In 1825, St. George Tucker's cousin, US Representative George Tucker, proposed

---

[17] Thomas Jefferson, *Notes on the State of Virginia* (Boston, 1802), 199.
[18] Christopher Michael Curtis, *Jefferson's Freeholders and the Politics of Ownership in the Old Dominion* (New York, 2012), 137; Christa Dierksheide, *Amelioration and Empire: Progress and Slavery in the Plantation Americas* (Charlottesville, 2014), 34–47; Guyatt, *Bind Us Apart*, 257–8; Brian Steele, *Thomas Jefferson and American Nationhood* (New York, 2012), 239.
[19] Robert Finley, *Thoughts on the Colonization of Free Blacks* (Washington, DC, 1816), 6–7.

a location west of the Rocky Mountains. Yet as white expansion into the far Northwest roved into view, Liberian colonizationists such as Henry Clay warned that internal resettlement "would again produce that very contact between discordant races which it is so desirable to avoid." Black resettlement in North America sank from a political mainstream that now flowed toward Africa, a far-flung location that Thomas Jefferson, the progenitor (and arch-betrayer) of colonization, had once ranked dead last.[20]

Through the 1850s, white Americans occasionally dredged up internal resettlement. In 1831, a Baptist preacher and abolitionist, John Leland, reviewed the plight of the slaves. "All their relations and attachments are here; why then ship them to Liberia? ... Why not liberate them, and let them form into states within the limits of other states?" he asked, either ignorant of the US Constitution's ban on forming one state from another without the latter's consent or unduly hopeful of the same.[21] Those advocates of internal colonization more willing than Leland to reject black statehood sometimes suggested parceling out the public lands. "The black man looks to Liberia but desires not a home on her pestilential shore," noted an 1837 petition from Washington County, Ohio, which asked Congress "to provide speedily a city of refuge in some one of your territories."[22]

Like the Louisiana Purchase nearly half a century earlier, the Mexican Cession at first seemed an obvious outlet for African Americans. "Texas with New Mexico and Upper California in her train, should be particularly welcome, if they came in ... planting colonies of free colored people on their western borders," claimed one New Englander.[23] In 1848, a New York Whig, Representative William Duer, moved that the House Committee on Public Lands plan a reservation open to any black man over the age of twenty-one, but a Democrat, William Sawyer, accused him of misplaced benevolence for awarding lands to African Americans while resisting a homestead law that would have reduced the price of land for white settlers. Sawyer also charged Duer with plotting a black state, so Duer clarified that he meant to cap the settlement at the purely local

[20] Ikuko Asaka, *Tropical Freedom: Climate, Settler Colonialism, and Black Exclusion in the Age of Emancipation* (Durham, 2017), 39–41.
[21] J. Leland, address, March 4, 1831, in L. F. Greene, ed., *The Writings of the Late Elder John Leland* (New York, 1845), 612–13.
[22] J. Tuttle et al., petition, September 19, 1837, U.S. House Records, RG233/25A-G18.2/2, NARA.
[23] Massachusetts Junior, pseud., *A Plea for the South* (Boston, 1847), 27.

powers of a US territory.[24] Reluctance to use the public lands to *place* black colonies crossed party lines, however: even Whigs preferred to *sell* the national domain to whites, and to contribute the proceeds to the ACS.[25]

Absent legislative support, those minded to found an internal colony would have to do it themselves. In 1825, the Scottish reformer Frances Wright, then accompanying Lafayette on his feted tour of the United States, announced an experimental settlement of her own, at Nashoba, Tennessee. She established a training school for prospective manumittees, who would be expatriated in due course, but she doomed the community from the moment she confessed that it would encourage racial amalgamation.[26] Colonies looking only to manumission, not "miscegenation," were easier to establish – but barely. In 1819, ex-President Madison's private secretary, Virginia planter Edward Coles (who, like John Page, had appealed in vain to Jefferson's supposed colonizationism), freed his own slaves and accompanied them to Illinois, on the cusp of entry to the Union. Three years later, the precocious Coles found himself in the governor's office, countering a local campaign to celebrate statehood (and, therefore, sovereignty) by introducing slavery to the future "Land of Lincoln." That a free state could even contemplate importing an institution that the slave states lamented as an inherited evil converted Coles to the cause of Liberia, evidently the only true refuge for African Americans.[27]

Yet Edward Coles's manumittees were indeed free, thanks in no small part to the fact that he had been alive to oversee the process. By the 1850s, however, the same judicial reaction that invalidated wills sending slaves to Liberia annulled those freeing them in a different state of the Union. In 1833, another Virginia slaveowner, John Randolph, had died leaving three wills, the second of which instructed his executor to relocate almost 400 slaves. In 1844, the courts finally ruled that version the legitimate one, and in 1846, his administrator sent the manumittees to Ohio, where an agent had bought lands for them in Mercer County.[28] Having

---

[24] *CG* 30 Cong., 1 Sess., Appendix, 727–31 (June 22, 1848).
[25] *CG* 32 Cong., 1 Sess., Appendix, 508 (April 28, 1852).
[26] Steven Hahn, *A Nation without Borders: The United States and Its World in an Age of Civil Wars, 1830–1910* (New York, 2016), 71–2; William H. Pease and Jane H. Pease, *Black Utopia: Negro Communal Experiments in America* (Madison, 1963), 33–7.
[27] Guyatt, *Bind Us Apart*, 308–10.
[28] Frank F. Mathias, "John Randolph's Freedmen: The Thwarting of a Will," *Journal of Southern History* 39 (1973), 263–72.

withstood the prejudices of the Virginia bench, the "Randolph Negroes" could not escape those of Ohio's whites, who scattered not only the recent immigrants but also the residents of Carthagena, an older black colony run by an abolitionist, Augustus Wattles.[29] It was almost certainly the Randolph experiment that inspired a famous episode in William Wells Brown's eclectic *Clotel* (1853), the first novel published by an African American.[30]

Despite the violence that they had suffered, Randolph's manumittees had at least managed to circumvent the Ohio black laws by even entering the state. The slaves of Abram Earhart, of Tennessee, and Robert Bledsoe, of Georgia, were not as lucky: slated for freedom in the Old Northwest, they ended up remaining in southern slavery. The courts noted that the states of the Ohio Valley forbade free blacks from entering their bounds, and, since Tennessee and Georgia mandated that manumittees' (successful) emigration *precede* emancipation, the slaves stayed just that.[31] In 1858, Georgia's supreme court upheld a similar will that had failed to specify a destination for its manumittees, thereby preserving lawful options for their internal emigration. Still, Justice Joseph Lumpkin could not hide his dislike for internal colonies: "in case of civil war, they would become an element of strength to the enemy."[32] It was a judicious opinion.

Black Antecedents

African Americans' interest in continental resettlement peaked later than whites', but also diminished during the 1850s, the heyday of foreign schemes. As early as 1774, a number of Massachusetts slaves petitioned Governor Thomas Gage (1774–5) for their freedom and "some part of the unimproved land belonging to the province."[33] Yet the major projects of the Revolutionary era were otherwise those of white reformers. It took the founding of the ACS for black Americans to start debating domestic colonization, a deliberate riposte to the society's overseas scheme, albeit a riposte that conceded that they might indeed have to migrate. In January

[29] Pease, *Black Utopia*, 26–7.
[30] William Wells Brown, *Clotel; or, the President's Daughter* (London, 1853), 186–8.
[31] *Nancy v. Wright*, 9 Humphreys 597 (TN.1848); *Adams v. Bass*, 18 Cobb 130 (GA.1855).
[32] *Sanders v. Ward*, 25 Martin 109 (GA.1858).
[33] Anon. to T. Gage, June 1774, *Collections of the Massachusetts Historical Society*, s5.v3 (1877), 434–5.

1817, meetings in Georgetown and Richmond condemned the ACS, while, however, memorializing Congress for lands on the Missouri River, which black settlers would hold under US jurisdiction.[34] In a statement that he would later try to erase from the record, the Philadelphia sailmaker and subsequent opponent of the ACS, James Forten, declared for Africa instead: should blacks "settle anywhere in the vicinity of the whites, their condition must become before many years as bad as it is now, since the white population is continually rolling back."[35] Black fears of white encroachment echoed down to the Civil War, but were never enough to drown out support for internal colonization.[36]

The 1829 exodus of black Cincinnatians to Wilberforce, Canada, inspired similar agrarian schemes for the interior of the United States, as well. "Those who may be obliged to exchange a cultivated region for a howling wilderness ... [should] retire back into the western wilds ... where the plough-share of prejudice has as yet been unable to penetrate the soil," reported the third national convention's committee on colonization.[37] During 1838–9, a Pittsburgh minister (and mentor of Martin Delany), Lewis Woodson, debated the niceties of agrarian resettlement with Samuel Cornish in the columns of the *Colored American*.[38] "Too many of our people have crowded themselves into the larger towns and cities of the free States," observed Woodson. "*You* would have them ... 'mix' and 'scatter' themselves among the whites in the country ... [and] *I* would have them ... settle themselves in communities in the country, and establish society, churches and schools of their own." Woodson denied that his plan was "colonization magnified": purchasing tracts adjacent to those of the ethnic majority, within the territory of one's native land, was not the same as choosing exile in Africa.[39]

Having conceded the merits of long-range migration, Cornish would not also admit those of local segregation once black settlers had reached

[34] Ousmane K. Power-Greene, *Against Wind and Tide: The African American Struggle against the Colonization Movement* (New York, 2014), 1.

[35] Isaac V. Brown, *Memoirs of the Rev. Robert Finley* (New Brunswick, NJ, 1819), 101–2.

[36] R. J. M. Blackett, *The Captive's Quest for Freedom: Fugitive Slaves, the 1850 Fugitive Slave Law, and the Politics of Slavery* (New York, 2018), 118; John Hope Franklin, *The Free Negro in North Carolina, 1790–1860* (Chapel Hill, 1943), 217–18.

[37] Anon., pub., *Proceedings of the Third Annual Convention for the Improvement of the Free People of Colour* (New York, 1833), 27–8.

[38] Floyd J. Miller, *The Search for a Black Nationality: Black Emigration and Colonization, 1787–1863* (Urbana, 1975), 94–103.

[39] "Augustine" to S. E. Cornish, *Colored American*, July 28, 1838.

their destination. Woodson rejoined that white respect would increase, and the sway of the ACS decrease, at the sight of industrious black settlements.⁴⁰ For those readers of the *Colored American* who dreamed of landownership, however, another alternative to Africa suddenly emerged: Trinidad, which, unlike the West, was out of range to white pioneers' wagons.⁴¹ In the fall of 1839, as others turned to the West Indies, Martin Delany suspended his medical practice to scour the North American continent for a site suitable for a black nation. He went at least as far as the Indian Territory (modern Oklahoma), but was troubled to find an exploitative white presence throughout.⁴²

During the 1840s, one internal colony managed to secure near-universal black support: a settlement on the lands of the white philan-thropist Gerrit Smith, in New York's Essex, Franklin, and Hamilton Counties. From 1834, Smith had supported both the Anti-Slavery Society and the Colonization Society, but shunned the ACS after 1837. As such, he intended no parallel between the Liberian project and his own when, in 1846, he announced a plan to bestow 120,000 acres, free of charge, on 3,000 poor black New Yorkers. Smith had been moved by a fellow reformer's criticism of his huge landholdings (for denying poor whites their economic freedom), and had started to sell off his domains several months earlier. Once Smith had covered his debts, he appointed James McCune Smith and two black ministers, Charles Ray and Theodore Wright (the coauthor of Cornish's censorious *Colonization Scheme Considered*), to choose beneficiaries from among the 18,000 black inhabitants of New York City. While Gerrit Smith was perfectly unoriginal in coaxing poor urban African Americans to the land, he *was* original in intending no community proper. His goal was utilitarian, not utopian: to qualify as many black men as possible for the vote, which New York based on ownership of real estate. His idea was no windmill-tilt in a state that had barely decided the 1844 presidential election for James Polk. Surprisingly, perhaps, Smith referred to his venture as "the colored colony," or North Elba.⁴³

"It has been said that Mr. Gerrit Smith was governed by selfish motives, and that it was to increase the value of the residue of his land,"

---

⁴⁰ "The West," ibid., February 16, 1839.
⁴¹ B. Clark to C. B. Ray et al., ibid., October 5, 1839.
⁴² Vincent Harding, *There Is a River: The Black Struggle for Freedom in America* (New York, 1981), 131–2.
⁴³ John Stauffer, *The Black Hearts of Men: Radical Abolitionists and the Transformation of Race* (Cambridge, MA, 2001), 101–2, 135–42.

reported that future apostate of black abolitionism, Lewis Putnam, who scolded such ingratitude.[44] Yet Smith had been frank that his Adirondack holdings were, in places, a wilderness. For their part, black New Yorkers saw nothing offensive in a project that would keep them in their native state, let alone their native country. The national convention, held at Troy in 1847, thanked the philanthropist, with Frederick Douglass "fearful [only] that the munificence of Mr. Smith would operate as an injury unless the lands bestowed by him be occupied."[45] There was the rub. The lands needed improving as well as inhabiting, and the land-rich, cash-poor Smith was unable to meet the settlers' start-up costs. Perhaps thirty black families moved to the "Smith Lands," but by 1860, only two or three colonists remained, the others having foreclosed due to the major drawback of landownership: taxes.[46] Moreover, most of Smith's settlers opted for his estates in Florence, Oneida County, well to the west of his main holdings. As early as 1849, Douglass had curbed his enthusiasm for Smith's scheme, striking his own name from the trustees of the Florence Association. "My knowledge of the locality, derived only from the map, is altogether too limited," he admitted, a lesson that many a colonizationist would have done well to learn.[47] In 1853, Douglass reminisced to Harriet Beecher Stowe about Smith's venture. "I have far less confidence in such efforts, than I have in the benevolence which prompts them. Agricultural pursuits are not ... suited to our condition," explained Douglass.[48]

Yet Smith's scheme was important as a solvent, breaking down blacks' old stances against emigration, bloodshed (in a just cause), and participation in politics. When, in 1849, the radical abolitionist Henry Highland Garnet came out for colonization in Liberia, he did so at the same time for the West, while a Connecticut photographer, Augustus Washington, "compelled to abandon [his] plan of a separate State in America," moved to Monrovia in 1853.[49] Having backed Gerrit Smith's scheme, which had suffrage at its heart, even stay-and-fighters such as James McCune Smith

---

[44] Lewis H. Putnam, *A Sketch of Hamilton County* (New York, 1847), 13.
[45] J. C. Kneeland, pub., *Proceedings of the National Convention of Colored People* (Troy, 1847), 13.
[46] Robert M. De Witt, pub., *The Life, Trial, and Execution of Captain John Brown* (New York, 1859), 9.
[47] F. Douglass to S. Myers, March 15, *Impartial Citizen*, April 11, 1849.
[48] Douglass to H. B. Stowe, March 8, 1853, in Frederick Douglass, pub., *Proceedings of the Colored National Convention* (Rochester, 1853), 35.
[49] "The West – The West!," *North Star*, January 26, 1849; "African Colonization," *New-York Colonization Journal*, July 1851.

and Douglass drifted from the Garrisonians and toward the political abolitionists of the Free Soil Party. For critics of segregation, another virtue of the Gerrit Smith settlement was that it was not, in fact, mono-racial: Smith had spared a place at North Elba for a white settler, John Brown, who used it to plan his invasion of the South. From the 1850s, Frederick Douglass and Gerrit Smith echoed Brown by treating violence as a legitimate weapon in the abolitionist arsenal.[50]

When John Brown came to Chatham, Canada, in 1858, proposing a black republic within the boundaries of the United States, one of the town's residents, Martin Delany, cited the *Dred Scott* decision to refrain from joining him: "according to American jurisprudence, negroes, having no rights respected by white men, consequently could have no right . . . to sovereignty."[51] Where Delany kept looking for the answer in emigration, Brown found it in insurrection, losing his life in the process. Yet the Supreme Court's infamous ruling, which foreclosed black citizenship, was only the latest sign from Washington that migration-minded African Americans should look abroad. "We ask that the right of pre-emption, enjoyed by all white settlers upon the public lands, shall also be enjoyed by colored settlers," the Rochester Convention had vainly peti-tioned Congress in 1853.[52] The next year, a whites-only homestead bill passed the House. It then failed in the Senate, but only because of the distraction created by the Kansas–Nebraska Act.[53] During the 1850s, then, when black Americans invoked internal colonization, it was usually to silence opponents of its foreign variant with an instructive comparison. "God placed you in Maryland, right by the side of your 'brethren in bonds,'" James Whitfield reminded Frederick Douglass in 1853, ruing that free blacks had not heeded his own advice, in 1838, to move to a California now filled with white immigrants. "Was it not . . . by removing to a free *State* you could do more to elevate yourself . . . [and] benefit your brethren also?" Whitfield asked Douglass.[54] "Seven thousand of our people have emigrated to California, which is five times further off than

---

[50] Stauffer, *Black Hearts*, 152–8, 173, 180.
[51] Frank A. Rollin, ed., *Life and Public Services of Martin R. Delany* (Boston, 1883), 85–9.
[52] "Address of the Colored National Convention," *FDP*, July 15, 1853.
[53] Leon F. Litwack, *North of Slavery: The Negro in the Free States, 1790–1860* (Chicago, 1961), 48–50; Gerald Wolff, "The Slavocracy and the Homestead Problem of 1854," *Agricultural History* 40 (1966), 101–12.
[54] J. M. Whitfield to Douglass, November 15, *FDP*, November 25, 1853; M. T. Newsom, pub., *Arguments, Pro and Con, on the Call for a National Emigration Convention* (Detroit, 1854), 16–17.

Hayti, and we have yet to hear the first word uttered against their going there," noted "XYZ," in an unwitting reminder to historians not to consider internal resettlement the easier option, given that travelers could still only traverse the United States via the Central American isthmus (at least, in any comfort).[55]

Just as their forebears had hoped that a waterway from the Mississippi to the Pacific might lie beyond the edges of the map, so antebellum Americans, black and white, fitfully assumed that the answer to the "race question" lay somewhere out west. The process that that deliverance would entail was as enigmatic, however, as the place where it would unfold. Accordingly, by 1861, white colonizationists had vested almost all their hopes of inducing migration in the attraction of foreign lands and the repulsion of domestic laws.

BACKWARD AND FORWARD: COLONIZATION POLICY, THE BLACK LAWS, AND INDIAN RESERVATIONS, 1861–1865

During the Civil War, the polar forces of emigration and exclusion lost their magnetism. Through a combination of moral principle, political pragmatism, and sheer probability – and far less of the first than historians have liked to think – colonization schemes and the black laws had failed alike by 1865.

Colonization: Future Foundations

Although Abraham Lincoln's White House had suffered nothing but setbacks in its resettlement projects, it would have been ready, willing, and able to resume them once peace returned, had Capitol Hill only proved more cooperative during 1864. That year, Congress failed to reinforce the institutional basis that colonization would have needed in the future. It also repealed most of the policy's funding, though that deed was more accidental than antagonistic.

The executive's colonization brief, as set out by the legislation of 1862, almost became part of the office that, by 1865, emerged as the Freedmen's Bureau. In January 1863, Representative Thomas Eliot of Massachusetts had moved for a central agency to coordinate Unionists' diverse efforts to

---

[55] "A Note from Philadelphia," *WAA*, April 13, 1861.

help former slaves.[56] In its earliest iterations, the office was to encompass the work of Senator James Doolittle's mooted bureau of migration, the founding of which had been delayed by the previous summer's recess. In February 1863, the House Select Committee on Emancipation "agreed upon a bill to establish a board of emigration and colonization in connection with the War Department."[57] At the same time, the Select Committee on Immigration, which James Mitchell approached in an attempt to upgrade his own agency to a full bureau, decided to devote itself to importing white Europeans, not exporting black Americans.[58]

In December 1863, Eliot, who chaired the Committee on Emancipation, reintroduced his bureau bill. Even his second draft still provided for colonization, but in February 1864, he announced that he would no longer support that aspect of it. Hailing the efforts of the Committee on Immigration to attract the "studious German," "impetuous Irish," and "canny Scotch," Eliot explained, "we cannot spare the freedmen ... the industrial interests of our country require that their compensated labor should enrich the land which has been cursed by their unpaid toil." His opinion was a common one: northerners worried how to fill the factories and fields of a nation blessed, through war, with full employment. Criticizing the Direct Taxes Act (1862), Eliot contended that a better use of southern soil would be to support former slaves, not swell a frozen colonization fund: "we have provided for the expatriation of the freedman, but not for his relief."[59] Opponents of the bureau were quite happy to keep it that way. A New York Democrat, Martin Kalbfleisch, cited the Randolph colony as the only precedent for Eliot's estates of free blacks: "sanctioned by law, it proved nevertheless a total failure." Another Democrat, Chilton White of Ohio, called colonization (in all its forms) "impracticable and impossible," which, in his opinion, left perpetual slavery as the only answer.[60] Republicans replied by quoting the American Freedmen's Inquiry Commission (AFIC), a three-man body appointed in 1863 that, following interviews with US officials in the occupied Confederacy, had reported

[56] Herman Belz, *A New Birth of Freedom: The Republican Party and Freedmen's Rights, 1861 to 1866* (New York, 2000), 75.
[57] "Washington," Philadelphia *Press*, February 16, 1863.
[58] A Bill to Establish an Emigration Bureau (n.d.), RG233/38A-E23.3, NARA.
[59] CG 38 Cong., 1 Sess., 569 (February 10, 1864).
[60] Ibid., 760, 766 (February 19, 1864).

that former slaves would stay south and work the same land, in freedom or in slavery.[61]

But would they? In March 1864, the Freedmen's Bureau bill passed the House, 69-67. It then failed in the relevant Senate committee, headed by Charles Sumner, which was less minded than the House to recognize freedpeople's claims to the land, but more so those to their personal liberty. On the Senate floor, the very geography of freedom generated friction. Iowa Republican James Grimes protested the "general superintendence" that the Senate's own bill prescribed, which treated freedpeople as though they were Indians who had to be governed separately. The slaveholding founder of the loyal state of West Virginia (1863), Waitman Willey, made strange bedfellows of other senators by amending the text to allow the bureau's commissioner to cooperate with northern governors in relocating unemployed freedpeople to the free states.[62] It was not the first time that an opponent of the Republicans had embarrassed them by proposing to send the contrabands north: just before the fall elections of 1862, the superintendent of Fort Monroe (and a Democrat), Major General John Dix, had asked Governor John Andrew of Massachusetts (1861–6), a Republican, whether his state could grant asylum to 2,000 African Americans encamped in Virginia.[63] Around the same time, Edwin Stanton's Department of War had abandoned an unpopular initiative to send contrabands to Illinois.[64] Yet with northern employers clamoring for hands, recruiters for draftees (from 1863), and humanitarians for an end to the needless suffering in the South, provocateurs such as Dix and Willey succeeded in casting shame on the many Republicans terrified of a white backlash at the polls.

Indeed, for most Republicans, the only question was whether to forbid the migration from South to North of freedpeople, or just to avoid the issue altogether. At a December 1863 meeting of the House Select Committee on Emancipation, an Indiana Republican, Godlove Orth, had moved that the federal government take no action to encourage

---

[61] Matthew Furrow, "Samuel Gridley Howe, the Black Population of Canada West, and the Racial Ideology of the 'Blueprint for Radical Reconstruction,'" *Journal of American History* 97 (2010), 368.

[62] Belz, *New Birth of Freedom*, 78–83.

[63] V. Jacque Voegeli, "A Rejected Alternative: Union Policy and the Relocation of Southern 'Contrabands' at the Dawn of Emancipation," *Journal of Southern History* 69 (2003), 765–90.

[64] Bruce Tap, "Race, Rhetoric, and Emancipation: The Election of 1862 in Illinois," *Civil War History* 39 (1993), 101–2.

freedpeople to move north, while Anthony Knapp, an Illinois Democrat, had proposed that the Freedmen's Bureau bill renounce introducing people of color into any state whose laws forbade it. In the election year of 1864, many of the Republicans who had opposed Senator Waitman Willey's amendment hoped to stifle all talk of black migration, while those Republicans who had supported it wished to rein in the (duly embarrassed) radicals in their own party. In late June 1864, in a 19-15 vote defying all normal alignments, the Senate adopted Willey's amendment, but Henry Wilson, of Massachusetts, managed to delete its explosive reference to the northern states. The Senate then passed its own Freedmen's Bureau bill, but the House refused to concur, thereby postponing debate until the December session.[65]

Meanwhile, the most senior US official dedicated to black Americans, James Mitchell, gathered letters of recommendation for the role of commissioner, whether the bureau's brief ultimately extended to colonization or not. He won the confidence of, among others, Senator James Harlan of Iowa; Governor Richard Yates of Illinois (1861-5); ex-Governor Joseph Wright, and Representatives Albert Porter, Schuyler Colfax, and Godlove Orth, of Indiana; and James Speed of Kentucky, who would succeed Edward Bates as US attorney general. The Rev. Mitchell also harnessed his Methodist connections, especially Bishop Matthew Simpson, a confidant of Abraham Lincoln.[66] Yet Mitchell's midwestern and border-state contacts, many of them mutual friends of the president, availed him nothing. When Congress resumed the bureau bill during the winter of 1864-5, its debates turned from questions of migration to those of jurisdiction: whether the office would count as civilian, under the Department of the Treasury, or military, under the Department of War.[67] "I repudiate this substitute for colonization, this tissue of folly," reiterated a Kentucky Unionist, Representative Henry Grider, but most conservatives had entered upon more urgent contests, such as immediate abolition and black suffrage.[68] In March 1865, Congress finally passed the Freedmen's Bureau Act, placing that office in the Department of War. While the law did not mention black migration, the bureau would go on

---

[65] Belz, *New Birth of Freedom*, 83-5.
[66] R. Yates and J. K. Dubois, J. A. Wright et al., and M. Simpson et al., letters of recommendation, August 9, 1864, March 6, 1865, and n.d., respectively, Letters Received by the Commissioner of the Bureau of Refugees, Freedmen, and Abandoned Lands, RG105/M752/16, NARA.
[67] Belz, *New Birth of Freedom*, 92-106.
[68] CG 38 Cong., 2 Sess., Appendix, 100 (February 21, 1865).

to consider that policy – just not under Mitchell. "The death of Mr. Lincoln and the inequitable and unreasonable demand made by New England to have the entire control of the Negro Question," as Mitchell put it, saw President Andrew Johnson (1865–9) appoint Oliver Howard, the "Christian General" of Maine.[69]

Colonization: Future Funding

Mitchell's failure to secure the post of bureau commissioner hurt all the more because his old one had been abolished, according to Attorney General Speed, by what Congress had done in July 1864: repeal $600,000 of the colonization fund, of which only $38,000 had ever been spent.[70] That outcome had become possible, even probable, because of a number of confrontations: in private, between James Mitchell and his superior (or was he?), John Usher, and in public, between the Blair brothers and virtually every Republican who had the misfortune to cross their path.

Although Mitchell had worked smoothly under Usher's predecessor, Caleb Smith, his position within the Department of the Interior had always been tenuous. Salaried as a chief clerk, Mitchell had been in the department's employ as an "agent" even prior to his August 1862 "commission" from Lincoln, an appointment that, Mitchell claimed, had granted him substantial independence.[71] For reasons originating in pre-war Indiana, Mitchell and Smith's successor, Usher, harbored an intense dislike for each other. As early as May 1863, Usher took Edwin Stanton's refusal to issue passes to the West Indian and Liberian canvassers of contraband camps as the perfect opportunity to rid himself of a turbulent priest. "The recent action of the War Department prevents the further emigration ... of persons of African descent," Usher told Lincoln. "The further attention of the Rev. Mr. Mitchell to that business [should] be dispensed with."[72] Lincoln ignored Usher, whom Mitchell taunted with, "I have either the charge of the Colonization work in this Department or I am independent of the Secretary of the Interior, and assigned here for

[69] J. Mitchell to U. S. Grant, February 16, 1871, Communications from the Department of War, Records Relating to the Suppression of the African Slave Trade and Negro Colonization, RG48/M160/3, NARA II.
[70] J. Speed to J. Harlan, June 2, 1865, 11 Op. Att'y Gen. 241 (1869).
[71] Phillip W. Magness and Sebastian N. Page, *Colonization after Emancipation: Lincoln and the Movement for Black Resettlement* (Columbia, MO, 2011), 88–9.
[72] J. P. Usher to A. Lincoln, May 18, 1863, S. Exec. Doc. 55, 39 Cong., 1 Sess. (1866), 33.

office room."[73] Yet Usher could stymie his (in)subordinate by intercepting his mail and refusing drafts on the colonization fund, which, if disbursed by the letter of the law, applied to few but the former slaves whom Stanton had placed beyond reach. Secretary Usher also benefited from being the public face of a department whose internal turmoil was unknown even to fellow members of the cabinet. "The experience the country has derived ... render[s] it a question of great importance whether the effort to colonize ... should be continued," announced Usher in his departmental report for 1863, even as he made a coded, last-ditch appeal for the Chiriquí scheme.[74] The secretary did not even reveal the existence of the British West Indies projects, whose progress Mitchell had shrouded in a secrecy that suited Usher just fine.

While James Mitchell tainted colonization's reputation with his superior, the Blairs did so with their erstwhile allies in the Republican Party. Although Abraham Lincoln never again used the word "colonization" in public after December 1862, he also did not need to: that "family of ... execrable selfishness," as Representative Thaddeus Stevens called the Blairs, was quite willing to risk the unpopularity that the president dared not.[75] While there is no evidence that Lincoln asked them to act as hatchet men, he also refrained from repudiating their increasingly pungent remarks, even as congressmen begged him to. In a speech of June 1863 at Concord, New Hampshire, Montgomery Blair rued that slavery's doom was not enough for abolitionists of the "Wendell Phillips school," who, he alleged, viewed the continued presence of African Americans in the United States as essential to their own political ambitions. Calling for "gradual segregation," Blair demanded, "shall we take Phillips for a guide, or Jefferson and Lincoln?"[76] Senator Wilson warned the president that Blair's speech was "universally denounced in New England," but a Washington insider, Thomas Barnett, suspected that Blair had in fact spoken for Lincoln.[77] Another of the president's interlocutors, Edward Bates, made a similar claim.[78]

---

[73] Mitchell to Usher, October 22, 1863, Communications Relating to James Mitchell, RG48/M160/8.
[74] CG 38 Cong., 1 Sess., Appendix, 26 (December 5, 1863).
[75] "Programme of the Exterminators," *American Citizen*, October 4, 1865.
[76] Montgomery Blair, *Comments on the Policy Inaugurated by the President* (New York, 1863), 16–20.
[77] H. Wilson to Lincoln, August 21, 1863, AL; T. J. Barnett to S. L. M. Barlow, October 6, 1863, Samuel L. M. Barlow Papers, Huntington Library.
[78] E. Bates to J. O. Broadhead, September 26, 1863, James O. Broadhead Papers, Missouri History Museum.

Congressmen had already asked Lincoln to renounce the Blair clan, when, in February 1864, its soldier-politician, Frank Blair, returned from the field to announce to the House, "I take my stand on the Lincoln platform ... the segregation of the white and black races."[79] Three weeks later, Representative Henry Winter Davis took to the floor to explicitly connect Abraham Lincoln to the Blairs' remarks, citing peaceful race relations in his own state, Maryland, as proof of colonization's folly.[80] Davis's reference to the Old Line State moved Frank Blair to a splenetic rejoinder, a speech entitled "The Jacobins of Missouri and Maryland," which decried how radicals had commandeered the cause of emancipation in those states, and claimed Lincoln once more for colonization.[81] Still without word to the contrary, congressmen gave up distinguishing the president from his proxies.[82] With relations between the White House and Capitol Hill already strained by their different visions of Reconstruction, their dispute over colonization was a serious one. By July 1864, Henry Winter Davis had joined Senator Benjamin Wade in penning a notorious "manifesto" against Lincoln, who, in September, would have to request Montgomery Blair's resignation as the price of ending a third-party challenge for the presidency by the radical John Frémont.[83] Lincoln relinquished Blair sooner than the policy that they each espoused – but, for that very reason, Blair quite understood.

It was under these circumstances that a routine request from the Senate to the White House – and from there, to the Department of the Interior – became a tussle between John Usher and James Mitchell that took the entire colonization policy (and many of its records) with it.[84] In January 1864, the Senate Committee on Territories, which had tasked itself with researching internal resettlement, had asked the administration for a breakdown of colonization expenditure to date. Instructed by Usher to present his accounts, Mitchell reminded the secretary that "I know little or nothing about the disbursement of the Colonization fund ... as you

---

[79] T. Stevens to S. P. Chase, October 8, 1863, Salmon P. Chase Papers, Historical Society of Pennsylvania; W. D. Kelley to Lincoln, October 20, 1863, AL; CG 38 Cong., 1 Sess., 513 (February 5, 1864).
[80] CG 38 Cong., 1 Sess., Appendix, 44–6 (February 25, 1864).
[81] Ibid., 46–51 (February 27, 1864).   [82] CG 38 Cong., 1 Sess., 2042 (May 2, 1864).
[83] James M. McPherson, *Battle Cry of Freedom: The Civil War Era* (New York, 1988), 776.
[84] B. F. Wade to Lincoln, January 18, 1864, Communications Received from the President, RG48/M160/3; Phillip W. Magness, "James Mitchell and the Mystery of the Emigration Office Papers," *Journal of the Abraham Lincoln Association* 32 (2011), 50–62.

have controlled [it]."[85] In March 1864, Usher sent Lincoln a provisional total of $33,000, most of it advanced to Samuel Pomeroy in 1862, but advised the president that nobody yet knew the full expense of the Île à Vache expedition, then in the throes of its ignominious rescue.[86] But Minnesota's Senator Morton Wilkinson already knew the cost: too much. On March 15, he moved to annul the appropriations and, on May 11, reported a repeal bill from the Committee on Territories.[87] With the Haiti fiasco now public knowledge, Wilkinson asked senators to abolish the $600,000 fund that had accompanied the District Emancipation and Second Confiscation Acts. In his broadside against the "hazardous and disgraceful" policy of colonization, Wilkinson overlooked two facts: that he had personally introduced all but $100,000 of that budget, and that Congress had made a third appropriation, under the Direct Taxes Act, which would accrue funds for colonization until repealed or rendered obsolete.[88]

Remembering an official report that James Mitchell had issued in 1862, Senator James Lane, a Kansas Republican and mainstay of the Committee on Territories's enthusiasm for internal resettlement, and Senator Lazarus Powell, a Kentucky Democrat eager to save colonization from its impending tomb, each stalled Wilkinson by requesting an update from the "commissioner of emigration."[89] John Usher replied that no such office existed, effectively muzzling Mitchell with semantics.[90] As session's end loomed, Lincoln could send the Senate only Usher's stunted packet of papers, which conveyed an impression that has persisted to this day: that the administration had pursued no schemes beyond those for Chiriquí and the Île à Vache.[91] When colonization came up for what turned out to be a cursory debate, James Lane declared for abolishing the fund as long as it was reassigned to internal resettlement; Henry Wilson ridiculed Montgomery Blair and his "exploded idea" of colonization; and Morton Wilkinson informed colleagues that Usher himself had advised repeal, which, presumably, the secretary hoped would starve Mitchell out of office.[92] Senators voted to terminate the colonization fund, and on July

[85] Mitchell to Usher, January 21, 1864, Mitchell Communications.
[86] Usher to Lincoln, March 7, 1864, S. Misc. Doc. 69, 38 Cong., 1 Sess. (1864), 1–2.
[87] CG 38 Cong., 1 Sess., 1108 (March 15, 1864).   [88] Ibid., 2218 (May 11, 1864).
[89] Ibid., 3169 (June 22, 1864).
[90] Usher to Lincoln, June 29, 1864, S. Exec. Doc. 55, 39 Cong., 1 Sess. (1866), 56–7.
[91] Lincoln to the Senate, June 29, 1864, AL.
[92] CG 38 Cong., 1 Sess., 3261–3 (June 25, 1864).

2, 1864, the president signed the bill in question. It was a fitting coda for a policy no longer relevant to race relations in the United States.

Only, it was nothing of the sort. By 1865, the (extant) Direct Taxes Act had earmarked more than $200,000 for colonization.[93] Careful observers such as James Mitchell, Thomas Malcom, of the Pennsylvania Colonization Society, and Ambrose Thompson, of the Chiriqui Improvement Company, would all inquire into accessing that money.[94] Moreover, congressmen had repealed even the major, $600,000 fund only as part of a sundry appropriations bill, with all the desultory debate and rushed compromise that that implied. So, when President Lincoln signed the bill, it was no more a sign of his opposition to colonization than it was of his support for lighthouses, sewers, and the purchase of a set of historical maps by the Library of Congress.[95] Nevertheless, the repeal rider did prompt some speculation by his private secretary. "I am glad the President has sloughed off that idea of colonization," John Hay told his diary. "I have always thought it a hideous and barbarous humbug and the thievery of Pomeroy and [Bernard] Kock have about converted him to the same belief."[96] Hay's thoughts, already more nuanced than their first sentence might suggest, must be further qualified by his ignorance, as betrayed in his later biography of Lincoln, of the colonization schemes in the British West Indies.[97] In his own postwar writings, Secretary of the Navy Gideon Welles would concur that it was corrupt agents who, more than anything, had frustrated the president, adding that "though disappointed in these [colonization] experiments, [Lincoln] by no means abandoned the policy."[98]

Accordingly, in September 1864, Lincoln refused to accept Mitchell's resignation, deeming it the product of an "unfriendly" legislative amendment, and asked the outgoing attorney general, Edward Bates, whether the White House could lawfully retain Mitchell's services.[99] "Notwithstanding the act which repeals the appropriation contingently,

---

[93] James Mitchell, *Brief on Emigration and Colonization* (Washington, DC, 1865), 2.

[94] T. S. Malcom to W. Coppinger, May 16, 1864, reel 95, ACS; J. Bigelow to A. W. Thompson, February 24, 1879, box 24, Ambrose W. Thompson Papers, LC.

[95] An Act Making Appropriations for Sundry Civil Expenses of the Government (July 2, 1864), 13 Stat. 352.

[96] Entry, July 1, 1864, in Michael Burlingame and John R. Turner Ettlinger, eds., *Inside Lincoln's White House: The Complete Civil War Diary of John Hay* (Carbondale, 1997), 217.

[97] John G. Nicolay and John Hay, *Abraham Lincoln: A History* (New York, 1890), 6:367.

[98] Gideon Welles, "Administration of Abraham Lincoln," *Galaxy* 24 (1877), 439.

[99] Mitchell, "Brief on the Office of Emigration," in J. Hughes and J. W. Denver to A. Johnson, June 16, 1865, Miscellaneous Letters of the Department of State, RG59/M179/457, NARA II; Lincoln to Bates, September 9, 1864, Registers of Letters Received,

you still have *something* to do, under those acts; and therefore ... the same right to continue Mr. Mitchell," conjectured Bates, unable to draft a formal opinion on his last day in office.[100] That winter, Mitchell himself asked Lincoln whether they should persist with an indisputably stalled policy, but they settled on merely suspending colonization until they could be sure that the Confederacy's slated enlistment of slaves into its own armies would not spark a last-minute contest for black manpower. Incongruously, Mitchell found an ally in the racial egalitarian, Representative Thaddeus Stevens, who, intrigued by internal colonization and inclined to thank Mitchell for encouraging his own House contacts to pass the Thirteenth Amendment (which abolished slavery), endorsed a continued role for the colonization office.[101] But in June 1865, Attorney General Speed, acting in less haste than had Bates, determined that Congress's repeal proviso had in fact revoked Mitchell's commission along with his means.

Quite apart from his personal support for Mitchell, Lincoln left other signs that he meant to revive colonization after the war. In his annual message of December 1864, the president noted that Liberia "may be expected to derive new vigor from American influence, improved by the rapid disappearance of slavery in the United States."[102] He also surprised the ACS with an unsolicited recommendation to Congress to sell Monrovia a gunboat at reduced cost.[103] In two meetings over the spring of 1865, Lincoln discussed colonization with a "favorite," the hero of the "contrabands" precedent, Major General Benjamin Butler.[104] "What shall we do with the negroes after they are free?" wondered Lincoln, the question that had perplexed him since at least 1854.[105] He listened attentively as Butler proposed taking black troops to Panama, where they could dig an isthmian canal. "There is meat in that," replied Lincoln, who

Records of the Attorney General's Office, RG60/7/2, NARA II. The first item is misfiled for date, and is courtesy of Magness.

[100] Bates to Lincoln, November 30, 1864, AL.

[101] Mitchell to Lincoln, February 1, 1865, Miscellaneous Letters Received at the Department of the Treasury, RG56/179/"M" (1864–5), NARA II; Mitchell, *Brief*, 7; Lemuel D. Evans, *Speech of Hon. L. D. Evans* (n.p., 1869), 4–5.

[102] "Annual Message to Congress," December 6, 1864, *CWAL*, 8:138.

[103] Coppinger to E. S. Morris, December 12, 1864, reel 209, ACS.

[104] William O. Stoddard, *Inside the White House in War Times* (New York, 1890), 147.

[105] Paul D. Escott, *"What Shall We Do with the Negro?": Lincoln, White Racism, and Civil War America* (Charlottesville, 2009), 223.

was killed before he could confer with Butler a third time.[106] From the mid-twentieth century, the general's account of his conversation with Lincoln, which he repeated several times until his own death in 1893, fell from the canon. Troubled by the challenge that Butler's anecdote posed to an emerging narrative of wartime progress in race relations, and unable to understand how Lincoln could suggest the vote for some black soldiers and a voyage for others, historians began to argue that Butler had left a rogue source, two years removed from the last evidence implicating Lincoln in colonization.[107] That claim is evidently untenable, and placed on Butler's story a burden that it need not bear. Other than the inevitable imprecision of recollections dictated to an amanuensis years later, Butler's story is consistent with the evidence, not only in its outline but in several details. Notably, Butler recalled William Seward's exasperation when he told the secretary of the president's recurrence to colonization. Indeed, when Seward learned of Lincoln's death, he would divulge to an acquaintance his only substantive dispute with the president: "his 'colonization' scheme . . . which I opposed on the self-evident principle that all natives of a country have an equal right in its soil."[108]

The Black Laws

If only Seward's thoughts on African American birthright had been shared by state legislators, who, during the first two years of war, tightened the black laws with the conviction of men whose president all but suggested doing so.[109] Lawmakers were quick to pass proscriptive laws whenever they doubted colonization's potential – but if exerting a pull on African Americans failed, could giving them a push ever succeed? For the first half of the Civil War, legislators tended to think so; for the

[106] Benjamin F. Butler, *Butler's Book* (Boston, 1892), 903–8; Allen Thorndike Rice, ed., *Reminiscences of Abraham Lincoln by Distinguished Men of His Time* (New York, 1886), 149–54.

[107] For Butler's skeptics, see Eric Foner, *The Fiery Trial: Abraham Lincoln and American Slavery* (New York, 2010), 401–2n52, and Mark E. Neely, Jr., "Abraham Lincoln and Black Colonization: Benjamin Butler's Spurious Testimony," *Civil War History* 25 (1979), 77–83. For Butler's believers, see Henry Louis Gates, Jr., and Donald Yacovone, eds., *Lincoln on Race and Slavery* (Princeton, 2009), liii–lv, and Phillip W. Magness, "Benjamin Butler's Colonization Testimony Reevaluated," *Journal of the Abraham Lincoln Association* 29 (2008), 1–28.

[108] F. B. Carpenter, *The Inner Life of Abraham Lincoln: Six Months at the White House* (New York, 1867), 291.

[109] "Annual Message to Congress," December 1, 1862, CWAL, 5:536.

second half, to think not, whether on account of the dubious ethics or the doubtful efficiency of the black laws.

As early as the winter of 1860–1, the lower Midwest moved to check black immigration.[110] In Ohio, template petitions demanding that lawmakers reintroduce the black laws bore thousands of signatures, but met the obstacle of a solidly Republican statehouse.[111] "If other States should disregard their constitutional obligations ... it is no good precedent for Ohio to follow," advised the committee charged with such memorials.[112] Yet those states that did have black laws worried that they would not prove potent enough. In Illinois, in 1862, a fresh constitutional convention approved a text with stricter bans on black immigration, suffrage, and officeholding. As in 1847, delegates put those articles to a separate ballot, and voters approved them overwhelmingly; unlike in 1847, voters rejected the main document, annulling the new "negro clauses" with it.[113] In 1865, having regained the Republican majority that he had lost two years earlier, Governor Richard Yates advised legislators to "sweep [the black laws] from the statute books with a swift, relentless hand."[114] The assemblymen of Illinois did as he asked, but when his Hoosier counterpart, Governor Oliver Morton (1861–7), confessed his shame that his own black laws barred the warriors of the Twenty-Eighth Indiana Regiment from reentering the state, he did so in vain.[115] Legislators took until 1867 to repeal the offending statute, though the US Civil Rights Act (1866) had already obviated Indiana's Article XIII. Even then, they removed only the law enforcing the article, and not the article itself. Showing a luck that belied its numeration, Article XIII remained in the state constitution until 1881.[116]

Bills for black laws emanated from statehouses beyond the Ohio Valley, though not from the upper Midwest, whose northerly latitude

[110] V. Jacque Voegeli, *Free but Not Equal: The Midwest and the Negro during the Civil War* (Chicago, 1967), 85–6, 89, 166.
[111] David A. Gerber, *Black Ohio and the Color Line, 1860–1915* (Urbana, 1976), 28.
[112] P. Zinn et al., report, n.d., in Richard Nevins, pub., *Journal of the House of Ohio* (Columbus, 1862), appendix, 34.
[113] O. M. Dickerson, *The Illinois Constitutional Convention of 1862* (Urbana, 1905), 23–4.
[114] John Jones, *The Black Laws of Illinois, and a Few Reasons Why They Should Be Repealed* (Chicago, 1864), 16; R. Yates, message, January 3, 1865, in Baker and Phillips, pub., *Journal of the Senate of Illinois* (Springfield, 1865), 30.
[115] Oliver P. Morton, *Reconstruction and Negro Suffrage: Speech at Richmond, Indiana* (n. p., 1865), 15.
[116] Emma Lou Thornbrough, *The Negro in Indiana: A Study of a Minority* (Indianapolis, 1957), 233–6.

allowed politicians to move the debate to a higher plane.[117] In 1864, Iowa repealed its black law – the senate, by a 40-0 vote. "The men through whose truculency to the slave power this black code was adopted, have long since been consigned to their political graves," proclaimed Governor William Stone (1864–8).[118] Meanwhile, Wisconsin, like Ohio, refused to adopt exclusion. If "those so exercised about the influx of negroes ... would exhibit equal zeal in trying to restore the Union, they would do far more to effect their object," scolded a select committee at Madison, arguing that it had only ever been flight from an institution now under attack by US forces that had driven slaves north.[119] Farther east, sarcastic Pennsylvania Republicans dismissed pro-exclusion petitions by suggesting that any new black law provide for microscopes, so that officials could scrutinize the scalps of immigrants with ambiguously "wooly" hair.[120]

Still, such equanimity was the exception, not the rule. In the loyal South, conservatives in Missouri and Maryland clung onto colonization and exclusion, even as their states abolished slavery itself.[121] As late as 1865, Kentucky's governor called on legislators to repeal the state's black law purely to forestall congressional ire, which might otherwise impose black suffrage on the state.[122] Two creations of federal favor, the restored governments of Arkansas and West Virginia, were also reluctant to forfeit their sovereign right to a ban on black immigration. Delegates at Little Rock made a gracious exception, however, for those African Americans who had entered the state under US auspices, namely, the black soldiers guarding their session, while those at Wheeling yielded to federal pressure and excised the black law from their draft constitution.[123] Ironically,

---

[117] Leslie A. Schwalm, *Emancipation's Diaspora: Race and Reconstruction in the Upper Midwest* (Chapel Hill, 2009), 81–106.

[118] W. M. Stone, message, January 11, 1866, in F. W. Palmer, pub., *Journal of the House of Iowa* (Des Moines, 1866), 50.

[119] L. B. Caswell and J. H. Rountree, report, March 13, 1863, in S. D. Carpenter, pub., *Journal of the Assembly of Wisconsin* (Madison, 1863), 530.

[120] M. B. Lowry, report, April 1, 1863, in Singerly and Myers, pub., *Journal of the Senate of Pennsylvania* (Harrisburg, 1863), 525.

[121] Donnie D. Bellamy, "The Persistency of Colonization in Missouri," *Missouri Historical Review* 72 (1977), 19–21; D. Kerr et al., report, February 2, 1864, in Bull and Tuttle, pub., *Journal of the House of Delegates* (Annapolis, 1864), appendix, doc. E, 3–6.

[122] T. E. Bramlette, message, December 5, 1865, in George D. Prentice, pub., *Journal of the House of Kentucky* (Frankfort, 1865), 31–3.

[123] Ordinance, January 20, 1864, in Price and Barton, pub., *Journal of the Convention of Arkansas* (Little Rock, 1870), 38; Forrest Talbott, "Some Legislative and Legal Aspects of the Negro Question in West Virginia during the Civil War and Reconstruction," *West Virginia History* 24 (1962), 15.

several of the Confederate states had been the quickest to amend their exclusion laws, in order to readmit black laborers who had left home to aid the war effort.[124] For all their antebellum restrictions on black locomotion, Confederate lawmakers were, even if only through the exigencies of war, keener than their Unionist counterparts to encourage laborers of all colors to go where needed.

Native Americans and African Americans

As the staying power of the black laws showed, loyal states could never be blank slates, but polities that had committed treason gave the federal government no reason to preserve the racial status quo. For US lawmakers, that meant, more than the Confederacy itself, the Native American nations that had allied with it at the war's outbreak. "Why should there not be, at need, a negro State by the side of an Indian State?" asked a French champion of the Union, Agénor de Gasparin, in 1861.[125] The Blair family agreed with him (except for the statehood part), and promptly made plans to move freedpeople to the forfeit lands of disloyal tribes.[126]

For such an obvious expedient, the Blairs' thinking was remarkably original. From the 1810s to the 1860s, politicians had rarely combined black colonization with Indian resettlement; if anything, they had tried to keep them separate. The reforming slaveholders of the early republic had rejected black colonies in the US interior, which, as the cooperation between fugitive slaves and Native Americans in the First Seminole War (1816–19) showed, risked combining the growing instances of slave revolt and indigenous resistance. In the 1820s, colonizationists cited the federal government's recognition of the Indian nations as grounds for acknowledging Liberia, but Jacksonians countered that the issues were quite distinct.[127] During the 1830s, the emerging Second Party System widened the gap between supporters of Indian and of black removal,

---

[124] No. 68 (December 11, 1861), in Boughton et al., pub., *Acts of Georgia* (Milledgeville, 1862), 71–2; No. 4583 (December 21, 1861), in Charles P. Pelham, pub., *Acts of South Carolina* (Columbia, 1862), 53; No. 9 (January 7, 1862), in William F. Ritchie, pub., *Acts of Virginia* (Richmond, 1862), 146.

[125] Agénor de Gasparin, *The Uprising of a Great People* (New York, 1861), 215.

[126] F. P. Blair, Sr., to M. Blair, May 31, 1861, reel 2, BF.

[127] Brandon Mills, "Situating African Colonization within the History of U.S. Expansion," in Beverly C. Tomek and Matthew J. Hetrick, eds., *New Directions in the Study of African American Recolonization* (Gainesville, 2017), 169–74.

with, by and large, Democrats for the former and Whigs for the latter. The Whigs echoed Jefferson's belief – ironically, in view of their political lineage – that Native Americans were scarcely degraded specimens of Europeans, a case that they hesitated to make for African Americans. Neither anticipating nor advocating Native Americans' extermination, the Christian reformers at the heart of the Whig Party accordingly argued that the forced migration of Indians would only delay the day of renewed contact with whites.[128] Those Americans excluded from formal politics were quicker, however, to discern similarities between African and Native American colonization.[129] The black inhabitants of Providence protested the "inconsistent conduct of those who so strenuously advocate our removal ... [but] contend against the cruelty and injustice of Georgia in her attempt to remove the Cherokee Indians," while James Whitfield interpreted the Cherokee's "Trail of Tears" (1838–9) as a warning to blacks to migrate on their own terms while they could.[130] But neither the antebellum revival of colonization nor the emergence of new political parties transformed the practical disconnect between the two policies. From 1857, the federal government recognized both African Americans and Native Americans as noncitizens, a status that it had long accorded the latter. Yet a lack of US citizenship left African Americans liable, as 4,500,000 individuals, to the states' black laws, while entitling Native Americans, as a limited number of sovereign nations, to treat with the United States as notional equals.[131]

When the Civil War broke out, Native Americans fell as far down Washington's agenda as African Americans went up it. That was a predictable development, though still a notable one in that both constituencies came under the Department of the Interior, which pursued a policy premised on migration for both. (Moreover, in 1863, Lincoln reprised segments of his meeting with the black Washingtonians by informing a delegation of tribal leaders that "there is a great difference between ... palefaced people and their red brethren.")[132] The Five Civilized Tribes,

---

[128] Lawrence J. Friedman, *Inventors of the Promised Land* (New York, 1975), 200–5.
[129] Emily Conroy-Krutz, *Christian Imperialism: Converting the World in the Early American Republic* (Ithaca, 2015), 211.
[130] William Lloyd Garrison, *Thoughts on Colonization* (Boston, 1832), 44–5; Whitfield to Cornish and J. M. Smith, April 1, *Colored American*, May 18, 1839.
[131] Martha S. Jones, *Birthright Citizens: A History of Race and Rights in Antebellum America* (New York, 2018), 43–4.
[132] "Speech to Indians," March 27, 1863, *CWAL*, 6:151.

which the federal government had removed in the 1830s to lands lying between Texas and Arkansas, did well, in the short term, to align with the Confederacy, which, moreover, commanded the sympathies of those members who held slaves.[133] Farther north, in 1862, the Minnesota Sioux (or Dakota) also rebelled against the United States, but their location did not permit such an alliance, and Union forces swiftly defeated them. "For the sake of slavery, we colonized the Indians, and was it not *singular*, that [they] should turn upon us ... in the N. West at the very moment when our good President was proposing a similar colonization of the Negroes?" asked a member of the US Sanitary Commission.[134] His point was lost on his contemporaries, some of whom proposed colonizing the restive Sioux on an island in Lake Superior.[135]

Ultimately, the federal government transferred Indians only to lands already occupied by Indians, whether of their own tribe or others. From early 1862, reports appeared that the United States would, as the price of readmitting the disloyal nations to their former standing, compress them further by demanding the right to settle African Americans within their boundaries.[136] Shortly afterward, Union forces invaded the Indian Territory at the instigation of James Lane, the US senator for its neighbor, Kansas, to which many of its inhabitants had fled. Lane would duly encourage his fellow congressmen to allow the destitute peoples back, but his vision went further than restoring the former reservations. "The amalgamation of the Indian and the black man advances both races," he told the Senate in 1865. "I should like to see these eighty thousand square miles, almost in the geographical center of the United States, opened up to the Indian and to the black man."[137] The next month, the Senate passed the so-called Harlan Bill, which reintroduced superintendents – and land speculators – to the Indian Territory.

In September 1865, a peace council met at Fort Smith, Arkansas, between federal and tribal delegates. Wartime colonization schemes had usually struggled for consent from sovereign nations, and things were no different now. The Chickasaw, Choctaw, Osage, and Seminole, already

---

[133] Francis Paul Prucha, *The Great Father: The United States Government and the American Indians* (Lincoln, 1984), 415–16.
[134] [Illegible] to J. A. Andrew, November 5, 1862, John A. Andrew Papers, Massachusetts Historical Society.
[135] "The Sioux War," *Continental Monthly* 3 (1863), 205.
[136] "The Colonization of Contrabands," *Douglass' Monthly*, February 1862.
[137] *CG* 38 Cong., 2 Sess., 1024 (February 23, 1865).

aggrieved at being treated as traitors when in fact from those tribes' pro-Union factions, balked at US demands that they accept African American settlers.[138] "We are willing to provide for the colored people of our own nation, but do not desire our lands to become colonization grounds for the negroes of other States," clarified the Seminole.[139] Although that nation's eventual treaty with the United States conceded the latter's right to settle African Americans, the federal government refrained from exercising the same. In 1869, Ely Parker, the commissioner of Indian affairs (and himself an Indian), notified Jacob Dolson Cox, the secretary of the interior, that the lands scheduled for black settlers had never been surveyed, and so could not be occupied.[140]

After 1865, the Blairs kept trying to amalgamate the policies of black and Indian resettlement. They deemed Native American reservations, which radical Republicans readily endorsed, the perfect *precedent* for new black colonies, while James Doolittle continued to consider Oklahoma the perfect *place* for them. Other Americans remained loath, however, to see such connections.[141] Even Frederick Douglass, long a believer in the unity of humankind and a critic of forced migration, claimed that the native physique was more "fragile" than that of the African American and that Indians *chose* to scurry for reservations whenever "civilization" crept too close.[142]

With that failed merger of two cognate policies, could white Americans keep denying that peace must find blacks and whites inhabiting the same space? Colonization in other countries, expulsion from the states, and resettlement in the territories – none had succeeded. Yet such solutions' failure lay partly in whites' waning commitment to them. From the outset of the war, even Doolittle, Lane, and the Blairs had discerned a higher law: nature itself would keep African Americans in the South. In other words, the North could free the slaves without suffering the consequences itself.

[138] Annie Heloise Abel, *The Slaveholding Indians* (Cleveland, 1915–25), 3:191–3.
[139] J. Chupco et al., response, September 12, 1865, in United States, pub., *Report of the Commissioner of Indian Affairs* (Washington, DC, 1865), 325.
[140] E. S. Parker to J. D. Cox, May 21, 1869, Report Books of the Office of Indian Affairs, RG75/M348/18, NARA.
[141] F. P. Blair, Sr., to F. P. Blair, Jr., December 12, 1866, and January 18, 1867, reel 2, BF; J. R. Doolittle to Johnson, September 9, 1865, Andrew Johnson Papers, LC.
[142] "Black Freedom is the Prerequisite of Victory," January 13, 1865, in John W. Blassingame and John R. McKivigan, eds., *The Frederick Douglass Papers* (New Haven, 1979–92), 4:57.

SOUTHWARD HO: CLIMATIC MIGRATION, WARTIME
RECONSTRUCTION, AND RESURGENT COLONIZATION,
1861–1868

Climate Control

Climatic ideology, or "isothermalism," was a strain of science – and strained science – that had existed for decades but that became popular during the Civil War. Cultivated in the laboratory of medical research and refined in the faculties of anthropology, ethnology, and sociology, an epidemic of geographic racialism had broken out with the 1847 arrival of a Swiss immigrant, Professor Louis Agassiz, who, from his chair at Harvard, propounded "zoological provinces" of humanity. That is to say, different races were physiologically suited to different latitudes: whites, to temperate zones, and blacks, to the tropics. Such theories spread with the boundaries of the United States itself, as white intellectuals began to doubt that African Americans could ever flourish in those parts of the West at the same latitude as the free states of the existing Union.[143] A proslavery publisher from New York, John Van Evrie, even claimed that the Old Northwest had become free soil not because of the 1787 ordinance but because of a climate "utterly uncongenial to the negro constitution."[144] During the 1850s, the Illinois Democrat, Senator Stephen Douglas, pinned his presidential ambitions on a similar determinism: Why *not* admit the new territories under his formula of popular sovereignty, given that their arid, continental climate was no more suited to slaves than it was to slavery? When enough Americans in both sections answered that their dispute was about pride, precedent, and due process, and that they could brook no more insults, the Union collapsed. Denied electoral vindication in 1860, Douglas could have claimed its intellectual (though posthumous) equivalent within a year, as his Republican opponents started to imagine that freedom would see African Americans stay south, or head there if currently located farther north.[145]

---

[143] George M. Fredrickson, *The Black Image in the White Mind: The Debate on Afro-American Character and Destiny, 1817–1914* (New York, 1971), 137–9.
[144] John H. Van Evrie, "Slavery Extension," *De Bow's Review* 15 (1853), 6.
[145] Mark E. Neely, Jr., "Colonization and the Myth That Lincoln Prepared the People for Emancipation," in William A. Blair and Karen Fisher Younger, eds., *Lincoln's Proclamation: Emancipation Reconsidered* (Chapel Hill, 2009), 64–5.

Strangely, it was, in part, Americans' colonization efforts that had fostered this vision of effortless colonization. By the Civil War, it was an axiom of Anglo-American science that black people descended to warmer climes, but a matter of dispute *where* such climes started. That raised an inextricable question: Where could Euro-Americans, whose expansionist proclivities commentators also assumed, *not* penetrate? For Liberian colonizationists, Africa was off-limits to people of European descent, but the entire Americas were open to them.[146] For the prewar Republicans, however, both Africa and the middle Americas were beyond the pale. "While the white man degenerates and withers in the glare of [the tropics]," announced Frank Blair in 1859, "the black man ... finds [it] an elixir for body and mind."[147] And for the labor recruiters of the British Empire, whites might survive in the Caribbean (for who else could govern its colonies?), even as nonwhites clearly did better – but blacks in Canada were in the wrong place.[148] Even a white abolitionist, Salmon Chase, was comfortable telling a black correspondent, Frederick Douglass, how the two races, "adapted to different latitudes and countries ... never have been brought together in one community, except under ... slavery."[149]

One group, at least, should have been immune to climatic ideology: African Americans. Yet they, too, could succumb to such mental miasmas. "If slavery were abolished tomorrow, there would be an overwhelming tide of emigration to the South, on the part of the colored people," claimed a black academic, William Allen, in 1852. "That is the soil ... which is congenial to their nature."[150] The following year, Allen and his white bride left New York State for the safety of temperate Britain, never to return. From Chatham, Canada West – slightly farther south than Allen's former home, whatever racial geographers might claim – Mary Ann Shadd echoed isothermalists' essentialism, even as she rejected how they applied it. Those "physically capable of resisting the influences of great heat, are also capable of enduring severe cold," she maintained as she surveyed locales for black emigration from Canada, her

---

[146] Asaka, *Tropical Freedom*, 151–4.
[147] F. P. Blair, Jr., *Colonization and Commerce* (n.p., 1859), 3.
[148] Asaka, *Tropical Freedom*, 165–6; Thomas C. Holt, *The Problem of Freedom: Race, Labor, and Politics in Jamaica and Britain, 1832–1938* (Baltimore, 1992), 235–6.
[149] S. P. Chase to F. Douglass, May 4, 1850, Salmon P. Chase Papers, Historical Society of Pennsylvania.
[150] "Letter from William G. Allen," *FDP*, November 5, 1852.

adopted home, to the Caribbean.[151] Yet when James Redpath's recruiters visited Chatham in 1861 to canvass for Haiti, she warned her neighbors not to risk abandoning the "healthy climate" of Canada.[152] Developments during the Civil War assuaged Unionists that they need not fear a black influx from the Confederacy, though the evidence in question was more the result of political decision-making than of providential design. Finally freed from southern obstructionism, congressmen passed the Homestead Act (1862), which opened vast expanses of public land to citizens of the United States (current or pending), a definition that excluded African Americans until the adoption of the Fourteenth Amendment (1868).[153] Having effectively restricted black movement westward, politicians proceeded to block it northward by rejecting the divisive schemes of John Dix and Waitman Willey, while military commanders tied freedpeople to the South with schemes of work, relief, and enlistment into the armies of that theater.[154] A number of settlements in the coastal Carolinas, which the Union occupied from the winter of 1861–2, staked a claim to the idea of "colonization" as one of restored plantations based on northern white ownership, southern black labor, and New England humanitarianism, in the form of missionaries who came south to educate the freedpeople.[155] As US forces entered Louisiana and Mississippi, administrators repeated the Carolina model, albeit with less of its (initial) idealism – and a lot less isolation from Confederate raiders. But with freedpeople bound, one way or another, to the southern soil, northern politicians began to think the statutory exclusion of African Americans unnecessary to keep "the Negro where he is," as a Democratic slogan of 1864 had it.

Again, though, statesmen did not see the laws of nature and laws of Congress as mutually exclusive.[156] For colonizationists had always viewed resettlement schemes as a mere catalyst for an inevitable process.

---

[151] Mary A. Shadd, *A Plea for Emigration, or Notes of Canada West* (Detroit, 1852), 37.
[152] "Haytian Emigration at a Discount in Chatham," *WAA*, October 19, 1861.
[153] Asaka, *Tropical Freedom*, 179.   [154] Voegeli, *Free but Not Equal*, 105–12.
[155] For the "transitional" colonies, see S. B. Brague, *Notes on Colored Troops and Military Colonies on Southern Soil* (New York, 1863); Patricia Click, *Time Full of Trial: The Roanoke Island Freedmen's Colony, 1862–1867* (Chapel Hill 2001); Horace James, *Annual Report of the Superintendent of Negro Affairs in North Carolina, 1864* (Boston, 1865); and Willie Lee Rose, *Rehearsal for Reconstruction: The Port Royal Experiment* (Indianapolis, 1964).
[156] Sidney George Fisher, *The Trial of the Constitution* (Philadelphia, 1862), 273–4.

"The colored race will go further and further south, and by ... amelioration and emancipation be removed," predicted James Doolittle in 1860.[157] Not two years later, his ally, Frank Blair, preempted congressional critics of colonization's "inadequacy": black movement to the tropics was "but a question of time," which the administration hoped only to expedite.[158] Yet colonization still appealed to climatic thinkers unreconciled to even the temporary loss of American soil to those ethnicities not destined to inhabit it forever.[159]

In 1863, one of Washington's many wartime committees captured the zeitgeist: the American Freedmen's Inquiry Commission, which comprised the social reformers Samuel Howe, James McKaye, and Robert Dale Owen.[160] Having interviewed scores of soldiers, slaves, and self-appointed experts, the commissioners reported "no disposition in [freedpeople] to go North," the icy domains of which had, they argued, only ever enticed fugitives with the warmth of freedom. Should "the South once offer the same attraction ... a few years will probably see half the free negro population now residing among us crossing Mason and Dixon's line to join the emancipated freedmen." Although the AFIC accepted that isothermal imperatives would drive African Americans south, it also rejected permanent government support for black colonies in the reconquered Confederacy, in that such measures would imply that "two races cannot in perpetuity inhabit the same country."[161] In a supplemental study, the commission's chairman, Robert Dale Owen, also warned freedpeople against "settling in colonies or suburbs by themselves," lest they worsen white prejudice. Otherwise, he reiterated the AFIC's initial findings: black Americans in the South would always reject colonization overseas, and those residing in the North and Canada would soon join them in that section.[162] That truth was so self-evident to the commissioners that when Samuel Howe, an apostle of Louis Agassiz,

---

[157] J. R. Doolittle to M. Doolittle, December 2, 1860, James R. Doolittle Papers, Wisconsin Historical Society.
[158] CG 37 Cong., 2 Sess., 1633 (April 11, 1862).
[159] E. B. Hunt, *Union Foundations: A Study of American Nationality as a Fact of Science* (New York, 1863), 49–57.
[160] Hahn, *Nation without Borders*, 277–8.
[161] United States, pub., *Preliminary Report Touching the Condition and Management of Emancipated Refugees* (New York, 1863), 22–3.
[162] Robert Dale Owen, *The Wrong of Slavery, the Right of Emancipation, and the Future of the African Race in the United States* (Philadelphia, 1864), 209–12.

interviewed the black residents of Canada West, he simply ignored the majority who told him that they planned on staying.[163]

Florida, Texas, and South Carolina

As white Unionists came to accept the domestic migration of African Americans as a benign force – namely, a southward one – and foreign colonization as a diminished prospect, they began to view the American tropics, that zone to which blacks were sure to sink, not as Antigua, Guiana, and Mexico, but Alabama, Georgia, and Mississippi. Three other states of the lower South stood out to Unionists as ideal destinations for African Americans: Florida, Texas, and South Carolina. Policy makers' interest peaked in that order, though outlasted the war for all three, since colonization in the (former) Confederacy seemed to offer the smoothest transition to whatever postwar order emerged. By 1865, one advocate of settling African Americans in the South Carolina Lowcountry even claimed to have solved the problem of Reconstruction – but had he gone out on a limb?

In a geographic sense, that was a charge that critics leveled at the Florida option, which captivated the northern public nonetheless from late 1861 to early 1863. During the first summer of war, a journalist and Republican from North Carolina, Daniel Goodloe, proposed the lower South at large as the "Eldorado of the negro," homing in on Florida that fall.[164] When Representative John Gurley broached colonization in the House in December 1861, he likewise suggested Florida. The following May, Gurley announced that, while he preferred internal to external resettlement, he preferred neither to whatever confiscation bill would pass the soonest.[165] Another man was eager to take Gurley's place as Florida's champion: Eli Thayer, the proud purveyor of internal colonization as an American cure-all – and one that northerners were desperate to buy. For in December 1861, a black minister from Trenton, William E. Walker, had started a petition to reduce the state of Florida to territorial status, at that point a popular approach to Reconstruction in general, and to reserve it for African Americans. ("Nothing herein [should be] construed as to require any compulsory emigration," added Walker.)[166] Unionists

---

[163] Furrow, "Samuel Gridley Howe," 353, 360; S. G. Howe, *The Refugees from Slavery in Canada West: Report to the Freedmen's Inquiry Commission* (Boston, 1864), 28.

[164] Daniel R. Goodloe, *Emancipation and the War* (Washington, DC, 1861), 5–6.

[165] CG 37 Cong., 2 Sess., Appendix, 234 (May 26, 1862).

[166] "Letter from William E. Walker," *Pine and Palm*, December 28, 1861.

hoped that Florida's low population and high proportion of public land would allow the federal government to hand black Americans sizable plots without violating private property rights.[167] In early 1862, Thayer enjoyed warm meetings with Abraham Lincoln and Edwin Stanton. That June's Direct Taxes Act prompted Thayer to bid for a bureau of migration under his leadership, since the Florida lands seized under its provisions could award homesteads to soldier-immigrants at no cost to the government.[168] By the fall, however, Thayer felt a chill: Stanton "assumed an asperity," though the pioneer also sensed the hand of William Seward, who had never forgiven Thayer for helping orchestrate his defeat for the 1860 nomination.[169] The provisional commander of the Florida expedition, Major General James Garfield, also clarified that he would prefer to be posted to South Carolina: "if they will send me where there is only to be fighting, I will choose it rather though I believe [in] the colonizing scheme."[170] Frustrated by the administration, Thayer mustered a Florida lobby within Congress, but Lincoln held firm against its entreaties, mothballing the plan by February 1863.[171] Although a seemingly unlosable military campaign had appealed to politicians during the grim winter of 1862–3, commentators now compared the idea to the Anaconda Plan, the passive blockade of the Confederacy that General Winfield Scott had proposed in 1861, since both strategies would have exerted worthless pressure on the unimportant peripheries of the seceded states. If devoting funds to the armies of the American heartland failed to crush the rebellion, argued a Kentucky congressman in February 1863, then "slower schemes of emigration, colonization, and substitution of populations," such as the Florida venture, *had* to fail, because they would cost more and take longer.[172]

Moreover, abolitionists had assumed that Thayer planned to arm and colonize African Americans from throughout the Union, but he now admitted that he intended nothing more than an expedition of white

---

[167] Nicholas Guyatt, "'An Impossible Idea?': The Curious Career of Internal Colonization," *Journal of the Civil War Era* 4 (2014), 240.

[168] George Winston Smith, "Carpetbag Imperialism in Florida, 1862–1868," *Florida Historical Quarterly* 27 (1948), 115–17.

[169] Franklin P. Rice, "The Life of Eli Thayer" (chap. 35), 23–4, Franklin P. Rice Papers, LC.

[170] J. A. Garfield to J. H. Rhodes, October 5, 1862, in Frederick D. Williams, ed., *The Wild Life of the Army: Civil War Letters of James A. Garfield* (East Lansing, 1964), 154.

[171] H. Rep. 5, 37 Cong., 3 Sess. (1863), 1–3; W. C. Bryant et al. to Lincoln, February 8, 1863, AL.

[172] CG 37 Cong., 3 Sess., Appendix, 158 (February 28, 1863).

settlers, who would employ Florida's existing black inhabitants as wage laborers.[173] Although black soldiers and white speculators would indeed enter the state from 1863, they did so without Thayer and in separate ventures. Yet the Florida fantasy persisted: the black emigrationist John Willis Menard, who found himself idle, in May 1863, between his (failed) departure for Liberia and (future) departure for the West Indies, petitioned Congress to reassign the state to African Americans.[174] (He remained keen on Florida, making Jacksonville his home from 1871 to 1889.)[175] But, themselves now skeptical of the military value of subduing a peninsula, supporters of colonization in Florida latterly imagined the state as part of a contiguous black settlement from South Carolina southward.

If the location of Florida had made it a dead end for colonization plans, then that of Texas made it a highway to the better part of the Americas. In 1861, a Maryland peacemaker mooted a grand compromise by suggesting that the slave states found new colonization societies, which would apply to the federal government for land on Texas's southwestern frontier.[176] The next year, a self-styled "practical phrenologist" from Cincinnati extolled Texas as an oubliette for the freedpeople: "completely isolated from the balance of the United States ... we should know but little more of their existence than we do of their red-skin neighbors."[177] Yet as long as Europeans meddled in Mexico, politicians pictured a more active role for any African Americans sent to its frontier.

The much-anticipated expedition to Texas should be "one of conquest and colonization," Frank Blair told Edwin Stanton in July 1862. Blair would have the United States readmit Texas and recognize its public lands, but only if ceded in part to black colonists, whose presence would "open the door for the exodus of the slaves into Mexico," while shutting it against the French until US forces were themselves ready to pass through it.[178] His father, Francis, took the idea to President Lincoln, who, as other colonization projects stalled during December 1862, asked a Treasury official to find a businessman with enough Yankee ingenuity to "remove the whole colored race of the slave states into Texas." One

---

[173] E. Thayer to C. E. Lester, February 1863, in C. Edwards Lester, *The Light and Dark of the Rebellion* (Philadelphia, 1863), 122.
[174] "For the Christian Recorder," *Christian Recorder*, May 16, 1863.
[175] Bess Beatty, "John Willis Menard: A Progressive Black in Post–Civil War Florida," *Florida Historical Quarterly* 59 (1980), 123–43.
[176] Lennox Birckhead, *A Voice from the South* (Baltimore, 1861), 226.
[177] L. M. Smith, *The Great American Crisis* (Cincinnati, 1862), 26.
[178] F. P. Blair, Jr., to E. M. Stanton, July 14, 1862, AL.

such contractor, John Bradley of Vermont, met with Lincoln, but both men decided that the plan was too problematic.[179] Just as Lincoln had trailed the Blairs in turning against Liberia, so he proved slow to join their intellectual migration to the American borderlands. In November 1863, a US expedition landed at the mouth of the Rio Grande, but black soldier-immigrants appeared only in the scaremongering columns of the *Houston Telegraph*.[180] Even Lincoln's own appointee as military governor of Texas, Andrew Hamilton, publicly reminded the president not to consider coerced colonization.[181]

From early 1864, Senator James Lane drew the public's attention to the Texas scheme. Envisioning black resettlement around the Gulf of Mexico, Lane reported a bill that February to demobilize black troops in the Lone Star State and have their families join them where the climate excluded whites.[182] "We may with negro regiments assert the Monroe doctrine, and drive Maximilian out of Mexico," Lane told an ecstatic audience in New York, which cheered all the louder when he claimed Abraham Lincoln for "emancipation, not amalgamation."[183] Lane's adjustments to the Indian Territory, and his vote to repeal the (foreign) colonization fund, should be understood in the context of that scheme. "The only effect of concentrating the negroes in Texas will be to make a very silly border war for future generations," wrote the president of the ACS, John Latrobe. "Since [Henry Winter] Davis and Lane's speeches, politicians here [Baltimore] are boasting that they have always been colonizationists – though it is news to me."[184] But until America's own civil war ended, Lane could make only plans for the Texas–Mexico frontier, even as Francis Blair presciently pitched Texan colonization to the vice president–elect, Andrew Johnson, lest "contingency" elevate him to the highest office.[185] Probably, Blair was thinking of colonization when he arranged the famous peace conference of February 1865 at Hampton

---

[179] F. P. Blair, Sr., to F. P. Blair, Jr., August 22, 1862, reel 2, BF; L. E. Chittenden, *Recollections of President Lincoln and His Administration* (New York, 1891), 335–40.

[180] Stephen A. Townsend, *The Yankee Invasion of Texas* (College Station, 2006), 17.

[181] Andrew J. Hamilton, *Letter of A. J. Hamilton of Texas* (New York, 1863), 5–6.

[182] CG 38 Cong., 1 Sess., 672–5 (February 16, 1864).

[183] William H. Moore, pub., *Speeches of Hon. James H. Lane* (Washington, DC, 1864), 13–14.

[184] J. H. B. Latrobe to Coppinger, February 29, 1864, reel 95, ACS.

[185] F. P. Blair, Sr., to Johnson, November 17, 1864, in LeRoy P. Graf and Ralph W. Haskins, eds., *The Papers of Andrew Johnson* (Knoxville, 1967–2000), 7:293–4.

Roads, Virginia, which he had initiated by proposing a joint Union–Confederate intervention in Mexico to an old friend, Jefferson Davis.[186] When peace returned north of the Rio Grande, observers on both sides of the border thought African Americans' emigration imminent – but also an unpredictable factor in Mexico's volatile situation. "Getting Maximilian to *take* them for colonizing Central America, involves [difficult] diplomatic considerations," warned Vermont's Brigadier General John Phelps, who evidently did not share his fellow Unionists' loyalty to the Juárez government. Phelps also regretted how black troops had not been contracted to serve in Africa once surplus to white requirements.[187] As the politics of summer 1865 would show, he was not the only soldier of abolitionist pedigree to have been converted to racial separatism by his time in the South.

But where colonization proposals for Florida had, by definition, eschewed expatriation, the expulsive premise of their counterparts for the Texas–Mexico borderlands offended African Americans. In June 1865, black troops sailed from Virginia to Texas in mutinous mood at rumors spread by former rebels that, once landed, they would be forced to migrate south.[188] A contest between the United States, France, and two Mexican governments was a white man's war, and should not become a black man's fight if it ended in emigration – or even enslavement. For the Mexican Empire now welcomed Confederates fleeing the reconstituted Union, and changed its laws against peonage with such ominous intent that the US minister, Thomas Corwin, advised black Americans against coming to Mexico, thereby reversing his stance of just three years earlier.[189] In a portent of changing alignments within the United States, too, Montgomery Blair now called for Mexican colonization in front of *Democratic* audiences, while his father accused the commissioner of the Freedmen's Bureau, Oliver Howard, of hostility to

---

[186] Don H. Doyle, *The Cause of All Nations: An International History of the American Civil War* (New York, 2014), 286–8; Nicholas Guyatt, "'The Future Empire of Our Freedmen': Republican Colonization Schemes in Texas and Mexico, 1861–1865," in Adam Arenson and Andrew R. Graybill, eds., *Civil War Wests: Testing the Limits of the United States* (Oakland, 2015), 106–7.

[187] J. W. Phelps to Sumner, April 20, 1865, series 2, John Wolcott Phelps Papers, NYPL.

[188] O. Brown to O. O. Howard, June 17, 1865, in Ira Berlin et al., eds., *Freedom: A Documentary History of Emancipation, 1861–1867* (Cambridge, UK, 1982–), series 2, 724–5.

[189] T. Corwin to W. H. Seward, No. 13, September 10, 1865, H. Exec. Doc. 73, 39 Cong., 1 Sess. (1866), 1:470–1.

the idea for thinning the presumptive ranks of future Republican voters.[190] Yet for Americans of all complexions, black emigration to Mexico appealed continually through the 1890s, when a former freedperson from Texas, William Ellis, enticed hundreds of Alabamians over the border.[191]

If most African Americans would have had to go a long way to reach Florida or Texas, then they would have struggled less to reach South Carolina, which Unionists would have had *whites* leave. A foreign observer of the United States, the Frenchman Alexis de Tocqueville, had once predicted that, should the lower South ever suffer the effects of civil war, its black population would prevail and "the white population ... will perhaps be forced to retire to the country whence its ancestors came."[192] Within a week of Fort Sumter's fall, a black Georgian had echoed Tocqueville's warning, while even James Doolittle wondered whether South Carolina's secessionists had thwarted foreign colonization by "preparing for a speedier work and that nearer home."[193] The Palmetto State was unique in its slight black majority (and in the white extremism that that demography had inculcated), which made expelling whites the more feasible option – and, northerners thought, the fairer one, too. Even radical Republicans could support this kind of separatism, which would, after all, grant African Americans land.[194] Citing the prominence of Florida, Georgia, and South Carolina in the chronicles of proslavery provocation, in 1864, Representative George Boutwell of Massachusetts demanded that those states be transformed into African American reservations, and recalled Virginia's St. George Tucker by setting the lure of black suffrage within their bounds. "The colored population, as rapidly as it can be spared from the industrial pursuits of the North, will aggregate upon the shores of the Atlantic and the Gulf of Mexico," claimed

[190] "Ratification Meeting at Cooper Institute," *New York Times*, October 19, 1865; F. P. Blair, Sr., to F. P. Blair, Jr., October 5, 1866, reel 2, BF.
[191] Hinton Rowan Helper, *Nojoque: A Question for a Continent* (New York, 1867), 14–15; S. Exec. Doc. 6, 42 Cong., 2 Sess. (1872), 18; H. Rep. 134, 46 Cong., 3 Sess. (1881); H. Doc. 169, 54 Cong., 1 Sess. (1896); Karl Jacoby, "Between North and South: The Alternative Borderlands of William H. Ellis and the African American Colony of 1895," in Samuel Truett and Elliott Young, eds., *Continental Crossroads: Remapping U.S.-Mexico Borderlands History* (Durham, 2004), 209–40.
[192] Alexis de Tocqueville and Henry Reeve, trans., *Democracy in America* (New York, 1839), 373.
[193] J. Peters to G. Lawrence, Jr., April 20, *WAA*, May 11, 1861; Doolittle to Lincoln, April 18, 1861, AL.
[194] J. M. Thompson to Johnson, May 5, 1865, Johnson Papers.

Boutwell.[195] In order to materialize, though, the plan would require the right man, in the right place, at the right time.

That man was Major General William Sherman, who, in early 1865, assigned swathes of the South Carolina Lowcountry to the thousands of African American refugees who had followed his famous march from Georgia. While skeptical of racial equality, Sherman was no less critical of the Union colonies along the Mississippi River, whose remoteness had exposed them to Confederate attacks. Aware of the limited capacity of the coastal colony at Port Royal, South Carolina, Sherman entered Savannah, Georgia, in January 1865. Sitting next to Secretary of War Stanton, who had come south to investigate allegations of Sherman's hostility toward his black camp followers, the general conferred with a deputation of twenty local African Americans.[196] When Stanton asked whether they would prefer being "scattered among the whites, or in colonies," their spokesperson plumped for the latter, with only one dissenting vote. "There is a prejudice against us in the South that will take years to get over," they explained. Days later, Sherman issued Special Field Order No. 15, which reserved the Sea Islands and rice fields of Florida, Georgia, and South Carolina for African Americans. Unlike the earlier Union colonies within Confederate territory, blacks would own the land and manage their own affairs.[197] Over the following months, 40,000 African Americans moved to "Sherman's Land."

In the North, Sherman's actions worried conservatives but divided radicals. "Giving the land to the negros will . . . make them for the time [being] landed paupers, who will occupy the land and yet not cultivate it," a veteran of Gettysburg told the president.[198] "What just freedom is it to be . . . shut up in a rice swamp, and not be allowed to see the face of their white fellow-citizens?" demanded Benjamin Butler, whose own solution, of having African Americans dig a canal across Central America, was more cosmopolitan for *location*, at least.[199] Frederick Douglass raised similar objections, while William Lloyd Garrison applauded Sherman's precedent: "it is conceded that the prime duty of the black man is not to . . . [grow] government cotton for insufficient wages, but to look after

[195] *CG* 38 Cong., 1 Sess., 2104–5 (May 4, 1864).
[196] Guyatt, "An Impossible Idea?," 242–3; Hahn, *Nation without Borders*, 290–1.
[197] William T. Sherman, *Memoirs of General William T. Sherman* (New York, 1875), 2:242–52.
[198] J. C. Robinson to Lincoln, February 1, 1865, AL.
[199] Benjamin F. Butler, *Speech of Maj.-Gen. Benj. F. Butler, upon the Campaign before Richmond* (Boston, 1865), 84.

his own interests like any other freeman."[200] And, in the background, one of Sherman's officers watched, waited, and wondered.

Colonization, Conservatism, and Reconstruction

When, in the summer of 1865, the future secretary of the interior, Major General Jacob Dolson Cox, ran for the governorship of Ohio, his Democratic opponents just assumed that he agreed with the latest heresy of the "Black Republicans": black voters.[201] Yet two residents of Oberlin, a town whose biracial college epitomized American abolitionism, urged the general, an Oberlin alumnus himself, to publicize his views. Despite the promise of that self-appointed "committee" not to print Cox's response without his consent, he was keen to disseminate what became known as the "Oberlin Letter."[202] In the postbellum South, Cox's reply prophesied, "the struggle for supremacy would be direct and immediate, and I see no hope whatever that the weaker race would not be reduced to hopeless subjection." Fortunately, he had an answer: "take contiguous territory in South Carolina, Georgia, Alabama, and Florida, and ... organize the freedmen in a dependency of the Union analogous to the Western territories."[203] All of a sudden, one state's politics turned national, even international, with the British liberal philosopher John Stuart Mill condemning Cox's "chimerical project."[204] From his Pennsylvania home, Thaddeus Stevens, who, just months earlier, had toyed with internal resettlement, now abandoned the idea: "I regret the course taken by your Genl. Cox ... colonization is an impossible idea – a Blair folly," Stevens wrote one Ohioan.[205] "The weak place in the plan is that it ignores the white man's greed for land wherever he can live," argued John Latrobe, reiterating that nowhere in the Americas was off-limits to the grasping Anglo-Saxon.[206] Cox "has thought for

---

[200] "Letters from New York," *Liberator*, February 17, 1865.
[201] For Cox, see Wilbert H. Ahern, "The Cox Plan of Reconstruction: A Case Study in Ideology and Race Relations," *Civil War History* 16 (1970), 293–308; Guyatt, "An Impossible Idea?," 234–5, 244–55; and Eugene D. Schmiel, *Citizen-General: Jacob Dolson Cox and the Civil War Era* (Athens, OH, 2014), 176–92.
[202] E. H. Fairchild and S. Plumb to Cox, July 24, 1865, in Jacob D. Cox, *Reconstruction and the Relations of the Races in the United States* (Columbus, 1865), 3–4.
[203] Cox to Fairchild and Plumb, July 25, 1865, in Cox, *Reconstruction*, 10–11.
[204] William M. Dickson, *The Absolute Equality of All Men before the Law: The Only True Basis of Reconstruction* (Cincinnati, 1865), 22.
[205] Stevens to J. Hutchins, August 27, 1865, in Beverly Wilson Palmer and Holly Byers Ochoa, eds., *The Selected Papers of Thaddeus Stevens* (Pittsburgh, 1997–8), 2:11.
[206] *AR* 41 (1865), 300.

himself, and come to a conclusion different from the new creed of the East," William Sherman taunted his brother, John, the US senator for Ohio and a Republican.[207]

The Oberlin Letter unleashed a tornado across the torrid summer of 1865. Broadly speaking, moderates applauded Jacob Cox's ideas and radicals decried them, but the soldier-scholar's abolitionist credentials meant that nobody could ignore him. "The new policy of arming [blacks] has not been inaugurated a day too soon," Cox had assured a friend, Salmon Chase, in 1863.[208] Worried, however, by the treatment that vengeful rebels would mete out to black veterans once peace came, Cox's thinking outpaced events during the second half of the war. By 1865, Cox had concluded that emancipation must mean political equality, and political equality, demands for social equality, even racial amalgamation.[209] He concurred with Tucker, Boutwell, and a black Buckeye, A. D. Jones, in espousing a franchise exclusive to the settlement in order to attract colonists.[210] While on the campaign trail at Oberlin itself, Cox was cornered by a member of the audience into admitting that, if black suffrage were decided state by state, he would support it in Ohio. "General Cox is trying to conciliate the Democrats, by taking high anti-negro ground, thinking he is sure of the Republican vote," argued a new black newspaper in distant California, the *Elevator*. Invoking General George McClellan, the Janus-faced Democratic candidate who, in 1864, had contested (and lost) the White House by calling to prolong the war even as his platform demanded an armistice, the editor, Philip Bell, prayed that Cox would share McClellan's fate.[211] In the end, Cox won the governorship, though his margin of victory was one-third that of his predecessor.[212]

Across the North, radicals worried that Jacob Cox was a stalking horse for another man averse to forcing black suffrage on the states: Andrew Johnson, the Tennessee tailor who had reached the White House through a combination of his self-education, devotion to the Union, and good fortune in escaping assassination the night that Lincoln died. The bulk of Johnson's wartime remarks on colonization could have reassured the

[207] W. T. Sherman to J. Sherman, August 3, 1865, in Rachel Sherman Thorndike, ed., *The Sherman Letters* (New York, 1894), 252.
[208] Cox to Chase, April 24, 1863, Chase Papers.
[209] Guyatt, "An Impossible Idea?," 244–6.
[210] A. D. Jones to Johnson, May 23, 1865, in Graf, *Papers of Johnson*, 8:106–7.
[211] "Anti-Republicanism in Ohio," *Elevator*, October 6, 1865.
[212] Schmiel, *Citizen-General*, 191.

most fervent abolitionist, but closer inspection revealed someone who saw
the policy as merely untimely. "I am for the Government of my fathers
with negroes. I am for it without negroes. Before I would see this
Government destroyed I would see every negro back in Africa, disinte-
grated and blotted out of space," Johnson had told an audience at
Indianapolis in 1863.[213] In September 1865, President Johnson spoke to
Chase, now chief justice of the US Supreme Court, in terms that Chase
described thus: black southerners "must either be absorbed ... or they
must be kept separate. If allowed to vote they will necessarily be so
absorbed ... Is it not a great deal better that the two races should be
separated, and each control everything within their own limits?"[214] Yet
that was already the last sign of Johnson's willingness to consider internal
colonization, a measure that had met an impasse: the property rights of
those Confederates swiftly restored to US citizenship. Indeed, as early as
May, the new president had identified returning confiscated property as
the obvious lever to make rebels solicit his pardon.[215]

In October 1865, it fell to Oliver Howard, as commissioner of the
Freedmen's Bureau, to inform the settlers of Sherman's Land, who had
thought their title permanent, of their dispossession by the federal government.[216] "The negroes were overwhelmed with sorrow and dissatis-
faction," reported a northern journalist. Some "seemed willing to work
for fair wages, but the great body were anxious to rent or buy the lands,
to which the planters will not consent."[217] While freedpeople throughout
the South had little choice but to sign exploitative labor contracts, embit-
tered whites in Virginia would not offer even those, which left the bureau
just one answer: migration. Large holdings of public land remained in
Alabama, Arkansas, Florida, Louisiana, and Mississippi, where, humanitarians hoped, US authorities might make an equitable exception to the
racial exclusivity of the Homestead Act. In July 1865, Colonel Orlando
Brown of the Freedmen's Bureau suggested relocating to Florida those
"surplus" freedpeople on the York–James Peninsula, at least until wages
in Virginia rose. Despite his doubts about the quality of Florida's scrub-
land, Howard gave Brown his blessing, while Colonel Thomas Osborn,
the bureau's assistant commissioner in Florida, even suggested that the

[213] Graf, *Papers of Johnson*, 6:156, 489, 581–3, 7:227.
[214] Chase to W. Sprague, September 6, 1865, in John Niven et al., eds., *The Salmon
P. Chase Papers* (Kent, 1993–8), 5:67.
[215] Asaka, *Tropical Freedom*, 185–6.   [216] Hahn, *Nation without Borders*, 306–7.
[217] Sidney Andrews, *The South since the War* (Boston, 1866), 211–12.

United States assert eminent domain below 28°N to found a black colony.[218]

Yet the mooted migration never happened, because the Freedmen's Bureau lacked the authority to buy tools or to charter ships for the destitute freedpeople. Moreover, Howard was relaxed about former slaves laboring on their old plantations for wages: "the feeling of hostility now existing between the two races, I do not regard as permanent."[219] Even radical Republicans shared his unease about separating freedpeople from the fields where they could (and should) revive the cash crops so crucial to the US balance of payments. Accordingly, Howard was even less enthusiastic about colonization overseas, condemning an attempt by a Lima businessman to transport freedpeople to Peru and souring on the ACS by 1866.[220] Howard did support, however, a southern version of the Homestead Act, to make available to former slaves the public lands in those states rich in the same. In February 1866, the author of a bill to that end, a Maine Republican, Representative John Rice, proposed a refuge for African Americans from the oppression that they faced in the heart of the former Confederacy, but a New York Democrat, John Chanler, countered that the scheme amounted to colonization and predicted that its beneficiaries would prove incapable of self-government.[221] Although the law passed Congress, it misfired through would-be settlers' inability to meet the minimum purchase requirements, as well as through southern officials' reluctance to advertise its very existence. As for the Freedmen's Bureau itself, conservatives continued to deem it a waste of money better spent on colonization.[222]

The president, moreover, agreed with them. By the fall of 1865, Johnson had proclaimed colonization the "only alternative" to black citizenship, the prospects of which he doubted.[223] In February 1866, barely two weeks before vetoing a bill to renew the Freedmen's Bureau,

---

[218] Berlin, *Freedom*, s3.vi, 409–10.

[219] Howard to G. W. Nichols, December 29, 1865, series 7, Oliver Otis Howard Papers, Bowdoin College.

[220] Moon-Ho Jung, *Coolies and Cane: Race, Labor, and Sugar in the Age of Emancipation* (Baltimore, 2006), 129–30; Willis Dolmond Boyd, "Negro Colonization in the Reconstruction Era, 1865–1870," *Georgia Historical Quarterly* 40 (1956), 365.

[221] *CG* 39 Cong., 1 Sess., 716–18 (February 7, 1866).

[222] J. Worth, message, November 20, 1866, in William E. Pell, pub., *Journal of the House of North Carolina* (Raleigh, 1867), 32–3; R. Winn to Sister, March 10, 1866, Winn–Cook Family Papers, Filson Historical Society.

[223] "Interview with Alexander K. McClure," ca. October 31, 1865, in Graf, *Papers of Johnson*, 9:311.

President Johnson dispensed a virtual duty of the nineteenth-century executive: summoning a delegation of his compatriots and cajoling them to leave the country. Permitted, unlike Lincoln's captive audience of August 1862, not only to speak but to go first, the two New Yorkers, Frederick Douglass and George Downing, might have hoped that the encounter would mark an improvement on that infamous occasion. It did not. The president kept interrupting the delegates and fixated on racial strife in the South, claiming that "the colored people can live and advance in civilization to better advantage elsewhere." Douglass and Downing replied that even the nation's worst enemy could not impute a greater infamy to the United States than that the slaves must suffer exile for the crime of being free.[224]

Both parties to the exchange, which the newspapers published, received a flurry of supportive letters from their sympathizers, but neither had spoken with as much authority as it would have liked.[225] Although Johnson continued to call colonization the humane choice, advising black laborers to threaten emigration as a bargaining chip with the planters, congressional Republicans parted ways with him over his opposition to their version of Reconstruction.[226] The Civil Rights Act, which Capitol Hill imposed over the White House's veto and reinforced with the Fourteenth Amendment (1868), would confirm that African Americans were, as they had always maintained, birthright citizens of the United States. That ensured that their forcible expatriation, at least, could never again be part of state law. Yet while Douglass and Downing had spoken accurately enough for black northerners, many African Americans in the lower South, bearing the brunt of the hatred that Johnson had described (and perpetuated), thought seriously about emigrating.

Granted, they would have preferred that _whites_ move. "None of the negroes, either residing in Savannah or from the country ... had any desire to be colonized away from their present homes," reported Whitelaw Reid, a northern journalist who toured the postwar South. "Inquiry would always develope the fact that their idea of 'living by themselves' was to have the whites removed from what they consider

---

[224] "Interview with Delegation of Blacks" and "Reply of the Black Delegates to the President," February 7, 1866, in ibid., 10:47, 54.
[225] Ibid., 10:57–8, 60–3, 102; "Letter from L. Maria Child," _Independent_, February 28, 1866.
[226] "Interview with Pascal B. Randolph," July 21, 1866, in Graf, _Papers of Johnson_, 10:712.

their own country."[227] As Unionists had half-joked during the war: colonize the slaveholders, not the slaves.[228] But in that internal colonization had abjured the realm of political possibility by 1866, resettlement plans soon reassumed their old garb. The ACS transported hundreds of black southerners (on its new ship, the *Golconda*), who, unlike in antebellum times, no longer sought their personal freedom, but its economic equivalent: landownership.[229]

For the ACS, another outcome of emancipation was that the society gained the support of white southerners, even of onetime advocates of slavery such as James De Bow. As forced converts to free-soilism, former Confederates hoped that the Thirteenth Amendment would act as a sort of promissory note for hordes of European immigrants vying to take the place of the freedpeople. An optimistic ACS resumed its antebellum tactics, memorializing state legislators for appropriations as well as for joint resolutions asking congressmen to fund steamers to Liberia. The society also invited freedpeople's own emigration clubs to write petitions that did not name the ACS, a trick that it had used during the prewar struggle to secure the US recognition of Liberia. In 1867, the society even persuaded Thaddeus Stevens, via a veteran colonizationist and now-secretary of the interior, Orville Browning, to include $50,000 for emigrants to Liberia in an appropriations bill.[230] A Pennsylvania Republican, Representative Martin Thayer, moved to strike the House's support for the "chimerical experiment" of colonization, while Thayer's New York colleague, Thomas Davis, elicited laughter by demanding, in the spirit of the radicals, that Liberia first repeal its laws for racially exclusive citizenship. The colonization proviso failed, 22-77.[231]

If the postwar world was horribly unfamiliar to the ACS in some ways, it could at least take comfort in reminders of problems past. One was the substantial debt that the society accrued by dispatching more than 2,000 emigrants between 1865 and 1870. The other was the suffering that then befell those settlers, who, as during the 1850s, were mostly recent slaves of limited means. In 1869, John Pinney completed the work that he had begun in 1855 and withdrew the support of the New York auxiliary for

[227] Whitelaw Reid, *After the War: A Southern Tour* (New York, 1866), 146–7.
[228] "A New Colonization Society Proposed," *American Presbyterian*, July 16, 1863.
[229] Falechiondro Karcheik Sims-Alvarado, "The African-American Emigration Movement in Georgia during Reconstruction," dissertation, Georgia State University (2011), 3.
[230] Boyd, "Reconstruction Era," 362–76; O. H. Browning to Stevens, January 23, 1867, Letters Sent, RG48/M160/1.
[231] CG 39 Cong., 2 Sess., 1695–6 (March 1, 1867).

further emigration.[232] The same year, the national black convention refused to forgive Joseph Jenkins Roberts, then visiting the United States, who "ran away to Liberia in the time of our need . . . and cried colonization." It denied him honorary membership of the organization, a stigma that it had also placed on Henry Highland Garnet's African Civilization Society in 1864, when the first truly national convention since 1855 had met at Syracuse.[233]

If anyone was willing to speak for colonization, then three were: two brothers and their aging father. Like Andrew Johnson, the Blairs wished to see the states restored, their white yeomen elevated to power, and nothing more. Describing the politics of the new president, one abolitionist had, in 1865, remarked that it was "singular that the Blairs are on terms of friendship with so prominent a radical" – evidently forgetting that Frank had been "radical" once.[234] While Francis kept colonization in front of the amenable but powerless Johnson, Frank thought about stumping once more for the policy, but this time as a Democrat.[235] A new ally of the Blairs, the former vice president of the Confederacy, Alexander Stephens of Georgia, tried to persuade them that they would do better to let the freedpeople stay in the South and revive its staples.[236] For a moment, even Frank Blair might have agreed, since a lease that he had taken on Louisiana cotton lands had failed for want of black workers.[237] Yet his father swiftly put the old spirit back in him, persuading Frank that that setback reflected the "universal failure," in the United States, of all systems of nonwhite labor.[238] Even now, Blair, Sr., was not alone in his obsession.[239] "Separate the races, colonize the African, [and] elect General Grant President in 1868," an Illinois Republican implored the US House in 1867.[240] Noting that moderate Republicans talked of the war hero as their next nominee, Francis Blair secured a meeting with

[232] Eli Seifman, "Education or Emigration: The Schism within the African Colonization Movement, 1865–1875," *History of Education Quarterly* 7 (1967), 36–57.

[233] Anon., pub., *Proceedings of the National Convention of Colored Men of America* (Washington, DC, 1869), 18, 42; G. C. Rand and Avery, pub., *Proceedings of the National Convention of Colored Men* (Boston, 1864), 19–20, 26–8.

[234] "Washington Correspondence," *Independent*, April 20, 1865.

[235] F. P. Blair, Sr., to Johnson, August 1, 1865, and March 18, 1866, in Graf, *Papers of Johnson*, 8:517–18, 10:270; F. P. Blair, Jr., to F. P. Blair, Sr., June 22, 1866, BL.

[236] A. H. Stephens to M. Blair, February 5, 1867, reel 23, BF.

[237] William E. Parrish, *Frank Blair: Lincoln's Conservative* (Columbia, MO, 1998), 248.

[238] F. P. Blair, Sr., to F. P. Blair, Jr., December 23, 1867, reel 2, BF.

[239] J. S. Rollins to M. Blair, September 16, 1867, BL.

[240] CG 39 Cong., 2 Sess., 583 (January 18, 1867).

Grant, in which he outlined a black military colony spanning the Rio Grande. Grant listened, but "looked absent" when Blair ended by asking him to consider it a "compromise plan" for Reconstruction.[241] If there was one thing better than a candidate friendly to the Blairs, then it was a candidate from among them. While most Democrats fled the field in 1868 at the thought of facing "Unconditional Surrender" Grant, the Blairs charged ahead with their chosen one, Frank, who achieved what he almost had in 1860: the second slot on a presidential ticket headed by a former governor of New York, in this case Horatio Seymour (1863–4), whose stain of wartime disunionism Frank's military record might wipe.[242] As eight years earlier, the Blairs did not manage to insert colonization into the manifesto, an omission for which they compensated with politicking behind closed doors.[243] A Democratic campaign biography recalled how Frank Blair's scheme had once "commanded the assent ... of the leading statesmen of the abolition party."[244] But now that his colonization scheme had no chance of success, Blair could only spout such virulent racism that the Democrats even discussed replacing him on the ticket; "Blair, Blair, Black sheep, have you any wool?" teased Horace Greeley's *New-York Tribune*. Yet Blair remained in place, conjoined to a colorless candidate who had not even sought the nomination. Seymour and Blair went on to suffer an 80-214 Electoral College defeat that did no justice to the more than 47 percent of the popular vote that they took.[245]

The 1868 election was the last that a presidential candidate fought on overt white supremacism, as well as the first in which large numbers of African Americans cast a ballot. Given blacks' axiomatic loyalty to the party of Lincoln, the party of Blair probably won a slight majority of white voters. While there might be a time when white Americans rose above the prejudices that had birthed colonization, it was not yet.

[241] F. P. Blair, Sr., to F. P. Blair, Jr., December 8, 1867, reel 2, BF.
[242] Parrish, *Frank Blair*, 248–55.
[243] F. P. Blair, Jr., to F. P. Blair, Sr., July 11, 1868, reel 3, BF; F. P. Blair, Sr., to S. J. Tilden, July 11, 1868, BL; Francis P. Blair, Jr., *Speech of Gen. Frank P. Blair Delivered at Indianapolis* (n.p., 1868), 16, in reel 13, BF.
[244] David G. Croly, *Seymour and Blair: Their Lives and Services* (New York, 1868), 233.
[245] Parrish, *Frank Blair*, 256–60.

Epilogue

The year 1869 witnessed the inauguration of Ulysses Grant as the eighteenth president of the United States. A staunch Republican, Grant would not readily surrender the rights of black southerners to the intransigence of their white oppressors, but would prove keen to secure those rights by black resettlement of a different kind. At the same time, the shift of the Blair clan toward the racist end of the separatist spectrum confirmed a pattern discernible in the internal colonization schemes of the later war years, namely, that politicians could support either an inclusionary or an exclusionary form of black migration, aligned with the Republican and Democratic Parties, respectively. But the exclusionary form struggled to straddle the old Democratic dichotomy between white supremacism and fiscal conservatism. "Many persons wish the Negroes here all in Africa but they won't give a cent to remove them," a South Carolina pastor told the ACS in 1868.[1] Moreover, if Reconstruction rallied white southerners to the Democratic ticket, it also laid bare their aversion to dispensing with the labor of their black neighbors, however much they resented them.[2]

By contrast, the inclusionary form of migration crystallized with Grant's request to the Senate to accept the latest of the Dominican Republic's applications for annexation – this time, to the United States, not Spain. While his proposal would never recover from an 1871 defeat in Congress (which, however, few contemporaries imagined would mark its

---

[1] Willis Dolmond Boyd, "Negro Colonization in the Reconstruction Era, 1865–1870," *Georgia Historical Quarterly* 40 (1956), 370.
[2] George M. Fredrickson, *The Black Image in the White Mind: The Debate on Afro-American Character and Destiny, 1817–1914* (New York, 1971), 265.

zenith), the scheme succeeded in shedding light on deep divisions within Republican ranks about what the acquisition would mean for race relations in the contiguous United States. Before President Johnson had even left office, his Dominican counterpart, Buenaventura Báez (in his fourth of five nonconsecutive terms), had lobbied Washington to annex the Dominican Republic and thereby neutralize, once and for all, the threat posed by Haiti. As with the Latin American contracts of the Civil War, a whiff of speculation pervaded Báez's offer, but Johnson's successor, Grant, saw uncommon merit in his request.[3] "Caste has no foothold in San Domingo. It is capable of supporting the entire colored population of the United States, should it choose to emigrate," wrote Grant. He echoed Andrew Johnson, though with greater sincerity, in thinking that black laborers might use the threat of migration to cow exploitative planters, as well as the British abolitionist, David Turnbull, in predicting that such a fillip to the free Caribbean would undercut the slave produce of Brazil and Cuba. "If Providence designed that the two races should not live together," added Grant, lining up a fallback plan for Reconstruction, then African Americans would have a home waiting for them.[4]

Since President Grant had slated Santo Domingo for the US statehood that the Blairs had always shirked, he might have expected unanimous support from Senate Republicans. Slavery's demise had freed US expansionism from its southern connotations and pushed the Republicans toward the spread-eagleism that had once been the preserve of the Democrats. Furthermore, senators had indulged Secretary of State William Seward in his infamous "folly," the 1867 purchase of Alaska for more than $7,000,000, so surely they would not oppose the United States acquiring its long-desired Caribbean foothold? Even two former abolitionists, Frederick Douglass and Samuel Howe, whom Grant sent to the Dominican Republic on an investigative mission, could not conceive of the scheme as African colonization rehashed.[5] Yet Grant met a formidable opponent in the New England absolutist Charles Sumner, who still held the chairmanship of the Senate Committee on Foreign Relations. In early 1870, Sumner abruptly announced his opposition to annexation, justifying his stance in climatic terms: "to the African belongs the

---

[3] Nicholas Guyatt, "America's Conservatory: Race, Reconstruction, and the Santo Domingo Debate," *Journal of American History* 97 (2011), 977–78; Eric T. L. Love, *Race over Empire: Racism and U.S. Imperialism, 1865–1900* (Chapel Hill, 2004), 27–72.
[4] "Memorandum," ca. 1869–70, in John Y. Simon, ed., *The Papers of Ulysses S. Grant* (Carbondale, 1967–2012), 20:74–6.
[5] Guyatt, "America's Conservatory," 976–7, 990–1, 998–9.

equatorial belt, and he should enjoy it undisturbed."[6] While Sumner had meant to affirm the rights of the region's existing black population, the logic of his speech came close to advising African Americans to cross the Caribbean if they expected to exercise their own. Within the Republican Party, a new civil war broke out. The Chiriquí colonizationist Samuel Pomeroy took Ulysses Grant's side, hailing American republicanism as the perfect system for all peoples lucky enough to come under its sway.[7] When Carl Schurz of Missouri, taking the isothermalist line, backed Sumner instead, Oliver Morton, the former governor of Indiana, asked Schurz whether he knew that he was "restating the arguments which were made in behalf of slavery."[8] The debate was all the more bitter for splitting the abolitionists of Boston, a divide personified by the now-former friends, Sumner and Howe. James Redpath supported Sumner, sharing the senator's fears for the integrity of Haiti, as did William Lloyd Garrison (after a fashion), but Francis Bird, an influential radical of the 1850s, was torn by his friendship for both Sumner and Howe. Even moderate Republicans worried that US annexation, and the heavy-handed territorial government that must ensue, would intoxicate Washington with a degree of power that it had already tasted in order to suppress white violence in the South. In 1874, Dominican rebels briefly deposed Báez, which effectively annulled the republic's offer to the United States. In his final annual message, of 1876, and for the rest of his life, President Grant rued how senators had missed their opportunity to force former Confederates to "learn the crime of Ku Kluxism" as well as the worth of their black compatriots.[9]

By contrast, the major colonizationists of the Civil War opposed the US annexation of the Dominican Republic. Francis Blair, as hateful as ever as he neared eighty, accused Grant of plotting to use Hispaniola as a base for raising an army with which to subdue the South once more.[10] Gideon Welles, who had disliked colonization even in its classic form, agreed with Montgomery Blair that Grant's venture was doomed, claiming that, while Latins assimilated with other races, Anglo-Saxons simply annihilated them.[11] Alike horrified by radical Reconstruction, Blair and Welles became frequent correspondents. In 1875,

---

[6] "Washington," *New York Times*, March 25, 1870.
[7] CG 41 Cong., 3 Sess., 260 (December 21, 1870).
[8] Ibid., Appendix, 28 (January 11, 1871).
[9] Guyatt, "America's Conservatory," 980, 990, 994–8.
[10] F. P. Blair, Sr., "Essay on Annexation of Santo Domingo," 1869, BL.
[11] G. Welles to M. Blair, January 21, 1871, reel 24, BF.

Montgomery Blair informed Welles of Frank Blair's untimely death, musing that his brother had never truly left the Republican Party, but that it had left *him*, over racial separation. "The slaveholders were opposed to this of course when he advocated it, at first, and the radicals were all in favor," reminisced Blair. "But when slavery was abolished and the radicals got the negroes as voters, the slaveholders wanted to be rid of their new masters," and so reversed their own stance by turning to colonization.[12]

Another of Montgomery's Blair's collaborators, the Rev. James Mitchell, was among the unlikely allies that Sumner courted in his attempt to prove Grant downright wrong. Although Mitchell had since returned to the ministry, Sumner wrote him in 1871 to ask whether the late President Lincoln had intended black resettlement in the British West Indies either to amalgamate the races or to annex that region to the United States. "He did not covet [those colonies] as part of our dominion, quite otherwise, but desired that England should unite with us in creating an independent colored commonwealth," replied Mitchell.[13] Despite his withdrawal from active politics, the minister spoke on colonization from time to time, eventually conceding that "the deportation of the negroes is no longer considered a necessity."[14] He died at Mount Zion, Georgia, in 1903, taking with him much of the wartime White House's documentary record on colonization.[15]

The abolitionists and colonizationists of times past were not the only Americans to find themselves on shifting sands as the high tide of Reconstruction receded. During the late 1860s, the freedpeople of the Cotton Belt had shown an interest in Liberia; by the late 1870s, they had capitulated to a mania for Kansas. (In 1879, the Philadelphia contractor Ambrose Thompson wondered whether they might go to Chiriquí, too.)[16] Emigration, once a topic that well-known northerners had debated in national conventions, became something that obscure southerners

---

[12] Blair to Welles, July 25, 1875, Gideon Welles Papers, LC.
[13] "The Western Question," *Atlanta Constitution*, March 25, 1894.
[14] "Tide Marks," *Southwestern Christian Advocate*, February 14, 1878; "The New Issue," ibid., June 12, 1879; "Pertinent Talk by the Rev. Dr. James Mitchell," Louisville *Courier-Journal*, September 12, 1895; James Mitchell, *Historical Educational Brief of Work amongst the Whites of the South* (Atlanta, 1897), 3.
[15] Phillip W. Magness, "James Mitchell and the Mystery of the Emigration Office Papers," *Journal of the Abraham Lincoln Association* 32 (2011), 61–2.
[16] A. W. Thompson to B. F. Flanders, February 19, 1879, box 30, Ambrose W. Thompson Papers, LC.

planned in elaborate networks of local associations.[17] Hundreds of letters flooded into the American Colonization Society, which, from 1864 to 1892, was staffed by just one man, William Coppinger, who had transferred from the Pennsylvania auxiliary to allow the ACS's veteran secretaries, Ralph Gurley and William McLain, to retire. The society had depleted most of its funds on the expeditions of 1865–9, which would prevent it from meeting black demand for the rest of the century.[18] In 1878, a postwar settler in South Carolina, Martin Delany, requested the society's support on behalf of Charleston's Liberia Exodus Association, but with no better outcome than for his Niger Valley Exploring Party, two decades earlier.[19] By contrast, Delany's old rival, Henry Highland Garnet, successfully secured white patronage, albeit in the form of the US mission to Liberia. He died in 1882, shortly after taking up his post at Monrovia.[20]

Lacking such connections, black associations tried to fill the gap left by the ACS's inadequacy. Their activities became so frenetic as white paramilitaries "redeemed" the South that, in early 1879, a Minnesota Republican, Senator William Windom, moved that Congress assist "the partial migration of colored persons ... into such States as may desire to receive them."[21] Although Windom had meant well, his vague wording implied that some states wished to encourage African American immigration. Southern sharecroppers assumed that he had meant the grasslands of Kansas, which had absorbed a steady stream of black settlers ever since the Fourteenth Amendment had extended the Homestead Act to African Americans.[22] Perhaps 20,000 refugees, mostly Mississippians and Louisianans who imagined, as in 1865, that the federal government was about to redistribute land on a massive scale, passed through St. Louis in 1879, where they became stranded for months. Those who reached Kansas ended up either in cities or on the state's infertile uplands. Most northerners were unmoved by the plight of the so-called Exodusters:

[17] Steven Hahn, *A Nation under Our Feet: Black Political Struggles in the Rural South from Slavery to the Great Migration* (Cambridge, MA, 2003), 317–63.
[18] Kenneth C. Barnes, *Journey of Hope: The Back-to-Africa Movement in Arkansas in the Late 1800s* (Chapel Hill, 2004), 7–8.
[19] Cyril E. Griffith, *The African Dream: Martin R. Delany and the Emergence of Pan-African Thought* (University Park, 1975), 109–12.
[20] Martin B. Pasternak, *Rise Now and Fly to Arms: The Life of Henry Highland Garnet* (New York, 1995), 152–6.
[21] *Congressional Record*, 45 Cong., 3 Sess., 483 (January 16, 1879).
[22] Ikuko Asaka, *Tropical Freedom: Climate, Settler Colonialism, and Black Exclusion in the Age of Emancipation* (Durham, 2017), 196–8.

Frederick Douglass thought them cowards who had surrendered the South to white supremacists, while Democrats denied them federal relief, even accusing the Republicans of instigating the movement in order to pack one of the new swing states with black voters.[23]

Emigrationism revived in the late 1880s, as the racial segregation that the "Compromise of 1877" had augured, but not inaugurated, started to suffocate black southerners. Although a prominent champion of Liberia (and of the ACS) would emerge in an AME bishop, Henry McNeal Turner, the movement's mainstay remained rural laborers, one of whom even lamented the absence of laws to expel them (and so galvanize an all too inchoate impulse): "how much longer are we to be left hear to suffer and dy and wish to God that there was a Law Passed in the United States to day that would Compell Every collard man to leave the Southern States?"[24] White southerners were inclined to indulge him. Between 1887 and 1891, the Bourbon Democrats, who had once advocated political fusion with African American Republicans, turned to deportationism. Disappointed by the failure of the New South program of modernization, and challenged for office by insurgent whites, the Bourbon planter-paternalists became vocal colonizationists. Aware that white northerners would have to consent to (or at least acquiesce in) black expulsion, the deportationists cited nativists' hostility to immigrants as proof of the sections' shared aversion to "foreign" populations.[25] Observing that President Benjamin Harrison (1889–93) had accepted the Republican nomination with a call to ban unassimilable ethnicities, a Georgia journalist, Carlyle McKinley, announced that "our duty to expel alien races is as clear as the duty to exclude them."[26]

As ever, the expulsive urge proved fickle: by the 1890s, another period of three-party competition, white proposals for black removal dwindled as African Americans once more became an electoral prize in local struggles between populists and patricians. In general, the side that had more keenly courted black voters ended up regretting its short-termism, which exposed it to race-baiting by the opposition. (The backlash was far worse for African Americans themselves, who fell victim to lynch mobs.) But 1896 brought two important realignments. First, in that year's

---

[23] Nell Irvin Painter, *Exodusters: Black Migration to Kansas after Reconstruction* (New York, 1977), 137–255.
[24] Hahn, *Nation under Our Feet*, 452–4.   [25] Fredrickson, *Black Image*, 262–4.
[26] Carlyle McKinley, *An Appeal to Pharaoh: The Negro Problem, and Its Radical Solution* (New York, 1890), 202.

presidential election, the Democratic Party merged with the agrarian People's Party, an ill-fated alliance that ushered in a Fourth Party System of Republican domination. Second, in *Plessy v. Ferguson*, the US Supreme Court upheld racial segregation laws for public facilities. Its decision took a familiar philosophy of "separate but equal" – which, for a century, had meant the movement to give African Americans a land of their own – and recast it on an altogether more local scale. Yet some white southerners continued to worry that allowing their black neighbors to live by their side but, henceforth, without their supervision would worsen an antagonism resolvable only by colonization abroad.[27]

Still, if race war ever erupted in the former Confederate States, northern whites might choose to help their southern kin over their black onetime "wards." As the old battle wounds healed, as pseudo-science reached its apogee, and as the Spanish-American War (1898) pitted US troops against a shared, foreign, darker enemy, white Americans began to wonder what the events of 1861–5 had ever been about. And if a fight between the Blue and the Gray over slavery (if it really *had* been) were not tragic enough, what about that older, longer conflict between the Blue and the Blue over *anti*slavery?

At least, such was the thinking of a Massachusetts theologian and former abolitionist, Joseph Henry Allen. In 1891, between delivering lectures at Harvard, he took a moment to reminisce. "There was a strong feeling of regret, with my father as well as myself, that the current of antislavery feeling should have set so strongly against the colonization enterprise," Allen admitted to Samuel May, Jr., another veteran of the "Brothers' War" between reformers. "In 1848, when I had tried simply to give ... a fair account of the circumstances and anticipations in founding the Liberian Republic, some friends ... charged me, most unjustly, with writing in defence of Slavery!"[28] Allen's mind wandered to two antagonists: an abolitionist, Theodore Parker, who, despite opposing African colonization, had endorsed Frank Blair's project and thought emancipation likely to exterminate African Americans, and a colonizationist, Ezra Gannett, who, despite abhorring the Garrisonians' militancy, had

---

[27] Brainerd Dyer, "The Persistence of the Idea of Negro Colonization," *Pacific Historical Review* 12 (1943), 61–5; Fredrickson, *Black Image*, 266–8.
[28] J. H. Allen to S. May, Jr., December 29, 1891, Ms. 859, unnamed collection, Boston Public Library.

nonetheless admired the force of their convictions.[29] "Time has brought us all, I trust, to a kindlier mind," concluded Allen, "and in the kingdom of heaven, I have no doubt, Theodore Parker walks arm in arm with Dr. Gannett, two men whom I admired and loved alike."

But did they ever link arms with kindred spirits of a different complexion – the Rev. Dr. Gannett with the Rev. Dr. Garnet? Did the dictates of divine law, or the maxims of medical science, allow black Americans to reach the cold, lofty planes of their white compatriots' heaven? And if not, was their separate afterlife at least *equal*?

God only knew.

---

[29] Octavius B. Frothingham, *Theodore Parker: A Biography* (Boston, 1874), 467, 473; William C. Gannett, *Ezra Stiles Gannett: Unitarian Minister in Boston, 1824–1871* (Boston, 1875), 140–1, 293–4.

Index

Lightning Source UK Ltd.
Milton Keynes UK
UKHW041430100221
378467UK00011B/14

9 781107 141773